ALEXANDRIA

THE JOURNAL OF THE WESTERN COSMOLOGICAL TRADITIONS

EDITED BY DAVID FIDELER

3

PHANES PRESS
1995

ALEXANDRIA

David Fideler
EDITOR

Walter Bakes
PROOFREADING

David Fideler
GRAPHIC DESIGN

Mrs. Gillian K. Smith-Dennis
SUBSCRIPTIONS

The Members of
The Alexandria Society
FUNDING

Atrium Publishers Group (USA)
Airlift Books (UK and Europe)
DISTRIBUTION

PUBLISHED BY

Phanes Press
Post Office Box 6114
Grand Rapids, Michigan 49516
USA

ISBN 0-933999-54-2

Contents

Introduction:
Education and the Signs of the Times

IT IS INTERESTING how themes spontaneously arise when working on *Alexandria*, and it is even more interesting to see how the minds of many people are turning to the topic of education. Many contributors to this journal are educators in one way or another, and it's a good thing to see people questioning the underlying aims and assumptions of the educational system. As I point out in my article on "Reviving the Academies of the Muses," the fantasies reflected in the world of higher education are perhaps the most telling indicators of any culture's underlying ideals and mythologies. Therefore, if we want to understand the forces and aspirations at work in contemporary culture, the first place to look is toward the microcosm of education.

It has always been true, but now seems truer than ever, that the worlds of fact and value cannot be separated. If someone threatens your life with a knife, you are most certainly going to react, rather than sit back and think about it. The problem with the academic world is that it has, for far too long, acted otherwise, and shut itself off in monastic seclusion from larger cultural and social concerns. This was different in the Renaissance, with its emphasis on "civic humanism," which stressed the implicit relation between the *studia humanitatis* and the *civitas*. But today, in many universities, great works of literature are not studied for the perspectives and enrichment they can bring to contemporary life, but become the victims of computer-aided textual analysis and other forms of deconstructionism.

To add a personal voice to an otherwise conceptual analysis, I once participated in an upper level graduate seminar offered by the Religious Studies department of a well-respected Ivy League university. The topic of the seminar was Origen's work *Against Celsus*. Celsus, a pagan philosopher, had written a work against Christianity, and Origen's lengthy reply was a point-by-point refutation of Celsus's arguments against the emerging faith. Given such fertile material, one might imagine that there would be opportunity for fruitful discussion, but such was not the case. Despite the fact that Robert Wilken's book *The Christians as the Romans Saw Them* had just been published by Yale, we never once discussed the place of the Origen–Celsus debate in the history of ideas, nor did we discuss the ideas or viewpoints of either writer. Instead, the text was antiseptically held at an arm's length, and one entire session was devoted to discussing verbal "quotation formulas" used by Origen, the stylistic formulas he used to indicate that he was quoting another writer. Other sessions were characterized by participants cautiously and self-consciously making footnotes on isolated snippets of the text, without ever discussing the ideas, or the work as a whole. The unspoken implication was that this type of hairsplitting approach was the mark of true scholarship, while the integrative approach reflected in Robert Wilken's book was mere popularization. When Willis Barnstone's valuable, one-volume anthology of extracanonical texts entitled *The Other Bible* was published at the time, I passed it around the seminar. One professor in the department, who happened to be sitting in that day, sneered at the massive compilation for having such a "sensational title," thus effectively writing it off. Obviously, a *true scholar* would never write the type of book that ordinary people might want to read! One day in the seminar, after the typical flow of meaningless details, a graduate student jokingly suggested that we had ample material to compile a Religious Studies version of the popular board game, "Trivial Pursuit." Everybody laughed at the remark, but the comment was more revealing than anyone probably realized at the time.

Paradoxically, while little children are encouraged in every possible way to develop their innate potential, graduate level education, in the adult world, weeds out enthusiasm for a subject, isolates the topic from other disciplines, and encourages one to develop the affect of detached, academic reserve. The sense of wonder and enthusiasm is anesthetized, and the idea of presenting scholarship as a culturally viable enterprise is specifically discouraged. The upper echelons of the academic world are built upon the foundations of fear, and the reason that papers at most academic conferences are so boring is because participants have been indoctrinated into fearfulness of discussing questions of meaning and relevance, for such an approach is perceived as lacking scientific rigor.

Given the types of concerns which face the world today, this type of attitude is hardly viable, and that is why it is instructive to reconsider and revision the role of education in contemporary society. As Christine Rhone cogently observes in her article on the education of women (and the education of the true philosopher), our problems today are not at root political: they are philosophical. Speaking of the fact that the world population is scheduled to *double* over the next sixty years (mainly in Third World countries), Christine Rhone discusses how some suggest better education as a prophylactic measure, based on the fact that educated women have fewer children.

The idea of saving the world is an appealing messianic fantasy with which many people would like to identify. Given adequate resources, almost everyone would like to try their hand at it. But in actuality, no one person possesses the ability to singlehandedly change the course of things. Even if it were possible to significantly change our social institutions for the better, disease, human suffering, and the inevitability of death will always be with us. The readers of this journal are among the fortunate few, given the fact that they have the time, resources, and inclination to reflect on these matters. But the question remains, how can one's concern be translated into action when the momentum of the modern world seems so impervious to change? And how can one be a moral agent in society without falling into the trap of merely becoming a moralistic personality, a platitudinal thinker, or an ideologue?

There are myriad ways that any individual can care for others and care for the soul of the world. Initially, we must care for ourselves to some degree, because without adequate tools and inner resources, one can never provide service to others. But in the sense of providing service to society as a whole, once again the theme of education arises. For while it is impossible for a single individual to stop the destruction of the rainforests (and other problems that seem equally daunting), it is quite easy for every person to contribute something to our common welfare through the medium of "education," defined in the widest possible way. But in order to be effective moral agents in society, we need to possess the courage to both speak up and act at the proper moments, and not let those opportunities pass us by. Furthermore, if the world of higher learning wants to reclaim a sense of genuine integrity, it will once again have to make room for discussion which relates to authentic human and cultural issues. To borrow an analogy from James Hillman, in the same way that the Athenians had shrines to the most primitive deities on the slopes of the Acropolis, we need to make space for both the gods and demons of civilization within the halls of the Academy.

When we realize that social crises are ultimately philosophical rather than political issues, individuals immediately start casting around for the one philosophical perspective that will solve it all, and thus we are led from the realm of philosophy into the unhappy sphere of ideology. From this vantage point, the idea of the One Perspective that will solve everything is revealed as a leftover from monotheistic fantasies of literalistic Christianity: "just believe, and you will be saved." But once this bubble is burst, then the true work can begin: the negative side of Western philosophy as abstract system-building falls into rubble, so that the authentic, therapeutic voice of Socratic inquiry—the Voice in the City—can once again emerge. In this scenario, true philosophy is revealed not as a dogmatic undertaking, but as a practice of discussion. This is the type of *real* discussion that you can't get from the media (which exists to sell products) or from politicians (whose rhetoric is aimed at influencing public opinion); this is the type of discussion that can only arise among real people, in real communities, in daily life. If "man is a social animal" (in the tradition of Aristotle), perhaps we are most social in the context of conversation (in the tradition of Plato).

From this perspective, *Alexandria* and its contributors are engaged in a truly philosophical enterprise in a time when true philosophy, when true discussion, is only rarely to be found within the halls of Academe. In a society where there are few places to discuss ideas, *Alexandria* provides an extended Garden of Discourse, a pluralistic, imaginal meeting place for those interested in the Western traditions, the significance of these traditions in contemporary life, and what they have to contribute to the future. But *Alexandria* is only a publication, a fantasy—an *approximation* of living conversation. How, then, can we move serious dialogue into "the city"? And where are the real philosophers when we need them the most?

—DAVID FIDELER

Harmony Made Visible

MICHAEL S. SCHNEIDER

How can any educated person avoid the Greeks?

—Albert Einstein

GREEK ART has always been appreciated for its beauty, elegance, and power. But few admirers realize how much it owes to the influence of mathematical philosophy. A glimpse at Greek pottery design shows how art, philosophy, and mathematics once cross-pollinated to manifest harmony in everyday life.

In ancient Greece, as in Egypt and elsewhere, the purpose of any pottery can be identified by its shape and size. Pottery for holding oil was shaped differently than that for holding perfume, wine, water, or grain. Other shapes were used for mixing water with wine, for drinking from, for awarding in ceremonies, or for adorning tombs. (See Figure 1.)

Two questions arose over the centuries. First, how were these shapes designed? And second, why was the decoration painted on the vase where it was, often showing people and objects floating in midair? These questions can be answered by considering how the Greek philosophers were interested in ideals and archetypal principles, the nature of Truth, Beauty, and the Good, and Harmony which binds them together as one.

> [Artists should] fix their eyes on perfect truth as a perpetual standard of reverence, to be contemplated with the minutest care, before they proceed to deal with earthly canons about things beautiful.
>
> —Plato

Figure 1.
A selection of Greek pottery types.

The good, of course, is always beautiful, and the beautiful never lacks proportion.

—Plato

The principle of *harmony* (literally "fitting together") was so important to Plato that he suggested the education of youth emphasize an exposure to harmony in all its forms, including music, song, dance, sculpture, pottery, and architecture. In theory, people exposed throughout their lives to wholeness and harmony will develop a taste for these qualities and seek them in whatever they do. On the other hand, overwhelming exposure to fragmentation and discord inclines both individuals and societies to lose sight of guiding ideals and flounder about, as a glimpse at the nightly news will attest. Our modern "system" of education encourages this by imposing information from outside ourselves into memory. This brings "understanding," or "standing under" the weight of accumulated facts. It is mere "headucation" and gives no hint of the world's, or our own, ever present wholeness and harmony. But Plato recommended a different approach, of bringing knowledge of eternal ideals outward from deep memory to our awareness. Socrates called this *anamnesis* or "recollection." It is the original meaning of "education," from the Latin *educare*, "to lead out." The Greek word for "truth," *aletheia*, literally means "not forgetting" this innate wisdom.

> The aim of art is to represent not the outward appearance of things, but their inward significance.
>
> —Aristotle

The Greek philosophers recognized that the archetypal ideals, including wholeness, polarity, rhythm, and harmony, can be known through revelation by looking within ourselves, and also studied around us as expressions in nature. The artisans knew that when we see or hear harmony, whether its principles are mentally "understood" or not, we resonate with it in our deepest self. The purest expression of ideals is found in mathematics, in number and shape. Thus, the philosophers recommended the study of mathematics as a way to clear away confusion and become aware of the archetypal harmonies deep within ourselves. They accorded supreme importance to the study of number through arithmetic, geometry (number in space), music (number in time), and astronomy (number in space-time). The principles of mathematics and the eternal patterns inherent in numbers and shapes are available to anyone of any era who cares to examine them. Mathematics was honored as pure discovery, not as a human invention, or as a mere slave of commerce. As Cicero wrote, by the Greeks

> geometry was held in the very highest honor, and none were more illustrious than mathematicians. But we [Romans] have limited the practice of this art to its usefulness in measurement and calculation.

The artisans of ancient Greece, influenced by contemporary mathematical philosophers (see Figure 2), represented harmonious pro-

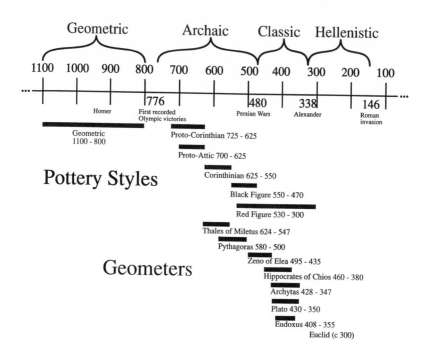

Figure 2.
Timeline of Greek pottery styles and geometers.

portions visually. Through number, shape, and proportion, divine harmony was expressed in mundane creations. Consequently, when we see the classical black and red figure vases which made Athens the ceramic center of the Mediterranean, we still internally resonate with the eternal, underlying principles of harmony on which they are based. Public exposure to harmony was carried out in all human-made creations, wherever it could be expressed. Harmonious designs evoke harmony in whoever sees them, and by building harmonious relationships into everyday objects, archetypal ideals quietly helped to guide society. Ancient cultures in general were ruled as much by the harmonious effects of music, song, dance, and crafts as by their legal codes. As Sallust wrote, "Harmony makes small things grow. Lack of it makes great things decay."

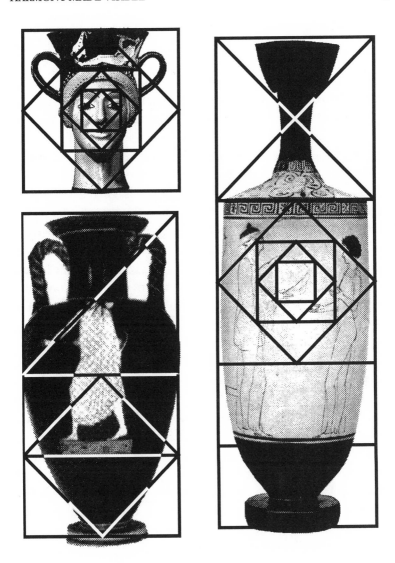

Figure 3.
Greek vases based upon the single, double, and triple square.

The hidden harmony is stronger than the visible.

—Heraclitus

The three vases shown in Figure 3 express the inner harmonies of the numbers one, two, and three, as the heights are equal, double, or triple their widest part. Since the vases are actually three-dimensional, they fit within stacked cubes. Whole-number relationships evoke concords within us, whether seen in the visual proportions of pottery or heard as musical intervals. By allowing the square to display its own natural geometry, we see how the dimensions of the vases were determined; we also see hints about the placement of the decorative elements. By the rules of "aesthetics" (from *aisthesis* or "sense perception"), figures are not placed exactly *on* the ideal geometric guidelines, but a little ahead, behind, above, or below to give the viewer a feeling of their motion, energy, action. Many vases are based upon one, two, and three stacked cubes, and other ratios including 2/3 (the musical fifth) and 3/4 (the musical fourth).

The Greek mathematical philosophers further realized that when harmony occurs in nature around us, and in human nature within us, it does so through the reconciliation of opposites. They tell us so in myth, as the goddess Harmonia was born of parents Aphrodite and Ares, Venus and Mars, the opposites love and war. The very words "mother" and "father" have etymological roots akin to "matter" and "pattern," and so all the designs of nature, and all human creations, were considered the result of the reconciliation of these primal "parents." The vase makers and painters (who were usually different but sometimes the same person) designed and adorned their vases using mathematics by interplaying the opposites of the rational "unit" and the irrational "square root." While the unit value, represented by the sides of the square, portrays all that is rational and can be "understood," the "square root" values found along diagonals represent its opposite, the irrational values which require "innerstanding," since they can't be described as any exact ratio of whole numbers. The diagonal allows the rational to extend beyond itself. The Unit and Diagonal symbolize all opposite pairs to be reconciled: the limited and unlimited, logic and intuition, divine and mundane, ideal and actual, outer and inner, male and female, matter and pattern, form and decoration, one and many, part and whole, the individual and society. The geometer's role, like the potter's, or the governor of a society, or the Self within the individual, is to find the proportions which reconcile discrete elements into their natural harmony.

That which is in opposition is in concert, and from things that differ comes the most beautiful harmony.

—Heraclitus

Geometers explored the philosophy of opposites in the figure of two circles whose centers touch each other's circumference forming an almond shape or *vesica piscis* ("bladder of the fish"). More than just a symbol, it is a birth portal through which ideal principles manifest as number and shape, which are seen in the harmonious forms of nature. Using only the trinity of geometer's tools—compass, straightedge, marker—a square is constructed and its diagonal unfolds to produce a root-2 rectangle. *Its* diagonal produces a root-3 rectangle, and so forth, producing rectangles whose sides are root-2, root-3, root-4, and root-5 times the side of the square, the distance between the circles' centers. (See Figure 4.) Using these "root rectangles" with their unique internal proportions gave the ancient Greek potters guidelines for harmonizing the overall shape with elements in the painting. The truths of timeless mathematical principles are beyond any authority or natural process to regulate, and so Greek art evokes subtle feelings in viewers many centuries later. Figure 5 displays the frames of root-2, side-by-side root-3, and root-5 vases. Readers are encouraged to place tracing paper over the pictures and use the geometer's tools to discover the vases' hidden guidelines.

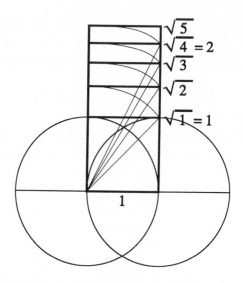

Figure 4.
The generation of the dynamic "root rectanges"
from the *vesica piscis*.

Sacred [art] is not, as our time chooses to see it, a "free" art,
developed from feelings and sentiment, but it is an art strictly
tied by and developed from the laws of geometry.

—Fredrik Macody Lund

A special case of the geometric reconciliation of opposites involves
the Golden Ratio, or "the section" as the Greeks referred to it, which
grows from the diagonal of the *half*-square. Quite a number of vases
display its proportions because it offers artisans a particularly powerful tool for guiding the viewer's attention around a spiral of squares
towards its "eye," the composition's visual "center of gravity" where
all diagonals cross. The architect, teacher, and writer Jay Hambidge
rediscovered this geometry and called it "dynamic symmetry." Figure
6 shows us figures which seem to float in mid-air, but which actually

Figure 5.
Greek vases based upon the root-2,
double root-3, and root-5 rectangles.

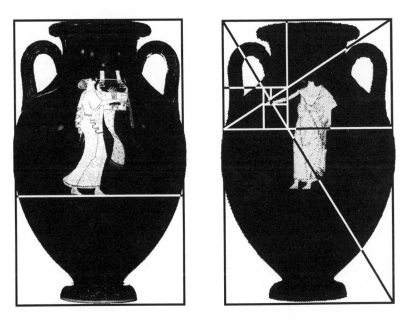

Figure 6.
Greek vases based on the Golden Rectangle of "whirling squares."

stand on unseen lines within the Golden Rectangle. One figure holds the spiral's eye in the palm of his hand where his attention, and ours, is directed.

The application of mathematical ideals to human creations seems to occur and recede in periodic rhythm over centuries and cultures. The ideals of Truth, Beauty, Goodness, and Harmony may again someday be widely appreciated, studied, longed for, cooperated with, and made manifest in everyday affairs to remind us of our own, and the world's, wholeness and harmonious diversity.

Most of the vases analyzed in this article are in the collection of the Metropolitan Museum of Art, New York City.

The Alchemy of Art

ARTHUR VERSLUIS

ALL TOO OFTEN we tend to think of knowledge as existing in distinct categories: we place alchemy as a predecessor of modern chemistry, for example, and do not recognize the ways in which various forms of knowledge interlink with one another. For most of us, alchemy means little, and has no relation to art. But I believe that by considering alchemical texts and their advice on the stages necessary to create the mysterious "philosopher's stone," and to achieve the magnum opus or consummation of the alchemical work, we will also recognize many insights into the nature of literary and artistic creation. In fact, through alchemy we will be able to begin developing a theory of creation.

In his book on the Jewish concept of the Golem, Moshe Idel writes of "ergetic" spirituality, referring to "a type of knowledge attained by action." He goes on to write that

> By creating an anthropoid the Jewish master is not only able to display his creative forces, but may attain the experience of the creative moment of God, who also has created man in a similar way to that found in the recipes used by the mystics and magicians. Paraphrasing a statement of Glanvill, we may describe the Golem practices as an attempt of man to know God by the art He uses in order to create man.... If our description of the meaning of the mystico-magical practices is adequate, then the creation of the Golem can be considered as anticipating the ergetic mode of knowledge, which consolidated only in the seventeenth century.[1]

While I have no intention of examining Jewish mysticism here—an attempt for which I am quite unqualified—Idel's comments about the

golem tradition in Judaism also describe very well the broader
European tradition of alchemy. For alchemy too is an ergetic gnosis
appearing through ritual action, and alchemy too "consolidated ... in
the seventeenth century."

Alchemy as a discipline can be traced back at least into Greco-
Egyptian civilization, and perhaps has roots in ancient Egyptian
religion.[2] Certainly alchemy can be traced through Greco-Roman
civilization and through the Christian and Islamic middle ages into
the Renaissance and modernity, always as a hidden tradition, transmitted from master to disciple. Although one may be able to trace such
roots back, eventually one must always lose sight of them in the haze
of antiquity. It is much more fruitful to look at the many relatively
recent alchemical treatises, and to consider their implications. For
one can think of few disciplines so profound and provocative that have
been more maligned and neglected than alchemy.

This is particularly so because the seventeenth and eighteenth
centuries in Europe saw an extraordinary consolidation and renaissance in alchemical works—indeed, this was the golden age of alchemical engravings and manuscripts. During these two centuries,
countless illustrations and treatises appeared, virtually all of them
claiming to reveal in highly elliptical and symbolic language the true
secrets of alchemical practice. Unfortunately, the proliferation of
would-be alchemists, even swindlers and fraudulent alchemists during this time led many to deplore and reject alchemy entirely. To
combat this proliferation, some alchemists published works like *The
Hermetic Museum*, a collection of authentic alchemical texts brought
out in Latin in 1678, whose authors included Basil Valentine, Helvetius,
Michael Maier, and Michael Sendivogius. And there were numerous
other valuable texts and engravings published during this time,
collected by Stanislav Klossowski de Rola and others in the twentieth
century.

There are many things I could note about these texts and illustrations, but among the most important must certainly be the way that
they tend to incorporate visual and literary arts together. Naturally,

there are many alchemical engravings that stand alone, without even accompanying mottos—the images and symbols are meant to carry the entire meaning. Among the most famous of these is the well known *Mutus Liber*. But there are also many works that incorporate images and words together, like Johann Daniel Mylius's *Opus medico-chymicum* of 1618, in which we see numerous charts, both circular and semi-circular, showing the angelical and elemental hierarchies as well as the various stages of divine creation. Here the words, the geometric structure, and the images all work together in artistic unity.

Probably the most remarkable and elaborate of alchemical works exemplifying this principle is *Atalanta Fugiens* (1618) by Michael Maier. Here we see a sequence of fifty alchemical images engraved by the master Johann Theodore de Bry to which are linked not only epigrams but poems and fugues. Thus we have not only the character-istic alchemical union of visual symbols and accompanying text, but what is more, the text set to music, so that one can read the epigrams, contemplate the images, and at the same time listen to the musical variations sung. *Atalanta Fugiens*, based in the myth of Atalanta, Hippomenes, and the golden apples, is a brilliant artistic union of visual, literary, and musical art.

Atalanta Fugiens draws upon the Greek myth of the fleet and beautiful Atalanta, who agreed upon a race with the youth Hippomenes. Hippomenes was given three golden apples by the goddess Venus, and during the race he tossed them aside to divert Atalanta, thus allowing his victory. Atalanta, having met her match, surrendered to him in love. But Maier does not simply recount this myth with his fugues, emblems, epigrams, and poems, he builds an entirely new, complex, and complete work that, while rooted in the Greek myth, flowers into an alchemical magnum opus of its own. Like any great work of art, in other words, *Atalanta Fugiens* assimilates and transmutes preexisting mythology and symbolism.

Let us look at examples of how *Atalanta Fugiens* works. The first epigram reads "The wind has carried him in its belly." And the accompanying illustration shows a naked male bearded figure whose hands and hair dissolve into turbulence above a landscape, while in his lower abdomen we see an embryo. The accompanying verses read, in part:

> The foetus, hidden in Boreas' womb,
>   Shall one day rise up, living, to the light;
> He only shall surpass all heroes' deeds
>   With art, with hand, with body's strength and mind.[3]

Here ancient mythological symbolism and alchemical symbolism together prepare the reader for the alchemical work ahead, the hero's journey "living, to the light." The foetus is the alchemist himself as spiritual embryo; the work to come is "with art" to purify and transmute the soul.

This is unquestionably ergetic spirituality, spirituality developed through creating. What Idel wrote about the creation of the golem in Judaism—that it entails mimicking divine creation of the cosmos—is clearly true of alchemy. There are numerous alchemical and theosophical texts of the seventeenth and eighteenth centuries in Europe that show the process of creation, from Mylius's *Opus medico-chemicum* to the illustrations of Robert Fludd to the many illustrations adorning the works of Jacob Boehme and his school during this same period. The exact illustrations I refer to sometimes depict the process of creation from a circle within a flaming triangle, in the center of which is the Tetragrammaton, through the creation of the waters, the entire cosmos, and man. Other series are more abstract, but still show transformations within a sphere, including the elemental lightning bolt of emanatory creation.

There is only one explanation for having such illustrations in alchemical texts, I would argue: the alchemist intends to be a creator in miniature, to have working through him the divine power that created the cosmos in the first place. One sees this virtually everywhere in alchemical works, as for instance in the *Escalier des sages* (1689) of Barent Coenders van Helpen, about which the author wrote

"The Wind has Carried Him in its Belly"
Emblem 1 from Michael Maier's *Atalanta Fugiens.*

that "I thought the title of Stairway of the Wise would not be inapt to this Philosophy," the ascent being in part a recapitulation of Creation itself, or a revelation of the essential principles informing Creation. Each illustration has appended a term like Sal [salt], short for *Solus Altiora Laboro* [Alone I work higher things], so that by contemplating the image and its epigrammatic formulation, we are also ascending toward God by understanding the principles of creation.[4]

Alchemical texts insist upon humility and the need for divine assistance: alchemy is not arrogant demiurgy by any means. Basilius Valentinus wrote in his treatise on "The Great Stone of the Ancient

Sages" that the philosopher's stone and the culmination of alchemy is "a gift which He [God] reserves for those favoured few who love the truth and hate falsehood, who study our Art earnestly by day and by night, and whose hearts are set upon God with unfeigned affection."[5] This is hardly an admonition uncharacteristic of alchemy as a whole. "The Sophic Hydrolith," another such text, is filled with similar advice to the aspirant, as are virtually all the treatises one might choose to consult. Alchemy, in other words, is by no means a science by which one seeks to "rival God"; one finds in these works that alchemy is a distinctly Christian science, a spiritual discipline.

Some scholars argue that alchemy exists outside Christianity, but this is only true if one defines "Christianity" as "orthodox, historicist Christianity" and excludes the entire range of mystical, Hermetic, and gnostic traditions that persist in every age in the Christian world. Carl Jung wrote that

> When I began to understand alchemy I realized that it represented the historical link with Gnosticism, and that a continuity therefore existed between past and present. Grounded in the natural philosophy of the Middle Ages, alchemy formed the bridge on the one hand into the past, to Gnosticism, and on the other into the future.[6]

While it is unclear what relationship alchemy has with ancient Gnosticism, both entail seeking a secret knowledge or gnosis. Thus although I doubt that many Renaissance or modern alchemists knew or cared much about Gnosticism in antiquity, one can see how there are parallels between alchemical Hermetism and ancient Gnosticism, even if there is an only tangential historical connection—and both certainly existed within a Christian context, broadly conceived.[7]

Indeed, if as Kurt Rudolph and Giovanni Filoramo hold, ancient Gnosticism is distinguished by a gnosis revealed by a *sôter* or a hierophant, so too alchemy is the art under the auspices of Hermes, who is, after all, the messenger of the Gods, and who therefore, like the Gnostic Revealer, joins the world above with the world below. Thus

Thomas Norton writes in his "The Ordinal of Alchemy" that "A most wonderful Magistery and Archimagistery is the Tincture of sacred Alchemy, the marvellous science of the secret Philosophy, the singular gift bestowed upon men through the grace of Almighty God."[8] We cannot achieve alchemical work without divine help, "*nor can anyone attain to this Art, unless there be some person sent by God to instruct him in it.*"[9] This person plays the role of Hermes, just as in ancient Gnosticism one was initiated into the Mystery of the Logos by one's spiritual guide or angelic revealer.

It is important to recognize that alchemy—according to its texts—exists in a religious context because without this recognition, one might be inclined to treat it as merely an ancestor of modern chemistry, whereas we are really looking here at a completely different paradigm than that of modern science. Alchemy is evidently a science of principles, and thus "all true enquirers into the Art of Alchemy should be well versed in the primary philosophy. Otherwise all their labour will be vain."[10] Alchemy involves physical experimentation, but this experimentation must be founded in spiritual knowledge, without which alchemy would be nothing more than toying with various substances in a furnace, neither a noble nor a useful occupation.

The culmination of alchemy is gnosis, secret knowledge of what transcends this mutable world, and it is here that alchemy and art may be seen to meet. For when we look at alchemical illustrations and treatises, we see artistic labor subordinated to what it is designed to express. Alchemical illustrations and treatises are not generally intended for aesthetic appreciation divorced from implications. Indeed, some illustrations are quite crude, and show only a little effort at and talent for verisimilitude; their significance lies in what they are attempts to convey. Their meaning lies beyond what one sees; one must look through the illustrations, read beyond the texts.

This is critical: alchemical texts—all of them—represent enigmas. The language is rarely direct, almost always elliptical, chiefly because the alchemical writers, while they want to convey their knowledge to a worthy aspirant, do not want that knowledge to reach the unworthy, those subject to overweening arrogance. Norton tells us, in fact, that alchemical knowledge could overthrow a kingdom and disrupt order throughout the cosmos—so he has good reason to keep this knowledge from those who might misuse it. Such warnings are visible throughout much alchemical literature. Consequently, we are given riddles, and even when alchemists tell us that they are being forthright, we are still presented with riddles like advice to search for "a thing which is depised and rejected by the multitude."[11]

In the anonymous treatise "The Glory of the World," we see the art of Hermeneutics in its purest form, for here all begins with proper reading:

> Hermes is right in saying that our Art is true, and has been rightly handed down by the Sages; all doubts concerning it have arisen through false interpretation of the mystic language of the philosophers. But, since they are loth to confess their own ignorance, their readers prefer to say that the words of the Sages are imposture and falsehood. The fault really lies with the ignorant reader, who does not understand the style of the Philosophers. If, in the interpretation of our books, they would suffer themselves to be guided by the teaching of Nature, rather than by their own foolish notions, they would not miss the mark so hopelessly.[12]

The art of alchemy is founded in right interpretation of the texts: without proper understanding from the beginning, one's entire course of action will be askew, and one's work will never be consummated. One must follow nature, rather than one's own "foolish notions."

The same holds true for literature. It is not for nothing that the troubadours of the thirteenth and fourteenth centuries spoke and wrote of a "secret language of love." For these poets and singers of love, as for the alchemists, language could reveal layers of meaning: one could see through the literal meaning to what an initiate would perceive. One sees this clearly in Dante's La Vita Nuova, which contains its own exegesis by its author. The poet writes of loving a particular woman, Beatrice, but he also writes about Love personified, and about religious experience. These are all bound into one, so that the language of individual love is compact with religious initiation.

In fact, this kind of hermeneutics is traditional within the Judeo-Christian world; according to kabbalistic tradition, scriptural exegesis can reveal numerous meanings from a single verse, even from single letters. Exegesis here is a creative art that can produce startling religious speculation, spin new doctrines out of verses that had never revealed such meanings before. Numerous love poems are interpreted also as poems of religious impulse; the Old Testament Song of Songs is the classic example. What we read literally not only has a higher meaning, in fact this other meaning conventionally is taken as the primary one; rarely is the Old Testament Song of Songs interpreted as an individual love song.

Literature is spun out of other literature, just as alchemical works derive from other alchemical works. Dante draws on Vergil and St. Bernard of Clairvaux; T. S. Eliot draws on Dante. The conventions exist; the poet renews them. So too, an alchemical writer inherits terminology, a specialized language, certain images, and tries to express through them what he has himself experienced. Borne out of the current of all that has come before them, both the literary and the alchemical writers embody a tradition that they exemplify and embrace. The greatest works of literature and the greatest alchemists exist among others, in relation to whom they largely define themselves.

Sometimes writing entails dismissing much of what one's recent predecessors have done, a "clearing of the ground." This happens, I think, mostly when a tradition has grown too conventionalized or hidebound—one finds alchemical writers attacking their contemporaries or recent predecessors only when they are perceived as not adequately conveying the secret tradition that it is the alchemical writer's primary duty to convey. One finds far more alchemical writers embracing their illustrious predecessors than one finds attacking. In general, this is true of authors and poets as well: Malcolm Lowry wrote that he could not understand any of his contemporaries, but that he was infinitely indebted to all who had gone before him. So too with Petrarch, and many others.

Of course, there is also an inverted exegesis, often associated with Gnosticism. The Gnostics of the second and third centuries C.E. were renowned for their inversions of orthodox exegesis: Marcion, for instance, held that since the God of the Old Testament was a jealous god, he must not be alone, and that indeed jealousy and ignorance marked him as a demiurge, inferior to the true God revealed by Christ. One is reminded of William Blake, who more than sixteen centuries later, in England, wrote that where the orthodox Christians see white, he sees black. The Gnostics, like William Blake, rebelled against an historicist religion, itself not far from what Blake called the "single vision" of Newton's sleep.

But as Simone Pétrement has argued, even if this inverted exegesis appears to oppose historicist Christianity, it still exists within a Christian context. Marcion sees the God of the Old Testament as an ignorant demiurge, but in this very placing, Marcion reveals himself as part of the tradition within which he rebels. Pétrement writes that "Not only can the Gnostic conception of the Demiurge be explained by Christianity, but it very much seems that it cannot be explained otherwise."[13] Marcion even went so far as to edit the Old Testament to eliminate parts that he felt inappropriate to the Christian revelation—again an exegetical act that could only take place if he had an agenda within a broadly Christian context.

In short, artistic and alchemical creation take place only within a traditional exegetic context—and this is true even of rebellious exegesis. I am not evaluating Marcionitic or other forms of Gnosticism, I am simply using them as extreme examples to test the principle here—that creation must unfold within a traditional ambience, an exegetic context that allows it to unfold. Even its harshest critics, Irenaeus and Tertullian, acknowledge that Gnosticism was an infinitely creative movement, a virtual "swarming ant-heap" of heresies, for each Gnostic formed his own system, had his own visionary experiences. But however many these movements, all of them did exist, broadly speaking, under a single rubric of Christian Gnosticism.

Likewise, when we gaze over the whole of European-American literary history, we see a continuously unfolding within a context, not just a series of discrete, isolated, brilliant creative moments. Interpretation, hermeneutics, defines each work by the way it interprets the past itself. Rebellious or devoted, every work that mentions other works or authors is not only placing them, but defining itself as well. The anonymous author of "The Sophic Hydrolith" lists his predecessors in the noble Art:

> Hermes Trismegistus, Pythagoras . . . Plato . . . Avicenna, Galen, Hippocrates . . . Mary the Prophetess . . . Dionysius . . . Morienus, Calid . . . Albertus Magnus . . . Arnold de Villa Nova, Geber, Raymond Lully, Roger Bacon . . . Thomas Aquinas. . . . and among moderns, Bernard of Trevisa, Frater Basil. Valentinus, Phillip Theophratus [Paracelsus].[14]

This is a multitraditional list that includes Christians like Dionysius [the Areopagite], Albertus Magnus, and Thomas Aquinas, but also some Islamic alchemists or theologians—Avicenna [Ibn Sina], and Geber [al-Jabir]—and some Greco-Roman figures.

Such definition by listing is hardly limited to alchemists. In nineteenth-century America Ralph Waldo Emerson tersely writes:

> Thou shalt read Homer, Æschylus, Sophocles, Euripides, Aristophanes, Plato, Proclus, Plotinus, Iamblichus, Porphyry, Aristotle, Virgil, Plutarch, Apuleius, Chaucer, Dante, Rabelais, Montaigne, Cervantes, Shakspear, Jonson, Ford, Chapman, Beaumont & Fletcher, Bacon, Herbert, Marvell, More, Milton, Molière, Swedenborg, Goethe.[15]

Here Emerson invokes a balance of ancient, medieval, and more recent authors, among whom we find far more Platonists than reputed alchemists, more essayists than theologians—but this is what we would expect, for Emerson invokes his own artistic kinfolk. One can imagine Emerson's own name in this list.

Yet I would not want such lists to diminish the mysterious uniqueness of creation. For each of these names invoked by our anonymous alchemist or by Emerson represents something like a constellation, each a remarkable individual whose works are stamped with particular genius. I have taught Dante's *Divine Comedy* and Rabelais's *Gargantua and Pantagruel* in the same course, and one can hardly find two authors whose deeply learned sensibilities were more removed from one another than the austere mystical visionary Dante and the earthy, fantastic Rabelais, whose influence can be felt through the whole of modern literature, as Emerson pointed out.[16]

Certainly there is something mysterious and extrahuman about artistic creation. Shelley wrote in his *A Defence of Poetry* that

> Poetry is not like reasoning, a power to be exerted according to the determination of the will. A Man cannot say, "I will compose poetry." The greatest poet even cannot say it: for the mind in creation is as a fading coal which some invisible influence, like an inconstant wind, awakens to transitory brightness: this power arises from within, like the colour of a flower which fades and changes as it is developed, and the conscious portions of our natures are unprophetic either of its approach or its departure.[17]

Alchemists too write that creation is not a function of reason: in the alchemical treatise "The Sophic Hydrolith" we read that "if any man desire to reach the great and unspeakable Mystery, he must remember that it is obtained not by the might of man, but by the grace of God, that not our will or desire, but only the mercy of the Most high, can bestow it upon us."[18] The alchemist and the artist both, like the farmer, "can do nothing but sow, plant, and water: God must give the increase."[19]

Thus one could argue that the literary artist and the alchemist both exist within a literary continuity, and that this continuity provides a kind of vessel within which the work can be created. Indeed, Goethe wrote exactly this:

> All productivity of the highest kind, every. . . great thought that bears fruit is beyond man's power, indeed, beyond all earthly power. These things man must regard as surprise gifts from on high, as pure children of God, to be received and honored with joyful gratitude. They are akin

to those all-powerful demoniac forces that do with him as they please, to which he unknowingly yields, even as he believes he is acting on his own. In such cases man must often be looked on as the instrument of a higher world order, *a vessel found worthy to receive the divine impulse.*[20]

The great poet is, in this view, one who is perfectly suited to channel and shape inspiring creative power. He can learn the nature of the art from what has been done before, he can train, and study, but in the end it is a matter of the power he conducts.

Yet this power does not create in defiance of nature's laws. Great literature, like alchemy, must work according to nature. Thus "The Only True Way"(1677) insists to alchemical aspirants that "if you desire success, you must . . . enlist under the standards of that method which proceeds in strict obedience to the teaching of Nature—in short, the method which Nature herself pursues in the bowels of the earth."[21] This is advice that closely resembles what Emerson wrote about Shakespeare—that his works are great because they reveal the creative power of nature herself. Emerson writes in *Nature* that

> The production of a work of art throws a light upon the mystery of Humanity. A work of art is an abstract or epitome of the world. It is the result or expression of nature, in miniature. The poet, the painter, the sculptor, the musician, the architect, seek each to concentrate this radiance of the world on one point, and each in his several work to satisfy the love of beauty which stimulates him to produce. Thus is Art, a nature *passed through the alembic of man.*[22]

The individual artist is the alembic in which the alchemy of art is performed.

While all artistic creation can be seen in light of alchemy, there are some authors whose work is a conscious attempt to embody alchemical principles. Among the greatest of these is Goethe, whose *Märchen*, or *Fairy Tale* undoubtedly reflects alchemy, which we know he studied in some depth. Goethe's *Fairy Tale* is an extraordinary surreal work whose luminous characters—the beautiful maiden Lily, the Young

Prince, the Green Snake—represent archetypes that linger in the
mind like dream images. Like *The Chemical Wedding of Christian
Rosenkreutz* (1616), this is a work whose haunting images seem more
than entertainment.

Goethe's *Fairy Tale* reveals a clear alchemical structure. In his
commentary on Goethe's *Fairy Tale*, Adam McLean writes:

> The alchemical process outlined in the *Fairy Tale* is quite traditional. It
> involves an initial bringing together of the substances for transmutation,
> the *prima materia*, the body of the Green Snake, which is worked upon
> by a reagent, the gold of the Will-o'-the-Wisps. This produces an initial
> spiritualization—the Snake becomes luminous from within. . . [But]
> through her experience in the Temple, the Snake knows she must be led
> through a sacrifical death process. This is, of course, the Nigredo. . . . the
> center of the process. . . .
>
> Other facets of the process are borne by the beautiful Lily. Initially, she
> wears a white robe, symbolizing the Albedo . . . but as the party awaits the
> exact moment of midnight, when the process will reach its crucial turning
> point she puts on a fire-colored veil. . . . This is the Rubedo, the formation
> of the Red Solar Stone. . . . The final stage is the Coniunctio, the
> Alchemical Marriage of the King and Queen, and the spiritualization of
> the material.[23]

The spiritualization of the material—this is the alchemical goal, but it
is also a succinct expression of Goethe's accomplishment in his *Fairy
Tale*. For in it, we see the natural world transmuted into a dreamlike
or symbolic interworld.

Is this not what the greatest literature often does? Rilke wrote in his
letters that

> It is our task to imprint this provisional, perishable earth so deeply, so
> patiently and passionately in ourselves that its reality shall arise in us
> again "invisibly." *We are the bees of the invisible. Nous butinons éperdument
> le miel du visible, pour l'accumuler dans la grand ruche d'or de l'Invisible.* [We
> are to gather the honey of the visible in order to accumulate it in the great

gold-hive of the Invisible.] The Elegies show us at this work, at the work of these continual conversions of the beloved visible and tangible into the invisible vibrations and excitation of our own nature, which introduces new vibration-frequencies into the vibration-spheres of the universe. (Since different elements in the cosmos are only different vibration-exponents, we prepare for ourselves in this way not only intensities of a spiritual nature but also, who knows, new bodies, metals, nebulae and constellations.)[24]

Rilke's comments on his own poetry here, particularly on the astounding *Duino Elegies*, reveal his views of his own work as transmuting the things of this world into inward ones, even as creating—who knows?— new bodies, constellations, invisible to us here.

Rilke sees his poetry as coming to him out of an invisible realm, a timeless realm of simultaneity that he calls "*open*," a community of those past, present, and future. "There" are "angels," but not angels in an orthodox Christian sense. "The angel of the elegies," he writes, "is that creature in whom the transformation of the visible into the invisible, which we are accomplishing, appears already consummated. For the angel of the Elegies all past towers and palaces are existent, *because* long invisible."[25] What is more, "The angel of the Elegies is that being who vouches for the recognition in the invisible of a higher order of reality.—Hence 'terrible' to us, because we, its lovers and transformers, do still cling to the visible." Thus "*we are*, let it be emphasized once more, *in the sense of the Elegies, we are these transformers of the earth; our existence, the flights and plunges of our love, everything qualifies us for this task* (beside which there exists, essentially, no other.)"[26]

This magnificent passage has very few parallels in literature, and none so far as I know written by a great poet. Rilke here is directly in the German tradition of Novalis and Goethe, and all three of these poets work to transmute the earthly into the invisible, spiritual; all three are mystics, but not necessarily Christian mystics. Indeed, Rilke feels himself moving further and further from a conventional Christian worldview, and seeks to distinguish his angels from the Christian

angels, writing to Witold von Hulewicz, in a passage startlingly close
to the angelological work of Islamic scholar Henry Corbin, that the
angels to which his poem refers are closer to those of Islam. But Rilke's
mysticism here ultimately is, I think, post-traditional.

Much has been written about Arthur Rimbaud's "alchemy of the
word," but it is in the German tradition represented by Rilke that we
see the alchemy of the word revealed most lucidly. Plato wrote in
Phaedrus that "where plagues and mightiest woes have bred in certain
families, owing to some ancient blood-guiltiness, there [poetic] madness has entered with holy prayers and rites, and by inspired utterances
found a way of deliverance." For one who has this gift is through these
mysteries "made whole and exempt from evil."[27] This is a similar
redemption to that which we see in Rilke, who also certainly had his
share of suffering, who was creatively paralyzed by the turmoil of the
First World War, and who nonetheless brought, out of his personal
suffering and the suffering of his generation, unearthly beautiful
poetic songs.

There are without doubt many other poets and artists whose work
may be seen as a transmutation of suffering into beauty; indeed,
perhaps this is the definition of the great modern artist. Certainly the
poetry of William Butler Yeats and T. S. Eliot have this quality. Yeats,
like Rilke, moved easily between the invisible and the visible worlds.
Eliot forged out of his own suffering, and that of his generation, not
only an expression of modern fragmentation in *The Wasteland*, but also
the Rilkean experience of the "still point of the turning world," a
mysticism that has its analogues in Christian gnostics like Julian of
Norwich, yet exists embedded in a modern, even secular context.

The modern poet, artist, author lives in a strange world, for open
before us are all the works of the past, yet to none of them do we
belong. Rilke held that it is our task to transmute the visible into the
invisible, precisely because all that we love in this world is mutable.
Perhaps this has always been the artist's work, and true not only of the
things we love around us—the taste of an apple, the azure sky, the way
a hat fits, the touch of our lover's hand—but of all the literature of the
past, too. For if all those works of Vergil and Apuleius, Dante and

Rabelais, Emerson and Rilke, are not become part of our consciousness, they remain just consumable objects on a shelf, separate and with little meaning.

To apply an alchemical aphorism to art: art consists in separating and joining. The poet begins separate from a given work from the past—Dante begins separate from Vergil, Eliot begins separate from Dante. Then the poet comes to know his predecessor intimately, more and more deeply. But this union only lasts so long before the poet must again separate himself from his predecessor—Dante cannot, as a poet, merely repeat Vergil's *Aeneid*. He must separate from his predecessor to become himself. Yet eventually he assimilates not only the work, but something of his predecessor's very consciousness. Vergil comes alive for Dante; Cicero comes alive for Petrarch.

This union of consciousness is the culmination of the artistic work, just as the *mysterium coniunctionis*, the mysterious union of the King and the Queen, is at the center of the alchemical work. What Rilke writes about angels—that they exist beyond time, and gather the visible into the eternal invisible—is true too of the great artist, whose presence we meet through his work. For art reflects consciousness, and consciousness is the process of assimilation and discrimination. We assimilate, separate, assimilate again in a deeper way, in the constant alchemical process of transmutation that is the deeper and deeper union of art. Art exists to transmute consciousness; it exists in order that we can join in that great invisible community whose presence we feel each time we enter under the spell of a great work of art.

Notes

1. Moshe Idel, *Golem: Jewish Magical and Mystical Traditions on the Artificial Anthropoid* (Albany: State University of New York Press, 1990), xxvii.

2. Jack Lindsay, *The Origins of Alchemy in Graeco-Roman Egypt* (New York: Barnes and Noble, 1970).

3. See Michael Maier, *Atalanta Fugiens*, translated by Joscelyn Godwin (Grand Rapids: Phanes, 1989). This astounding, highly illustrated book includes a cassette recording of the fugues, newly set in modern notation and sung in the original Latin.

4. See Stanislas Klossowski de Rola, *The Golden Game: Alchemical Engravings of the Seventeenth Century* (New York: Braziller, 1988), 298–300.

5. See Arthur Edward Waite, editor, *The Hermetic Museum* (Reprint. Two volumes in one. York Beach: Weiser, 1991), I, 315.

6. Carl Jung, *Memories, Dreams, Reflections* (New York: Vintage, 1962), 201.

7. See H. J. Sheppard, "The Origin of the Gnostic-Alchemical Relationship," *Scientia* 97 (1962), 146–149; H. J. Sheppard, "Gnosticism and Alchemy," *Ambix* 6 (1957) 86–101; Jung, *Psychology and Alchemy*, 295–316; cf. also Zosimos of Panopolis, *On the Letter Omega*, where gnostic, alchemical, and Hermetic streams converge. [Editor's note]

8. Waite, *The Hermetic Museum*, II, 11.

9. Waite, *The Hermetic Museum*, II, 12, italics added.

10. Waite, *The Hermetic Museum*, II, 14.

11. "The Glory of the World," in Waite, *The Hermetic Museum*, I, 228.

12. "The Glory of the World," in Waite, *The Hermetic Museum*, I, 228.

13. Simone Pétrement, *A Separate God: The Christian Origins of Gnosticism* (San Francisco: Harper, 1990), 40.

14. Waite, *The Hermetic Museum*, I, 73.

15. Ralph Waldo Emerson, *Journals*, 15? October 1842.

16. Ibid.: "Rabelais is not to be skipped in literary history as he is source of so much proverb, story & joke which are derived from him into all modern books in all languages. He is the Joe Miller of modern literature."

17. P. B. Shelley, "A Defence of Poetry," in D. Reiman, S. Powers, editors, *Shelley's Poetry and Prose* (New York: Norton, 1977), 503–504.

18. Waite, *The Hermetic Museum*, I, 74.

19. Waite, *The Hermetic Museum*, I, 76.

20. See *Goethe's World View*, translated by H. Norden (New York: Ungar, 1963), 165. Italics added.

21. Waite, *The Hermetic Museum*, I, 152–153.

22. Emerson, *Nature*, Chapter 3, in *Selected Writings of Ralph Waldo Emerson* (New York: Signet, 1965), 196. Italics added.

23. Adam McLean, "Commentary," in *Goethe's Fairy Tale of the Green Snake and the Beautiful Lily* (Grand Rapids: Phanes, 1993), 80.

24. See *The Letters of Rainer Maria Rilke (1910–1926)*, translated by J. Greene and M. Norton (New York: Norton, 1969), 374.

25. *The Letters of Rainer Maria Rilke (1910–1926)*, 375.

26. *The Letters of Rainer Maria Rilke (1910–1926)*, 376. Italics in original.

27. Plato, *Phaedrus* 245.

Editor's Introduction

ECOPSYCHOLOGY is an emerging, interdisciplinary field which draws upon the discoveries of cosmology, psychology, anthropology, environmental studies, and philosophy to investigate the question "What constitutes a healthy relationship between individuals, contemporary culture, and the natural world?" Inspired in part by historian Theodore Roszak's wide-ranging study *The Voice of the Earth: An Exploration of Ecopsychology* (New York: Simon and Schuster, 1992), ecopsychology provides a welcome alternative to the tendency present in psychotherapy which isolates the individual psyche from the context of the larger world and encourages psychic "adaptation" to a system that is itself destructive.

In 1994, a conference was held at the Esalen Institute on "Ecopsychology: Theory and Practice." During the conference, a group of environmental writers, activists, ministers, therapists, poets, media specialists, scholars, and teachers met to explore how our collective psyches interact with what David Abram called the "more-than-human world." This report, prepared by Melissa Nelson, may be more useful in raising questions than providing answers, but that is in the spirit of the gathering, which used the unstructured, leaderless format of the meetings as "invitations to dialogue."

Among the questions discussed were the following: What is the most effective way to encourage healthy environmental behavior? Is our consumer culture a form of psychopathology? Has the city become the implacable enemy of nature? Can modern industrial societies recapture the ecological insights that lay buried in their indigenous past? Can environmental law protect the sacred in nature? What is the best way to introduce ecopsychology into the universities?

This is the type of event one would like to see discussed on the nightly news.

—DAVID FIDELER

Ecopsychology in Theory and Practice: A Report on the 1994 Conference

EDITED BY MELISSA NELSON

The Gods of the City

James Hillman opened the conference by focusing on the psychological and ecological demands of the city. He asked, "How does the city fit into the green?" Because we have favored nature as the traditional home of the gods, the city is now often seen as the enemy of nature. We need to redefine "natural" to include the built environment so that we can rediscover the "gods of the city." The scale and population of cities are important, but the health of a city is not just a matter of size. It is a matter of *how* we live there and not just how many live there.

Jeff Golliher and Rachel Bagby pointed out that urban restoration is beginning to happen from within the city itself, often at the initiative of people of color in search of environmental justice. Inner city populations recognize that we cannot abandon the city to urban decay but must transform it into something that is more in touch with the natural cycles.

Theodore Roszak observed that "suburbs, with their urban sprawl are often a failed attempt to escape the city." If we don't find ways to honor the "gods of the city," then we lose the city as one of the liveliest forms of human habitat. Less than a century ago, people had many more non-urban living options. Today most of us are left with a choice between inner city and suburbs. Along with biodiversity, the diversity of our human habitat is disappearing. By creating healthy cities we may save rural life as well; we will decrease the desire to flee the city that now creates urban sprawl. But how do we create cities that fit into the local ecosystem and revitalize them as places of cultural creativity?

Can the city become an extension of organic values rather than a denial of them?

Towards an Environmentally-Based Definition of Mental Health

Patricia Cummings and Theodore Roszak raised the question, "Would it be useful to environmentalists and psychologists to have an environmentally-based, legally actionable definition of mental health?"

Laura Sewall offered an ecopsychological definition of mental health: "To be sane is to be integrated. This means being in touch with the whole, which means one must engage in reciprocal relationships with the natural world." Can such a definition of sanity be given legal force?

Patricia Cummings observed that one of the benefits of resorting to the law is to highlight issues and thereby encourage discussion in the media and general public. If the courts can legitimize and increase public awareness about our primary need to connect with the natural world, this effort is well worth pursuing. But at this point the sacredness of land is not a legally recognizable entity. Can the legal system recognize the sacred in nature and protect it?

The Way of Wyrd

Brian Bates, a scholar of European shamanic traditions, reminded us that all cultures were originally "indigenous." He then described the Way of Wyrd, recommending it as a source of ecopsychological insight for Europeans and Euro-Americans.

He explained that the root of the word "weird" comes from the Anglo-Saxon *wyrd*, the sacred unexplainable force of existence. Within pre-Christian traditions, nature was often illustrated by the image of a web. The web of nature was invisible to ordinary consciousness, but was revealed in altered psychological states. This image presented the universe as a network of fibers, where any movement anywhere affected everything else. The image of the self, in turn, was perceived as a life-force in touch with guardian spirits. When one was out of balance with the natural order, these spirits became inaccessible. Bates suggested that we can find remnants of an ecologically-based worldview in pre-Christian European traditions. Is it still possible to connect with our indigenous past? Can we create new rituals and meditative practices to revitalize the prehistoric sensibility?

The All-Consuming Self

Allen Kanner noted that the two most ecologically destructive forces on the planet today are consumerism and overpopulation. Moreover, consumerism is increasing due to highly sophisticated advertising that convinces us that we are inadequate unless we buy an endless array of consumer goods and services. Although modern advertising is the largest single psychological project ever undertaken by humankind, it is mostly ignored by Western psychology. Jerry Mander described how advertising takes advantage of the fact that inanimate objects, such as toasters and fax machines, *gain* appeal and aliveness in the two-dimensional field of TV and billboards, while animate objects, such as plants and people, *lose* their aliveness. Advertising makes technology seem superior and necessary. Mander observed, "We are co-evolving with the creations of our own minds in a sort of intraspecies incest!"

Consumer addiction becomes more pervasive in cities, where people do not have undeveloped land with which to interact. As a result they often feel resigned to, or even trapped in, a shopping mall culture.

Consumerism also gives people the illusion that they are participating in the sophisticated technological process that created the product. Technology is a major component of science and has become viewed as the highest achievement of humanity. But because few of us can be engineers or scientists, consuming their products becomes a way to feel involved with this highly valued process. On the other hand, the more in tune people are with their local ecosystem, the less likely they are to fall prey to the blandishments of consumerism.

Kanner asked, "How as therapists can we address consumerism as a form of psychopathology?"

Applying an Ecological Worldview to Psychotherapy

The trauma of being displaced from the natural world is finally beginning to emerge as an issue in the field of psychology. One of the roles of ecopsychology is to establish the importance of this issue in clinical work. Ralph Metzner reviewed several forms of psychopathology, including autism, post-traumatic stress disorder, amnesia, and addiction. Each captures a distinct component of modern alienation from nature. Common to many of these disorders is the psychological defense of disassociation, which Metzner believes describes the current relationship of the American psyche to the natural world.

He mentioned that exploring ecological consciousness necessitates that we recognize the "numbing process" of industrial society, which manifests in the psychological process of disassociation. We all agreed on the importance of overcoming psychic numbing by recognizing and expressing the pain below the "armor" of society. In this sense, depression and grief must be valued as signs of profound human concerns.

Can clinical psychology begin to pay attention to the urban habitat and how clients are psychologically affected by the ecological crisis? Which of the standard diagnostic categories used in psychotherapy helps illuminate our cultural condition?

Teaching Ecopsychology

Mary Gomes gathered together a group of undergraduate and graduate teachers, wilderness guides, and therapists to discuss a full ecopsychology curriculum. Everyone mentioned that students are hungry for courses and experiences that include an explicit emphasis on the human relationship to the natural world. However, there are also difficulties encountered in teaching ecopsychology. Instructors need to be prepared to help students deal with the strong feelings that arise when previously held cultural values are questioned or when grief, despair, and anger over the environmental situation come to the fore. Facilitating ecological awareness may require holding classes out of doors or scheduling wilderness trips so that students can experience both the richness of different ecosystems and the damage that industrial development has done to the landscape. Teaching that encourages ecological awareness should be based on experiential and interdisciplinary models of learning. Teachers need to share with students their honest concerns about environmental problems and make space for students to voice theirs.

There was a strong feeling that ecopsychology curricula need to include courses from environmental studies and ecological science. There was also great concern that ecopsychology not lose its political bite, experiential character, or spiritual dimension in order to be integrated into mainstream academia.

While many ecopsychology courses are now being taught, there is as yet no full curriculum in the field. Mary Gomes agreed to oversee a curricular clearinghouse. She will collect materials and answer inquiries through the Psychology Department, Sonoma State University, Rohner Park, CA 94928.

Our Bioregional Home

Jeff and Asha Golliher raised the question, "When we set out to change people's environmental habits so that they will become more ecologically sensitive, what are we actually asking them to do?"

The Gollihers believe that we are asking people to redefine "home," expanding its meaning both experientially and conceptually. Most people are sincerely concerned about the environment, but the global scale of the issue is too overwhelming to deal with. On the basis of ongoing work in small groups in community settings, it appears that the bioregional scale is the appropriate level on which to work. The household is too small, the nation is too large. This focus helps familiarize people with their local ecosystem, about which they are often surprisingly ignorant. Jeff Golliher mentioned that "watersheds and mountain ranges are inherently nonanthropocentric; they are larger than any institutional ego." The more communities begin to feel that these natural areas are their "home," the smaller the gap will be between nature and culture. Home should also include the mosaic of cultures one finds in bioregional community; it should be a place for a diversity of viewpoints.

In building an environmental ministry at the Cathedral of St. John the Divine, Jeff Golliher is asking churches to reexamine how they are addressing the ecological crisis. "How do we negotiate being in the world ourselves, in terms of our relation to institutions? Are institutions currently effective as vehicles for facilitating the emergence of an ecological way of being?"

Words on the Wind

Drawing upon his studies in the phenomenology of language, David Abram asked, "Are there ways of speaking that awaken our senses?" Speaking can bring us into the more-than-human world, but language can also constrain us and shut down our senses. We need to reacquaint ourselves with the reciprocity of the senses; as we feel the wind, the wind feels us. Among oral peoples, there is an amazing intimacy between language and the land. "For them, the visual counterpart to spoken language is the land itself and not the written word. Their cultural histories are stories embedded in the land. Land is text, and meaning is found everywhere, through movement, gesture, sound, rhythm. When you drive traditional people off the land, you drive them out of their mind."

The historical movement from oral speech to the written word has impoverished this soundscape and limited the meanings available to us through the senses. When we perceive meaning only in the written word, the world becomes less magical. James Hillman noted that the moment we start seeing natural things as "dead," "we need to look and look *again*, which is the root meaning of 're-spect.'" Must our deep psychological investment in literacy (the written word) censor our capacity to experience the animate and magical in nature?

Therapy, Law, and Ecopsychology

In a lively panel discussion that was opened to the whole Esalen community, James Hillman, Patricia Cummings, Mary Gomes, and

Theodore Roszak offered sharply contrasting views of our environmental condition. Their assessments were both sobering and hopeful.

James Hillman warned that our civilization may well be a "sinking ship" that leaves us with little choice beyond "going down with dignity, a largely forgotten virtue." He felt that the dark side of our situation needs to be frankly faced before we search for easy consolation. Patricia Cummings confessed that her many years of work as an activist left her deeply uncertain that the major environmental organizations have the leadership or moral force to solve the most urgent, global problems.

Mary Gomes offered a more optimistic possibility. Environmental sustainability may indeed require this particular ship called "industrial society" to sink, but perhaps, with the help of ecopsychology, we can find better, saner ways "to live in the water." Theodore Roszak pursued another ecopsychological issue. Is it possible that the self-regulating planet itself is now playing a major restorative role in defending life on Earth? Might this be the deeper reading of the controversial "Gaia Hypothesis"? Instead of asking, "What are we going to do about the environmental crisis?", perhaps we should ask, "What is the environmental crisis already doing about us?" He wondered if the more-than-human world may not be at work now, reshaping the human psyche to the needs of "the ecological unconscious." If so, where do we see signs of an emergent new form of sanity in the everyday lives of people?

The handsomely designed *Ecopsychology Newsletter* is published twice a year. Each issue contains resource information on programs, coursework, and conferences; articles dealing with ecopsychology; and descriptions of books, videos, and periodicals of special ecopsychological relevance. Subscriptions are $10 per year and should be sent to *The Ecopsychology Newsletter*, PO Box 7487, Berkeley, CA 94707.

A Note Against the Aristotelians

AFTER HAVING DEVOTED three years and six months to scholastic philosophy, according to the rules of our university: after having read, discussed, and meditated on the various treatises of the *Organon* (for of all the books of Aristotle those especially which treated of dialectic were read and re-read during the course of three years); even after, I say, having put in all that time, reckoning up the years completely occupied by the study of the scholastic arts, I sought to learn to what end I could, as a consequence, apply the knowledge I had acquired with so much toil and fatigue. I soon perceived that all this dialectic had not rendered me more learned in history and the knowledge of antiquity, nor more skillful in eloquence, nor a better poet, nor wiser in anything. Ah, what a stupefaction, what a grief! How did I deplore the misfortune of my destiny, the barrenness of a mind that after so much labor could not gather or even perceive the fruits of that wisdom which was alleged to be found so abundantly in the dialectic of Aristotle!

—PETER RAMUS (1515–1572)

The Divine Sophia:
Isis, Achamoth, and Ialdabaoth

LEE IRWIN

> Men use various consecrated symbols, some obscure, some more
> intelligible, in order to guide the understanding toward things
> divine, but never without a certain amount of risk. For some have
> completely missed their meaning and have slid into superstition;
> while others, flying from superstition as from a quagmire, have
> unwittingly fallen over a precipice into atheism.
>
> —Plutarch, *On the Mysteries of Isis and Osiris* 67

CERTAINLY THE NARRATIVE OF THE DIVINE SOPHIA, as told by the
followers of Valentinus (*c.* 180 C.E.), is a profound and difficult one for
those divorced from the complex, multi-religious milieu from which
it emerged. The figure of *Sophia* (Greek: "wisdom"), somewhat like
Athena with whom she has been compared, seems to leap forth
suddenly as one of the great Aeons of the Deep.[1] Further, this rather
abrupt historical appearance is embedded in a more complex creation
narrative in which Sophia plays a significant role as a divine female
creatress. While a great deal has been written about her role in the
Valentinian creation from both the Jewish and Christian perspectives,
very little has been written about her affinities within the Greco-
Roman and Egyptian religious world of those days.[2] By affinities, I
mean particularly her ties with the goddess Isis, both in terms of the
sacred stories of Isis and her mysteries, as well as ties with the current
and popular oracle traditions. In many ways, as I will try to show, the
Sophia mytheme appears as a *symbolon* incorporated into the Valentinian
creation narrative as an accommodation to the pervasive influences of

goddess worship within the Greco-Roman religious world.[3] I do not see the origins of the Sophia mytheme as either a development from Jewish or early Christian literary sources per se, nor as a consequence of myth-making by those fully identified with an exclusive Christian community.[4] This is not to say that Christian and Jewish texts or traditions may not have influenced the shaping of the Sophia myth, but rather that I see such influence (particularly from Jewish sources) as secondary to the more pervasive impact of the popular spread and development of the Isis mystery tradition. It is this relationship between the Goddess Isis and the mysterious figure of the divine Sophia in the creation story of the Valentinians that I wish to explore in this paper.

The Valentinian Creation

Perhaps one of the most influential developments in the synthesis of Greco-Roman religious ideas with those of early, emergent, and often conflicting Christians ideas and beliefs, were those of Valentinus (*c.* 100–175 C.E.). Born in Phrebonis, in the Egyptian delta, he was educated in the great cosmopolitan city of Alexandria. There he was certainly exposed to the very rich pluralism of the Hellenistic and Roman religious sects, temple worship, and an abundant number of devotees to various gods and goddesses. Also, he would have clearly been exposed to the Ptolemaic Isis tradition at the very time of its flourishing rise and development throughout the Mediterranean world.[5] His exposure to either Jewish or early, divergent Christian sects would not have been a central element in a Hellenic education, though proselytes from either sect were certainly present as minority practitioners. Oral traditions, sacred stories of many different gods and goddesses, and the various beliefs of their respective followers, would have circulated in a milieu in which Christian and Jewish ideas would have competed with the more culturally visible practices of the pervasive Greco-Roman temple traditions.

In about 135 C.E., Valentinus journeyed to Rome and became involved in the emergent, but disparate Christian *ekklesia* located there, assuming a leadership role through his persuasive speaking abilities and his articulation of a "gnostic" creation story probably developed in Alexandria. He gathered a number of students about him, lectured to the public, and was influential enough to be a contender for a position of leadership in the Roman church.[6] However, his interpretive stance, one long common in the Greco-Roman world, was to give allegorical interpretations that led to the discovery of underlying meanings, particularly in his creation story, that were unique and somewhat marginal to the emerging consensus within popular Christianity. His extensive stay in Rome led to the eventual formation of a number of Valentinian "schools," each with their own particular emphasis based on his original teachings.[7] Departing Rome in about 165 C.E., his death is shrouded in mystery, though Epiphanius suggests that he died in Cyprus, surrounded by devoted followers (*c.* 175 C.E.).[8]

The Valentinian creation narrative, obviously part of a widely diverse oral tradition, has survived primarily in the hostile and satirical writings of the early church fathers. Little of Valentinus's original works remain, though several Nag Hammadi tracts have been suggested as authored or influenced by him.[9] It was the later followers of Valentinus who disseminated the creation allegory, and this narrative has survived primarily in the form of the Italic school as recorded in the writings of Irenaeus (*c.* 180 C.E.), Bishop of Lugdunum, though at least six other versions are known.[10] It is this Irenaeus version, itself a synthesis of Valentinian thought, in which the figure of Sophia looms so large and plays such an important and creative role in the emanations of the cosmos. The following brief summary (*Adversus Haereses* 1.1.1–7.5) touches primarily upon the figure of Sophia, though the reader is referred to the accompanying illustration, "The Valentinian Cosmogenesis," which appears on the next page.[11]

With Bythos, the unengendered, invisible, and pre-existent Deep, was the inseparable Ennoia, silent, creative Contemplation, and for innumerable eons there was androgynous harmony and wholeness. Then Ennoia, stimulated by Bythos, gave birth to Nous, the self-

THE VALENTINIAN COSMOGENESIS

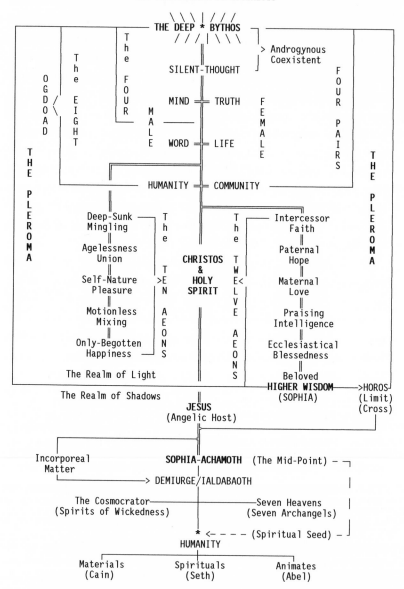

begotten Mind, who alone had knowledge (gnosis) of his origins, and to Aletheia or co-gendered Truth. This is the first Tetrad, the primal Four. Nous and Aletheia engendered Logos (the expressive Word) and Zoe (subsistent Life), who in their turn engendered Anthropos (Humanity) and Ekklesia (spiritual Community). This is the first Ogdoad, the four co-gendered, androgynous pairs, from which all other emanations proceeded.

By means of conjunction, Zoe and Logos then produced five more co-gendered pairs, the Ten Aeons, while Ekklesia and Anthropos likewise co-engendered six pairs, the Twelve Aeons. In this way thirty Aeons were manifest, derived from unengenered Deep-Contemplation, whose existence was known only to the self-begotten (*monogenes*) Mind. To the other Aeons, Deep-Contemplation was unknown and unperceivable. Together these Aeons constituted the realm of the *Pleroma*, the invisible fullness and higher domain of Light.[12]

The last pair of the Twelve was Sophia (Wisdom) and Theletos (the Long-desired or the Beloved). Sophia wished to know her unengendered origin and being aroused most deeply, in agony to know, with great pathos, extended herself before all the other Aeons, without the aid of her consort, and sought everywhere for the first creator, also known as First-Father, in order to honor his greatness. Extended to the point of being endangered by absorption into the sweetness of the absolute, she was purified and brought back by Horos, Limit or Boundary. She thereby recognized the unknowableness of the Deep and was reunited with her co-gendered consort, Theletos. However, her innate passions (*enthymesis*) continued to exist apart from her as a formless essence, separated from the Pleroma by Horos. This boundary, also called Veil and Cross, conceals the higher Pleroma from the lower cosmos.[13] Then, the self-begotten Nous-Aletheia, stimulated by the Deep, produced Christos and Holy Spirit, the final co-gendered Aeons, so that they might instruct all the Aeons of the Pleroma in the profound gnosis of the unknowability of the Deep.[14]

The passionate longing of the higher Sophia, which existed beyond the Pleroma, was called Achamoth (Hebrew: *chokmah*) or lower wisdom, and Christos-Holy Spirit, out of compassion, extended to give her form and substance, then withdrew back into the Pleroma.[15] Achamoth, desiring to be united with that luminous presence, sensing immortality, was held back by Horos. Thus, in longing for union with her own higher self (either as Sophia or Holy Spirit), Achamoth, lacking gnosis, experienced grief, fear, and uncertainty, as well as a constant turning back toward that higher light. From these passions all matter and substance was formed—from her tears and sorrows, all moist essence; from her laughter in remembering the light, all joys and luminescence; from bewilderment, darkness and the void. In response to her supplications, Christos-Holy Spirit and the other Aeons sent the Paraclete, Jesus, endowed with power and accompanied by angels, to the lower cosmos to comfort and still her passions. First veiling herself from shame, she then rejoiced receiving the true gnosis and was thus healed. The separated passions were transformed into incorporeal matter, mixed and mingled, to form two tendencies: one material, oriented to passion and evil; the other animal, oriented toward suffering and conversion. From her gnosis and ecstasy came a third essence, the spiritual (*pneuma*), reflecting her own higher nature.[16]

From the animal passions, inspired by her vision of the angelic hosts, Achamoth created the Demiurge (called Ialdabaoth in similar gnostic systems), father of the substances of the left (material) and right (animal) hands, creator of humanity and all the visible world.[17] Concealing herself at the midpoint above Ialdabaoth and below the Pleroma, Achamoth observed his creation of the seven heavens, the lower angelic hosts, Earth, humanity, and all the visible forms, both material and psychic.[18] Ignorant of other causes and origins, Ialdabaoth thus proudly claimed to be the only god, apart from whom there was no other (Isaiah 44.6). From the darker passions, he created the Cosmocrator, World-Ruler, Archon over all the troublesome daemons of the material world. Material humanity was created from material substance, into whom Ialdabaoth breathed animal vitality (psyche) and life, but Achamoth had secretly infused Ialdabaoth with spirit (pneuma) which he unknowingly passed on to humanity in mixed degrees. Thus human beings exist as variable combinations of the material, psychic and spiritual elements. These three mixed types were known respectively as the descendants of Cain, Abel, and Seth.[19]

The material nature will perish and not be resurrected, the psychic or animal nature will be informed and directed according to its learning and knowledge, and the spiritual remains as a seed deposited by Achamoth, Wisdom, to be cultivated according to the dispositions of the individual. Those who are the spirituals (*pneumatikoi*) and the perfected (*teloi*), having received the greater gift of spirit from Achamoth, have grown the seed to its full ripeness and maturity.[20] When all such seed has come to perfection, then Achamoth will ascend to the Pleroma and be united through the Holy Spirit and the higher Sophia, with Christos, as a holy bride. All the mature spiritual seeds will divest themselves of animal souls and, becoming intelligible spirits, will unite with the angels of the Christos. Ialdabaoth will ascend to the midpoint to oversee the souls of those who have disciplined their animal natures and are thus justified, while all remaining beings, the world, and matter itself shall be destroyed by an all-consuming inner fire. The advent of Jesus was to acquaint souls of the "spirituals" and "animates" with the spiritual seed within and to nourish its growth and development. During previous ages, the Mother also spoke many sacred utterances through the pneumatikoi, as did Ialdabaoth, and in this way the Valentinians denote three revelatory traditions: the direct oracles of Sophia/Achamoth, the illumined teachings of the pneumatikoi, and the writings of the prophets.[21]

The Isis Tradition

What were the origins of this Valentinian creation narrative? While its exact provenances will probably never be known, of the many strands that contribute to the pattern of its weaving (*mythoplokos*), some surely reflect the colors and weft of the popular Isis tradition. In particular, the figure of the divine Sophia stands forth as the most likely reincarnation of the late Ptolemaic goddess, so pervasively known and worshipped throughout the Roman Imperial era, including her approximately forty-plus temples in Egypt.[22] The sacred story (*hieros logos*) of Isis was also written in its most detailed surviving form about the time of the birth of Valentinus by Plutarch (*c.* 100 C.E.), in his letter to the priestess Clea at Delphi, where he attests to the popularity and pervasiveness of the Isis tradition.[23] In a more lofty and sublime sense, the Isis tradition of this period is also attested to by the Isis aretologies (200 B.C.E.–300 C.E.) in which the goddess assumes universal soteriological attributes connected with her higher status as a supreme goddess of the *oikumene*, the known world of the Greco-Romans.[24] Further, the Mysteries of Isis were pervasively practiced and highly popular during this same period as most cogently recorded by the Carthaginian philosopher and poet, Apuleius (*c.* 140 C.E.).[25]

In Alexandria, where Valentinus received his education, the Isis tradition had a long patronage and was a prominent part of the cultural and religious milieu. Beginning with the construction of the temples of Isis on the upper Nile at Philae and the great Sarapeum in Alexandria by Ptolemy Philadelphus (285–246 B.C.E.), the once ancient goddess of the Egyptian delta and the Greek isles rose to ever-increasing prominence that lasted well beyond the Isis processions described by eyewitnesses in late Rome (394 C.E.).[26] Royal Ptolemaic identification with the goddess was emphasized in the reign of Ptolemy Euergetes (246–221 B.C.E.) when his consort Berenice II claimed special affinity with Isis. Cleopatra III, wife of Ptolemy VIII (116–108 B.C.E.) fully represented herself as a living incarnation of the goddess, a tradition also embraced by Cleopatra VII, who shook the ancient *sistrum* to call her troops in the fateful battle of Actium.[27] Royal support for the Isis tradition lasted throughout the Ptolemaic period. For example, in Antioch (Syria) as early as the reign of Seleucus II (227 B.C.E.) an Isis festival was celebrated and there appears to have been a continuous Isis tradition there until the fourth century C.E.[28]

The Isis-Serapis tradition was also introduced in Rome (*c.* 86 B.C.E.) and in *c.* 38 C.E. the Emperor Gaius Caligula gave the first Imperial support to Isis; he had a temple constructed to Isis on the Campus Martius, which Domitian (81–96 C.E.) further enhanced and expanded. From this point on, Roman Imperial support was continuously granted the temple inhabitants and the popularity of Isis was pervasive in the major centers of the Greco-Roman world. In 215 C.E., an even more elaborate temple to Isis was constructed in the very heart of Rome (and elsewhere) by the Emperor Carcalla. Thus, during the lifetime of Valentinus and his followers, both in Alexandria and Rome, the Isis tradition was vitally alive and flourishing with the strongest popular and political support.[29]

The sacred story of Isis contains many provocative parallels with the Sophia of the Valentinian cosmogenesis. The oral traditions of Isis, pervasive in the Ptolemaic and Imperial age, provided a living resource for envisioning a potent female creatress within the context of an emergent religious worldview. Plutarch's account of the oral traditions makes an excellent foil against which the Sophia mytheme takes on richer and more complex associations. Was there a "higher" and "lower" Isis? In some ways it is not difficult to identify a tentative division between Isis, wife of the tragically murdered Osiris, and the universalized Queen of Heaven, the Isis of the aretologies. These two do not blend easily together or represent simply stages of religious development. Rather they reflect two distinctive images of the goddess, one tied to the formation of Isiatic rites of the dead and the other to an ecumenical mystery tradition. Together, they form, as does the Sophia tradition of the Valentinians, a reflexive and wholistic image of varying types of ontological manifestation. As an incarnate goddess, Isis manifests as a wifely companion caught in the turmoil of betrayal, loss, and death. As a universalized goddess of the mysteries, she manifests as a more transcendent ruler and exalted divine presence, as in Rome, where she was given such titles as *regina* (queen), *domina* (mistress), and *augusta* (exalted one).[30]

As Isis, mother and wife, her story has particular resonance with the emotional and passionate Sophia of the Valentinian narrative. Like the co-gendered creation of Sophia and Theletos (and all the Aeons), the intimate union of Isis and Osiris is reflected in the symbolon of their sexual union in the primeval womb of creation before their mutual birth.[31] This intimate bond is strengthened in a royal brother-sister marriage, an intimacy similar to that of each of the co-gendered Aeons. Traveling the known world after their birth, Osiris established the sacred rites of cultivation, civility, and worship through persuasion and song, but on his return to Egypt he was craftily entrapped in a coffin and set to sea by Typhon-Seth. Isis, on learning of his fate, sank into deep mourning and confusion, and, desiring to find her companion, searched everywhere, even to the ends of the known world where she sat in "dejection and tears."[32] Here we have a direct parallel motif, widely known in Alexandria and Rome, similar to the search and longing of Sophia for Bythos among the Aeons and reflected as well in Achamoth's search for the Christos. Each are cut off from their alter egos, isolated and alone, fearful and emotionally aroused; each experience deep pathos and conceive of the idea of seeking, particularly in the case of the lower Sophia, their lost companion, for whom they each long, and with whom, in the future, they will each be reunited. Each must wander outside their natal homes, seeking a male counterpart: Isis seeks Osiris, Sophia seeks Bythos, and Achamoth seeks the Christos.[33]

Isis must leave the sacred land of Egypt, the "home of the gods," in her search, just as Sophia extends herself beyond the boundary of the Pleroma, outside the domain of the Aeons. In this sense, the sacred land of the Egyptian *neters* or divinities—the sacred Nile valley bound by deserts—parallels the bound Pleroma of the Aeons. Isis must extend her power and magic into territories beyond the archetypal home of her birthplace. She is driven by passion and desire into "outer darkness," which in many ways reflects the lonely aspirations of Sophia's search for the first creator, but which also results in the lower creation.[34] Both wish to "honor the greatness" of their consorts. Inversely, just as Achamoth cannot enter the region of the Pleroma until the immortal seeds of the spirit have fructified, Isis is restrained from returning to Egypt until she rears the child of King Malcandor, who is mortal, but upon whom she tries to bestow immortality.[35] Here is another reflected image: Isis grants immortality to mortal humanity, secretly, without the knowledge of the royal parents, just as Achamoth secretly bestows immortality on humanity without the knowledge of the Kingly Demiurge. As the "mother of humanity," Achamoth is the potential savioress of all the rightly-guided animal and spiritual souls, just as Isis is a savioress of those who are faithful to her initiatic instructions.

Isis returns to Egypt with Osiris in the coffin but it is found by Typhon-Seth, who cuts the body of Osiris into fourteen pieces and scatters them far and wide. These pieces are symbolized by the many Osiris tombs scattered along the Nile where Isis held funereal rites for each piece, sometimes substituting an Osiris image, or a consecrated phallic effigy representing fertility and rebirth, to extend the worship of the god and to confuse her enemy, Typhon-Seth.[36] Here an analogy can be drawn between Osiris, Lord and Judge of the dead, and the Christos of Sophia who is also a judge and lord of the dead. The "lower Osiris" is murdered and entrapped within the confines of a material world (the coffin), but the "higher Osiris" sits in the judgement Hall of the Maati (Isis and Nephthys) over the resurrected dead and, upon weighing their hearts, assigns them their rightful places.[37] Similarly, the "lower Christos" is Jesus, the "fruit of the Aeons" who suffers, is crucified, entombed, and resurrected; the "higher Christos" is the bridegroom of Sophia, with whom she is united in the bridal chamber of the Pleroma, and to whom the pneumatikoi are assimilated at death and at the final judgement of the world.

Another analogy can be drawn between Horos, the Aeon of the boundary, and Hermes-Thoth, who is mentioned as parent, companion and son of Isis.[38] Hermes, from the *herma* or heap of stones set up to mark the boundaries, establishes the boundaries between the living and the (resurrected) dead and acts as a guide who can move between the realms. Hermes acts as escort of the dead, *psychopompos*, but only he can safely cross the boundaries; for this reason he also brings the messages of the gods to mortals, carrying the sacred *kerukeion* or herald's staff, thus indicating his special protected status as messenger in strange and alien courts.[39] Thoth was likewise a companion of Osiris, a reckoner of the heavens, a counter of stars, and one who measured the earth. As the scribe of Osiris, he was the inventor of writing, and was commanded by Osiris to act as counselor and assistant to Isis while he traveled the world beyond the boundaries of Egypt. It was also Thoth who taught Isis the words to briefly resurrect the dead Osiris. He is seen sitting on the top of the scale (often as a dog-headed baboon) between the two pans that weigh the hearts of the dead, and may be a symbol of the equinox, representing the balance point between extremes.[40] Thus Hermes-Thoth provides an exemplum of the divinity of the boundary *par excellence*, one quite similar to Horos, who, in the Valentinian narrative, stands at the boundary between the Pleroma and the lower cosmos as an escort to Sophia in both her higher and lower manifestations. He supports the boundary (as Stauros) and creates a separation from the Pleroma (as Horos).[41]

Another important figure in the Isis *mythologia* is the god Horus, who appears in two guises: the Elder Horus (some say, conceived by Isis while in the womb with Osiris) and the Younger Horus, Horus Harpocrates, conceived later.[42] When Isis recovered the scattered parts of the dismembered Osiris, she spoke magical words (taught by Thoth) over the body and Osiris was revived long enough for her to conceive a child, the Younger Horus.[43] This conception reflects an erotic element in the Isis narrative that was part of her connection with a phallic, procreative aspect in temple rites. In the Isis temples, the phallic images sometimes had a prayer written on them for fertility and conception; images of wombs and genitalia have also been found as offerings to the goddess. This more erotic side may correspond with the epithet of *Prunikos* ("impetuous") sometimes used in reference to Sophia, which has been translated as having erotic, sexual, or "lewd" connotations. Such connotations would have been wholly positive in the Greco-Roman milieu, where the goddess Isis-Hathor combined both maternal and erotic love.[44]

The pervasive image of Isis with a child at her breast depicts her nursing Horus Harpocrates, whom she reared in secret among the papyrus swamps of the Nile delta. The Elder Horus, or Horus Haroeris, was the ancient peregrine falcon god, also known as Horus Harakhty, whose eyes were the sun and moon, and who was assimilated to Re as a form of the underworld Osiris.[45] In Coffin Text 148, Isis, conceiving by Osiris, gives birth to the Elder Horus who then flies up beyond the gods and says, "My flight has reached the horizon. I have passed by the gods of Nut. I have gone further than the gods of old . . . I am Horus whose domain stretches far beyond gods or men and also I am son of Isis."[46] By contrast, the Younger Horus is born weak and feeble in the lower limbs and must be strengthened by his mother's magical breath (assisted by Thoth); the Younger Horus then fights and defeats Typhon-Seth. Plutarch specifically refers to the Younger Horus as being "contaminated in his substance because of the corporeal element."[47] In the Valentinian narrative, the lower Horus thus resonates with Ialdabaoth, the Demiurge, a more corporeal or material being, who is strengthened by the secret infusion of the pneuma (spirit-breath) into him by his mother, Achamoth, and who then contests with the *Cosmocrator* or World-Ruler for dominion over the lower or visible creation. The Elder Horus may reflect an image of Bythos, the Deep, as the god of the far-horizon, "beyond all gods and men," or may be considered a prototype of the Nous which alone knows the invisible, unengendered primal parents.[48]

While the Isis-Osiris myths contain many parallel motifs and certain structural resonances with Valentinian cosmology, the Isis aretologies (hymns describing her many virtues) provide a frame for considering the nature of the character and powers of the higher Sophia. Here the concept of "mother of god" (Egyptian: *mut-netjer*), used to refer to the Isis-Horus relationship, becomes extended to the entire realm of the oikumene, the Greco-Roman world and beyond. The title "Isis, Great Mother of the Gods" was used by the priests of Alexandria as early as 130 B.C.E., a title also used by Cleopatra VII.[49] Achamoth, who gives birth to Ialdabaoth, is also the "mother of god" or the mother of the supreme ruler of all visible creation, a term later assimilated into the Christian tradition of Mary (Theotokos) in her role as mother of Jesus. The higher Sophia also gives birth to Achamoth out of herself and thus is the supreme source and mother of the middle and lower cosmos. Isis, as engraved on the walls of her temple at Philae, also is the "Lady of Heaven, Earth, and the Netherworld."[50] From early times, Isis was a giver of life, able to heal and to grant immortality—certainly an attribute of Sophia who also gives life and immortality through the creation of the lower divinities and the divine seed implanted within human beings.[51]

Isis was also a goddess of wisdom, an epithet obviously held by Sophia. The wisdom of Isis is secret and hidden, "great in magical power," and her word is capable of causing transformation and miraculous changes.[52] In the Valentinian narrative, Sophia rarely speaks, except in prayer and supplication to the Father, and is stripped of the magical power of words so obviously intrinsic to Isis. Isis petitions Re to learn his secret name in order to heal him, thus providing a faint echo for the supplication of Sophia to the Fore-Father, but her wisdom seems to stem from seeking to understand her own origins and the causal source of the other Aeons, which results in a less magical creation, rather than by actively controlling the process through magical incantations.[53] Isis, in the Kyme aretology, is a cosmic creatress who "divides the earth from heaven, showed the path of the stars, and ordered the course of the sun and moon"; as the wisdom that secretly guides Ialdabaoth, Achamoth also provides the inspiration for the creation of the visible heavens.[54] The title *Soteira*, deathless savior, is a common and widespread epithet of Isis, she who saves from disaster, illness, and misfortune.[55] Sophia is also a soteriological figure who saves humanity by placing the divine seed within them, thus providing the means for spiritual rebirth.

In the Cyrene aretology, it says: "I am Isis, sole ruler forever, and I oversee the ends of the sea and the earth; I have authority, and though I am but One I oversee them." This motif announces the supreme rule and high position of Isis as the unique and singular guardian of all created beings.[56] While the higher Sophia does not succeed in her initial aspirations to know the source and origin of all creation, her lower manifestation, Achamoth, does indeed become the supreme authority over the created world. Her authority is higher than that of Ialdabaoth who is her active but limited creator (Horus-like) son; separated from the Pleroma, she must act autonomously from the other Aeons (like the separation of Isis from the other Egyptian divinities) to resuscitate the spiritual seed within humanity and thereby redeem the creation (with the help of the Osiris-like Christos). These correlations relate well to the soteriological functions assigned to Isis, which she clearly shares with Achamoth.

Isis of the aretologies is a supreme divinity who is *myrionumos* (of myriad names), *polyonumos* (many-named), and *polymorphos* (many-formed) who was assimilated with many other goddesses as a common practice in Greco-Roman religious hermeneutics. As such, her assimilation with the divine Sophia would have been an obvious interpretive strategy for those familiar with the Isis tradition.[57] In this sense, Sophia would be another manifestation of the Isis synthesis by which her priestesses, priests, and worshippers characterized many diverse Greco-Roman female divinities. The great Alexandrian goddess of the Serapeum, and the Isis Campensis of Rome, would be, in her royal patronage and support, a pervasive presence through celebration, seasonal rituals, and mystery rites, and, as a highly popular divinity for women, she would be easily identified as a female wisdom figure.[58] The Valentinian Sophia discussed in oral tradition among the various initiates would surely find a natural resonance with the Isis narratives, and from the perspective of the devotees of Isis, be an obvious manifestation of her wisdom and capacities. Conversely, the authors of the Valentinian creation would surely be sensitive to the pervasive role assigned to female divinities such as Isis and, in some way, rework the praise-motifs of the goddess to serve their own particular interests.

Another aspect of the Isis tradition that is also reflected in the Valentinian cosmogenesis is the mystery tradition and rites associated with Isis. These rites, popular and pervasive at the time of the emergent composition of the creation story, were well known and, while rarely openly discussed, impressed themselves deeply on the popular conception of the goddess. In the Kyme aretology Isis says, "I taught men the initiation into mysteries."[59] As early as Ptolemy II, the Isis tradition was conceived of as having a significant mystery aspect, both from the Egyptian point of view of the role of Isis in the underworld and at the judgement of the dead (as represented by the Egyptian priest Manetho) and from the Greek point of view in the ties between Ptolemaic Isis and the rites of Demeter (as represented by Timotheus, who belonged to a priestly family in charge of the Eleusinian mysteries).[60] The synthesis of the Isis-Osiris story, and its correlates with both the mysteries of Egyptian royal succession and the funerary rites of mummification, burial, and judgement blended with the Greek rites of renewal and the "blessedness of immortality" conferred at Eleusis, made a powerful combination. Eventually, Isis came to preside over the Eleusinian mysteries, as shown in the Maroenia aretology, though Isiatic magical influence at Eleusis may date to the early sixth century B.C.E.[61] Numerous associations (*thiasoi*) were formed of devoted followers of Isis (*Isiatai*) in both Greece and Rome, and worshippers without temple rank often formed communities near the temples to have access to the festivals and rites.[62]

The diverse participants in the Isis mystery rites, religious festivals, processions, and temple activities, and the pervasive interest in Egyptian religions by the lay and hieratic followers of Isis (the *Isiakoi*, or *Isiaci universi*) may have constituted more than ten percent of the Greco-Roman population. Thus the knowledge of Isis was by no means confined to merely oral narratives of the Isis-Osiris *mythologia*. The rich lore of the festivals, daily ceremonies, and mystery celebrations was also current and pervasive. Plutarch, in discussing these mysteries, notes:

> [Isis] was not indifferent to the contests and struggles which she had endured, nor to her own wanderings nor to her manifold deeds of wisdom and many feats of bravery, nor would she accept oblivion and silence for them, but she intermingled in the most holy rites portrayals and

suggestions and representations of her experiences at that time, and sanctified them, both as a lesson in godliness and an encouragement for men and women who find themselves in the clutches of like calamities.[63]

It is significant to note that the core themes of the Isis mystery are the wandering, sorrow, pain, and struggle involved in her search for the lost Osiris. Such themes would surely reinforce the search and longing motifs of the Valentinian Sophia for the Fore-Father and, even more cogently, of Achamoth's search for the Christos as directly reminiscent of the Isis mysteries.

Further, a Plutarch fragment recorded by Stobaeus (4.52.49), refers to the experience of the initiate in a likely Isis mystery:

> The soul suffers an experience similar to those who celebrate great initiations . . . wandering astray in the beginning, tiresome walking in circles, some frightening paths in darkness that lead nowhere; then immediately before the end all the terrible things, panic, and shivering and sweat, and amazement. And then some wonderful light comes to meet you, pure regions and meadows are there to greet you, with sounds and dance and solemn, sacred words and holy views; and there the initiate, perfect by now, set free and loose from all bondage, walk about, crowned with a wreath, celebrating the festival.[64]

Here we see a perfect exemplum of the circumstance of the higher Sophia, first searching in outer darkness, confused and afraid, then meeting with Horos and being turned back, then received into the Pleroma, reunited with her consort, instructed by the Christos-Holy Spirit, and finally blessed by the joy and harmony of the Aeons.

In a passage by Apuleius we read that the mysteries of Isis are to be accepted, as the priest informs Lucius, "in the form of a voluntary death and salvation by grace."[65] Surely the experiences of the higher and lower Sophia reflect just this soteriological motif, transposed now to the Christos as the redeeming Aeon, so that Sophia, rather than having the status of a goddess, is here given the role of an initiate and supplicant to the elder Aeons. Yet, the co-gendered nature of these Aeons, in their feminine manifestations as Holy Spirit, Community (Ekklesia), Life (Zoe), Truth (Aletheia), and Contemplative Thought (Ennoia), reflect feminine, creative presences at the highest stratum of the Valentinian ontology. Isis, as the redeeming goddess of the aretologies and as the goddess of holy rites of initiation, provides a powerful reflexive image that demonstrates clearly the redemptive power of the divine feminine at the highest levels of personal and social transformation. The rebirth and reintegration of the initiate into the "wonderful light of the pure regions" certainly articulates a *symbolon* of the reintegration of Sophia among the Aeons and is a foremarker of the promised reintegration of Sophia-Achamoth in the celestial marriage chamber with all the Valentinian spirituals and "perfected ones" (*teletoi*), a term used to explicitly describe those, according to Irenaeus, who have been "initiated into the mysteries of Achamoth."[66]

One final source must be briefly mentioned as yet another aspect of the Greco-Roman religious world that would also reflect written and oral traditions likely to influence the Sophia mytheme in the Valentinian creation. This is the widespread popularity and belief in the oracle traditions, increasingly so during the flourishing period of the Valentinians.[67] In the Greco-Roman period, the oracle traditions (such as the Sibylline and Chaldean) provided yet another exemplum of the connection between a higher and lower cosmological order in which a specially gifted woman functioned as intermediary with the higher Aeons. The sacred utterances of the Mother, referenced by Ireanaeus as mentioned above, provided an archetypal construct in which, as in heaven so on earth, a divinely appointed woman (*prophetis*) might act as interpreter and communicant of the gods. The tradition of an inspired teaching not only strengthened the concept of a specially appointed "elect," but it also provided a paradigmatic example of "inspired wisdom" that emphasized the prophetic gifts of women. As such, the image of Achamoth emerges as an oracular figure in the sense that she has connection with the highest Aeons through her relationship with the "fruit of the Pleroma," Jesus, and subsequently, with the Christos.[68] An excellent example of this is found in the representation of Hekate in the Chaldean Oracles, where the goddess is represented as conveying "noetic materials across the boundary into the sensible world. This role of transmitter had a complementary side, however; her position made her the 'girding membrane' that served as a limit between the Intelligible and Sensible realms."[69] This is very reminiscent of the role played by Achamoth in the Valentinian cosmology, cast in slightly more Platonic terms.

Conclusions

It has not been the point of this paper to convince the reader that the Valentinians necessarily shaped their cosmogenesis on a conscious emulation of the Isiatic tradition. I have nevertheless tried to outline the many points of similarity and resonance that clearly exist between the Sophia mythemes and mythologia surrounding the goddess Isis. By "resonance," a term I have used frequently, I simply mean a similarity and analogical harmony between structural elements within both narrative traditions. From my own point of view, I see the Valentinian narrative as a *syntagma*, a story which is "put together in order" and constitutes a reformulation of the role of the sacred female in the creation process. This reformulation does not, by any means, reproduce the high status and powers of a true creator goddess, but in fact subordinates the genetrix motif to a more dominant and implicit male hierarchical order. Yet, the prolific nature of the Isis tradition and the prevalence of other female divinities, both in Alexandria and Rome, certainly required some creative response that, while recognizing the power of the genetrix, cast that power into a more ambiguous light, and used the mytheme as a means for justifying a negative evaluation of the created and visible world. Yet, there remains an ambivalent quality to the narrative, because the spiritual potential for a true "gnosis" is a consequence of the seeds planted by the lower Sophia, who thus prepares the way for future spiritual illumination.

If we look briefly at the Isis aretologies from the perspective of those virtues which indeed are lacking in the divine Sophia, we can see immediately how reduced the role of Sophia has become in the Valentinian narrative. Already mentioned is Sophia's lack of "magical powers" or words and incantations which can have a direct creative sense. The cosmological prominence of Isis is well captured in the following statement made by the goddess in Apulieus's rendition of her epiphany to Lucius:

> I who am the mother of the universe (*rerum naturae parens*), mistress of all the elements, the first offspring of time, the highest of the deities (*summa numinum*), the queen of the dead, foremost of the heavenly beings (*prima caelitum*), the single form that infuses all gods and goddesses; I who order by my will the starry heights of heaven, the health giving breezes of the sea, and the awful silences of those in the underworld; my single godhead (*cuius numen unicum*) is adored by the whole world in varied forms, in different rites and with many diverse names.[70]

Sophia is not a mistress of the elements, nor the highest of the deities, nor queen of the dead, nor the single form that infuses all nature (though this might be debated); nor are the heavens ordered by her will except through her male offspring; nor are there rites carried out in her name. Nor, most certainly, is her godhood adored by the whole world, nor, necessarily, by even the Valentinians (though one suspects that female devotees might have had quite different ideas about the spiritual significance of Sophia).

In sum, Sophia is not the ruler of every land, a giver of law, the one who controls fate and destiny, she who established the temples and rites of the other gods, the most mighty in name, the all-bounteous guardian and guide, the provider of sweetness in assembly, the all-seeing truth, the all-powerful Good or the one of great renown—all of which are attributes of the goddess Isis.[71] Nor, more significantly, does Sophia establish that "the power of women is equal to that of men," as does Isis, a concept which struggles for significant expression in the Valentinian cosmogenesis but which never completely attains a genuine and unequivocal articulation.[72] Further, the attitudes of many Christian commentators expressed in the texts show a clear disdain for women in an era of increasing male religious hierarchy and emphasis on asceticism. This makes it doubly difficult to grasp the ways in which the Sophia figure would have been evaluated by the lay followers of the Valentinians and other competing neo-Christian sects.

In the broader and more popular context of the Greco-Roman, non-Christian and non-Jewish world, the evaluation of a female redeemer was extraordinarily high and positive. The Isis tradition significantly grew to its greatest popularity and expansion in the very same period that the new religious sects of Christianity were in a nascent but fertile period of development. Tragically, the growth of these new sects would result in the suppression and severe denial of a female deity, even though, at the popular level, the tradition was retained in the affirmation and spread of Mary Theotokos, Mother of God, in a much reduced symbolic role. At the time of the creation of the Valentinian *syntagma*, the Sophia story appears as a means to place a popular female divinity within a new context and to show her as not only subordinate within the hierarchy of the Aeons, but as having been the mother of an "inferior" creation, mother of the lower Demiurge and herself unable to return to the higher Pleroma.[73] The pervasiveness of the positive goddess traditions, and the Isis tradition in particular, represented a challenge that could not be ignored by the Valentinians. Their cosmogenesis narrative was a response, not to Jewish or Christian literary traditions per se, traditions from which they may have borrowed, but to a very widespread and popular goddess tradition, which compelled them to reformulate a new and more radical version "of the beginning," in order to affirm their own emergent synthesis of Christic and Greco-Roman religious ideals.

Notes

1. At the temple of Neith in Sais (delta nome), the androgynous warrior-goddess image was regarded as representing equally Athena and Isis, with the inscription, "I am all that has been, and is, and shall be, and my robe has never been uncovered by mortal man." See R. E. Witt, *Isis in the Graeco-Roman World* (London: Thames and Hudson, 1971), 67 and 122.

2. For Jewish studies see Carol R. Fontaine, "Wisdom in Proverbs," in *In Search of Wisdom: Essays in Memory of John G. Gammie*, ed. Leo G. Perdue, Bernard B. Scott, and William J. Wiseman (Louisville, Kentucky: Westminster/John Knox Press, 1993), 99–114; David Winston, "Wisdom in the Wisdom of Solomon," (ibid., 149–164); Steve Davies, "The Canaanite-Hebrew Goddess," in *The Book of the Goddess Past and Present*, ed. Carl Olsen (New York: Crossroad Press, 1985), 68–79; and Birger A. Pearson, *Gnosticism, Judaism, and Egyptian Christianity* (Minneapolis: Fortress Press, 1992), passim.

For basic Christian studies, see G. C. Stead, "The Valentinian Myth of Sophia," *Journal of Theological Studies* 20 (1969), 93–95; Deidre J. Good, "Sophia in Valentinianism," *The Second Century: A Journal of Early Christian Studies* 4 (1984), 193–201. Deirdre J. Good, *Reconstructing the Tradition of Sophia in Gnostic Literature* (Atlanta: Scholars Press, 1987) and Simone Petrement, *A Separate God: The Christian Origins of Gnosticism* (San Francisco: HarperSanFrancisco, 1990), passim, are both more in-depth studies.

3. For works comparing Sophia and Isis, most of which take a Judeo-Christian perspective, see John S. Kloppenborg, "Isis and Sophia in the Book of Wisdom," *Harvard Theological Review* 75 (1982), 57–84; W. L. Knox, "The Divine Wisdom," *Journal of Theological Studies* 38 (1937), 230–37; James M. Reese, *Hellenic Influences on the Book of Wisdom and its Consequences* (Rome: E Pontificio Instituto Biblico, 1970), passim.

Pheme Perkins has written most convincingly about the Isis-Sophia relationship; see Pheme Perkins, "Sophia and the Mother-Father: The Gnostic Goddess," *The Book of the Goddess Past and Present*, ed. Carl Olsen (New York: Crossroad Press, 1985), 97–109; and Pheme Perkins, "Sophia as Goddess in the Nag Hammadi Codices," in *Images of the Feminine in Gnosticism*, ed. Karen L. King (Philadelphia: Fortress Press, 1988), 96–112.

4. By use of the term "mytheme" I do not mean to denigrate, in any way, the religious content of the Sophia story. The Sophia aspect of the creation

story is a "theme" that is essential to the Valentinian creation process and around which cluster a number of divergent ideas and beliefs. Alternatively, the Sophia story does not stand as an independent "mythos" on its own, but is always embedded in a larger story. Therefore, the term "mytheme" refers to a specific structural content that has its own variable forms but is one strand of a large and more complex sacred narrative, oral or written.

5. For an excellent short survey on the Isis tradition, see Rory B. Egan, "Isis: Goddess of the Oikoumene," in *Goddesses in Religious and Modern Debate*, ed. Larry W. Hurtado (Atlanta: Scholars Press, 1990).

6. For an introduction to Valentinus, his life, and works see Bentley Layton, ed. and trans., *The Gnostic Scriptures: A New Translation* (New York: Doubleday, 1987), 117–222. Layton interprets Valentinian Fragment 1 as supporting the development of the creation mythos in Alexandria and notes that Valentinus may have "come into contact with the esoteric Hermetic literature of Greek-speaking Egypt" (Layton, *Gnostic Scriptures*, 220). It seems more likely to the present writer that this development would have been through oral, rather than written traditions. Pearson (*Gnosticism*, 200 note 23) suggests a Syrian origin, transmitted to Alexandria through the teacher Basilides, with whom Valentinus may have studied. The issue of the "gnostic" contribution is mentioned in Irenaeus, *Adversus Haereses* (1.11.1), ed. Alexander Roberts and James Donaldson, *The Ante-Nicene Fathers* (Grand Rapids: Eerdmans, 1987), I, 309–567.

7. For an excellent summary of the Valentinian worldview, see Pheme Perkins, *Gnosticism and the New Testament* (Minneapolis: Fortress Press, 1993), 44–45; Kurt Rudolph, *Gnosis: The Nature and History of Gnosticism* (San Francisco: Harper & Row, 1983), 317–24; and Hans Jonas, *The Gnostic Religion* (Boston: Beacon Press, 1972), 174–205.

8. Epiphanius, *Panarion* 31.7.1, trans. Philip R. Amidon, *The Panarion of St. Epiphanius, Bishop of Salamis* (Oxford: Oxford University Press, 1990), 108–114.

9. The writing of Valentinus are slight: the brief cosmological poem entitled "The Summer Harvest" and the nine Fragments (see Layton, *Gnostic Scriptures*, 230–247); some scholars consider the Nag Hammadi "The Gospel of Truth" as possibly written by Valentinus (Nag Hammadi Corpus I, 3), and the "Apocryphon of John" (Nag Hammadi Corpus II, 1) has been suggested

as a prototype of the Valentinian myth, though Simone Petrement (*A Separate God*, 418) argues that this document is a later Sethian development of the original myth. For Nag Hammadi documents, see James Robinson, ed., *The Nag Hammadi Library in English* (San Francisco: Harper & Row, 1977). See also G. C. Stead, "In Search of Valentinus," in *The Rediscovery of Gnosticism: The School of Valentinus*, ed. Bentley Layton (Leiden: E. J. Brill, 1980), I, 75–95.

10. See Jonas, *The Gnostic Religion*, 178; and Rudolph, *Gnosis*, 320. The primary classical texts are: Irenaeus, *Adversus Haereses* (1.1–8, 11–21); Hippolytus of Rome, *Refutatio Omnium Haeresium* (6.29–36); Origen, *Commentary on the Gospel of John* (cited from Heracleon), passim; Clement of Alexandria, *Ex Theodotos*, passim; Epiphanius, *Panarion* (31.5–8, 35–36); Tertullian, *Against the Valentinians* (1–39); also see Nag Hammadi Corpus XI, 2, "A Valentinian Exposition."

11. The classical Greek text for Irenaeus is found in: A. Rousseau and L. Doutreleau, eds., *Irenee de Lyon, Contra les Heresies: Livre I* (Paris: Le Cerf, 1979); the traditional English text is found in Alexander Roberts and James Donaldson, *Ante-Nicene Fathers*, I, 309–326. A recent English selected translation of the myth is also found in Layton, *Gnostic Scriptures*, 281–302.

The extended Irenaeus version has been attributed by some scholars to Ptolemy, a teacher and disciple of Valentinus, but Irenaeus (*Adversus Haereses* 1.12.1–3) calls Ptolemy "less skillful" and differentiates the Ptolemaic version from his own synthesis. My reading is given to clarify the exact nature of my interpretation of this text.

12. Irenaeus, *Adversus Haereses* 1.1.1–3.

13. Jonas, *Gnostic Religion*, 82–83; also see Hippolytus, *Refutatio* 6.30.6. Horos, as maker of the boundary, "divided the cosmos from the Pleroma" (Clement of Alexandria, *Excerpta ex Theodoto* 42.1). See also Rudolph, *Gnosis*, 72–73 (Nag Hammadi Corpus II, 4.94.5–13); and Giovanni Filoramo, *A Short History of Gnosticism* (Oxford: Basil Blackwell, 1991), 74 and 79.

14. Irenaeus, *Adversus Haereses* 1.2.1–6; the instruction of the Aeons by Christos-Holy Spirit emphasizes the "apophatic" aspects of mystical knowledge—that all qualities and descriptions of the divine Deep prove inadequate and therefore silent contemplation is the only means for true knowledge or gnosis.

15. Among the Anatolian Valentinians, the knowledge bestowed on the lower Sophia was initiated by the "Mother" who brought forth the Christos according to the idea of the Better. See Clement of Alexandria, *Excerpta ex Theodoto* 23.2, 32.2, 39; also Jonas, *Gnostic Religion*, 186. For the Hebrew origins of the name Achamoth, see Davies, "Canaanite-Hebrew Goddess," 75.

16. Irenaeus, *Adversus Haereses* 1.4.1–5, 5.1–1. For discussion of the three essences, see Jonas, *Gnostic Religions*, 190 and Rudolph, *Gnosis*, 321. Perkins, "Sophia and the Mother-Father," 100, writes: "Valentinian traditions have several pictures of Sophia. While Sophia is most commonly the young 'fallen' aeon who must be restored to the Pleroma, or Achamoth, the lower Sophia, who will be restored to the aeon along with the Gnostics, there are traditions in which she appears as the perfect consort of God."

17. Irenaeus, *Adversus Haereses* 1.30.5–6. Concerning the name Ialdabaoth, Pearson, *Gnosticism*, 30, writes: "The name 'Ialdabaoth' has often been taken to reflect the Aramaic 'child of chaos.'" According to Kurt Rudolph, *Gnosis*, 73, the name is of Aramaic origin and "probably means 'begetter of Sabaoth (=Abaoth)' i.e. 'the (heavenly) powers'; evidently an esoteric description of the God of the Jews who corresponding to the biblical tradition occupies in the gnostic systems the role of the creator."

18. Hippolytus, *Refutatio* 6.33, writes, "The Sophia is called 'pneuma,' and the Demiurge, 'psyche.'" The relationship between Achamoth (Hebrew: *Hochmah*) as wisdom and Ialdabaoth as Yahweh is here linked to the Sophanic literary materials of Judaism, cf. Proverbs 1.20–33; 8.1–36; 9.1–6; Wisdom of Solomon 6.12–16; 6.21–10.21; and Ecclesiasticus (Wisdom of Sirach) 1.1–20, 24. The last two can be found in Edgar Goodspeed, trans., *The Apocrypha: An American Translation* (New York: Vintage Books, 1959). See also David Winston, *The Wisdom of Solomon: A New Translation and Commentary* (New York: Doubleday, 1979), 34–38, 59–60.

19. Irenaeus, *Adversus Haereses* 1.5.1–6, 1.7.5; for the destinction between the Demiurge and the Cosmocrator, see Irenaeus 1.5.4. The Laws of Moses were interpreted by Ptolemy, the follower of Valentinus, as divisible into three parts: one part from God (Ialdabaoth?); one part from Moses, without inspiration; and one part from the Jewish elders. See Ptolemy's "Letter to Flora" in Layton, *Gnostic Scriptures*, 308–315.

20. For a discussion of the Gnostic concepts of "types" of humanity, see Pearson, *Gnosticism*, 168–69. Such types were known and argued about within other Christian communities as well, such as in 1 Corinthians 1–4, also 12.8.

21. Irenaeus, *Adversus Haereses*, 1.6.1–7.5; regarding the prophecies of past times, Irenaeus writes (1.1.73), "They divide the prophecies, maintaining that one portion was uttered by the Mother, a second by her seed, and a third by the Demiurge."

22. Basic secondary sources for the Isis tradition may be found in the following: C. J. Bleeker, "Isis as Saviour Goddess," in *The Saviour God*, ed. S. G. F. Brandon (New York: Barnes & Noble, 1963), 1–16; C. J. Bleeker, "Isis and Hathor, Two Ancient Egyptian Goddesses," in *The Book of the Goddess Past and Present*, ed., Carl Olsen (New York: Crossroad, 1985), 29–48; Hans Conzelmann, "The Mother of Wisdom," in *The Future of Our Religious Past*, ed., James Robinson (New York: Harper & Row, 1971), 231–243; Howard Clark Kee, "Isis," in *Miracles in the Early Christian World*, ed., Howard Clark Kee (New Haven: Yale University Press, 1983), 105–145; David Kinsely, "Isis, Heavenly Queen," in *The Goddesses' Mirror: Visions of the Divine from East and West*, ed., David Kinsely (Albany: SUNY Press, 1989), 165–183; R. E. Witt, *Isis in the Graeco-Roman World* (London: Thames and Hudson, 1971); Sharon Kelly Heyob, *The Cult of Isis Among Women in the Graeco-Roman World* (Leiden: E. J. Brill, 1975); and Friedrich Solmsen, *Isis Among the Greeks and Romans* (Cambridge: Harvard University Press, 1979) each give more in-depth surveys of the Ptolemaic and Imperial Roman eras. The forty-two temples dedicated to Isis are mentioned in Witt, *Isis*, 54.

23. See Frederick C. Babbitt, trans., *Plutarch's Moralia*, vol. 5 (Cambridge: Harvard University Press, 1936), *De Iside et Osiride* (hereafter *De Iside*), but more specifically sections 12–19, 27–29, 32–36, 52–55, 64, 66 (for the popularity of Isis), 79. Also see Marvin Meyer, ed., *The Ancient Mysteries: A Sourcebook* (San Francisco: Harper & Row, 1987), 157–196, for a brief resume of primary sources. Regarding the popularity of Isis, Plutarch echos the sentiments expressed by Diodorus (*fl.* 60–30 B.C.E.) who wrote, "The whole inhabited world (*oikoumene*) bears testimony to her [Isis] and offers her honors because of her self-disclosures through healing." See C. H. Oldfather, trans., *Diodorus of Sicily in Twelve Volumes* (Cambridge: Harvard University Press, 1968), 1.25.4. For a review of the Isis religious practices, see: J. Leclant, "The

Cults of Isis among the Greeks and in the Roman Empire," in *Greek and Egyptian Mythologies*, eds., Yves Bonnefoy and Wendy Doniger (Chicago: University of Chicago Press, 1992), 245–251.

24. Louis V. Zabkar, *Hymns to Isis in Her Temple at Philae* (Hanover: University Press of New England, 1988), 135–160, discusses the aretologies and gives abundant translations. He also writes (135): "Today six aretologies proper, and about ten other texts closely related to them, are known. By their style and contents these constitute a specific literary genre in which the virtues and powers of Isis as a universal goddess were praised and proclaimed to the entire Greek world." For an alternative rendition of the Kyme aretology, see Fredrick C. Grant, ed., *Hellenistic Religions: The Age of Syncreticism* (Indianapolis: Bobbs-Merrill, 1953), 131–33; also pages 128–30, gives a partial translation of the Oxyrhynchus Papyri XI, 1380, dated to the second century C.E., which describes the many titles and locations of Isis and her temples. Vera Frederika Vanderlip, *The Four Greek Hymns of Isidorus and the Cult of Isis* (Toronto: A. M. Hakkert, 1972), gives four complete aretologies with extensive commentary (hereafter, Isidorus, *Hymns*). See also Diodorus 1.27.3–4.

25. See J. Gwyn Griffiths, *Apuleius of Madauros, The Isis-Book (Metamorphoses, Book XI): Introduction, Translation and Commentary* (Leiden: E. J. Brill, 1975); also Myers, *Ancient Mysteries*, 176–193. For an overview of the Isis mysteries, see Walter Burkert, *Ancient Mystery Cults* (Cambridge: Harvard University Press, 1987), passim.

26. Franz Cumont, *Oriental Religions in Roman Paganism* (New York: Dover Publications, [1911] 1956), 85. Bleeker, "Isis and Hathor," 35–36, notes: "Already in the fourth century B.C.E. Isis had a sanctuary in Piraeus, near Athens. Her cult spread also to the Greek Islands."

27. Kee, "Isis," 117; Witt, *Isis*, 222.

28. On Isis in Syria, see Frederick W. Norris, "Isis, Sarapis and Demeter in Antioch of Syria," *Harvard Theological Review* 75 (1982), 189–207. If Pearson's thesis of the Syrian origin of Valentinianism, transmitted through Basilides, is correct, the Isis tradition that was highly visible in Antioch may have influenced the Valentinian creation narrative (see note 6).

29. Cumont, *Oriental Religions*, 84–85; Witt, *Isis*, 70–88, 222–242.

30. Kelsey, "Isis, Heavenly Queen," 181.

31. Plutarch, *De Iside* 12.

32. Plutarch, *De Iside* 13–14, 15; Diodorus 1.20.3–22.7.

33. In is also interesting to consider that according to Irenaeus (*Adversus Haereses* 1.12.1), Ptolemy, a prominent follower of Valentinus, taught that Bythos had "two consorts" (Ennoia and Thelesis), reminiscent perhaps of Osiris's relationship with Isis and her sister, Nephthys (Plutarch, *De Iside* 14). The pathos of Isis is similar to that of the initiates in the mysteries, see below.

34. Conzelmann, "Mother of Wisdom," 236, writes: "Osiris the primordial God abides, i.e. symbolically, he is Being (*das Sein*). Isis is movement. This is represented mythically in our text as walking the circuit of the world. This means: Isis creates the Cosmos and consequently rules it."

35. Plutarch, *De Iside* 15–16.

36. Plutarch, *De Iside* 17–18; Diodorus 1.21.1–22.7; he writes (21.2) that the body of Osiris was divided into twenty-six pieces.

37. See E. A. Wallis Budge, *Egyptian Religion: Egyptian Ideas of the Future Life* (New York: Routledge & Kegan Paul, [1899] 1987), 124, passim.

38. Plutarch, *De Iside* 12. For more on the complex relationship between Hermes and Isis, see Michel Tardieu, "Isis the Magician, in Greek and Coptic Papyruses," in *Greek and Egyptian Mythologies*, eds., Yves Bonnefoy and Wendy Doniger (Chicago: The University of Chicago Press, 1992), 252. Tardieu equates the two Horus deities (see below) with Hermes the Elder (parent of Isis in the Paris Codex) and Hermes the Younger (child of Isis in the Leiden Scroll). Interestingly, Irenaeus (*Adversus Haereses* 1.11.1) notes that Valentinus taught that there were two Horos figures, the guardian of the lower boundary (between Achamoth and the Aeons) and the guardian of the upper boundary (between Bythos and the Aeons). Might this not reflect the Hermes mythos? While Horos ("limit, boundary, frontier") in Greek is a homonym with the Greek spelling of Horus (Greek: *Horos*), there appears to be little ideological connection between the two in the Valentinian mythos.

39. Walter Burkert, *Greek Religion* (Cambridge: Harvard University Press, 1985), 156–59.

40. Plutarch, *De Iside* 12; Diodorus 1.15.9–17.3. See also E. A. Wallis Budge, *The Gods of the Egyptians* (New York: Dover, [1904] 1969), I, 400–415.

41. Irenaeus, *Adversus Haereses* 1.3.5. Another interesting symbolon of the boundary is the "veil" or curtain. In Nag Hammadi Corpus II, 4.94.5–12, it states, "Sophia, who is called Pistis, wanted to create something, alone

without her consort; and her product was a celestial thing, a veil, existing between the World Above and the realms that are below." Might this concept not have some resonance with the veil of the initiates, worn by them in the sacred rites to inhibit their *epopteia* or vision of higher truth, until the moment of revelation? This idea is particularly strenghtened by Achamoth's veiling herself before fully facing Jesus when he descends to heal her of her distresses (*Adversus Haereses* 1.4.5). See also Burkert, *Ancient Mystery Cults*, 94, and Figure 3 of the Lovatelli Urn. In such a case the boundary becomes an ontological marker, distinguishing between those who have "seen" and those who have not seen.

42. Plutarch, *De Iside* 12, 26.

43. The Kyme aretology mentions Isis being taught by Hermes (ibid., 140).

44. Witt, *Isis*, 85. For more on Prunikos, see: Anne Pasquier, "Prunikos: A Colorful Expression to Designate Wisdom in Gnostic Texts," in *Images of the Feminine in Gnosticism*, ed., Karen L. King (Philadelphia: Fortress Press, 1988), 47–66; Isis as erotic goddess of love magic is also discussed in Tardieu, "Isis the Magician," 255. See also Zabkar, *Hymns to Isis*, 154.

45. Richard H. Wilkinson, *Reading Egyptian Art: A Hieroglyphic Guide to Ancient Egyptian Painting and Sculpture* (London: Thames & Hudson, 1992), 33.

46. For Coffin Text 148, see R. T. Rundle Clark, *Myth and Symbol in Ancient Egypt* (London: Thames and Hudson, [1959] 1978), 213–217; texts date from the Egyptian Middle Kingdom period.

47. Plutarch, *De Iside* 54; Kinsley, "Isis," 169; see also Budge, *Gods*, I, 486–95.

48. Witt, *Isis*, 194, suggests a parallel between Harpocrates and the Logos of the Sophia narrative; he writes (218): "The Valentinian Gnostics can plausibly be said to have evolved a doctrine in which Isis fulfils the role of Sophia and Horus/Harpocrates that of the Logos."

49. Witt, *Isis*, 131.

50. Zabkar, *Hymns to Isis*, 51, Hymn IV.

51. Witt, *Isis*, 187. In the Greek Magical Papyri, Isis is called the "seed of the ancestral gods . . . and breath of Amon," a perhaps Greco-Roman echo of the concept of the divine spark or presence; see also Tardieu, "Isis the Magician," 253; *Papyri Graecae Magicae* (PGM) 2978–89, in H. D. Betz, *The*

Greek Magical Papyri in Translation (Chicago: University of Chicago, 1985). Healing remedies and care of the sick are the special provenance of Isis, particularly in the PGM.

52. Bleeker, "Isis and Hathor," 32–33; Kee, "Isis," 109.

53. Tardieu, "Isis the Magician," 254.

54. Meyer, *Ancient Mysteries*, 173.

55. Isidorus, *Hymns* 1.26; Oxyrhynchus Papyri XI, 1380.20, 55.

56. Conzelmann, "Mother of Wisdom," 237; also see note 34.

57. Plutarch, *De Iside* 53; Witt, *Isis*, 112, 121; Tardieu, "Isis the Magician," 252.

58. See Heyob, *Cult of Isis Among Women*, passim.

59. Zabkar, *Hymns to Isis*, 140–141.

60. Plutarch, *De Iside* 28; Egan, "Isis: Goddess of the Oikoumene," 127–28; see also Witt, *Isis*, 52–53. Ptolemy II is said to have asked Manetho and Timotheus for direction in the development of the Isis rites at the Sarapeum.

61. Burkert, *Ancient Mystery Cults*, 20–21, 25–27, 41; Meyers, *Ancient Mysteries*, 157.

62. Burkert, *Ancient Mystery Cults*, 38–39.

63. Plutarch, *De Iside* 28.

64. Burkert, *Ancient Mystery Cults*, 91–92, also 162 n. 11.

65. Apuleius, *Metamorphosis* 11.21; see also Bleeker, "Isis as Saviour Goddess," 13.

66. Use of mystery language and concepts by the Valentinians was apparently common, and a source of constant irritation to Irenaeus; see *Adversus Haereses* 1.Preface.2, 1.6.1 (where the "mysteries of Achamoth" are cited), 1.6.4, 1.7.3 ("seed of Achamoth").

67. See H. W. Parke, *Sibyls and Sibylline Prophecy in Classical Antiquity* (New York: Routledge, 1992), 160ff.

68. Painting on a broader canvas, the Isis tradition also maintained a temple tradition for dream oracles that might be received by the sickly, needy, or disturbed, by sleeping in the temple. This too would reinforce the idea of a higher female divinity who functioned (at least) in the lower cosmos in terms of the needs of *Isiakoi* by appearing to them in dreams and healing them. It would be interesting to discover if Achamoth appeared to the Valentinian

elect in dreams—my guess is that such dreams did occur and were given special regard. See Burkert, *Greek Religion*, 114–118 and Parke, *Sibyls*, 125–173. In Apuleius, *Metamorphosis* 11.5, the revelation of Isis is explicitly called an oracle.

69. Sarah Iles Johnston, *Hekate Soteria: A Study of Hekate's Roles in the Chaldean Oracles and Related Literature* (Atlanta: Scholars Press, 1990), 69, passim.

70. Zabkar, *Hymns to Isis*, 143; Meyers, *Ancient Mysteries*, 179–180.

71. From the various Isis Aretologies.

72. Oxyrhynchus Papyri XI, 1380 in Grant, *Hellenistic Religions*, 129.

73. See Asphodel Long, *In a Chariot Drawn by Lions: The Search for the Female in Deity* (Freedom, California: The Crossing Press, 1993), 97–100.

Professor Peter Russell

Ruminations on All and Everything

PETER RUSSELL

I MYSELF am both by nature and by profession a poet and I have come to realize that no poetry of any serious value can be written by anyone who has no ultimate faith or belief, or at least an intimation of some kind of knowledge of the "whole." My own mentor, Ezra Pound, held that poetry "has to do with beliefs."

Modern philosophers of the better sort have seen and considered some, perhaps all, the separate "parts of a world" but have, not surprisingly, been unable to put them together, to synthesize a single vision. Hence they analyze things in ever-smaller divisions. Concepts like Unity, Love, the Good, Justice, Truth, Wisdom, Virtue, which for nearly three thousand years have been at the core of philosophical thinking, have ceased to have any meaning whatever for the professional philosophers, but continue to mean something very real to the human race in general. Children even pick up immediately on these basic concepts, but the professionals ignore, evade, or scorn them.

In the absence of any kind of metaphysical view these concepts may well seem purely illusory, and the "professori" being employees of the State can hardly expect to ingratiate themselves with the authorities by talking of values of the spirit. The State is infinitely permissive but the one thing it will not tolerate is any kind of speculation based on non-quantitative, non-measurable, non-sensorial evidence. In fact the State has no values whatsoever apart from the contingent, the convenient. Bearing this in mind, one can see clearly why "deconstruction" has become the order of the day!

* * *

83

Today, the poetry nabobs have thrown over all the values embodied in great poetry from Gilgamesh, Homer, Tyrtaeus, Sappho, to T. S. Eliot and Pound. The reasons for all this are infinitely various but in the pseudo-intellectual spheres of today one of the prime movers has been the deliberately malicious and erroneous reading of a perfectly respectable philologist and linguist, de Saussure, who at the beginning of this century, quite rightly, shifted the emphasis in linguistics from the diachronic to the synchronic. De Saussure was an exemplary diachronic linguist, that is a scholar in historical philology, but he realized that after a century and a half of chronological study of comparative language, it was high time to study language in the synchronic sense. His followers, dwarfs on the shoulders of a giant, made this the excuse to ignore historical studies and the variety of languages in the world, and to study language solely "as it is now." In the century that has passed since then, nine-tenths or more of our knowledge about language and languages has been ditched by the savants (now known as "linguisticians" rather than "linguists" because most of them don't know their own language, let alone a second or a third one).

As a parallel phenomenon I would quote my own mentor, Ezra Pound, and his "Imagist" movement, which around 1912 tried to revivify the poetic language by inculcating the clear image taken by the senses directly from sensorial observation. This was a stylistic tactic necessary at the time. But being a *tactic*, it was essentially limited. Pound himself continued with a *strategy* of the whole vision. *Imagisme*, a very limited and partial approach to writing poems, has remained the most influential element in modern poetry, the very thing that has reduced poetry from something respectable and serious to the silly little game it is now. If Pound's little sideshow, *Imagisme*, turned into the mass production of aborted poems in which the meaningless image is the central element and the poetic is solely a matter of *mimesis* (thus removing the poem one more stage away from reality instead of going out to meet reality), the linguisticians' brood, whose grandchildren call themselves proudly "postmodernists," have so twisted and will-fully misrepresented de Saussure's dictum "the signifier is arbitrary" that it has degenerated into the global assumption that "the signified itself is arbitrary." De Saussure's original *bon mot* was valid enough for a descriptive cross-section of any language as it is at any one moment of time, but of course would be wholly inadequate, even totally untrue, if you examine language in the light of its whole knowable history. This would require much more than the science of etymology and the valuable art of folk etymology, for language and the coining of words obviously arises out of the whole condition of man. A real science of etymology would demand a universal anthropology and archaeology which mankind has never been capable of developing.

The conventional model of the postmodernist linguisticians' concept of speech and language is the simplistic diagram of the function of transmitter and receiver in a Field Signals Unit. This is, to put it mildly, a somewhat minimal description of a faculty, speech, which is infinitely complex. It is also quite perversely inadequate and wrong-minded because it bases its description, and its subsequent prescriptions, on a mechanical process of transmission, a function, rather than on the very nature of the contents of human communication. But then, most people's ideas are based more on their gadgets and electronic toys and their functions than on a contemplation of the nature of things!

There is another class of slightly more traditional educators, especially in high schools, who put the greatest emphasis in their "teaching" of poetry, in the "meaning." The postmodernist view leads us inevitably to the conclusion that everything and everybody, including their idol, Mr. John Ashbery, is meaningless. The "meaning-mongers," on the other hand, insist that their students search for a verbal equivalent in straight prose for the poetic production of, say, Keats or Shelley, which shall be the "real" meaning, as though the poet hadn't said just what he "meant." Archibald McLeish's now proverbial dictum—"The poem should not mean but *be*"—is far more to the point, but like all wise saws and modern instances, both to say traditional proverbs, is on anything but a superficial glance, extremely ambiguous, and however well-known, is ignored anyway. The poem that is worth the name of poem offers multiple, often contradictory, meanings, but these are only parts or individual functions of it, since the poem is not devised on the basis of an intended meaning. If it were, the "poet" would have written in good straightforward, logical and grammatical prose and have avoided all ambiguity and risky suggestiveness. Good prose is equivalent to simple algebraic equations, and let us bless the Gods for it. A great poet like Shelley or Goethe or Dante often writes the best prose. A famous prose writer like, say, Trollope, often writes the worst. The achieved poem is in a different semantic category: it is infinitely more complex than simultaneous quadratic equations. The good poem really is an equation in complex numbers—no one can or should reduce it to a "meaning" or even a series of meanings. If the meaning-mongers would only think of music (which, after all, is at least as compelling and vital to us as is poetry), they might avoid their lightheaded pedantries. When you listen to good music, surely you don't ask "What does it mean?" And yet, surely a fugue of Bach or a quartet of Beethoven "means" something extremely profound to us.

*   *   *

This would-be dialectical ramble inevitably brings me to the problem of pluralism. Not of course that there ever was a period when there was one monolithic faith alone. Every era, and ours is no exception, has had an officially dominant "religion" or set of beliefs, and a whole series of sophists, heretics, meddlers, and tricksters, as well as an exiguous number of mystics and metaphysicians who have thought primarily in universal terms. Dante and Meister Eckhart, like Pythagoras and Plato, were of this last class of universal truth-seekers. They were surrounded by innumerable self-contradictory dogmas and ideologies which were the *sine qua non* of acceptance (and so "tenure and promotion") by the many political parties that masqueraded as churches and "schools." For all of them there was only one truth. The difference today lies in the fact that the dominant power is the party of parties who believe that all "truths" are equally true (or untrue) and that anyone who holds to a particular belief (a "presence" as they say) is suspect, and so worthy only of being eliminated from the rat-race. This they call pluralism and hold to be the One Truth. In the words of Auguste Comte, "There is only one absolute maxim: There is absolutely no absolute."

Dr. Paul Dean, reviewing T. S. Eliot's recently published "Varieties of Metaphysical Poetry," quotes from Eliot's earlier essay on the Metaphysicals: "A philosophical theory which has entered into poetry is established, for its truth or falsity in one sense ceases to matter, and its truth in another sense is proved." This might sound like a dangerous pluralism, but that is far from the case when the passage is read in its context. It means rather that the momentary articulation of a particular idea (true or untrue in itself) is powerfully suggestive or evocative of the Universal Truth, the *presence* of the Transcendent One. Mr. Dean goes on: "As the unity of belief fragments historically—the Reformation being the great watershed, the consequences of which are still being worked out in our pluralistic and relativistic world, so the likelihood of an artist's attaining intellectual coherence recedes. In the absence of commonly accepted acknowledged standards, it is unlikely; in the absence even of an agreement that some standards are necessary, it is virtually impossible" (*The New Criterion*, October 1994, p.77).

As I see it there are two quite different types of pluralism. One is *necessary* in the overall divine plan, the other is quite gratuitous.

This latter for me represents a mere amorphous relativism based on a minimal cultural experience and an almost closed mind: "My guess is as good as yours"; or "Nothing is admissible if there is in it any 'presence,'" that is, if it includes any dogma or magisterium accepted in the past, any traditional teaching; or again, "Things only have meaning in as far as they are considered in the *différance* from other particular things," that is, that there is no meaning in anything "in itself." These infantile conclusions are the result of the exclusion of traditional metaphysic from all thought. By examining solely sublunary things and comparing them with each other, without any reference whatever to the celestial and supracelestial realms, quite obviously nothing but meaninglessness results. Plato in *Parmenides* proved quite logically that if the concept of the Transcendent One was ignored or denied, everything from abstract ideas to material phenomena would be reduced to a shadowy and insubstantial nullity.

The first or necessary type of pluralism is quite simply due to the fact that the infinitely multitudinous phenomena are all situated, as it were, at different distances from the One collected truth, which itself contains without contradiction or diversion, the Whole. The truly aware man, one versed in Plato's four levels of discourse, need find no difficulty in holding plural beliefs or faiths, different and even contradictory just because each participates more or less of Truth at one or other of very many hierarchic levels of *Intelligentia*. My tobacco shopkeeper, who when I buy ten packs of *Alfa* writes down in a vertical column the price ten times and solemnly adds all these figures up (unaware that all you have to do is to add one zero), has a much more limited view of things in general than my neighbor who has studied Dante's use of numbers in the *Commedia*. I need hardly say that society rewards the tobacconist with far more cash per annum than the learned schoolmaster, who in fact is himself a sort of broody owl. I have noted that almost all the great mystics have been outstanding mathematicians.

In the nineteenth century the hierarchical system of social class was based on a combination of economic status and educational attainment, because of course only the fairly well-off could get at least some education and some social polish. In our time we boast of our classless society, but the trouble with the classless society is, to put it vulgarly, that "It has no class." For the purposes of a social taxonomy, I class people into those who intuitively know more or less *qualitatively* of the nature of things. I envisage, in my rather naïf fashion, a series of concentric spheres representing the intellectual (= *noetic*) reach or range of the different types of individual towards that sublime concept of the Transcendent One. These imaginary concentric spheres are not at all unlike the concentric spheres of the Heavens envisaged by the Jewish apocalyptics, the Islamic spiritual space-travelers who anticipated Dante by more than half a millennium, and indeed the shamans who preceded, and who have survived, these highest schools of intelligence. But please note that my hierarchy of concentric spheres represents degrees of qualitative intellection, not just arithmetical progressions of *quantities* of knowledge. As my neighbor X says of my neighbor Y, "He knows everything, he understands nothing."

In this latter sense of plurality I have less and less difficulty on holding in my mind and simultaneously balancing qualitatively very different ideas. In my youth I searched always for the one formula, in my case a Roman Catholic orthodoxy, as the one final Truth. Having not merely studied academically but also to some extent "lived out" the Christian, Jewish, Islamic, Hindu, Buddhist, Taoist, Confucian, and many other "religious" experiences, not to say quite a number of non-deistic philosophies, now I am well into my seventies and can live with all of these images or archetypes and be quite undisturbed by the apparent contradictions between them. For me, *Isshi*, the woman, is at once the mythical Eve; the Hokhmah or Sophia; the "femina qui circumdabit cirum" (Jeremiah 31.22); Blessed Mary the Mother of God; as well as sublime feminine images from Islam and other religions; and further even than this identify her with Isis herself or the many other Mother Goddesses of antiquity, like Mary with their rod and triple orb, Mistresses of Heaven, Earth, and Hell. On the level of religiosity and poetry I perceive all these beautiful figures as equivalent, analogous if you prefer the word. On the level of dogma, of course it would be quite inadmissible to identify them. Dogma has its place but it is much lower than the poetic. The different religions all have their dogmas, which really are *figured* representations of ineffable and informal truths. These figures or dogmas are necessary for us to grasp enough to rise to higher levels, such as the poetic or prophetic vision. I am not concerned to encourage some sort of syncretic dogma or dogmatic syncretism, as it seems to me that the Bahai and the Masons and Rosicrucians have done, but rather to be hyperconscious of that One truth which all the religions and dogmas subsume. I don't ask myself any more "Is it true? Is it correct?" any more than I do when I listen to music of Monteverdi, Bach, or Beethoven.

Religiosity rather than dogmatic religion is what I am concerned with and is what releases poetry, inspiration, even perhaps revelation in us. In my Quintillius poems (an imaginary late Roman poet), I have uttered what on the dogma level are shocking blasphemies, but these utterances, like many of the so-called blasphemies of Baudelaire, are bridges to the Divine. In this sense they are genuinely *pontifical* utterances.

The religious and the poetic not only border on each other and are consequent on each other, but they very largely overlap each other. Poetry is a subtle intuition of analogies and harmonies that evoke hidden truths which by their nature are undefinable and ineffable. Dogmatics cannot define such things for they represent the most profound dimensions of consciousness, and are essentially religious. What makes Poetry Poetry is the harmonious sound of word chains that echo and correspond to, in musical terms, the prelinguistic and prelogical spiritual content which we perceive as an overwhelming Presence, but which logical analysis cannot describe. Poetry thus goes to the very root or ground that is held in common by Man and the Infinite.

Authentic poetry need not be specifically religious in content. It consists in letting go of oneself (or a letting oneself go) and intuiting the profound deeps in which the Eternal Mystery manifests itself. This sort of poetry does not come from stating or formulating some idea but from evoking in rhythm and harmony and the eternal images this Presence ("pre-sense" or even "forebeing") and with it one's whole being vibrates like strings brushed by an invisible wind. There can be no poetry without the Spirit (Pneuma, Spiritus, *Nous*). For the Christian that Spirit will be the Holy Spirit, the Holy Ghost; for the Jew or Muslim it will be *ruh* or *ruah*; for the Hindu it will be *atman* (and does not *atmen* in German mean to *breathe*, respiration, aspiration, inspiration?). The views put forward in this last paragraph represent not my own "original" ideas, but my own actual experience over fifty years and more, and only this week I find an extraordinary congruence with them in a brief article in a local journal by the Bishop of Postoia, Simone Scatizzi. The article was written in the simplest and clearest language possible, not for intellectuals or poets or professors, but for the old people in the Valdarno, many of them almost illiterate, but I find it extremely beautiful and true. The good Bishop never once mentions God, or the Blessed Virgin, the Eucharist, and certainly never the Church, but seems to me to touch on the very ground of Being.

All these basic ideas I find fully developed in the Orphic, Pythagorean, Platonic tradition. The subsequent Christian synthesis which existed side by side with the later Platonism and in a state of reciprocal osmosis with it, is not merely a fusion of Jewish and Greco-Roman ideas, but is a sort of harmonic progression arising out of a world in which Jewish Messianic ideas and Hellenistic philosophies interpenetrated one another to a point at which an entirely new composition (or compound) seems to emerge. With Dionysius the pseudo-Areopagite, the legions of pagan Gods, daimons, geniuses, and heroes are finally totally absorbed into the Christian cosmology and the remains of so-called paganism for the next thousand years are fragmentary and degenerate, only to be revived in the humanism of the Italian Renaissance. I would say that it is not just a matter of belief or faith in a specific dogma which leads to "salvation," but rather an opening-up to the Spirit, the Universal Mind or consciousness, in which all these sublime ideas can cohabit peacefully and even resonate with each other like some celestial choir.

* * *

I have just recently given a lecture entitled (in Italian) "Courtly Love, bourgeois love, uncourtly love" (or "discourteous love") and among many themes in it is the way the ancient Greek conception of Eros is a cosmic principle, which has its own validity at all levels from the most animal-like love-making (the North French "ameur" rather than the troubadours' "amour") right up to the highest level we can envisage the *nous*, or First Cause. My "uncourtly love" is of course the contemporary idea of Eros as merely sex (bumper stickers like "Make sex not love"). My central thesis (or rather, conviction) is that you can't experience Love without religiosity, and you can't have religiosity and love without poetry.

In her fine book on Plato's ideas on Beauty and the Arts, *The Fire and the Sun*, Iris Murdoch declares "Plato's Eros is a principle that connects the commonest human desire to the highest morality and to the pattern of the Divine Creativity in the Universe." At the same time, the learned lady draws attention to the fact that Pherekydes (the teacher of Pythagoras!) held that "Zeus became eros in order to create the world." This astounding statement adumbrates or subsumes, seven hundred years before the event, the Incarnation, that is of the Christ Jesus as the Logos (already a very ancient concept), as Love itself, and as the demiurge or creator. There are moments when one simply shudders with ecstatic recognition. And this is one of them for me. It is full of an overwhelming *presence.* Just the thing our postmodernists most actively condemn!

The modern scientific mind holds that it is the simplest and most economic explanation of a phenomenon which is the most likely to be the right one, and I see no objections to that, seeing that science should strictly be concerned with the behavior of concrete material things which are measurable. When we come to moral and spiritual matters (which are not measurable or quantifiable), scientific guidelines don't help us. If poetry, religiosity, and Love itself require some sort of faith in an ultimate transcendent Truth, then as an analogy to the scientific formula, I would suggest the principle devised by the Vedantist Gerald Heard, the friend and sometime mentor of Aldous Huxley:

> Faith . . . is the choice of the nobler hypothesis. It is the resolve to place the highest meaning on the facts which we observe.

I would hazard the opinion that only Love, in the quite archetypal sense, can determine what is "higher" or "lower." Huxley himself in *Grey Eminence* maintains that

> Ultimate reality cannot be understood except intuitively, through an act of the will and the affections. *Plus diligitur quam intelligitur.*

If the Church theologized away the Spirit of Man in the Council of

869, it seems to me that the academic Establishment and especially the postmodernists have eliminated, or at least tried to eliminate, the will and the affections. Hence there is neither Beauty, nor Love, nor Truth in their art or their criticism.

Plato maintained that the Good (which he equated with the One) comes to man in the form of Beauty, and Ezra Pound in his truly beautiful study of medieval poetry, *The Spirit of Romance*, written at the tender age of twenty-three, said:

> Great art is made to call forth an ecstasy. The finer the quality of this ecstasy, the finer the art; only secondary art relies on its pleasantness.

What are we to say of contemporary arts which appeal through their unpleasantness? I don't think the good Pound ever envisaged that possibility, at least until the end of his life, when in fact one day he gave me a copy of Burroughs's *The Naked Lunch* and asked me to tell him what I thought of it. Shortly after, I expressed the opinion that, while it was very well written, it was "shit." The old man gave me a quizzical look but said nothing in favor or against my carefully chosen expression.

We hear a lot in the academic world about methodology, a term which has meaning in scientific research but which in literary studies is little more than an empty semanteme. Aristotle, no fool he, started his *metaphysica* with the dubious pronouncement "All men desire knowledge." I hesitate to correct the great Stagirite, but surely he ought to have said "All men ought to desire knowledge"? Alas, most men don't. They wallow in their ignorance.

In my own experience, in a very wide range of studies I came to realize about twenty years ago, with great joy and delight, that *Knowledge increases ignorance*. In my image of the concentric spheres representing the fields of knowledge of different classes of men, the larger the sphere of knowledge you have conquered, the larger the outer surfaces of the sphere, and consequently the larger the interface between it and the space outside it which represents the volume of your ignorance. Rather than being discouraged by this, I was excited and yearned for more and more! This is a valid form, I believe, of Love. Everyone has read the *Symposium* where Plato defines Love as a form of indigence and intimates that the more you get of it the more you want. If this principle were applied to material things—Midas's love of gold, for instance—we would be very miserable indeed and our ass's ears would keep growing larger. But in the realm of Spirit, the opposite is the case. The more knowledge we get, the more we want, and the more we become aware of the infinite extent of our ignorance; and yet, it all delights us beyond measure. When the quality of Knowledge reaches a certain pitch it is known as Wisdom rather than mere Knowledge, and Wisdom is Sapientia, Sophia, Hokhmah—Isis, Athena, Mariam—and when you catch a glimpse of those resplendent Divinities you begin to learn what falling in love really is. All the Kates and Nells fall away into insignificance, nice as they were.

Three hundred years and more after St. John the Evangelist said that Jesus said "God is love," St. Augustine wrote, "By the Word we mean Knowledge joined with Love" (*De Trin.* 9.10) and a recent contemporary theologian, Don Luigi Sturzo, has said that Knowledge is a principle of Love. That gives the Logos concept a history as long as the history of writing in the West. It is as alive today as ever it was, though perhaps in comparatively few people. As I see it, Love is the recognition of the knowledge of the good attained simultaneously in the memory, the understanding, and the will. And of course, *recognition* was a key concept in Aristotle's *Poetics*.

Ultimately, of course, all the higher spiritual faculties depend on the archetypes or Universals. We can never know what they are because they are divine mysteries. As Thomas Taylor, quoting Proclus, says in the introduction to his translation of *Parmenides*, we can only perceive living mysteries under the veil of symbols and figures. A sober modern and even rather positivistic scholar, F. M. Cornford, in his valuable and learned introduction to *Plato and Parmenides* wrote some seventy years ago that:

> historians of ancient philosophy have paid far too little attention to

traditional images, like these of the father, the mother, and the seed. They are preserved in poetry long after philosophers of the more prosaic sort have discarded them and grammarians have come to treat them as mere arbitrary "metaphors." They are in fact survivals from a time when they were the only language available for speculation and were much more literally meant than we imagine. It is a commonplace of analytical psychology, confirmed by daily experience, that they still remain as the language of dreams. That is why they are charged with emotion in the poetry which preserves them, and also why the modern poets who renounce them and rack their brains to invent images never used before fail to produce the proper effect of poetry. The Greek poets thought otherwise. There is much light to be gained from a study of their traditional store of so-called metaphors, on the assumption that they embalm the philosophy of pre-scientific ages.

Contemporary poets could learn more from this than from almost the whole vast bulk of literary history and criticism published in the interim. The same Professor Cornford wrote in this essay "The Harmony of the Spheres" (now to be found in the collection of essays *The Unwritten Philosophy*):

Seek truth and Beauty together—you will never find them apart.

When I was about twenty-five years old, I read an essay by some British critic tearing to pieces Keats's "Ode on a Grecian Urn" and persuading the young and inexperienced (like me) that Keats's "Beauty is Truth, Truth Beauty" was absolute rubbish, mere rhetoric. This set me back twenty-five years. Perhaps the author of that article is the only person I have ever wanted premeditatively to murder.

Cornford's call for a poetic language of natural symbols based on what Plato defined as the "ideas" has been echoed considerably more eloquently in recent times by our editor, Mr. David Fideler, who writes in his book *Jesus Christ, Sun of God*:

Without the symbolic language offered by a living mythology, poets grow silent, alienated from the springs of inspiration, or resort merely to describing aspects of the physical world or their own neuroses. The artist, who in a healthy civilization, presents us with ways of seeing the world, without a living vision resorts to mere technique, "photorealism," or interior decoration.

The language of universal analogy, which is the *sine qua non* of serious poetry, is in origin pre-verbal because it consists of images and symbols representing events and states of mind at a level of the soul or Intellect closer to the Archetypes than the language of logical discourses can penetrate. William Blake knew this and more or less everything too!

In late antiquity and the Middle Ages the Church for all its appalling faults and failures did all it could to build up and renovate the soul of man. In our own time the dominating powers have done all they can with the unambiguous purpose of *soul-wrecking*, whether in Moscow or on Wall Street or Threadneedle Street. Blake, repeating Boehme and the whole Hermetic and Gnostic tradition, held that "Every natural effect has a spiritual cause" but the modern soul-wrecking view, the dominant recent view, that "everything" is *only* natural leads, as Plato in *Parmenides* made abundantly clear, to the position where "everything" is virtually nothing, shadowy and meaningless. On the other hand, the traditional concept of "Spirit" represents the interface or meeting point between the individual soul's highest intellect and the universal soul or Intellect or consciousness (the Indian concept of Atman).

But just how is one to reconcile all this *poetic* view with non-poetic man's crowning need for faith and certainty (the Qurânic *yaqîn*)? Are all these elements of Faith simply metaphors? Christian Fundamentalists get very angry if you suggest such a thing. The most prophetic spirit of recent times, the young Count von Hardenberg, known as Novalis, "the new-ploughed field," amongst his many profound aphorisms left us one which for me is quite fundamental:

Illusions are essential to (the searching out of) Truth.

I was seventeen when I first read that and I was profoundly shocked, or perhaps I simply dismissed it as so much nonsense or French *esprit.* Over the years I have come more and more to understand this profound observation.

Yeats, the very great Irish poet, never tired of quoting from the Kabbalah that "The Truth cannot be known but it can be represented."

Myths, poems, and great works of art are all Mysteries. Their elements are the most improbable, fanciful, and even contradictory images, and they rarely represent things as they appear (mimesis, the photographic non-art), and yet in some way few of us can explain they carry us into the very presence of Truth and Mystery. Any purely rational attempts to explain such great imaginative works are doomed to ludicrous failure. Quite simply, in contemplating or experiencing them we discover worlds of new experience of which we were unaware before. Worlds of new experience the validity, the beauty, and the Truth of which we cannot doubt. The "illusion" itself may not be true, but it opens to us the possibility of perceiving and receiving profoundly moving experiences, the truth of which quite simply is self-evident.

Whatever it is that catalyzes and makes possible these marvelous experiences can only be Love. There is a wonderful passage in Proust which I can only paraphrase lamely from a very defective memory:

> Among all the many other things necessary for Love to be born is the conviction that in it one participates in *an unknown life* which Love alone permits us to penetrate.

What was Dante's *La Vita Nuova* if not the sweetest and profoundest discovery of a hitherto "unknown life"?

Clement of Alexandria's Letter to Theodore Containing Fragments of a Secret Gospel of Mark

TRANSLATED BY MORTON SMITH*

From the letters of the most holy Clement, the author of the *Stromateis*. To Theodore.

You did well in silencing the unspeakable teachings of the Carpocratians. For these are the "wandering stars" referred to in the prophecy, who wander from the narrow road of the commandments into a boundless abyss of the carnal and bodily sins. For, priding themselves in knowledge, as they say, "of the deep things of Satan," they do not know that they are casting themselves away into "the nether world of the darkness" of falsity, and, boasting that they are free, they have become slaves of servile desires. Such men are to be opposed in all ways and altogether. For, even if they should say something true, one who loves the truth should not, even so, agree with them. For not all true things are the truth, nor should that truth which merely seems true according to human opinions be preferred to the true truth, that according to the faith.

Now of the things they keep saying about the divinely inspired Gospel according to Mark, some are altogether falsifications, and others, even if they do contain some true elements, nevertheless are not reported truly. For the true things being mixed with inventions, are falsified, so that, as the saying goes, even the salt loses its savor.

As for Mark, then, during Peter's stay in Rome he wrote an account of the Lord's doings, not, however, declaring all of them, nor yet

---

* From Morton Smith, *Clement of Alexandria and a Secret Gospel of Mark* (Cambridge: Harvard University Press, 1973).

hinting at the secret ones, but selecting what he thought most useful for increasing the faith of those who were being instructed. But when Peter died a martyr, Mark came over to Alexandria, bringing both his own notes and those of Peter, from which he transferred to his former book the things suitable to whatever makes for progress toward knowledge. Thus he composed a more spiritual Gospel for the use of those who were being perfected. Nevertheless, he yet did not divulge the things not to be uttered, nor did he write down the hierophantic teaching of the Lord, but to the stories already written he added yet others and, moreover, brought in certain sayings of which he knew the interpretation would, as a mystagogue, lead the hearers into the innermost sanctuary of that truth hidden behind seven veils.

Thus, in sum, he prepared matters, neither grudgingly nor incautiously, in my opinion, and, dying, he left his composition to the church in Alexandria, where it even yet is most carefully guarded, being read only to those who are being initiated into the great mysteries.

But since the foul demons are always devising destruction for the race of men, Carpocrates, instructed by them and using deceitful arts, so enslaved a certain presbyter of the church in Alexandria that he got from him a copy of the secret Gospel, which he both interpreted according to his blasphemous and carnal doctrine and, moreover, polluted, mixing with the spotless and holy words utterly shameless lies. From this mixture is drawn off the teaching of the Carpocratians.

To them, therefore, as I said above, one must never give way; nor, when they put forward their falsifications, should one concede that the secret Gospel is by Mark, but should even deny it on oath. For, "Not all true things are to be said to all men." For this reason the Wisdom of God, through Solomon, advises, "Answer the fool from his folly," teaching that the light of the truth should be hidden from those who are mentally blind. Again it says, "From him who has not shall be taken away," and, "Let the fool walk in darkness." But we are children of light," having been illuminated by "the dayspring" of the spirit of the Lord "from on high," and "Where the Spirit of the Lord is," it says, "there is liberty," for "All things are pure to the pure."

To you, therefore, I shall not hesitate to answer the questions you have asked, refuting the falsifications by the very words of the Gospel. For example, after "And they were in the road going up to Jerusalem," and what follows, until "After three days he shall arise," the secret Gospel brings the following material word for word: "And they come into Bethany. And a certain woman whose brother had died was there. And, coming, she prostrated herself before Jesus and says to him, 'Son of David, have mercy on me.' But the disciples rebuked her. And Jesus, being angered, went off with her into the garden where the tomb was, and straightway a great cry was heard from the tomb. And going near Jesus rolled away the stone from the door of the tomb. And straightway, going in where the youth was, he stretched forth his hand and raised him, seizing his hand. But the youth, looking upon him, loved him and began to beseech him that he might be with him. And going out of the tomb they came into the house of the youth, for he was rich. And after six days Jesus told him what to do and in the evening the youth comes to him, wearing a linen cloth over his naked body. And he remained with him that night, for Jesus taught him the mystery of the kingdom of God. And whence, arising, he returned to the other side of the Jordan."

After these words follows the text, "And James and John come to him," and all that section. But "naked man with naked man," and the other things about which you wrote, are not found.

And after the words, "And he comes into Jericho," the secret Gospel adds only, "And the sister of the youth whom Jesus loved and his mother and Salome were there, and Jesus did not receive them." But the many other things about which you wrote both seem to be and are falsifications. Now the true explanation and that which accords with the true philosophy . . .

[Here the fragment ends.]

The Strange Case of the Secret Gospel According to Mark: How Morton Smith's Discovery of a Lost Letter by Clement of Alexandria Scandalized Biblical Scholarship

SHAWN EYER

"DEAR READER, do not be alarmed at the parallels between . . . magic and ancient Christianity. Christianity never claimed to be original. It claimed . . . to be *true!*" With these words in the *New York Times Book Review*, Pierson Parker reassured the faithful American public that it need not be concerned with the latest news from the obscure and bookish world of New Testament scholarship.[1] It was 1973, and the Biblical studies community, as well as the popular press, was in a stir over a small manuscript discovery that—to judge from the reactions of some—seemingly threatened to call down the apocalypse. A newly-released book by Columbia University's Morton Smith, presenting a translation and interpretation of a fragment of a newly-recovered Secret Gospel of Mark, was at the center of the controversy.

The Discovery: 1958–1960

In the spring of 1958, Smith, then a graduate student in Theology at Columbia University, was invited to catalogue the manuscript holdings in the library of the Mar Saba monastery, located twelve miles south of Jerusalem. Smith had been a guest of the same hermitage years earlier, when he was stranded in Palestine by the conflagrations of the second World War.

What Smith found in the tower library surprised him. He discovered some new scholia of Sophocles, for instance, and dozens of other manuscripts.[2] Despite these finds, however, the beleaguered scholar soon resigned himself to what looked like a reasonable conclusion: he would find nothing of major importance at Mar Saba. His malaise evaporated one day as he first deciphered the manuscript that would always thereafter be identified with him:

> One afternoon near the end of my stay, I found myself in my cell, staring incredulously at a text written in a tiny scrawl. [. . . I]f this writing was what it claimed to be, I had a hitherto unknown text by a writer of major significance for early church history.[3]

What Smith then began photographing was a three-page handwritten addition penned into the endpapers of a printed book, Isaac Voss' 1646 edition of the *Epistolae genuinae S. Ignatii Martyris*.[4] It identified itself as a letter by Clement of the *Stromateis*, i.e., Clement of Alexandria, the second-century church father well-known for his Platonic approach to Christian belief. Clement writes "to Theodore," congratulating him for success in his disputes with the Carpocratians, an heterodoxical sect about which little is known. Apparently in their conflict with Theodore, the Carpocratians appealed to Mark's gospel.

Clement responds by recounting a new story about the Gospel. After Peter's death, Mark brought his original gospel to Alexandria and wrote a "more spiritual gospel for the use of those who were being perfected." Clement says this text is kept by the Alexandrian church for use only in the initiation into "the great mysteries."

However, Carpocrates the heretic, by means of magical stealth, obtained a copy and adapted it to his own ends. Because this version of the "secret" or "mystery" gospel had been polluted with "shameless lies," Clement urges Theodore to deny its Markan authorship even under oath. "Not all true things are to be said to all men," he advises.

Theodore has asked questions about particular passages of the special Carpocratian Gospel of Mark, and by way of reply Clement transcribes two sections which, he claims, have been distorted by the heretics. The first fragment of the Secret Gospel of Mark, meant to be inserted between Mark 10.34 and 35, reads:

They came to Bethany. There was one woman there whose brother had died. She came and prostrated herself before Jesus and spoke to him. "Son of David, pity me!" But the disciples rebuked her. Jesus was angry and went with her into the garden where the tomb was. Immediately a great cry was heard from the tomb. And going up to it, Jesus rolled the stone away from the door of the tomb, and immediately went in where the young man was. Stretching out his hand, he lifted him up, taking hold his hand. And the youth, looking intently at him, loved him and started begging him to let him remain with him. And going out of the tomb, they went into the house of the youth, for he was rich. And after six days Jesus gave him an order and, at evening, the young man came to him wearing nothing but a linen cloth. And he stayed with him for the night, because Jesus taught him the mystery of the Kingdom of God. And then when he left he went back to the other side of the Jordan.

Then a second fragment of Secret Mark is given, this time to be inserted into Mark 10.46. This has long been recognized as a narrative snag in Mark's Gospel, as it awkwardly reads, "Then they come to Jericho. As he was leaving Jericho with his disciples . . ." This strange construction is not present in Secret Mark, which reads:

Then he came into Jericho. And the sister of the young man whom Jesus loved was there with his mother and Salome, but Jesus would not receive them.

Just as Clement prepares to reveal the "real interpretation" of these verses to Theodore, the copyist discontinues and Smith's discovery is, sadly, complete.

Smith stopped briefly in the Hebrew University in Jerusalem to share his discovery with Gershom Scholem.[5] He then returned to America where he sought the opinions of his mentors Erwin Goodenough and Arthur Darby Nock. "God knows what you've got hold of," Goodenough said.[6] "They made up all sorts of stuff in the fifth century," said Nock. "But, I say, it is exciting."[7]

At the 1960 annual meeting of the Society of Biblical Literature,

Morton Smith announced his discovery to the scholarly community, openly presenting a translation and discussion of the Clementine letter. A well-written account of his presentation, with a photograph of the Mar Saba monastery, appeared the next morning on the front page of *The New York Times*.[8] A list of the seventy-five manuscripts Smith catalogued appeared the same year in the journal *Archaeology*[9] as well as the Greek Orthodox Patriarchate journal, *Nea Sion*.[10] And Morton Smith embarked on a decade of meticulous investigation into the nature of his find.

The Reaction: 1973–1982

While there may seem nothing particularly scandalous about the apocryphal episodes of Secret Mark in and of themselves, the release of the material to the general public aroused a great deal of popular and scholarly derision. Smith wrote two books on the subject: first, the voluminous and intricate scholarly analysis *Clement of Alexandria and a Secret Gospel of Mark*, and then *The Secret Gospel*, a thin and conversational popular account of the discovery and its interpretation. The first book was delivered to the Harvard University press in 1966, but was very slow at going through the press.[11] Smith's popular treatment, however, was released by Harper and Row in the summer of 1973. This is the version that most scholars had in their hands first. What did it say that was so shocking?

Smith's analysis of the Secret Mark text—and consequently the wider body of literature bearing on the history of early Christianity— brought him to consider unusual possibilities. Because Secret Mark presents a miracle story, this meant a particular concentration upon material of a like type. Smith was working outside of the traditional school of Biblical criticism which automatically regarded all miracle accounts as mythological inventions of the early Christian communities.[12] Instead of taking as his goal the theological deconstruction of the miracle traditions, Smith asked to what degree the miracle stories of the gospels might in fact be based upon actions of Jesus, much in the same way scholars examine the sayings traditions.

It has been typical for critical scholars of the Bible to reject any historical foundation for the "miracle-worker" stories about Jesus. Because such tales would tend to rely on the supernatural, and scholars seek to understand the origins of the Bible in realistic terms, it is more plausible for the modern critic to propose reasons why an early Christian community might have come to understand Jesus as a miracle-worker and subsequently engage in the production of narratives that depict him in that mold. Smith's understanding of the kingdom language in the Christian writings, with its well-known ambivalent (and yet emphatically present or "realized") eschatological tendencies, evolved to the conclusion that:

> [Jesus] could admit his followers to the kingdom of God, and he could do it in some special way, so that they were not there merely by anticipation, nor by virtue of belief and obedience, nor by some other figure of speech, but were really, actually, in.[13]

Smith held that the best explanation for the literary and historical evidence surrounding the mircles of Jesus was that Jesus himself actually performed—or meant to and was understood to have performed—magical feats. Among these was a baptismal initiation rite through which he was able to "give" his disciples a vision of the heavenly spheres. This was in the form of an altered state of consciousness induced by "the recitation of repetitive, hypnotic prayers and hymns," a technique common in Jewish mystical texts, Qumran material, Greek magical papyri and later Christian practices such as the Byzantine liturgy.[14] This is a radical departure from the mainstream scholarship which seeks to minimize or eliminate altogether any possible "supernatural" elements attached to the Historical Jesus, who is most often understood as a speaker on social issues and applied ethics—an Elijahform social worker, if you will.

Morton Smith did not begin with that assumption, nor did his reinterpretation of Christian history arrive at it. Thus, the new theory summarized in his 1973 book for general readership displeased practically everyone:

From the scattered indications in the canonical Gospels and the secret Gospel of Mark, we can put together a picture of Jesus' baptism, "the mystery of the kingdom of God." It was a water baptism administered by Jesus to chosen disciples, singly and by night. The costume, for the disciple, was a linen cloth worn over the naked body. This cloth was probably removed for the baptism proper, the immersion in water, which was now reduced to a preparatory purification. After that, by unknown ceremonies, the disciple was possessed by Jesus' spirit and so united with Jesus. One with him, he participated by hallucination in Jesus' ascent into the heavens, he entered the kingdom of God, and was thereby set free from the laws ordained for and in the lower world. Freedom from the law may have resulted in completion of the spiritual union by physical union. This certainly occurred in many forms of gnostic Christianity; how early it began there is no telling.[15]

In an interview with *The New York Times* just before his books were released onto the market, Smith noted with appreciation, "Thank God I have tenure."[16]

The Inquisition: Let's Begin

Not a moment was lost in the ensuing backlash. Smith had laid aside the canon of unwritten rules that most Biblical scholars worked by. He took the Gospels as more firmly rooted in history than in the imagination of the early church. He refused to operate with an artificially thick barrier between pagan and Christian, magic and mythology. Not only did he promulgate his theories from his office at Columbia University via obscure scholarly periodicals, he had now given them to the world in plain, understandable, and all-too-clear language. Thus there was no time for the typical scholarly method of thorough, researched, logical refutation. The public attention span was short. It was imperative that Smith be discredited before too many Biblical scholars told the press that there might be something to his theories. Some of the high-pitched remarks of well-known scholars are amusing to us in retrospect:

Patrick Skehan: "a morbid concatenation of fancies"[17]

Joseph Fitzmyer: "venal popularization"[18] "replete with innuendos and eisegesis"[19]

Paul J. Achtemeier: "Characteristically, his arguments are awash in speculation."[20] "an *a priori* principle of selective credulity"[21]

William Beardslee: "ill-founded"[22]

Pierson Parker: "the alleged parallels are far-fetched"[23]

Hans Conzelmann: "science fiction"[24] "does not belong to scholarly, nor even . . . discussable, literature"[25]

Raymond Brown: "debunking attitude towards Christianity"[26]

Frederick Danker: "in the same niche with Allegro's mushroom fantasies and Eisler's salmagundi."[27]

Helmut Merkel: "Once again total warfare has been declared on New Testament scholarship."[28]

The possibility that the initiation could have included elements of eroticism was unthinkable to many scholars, whose reaction was to project onto Smith's entire interpretive work an imaginary emphasis on Jesus being a homosexual:

> The fact that the young man comes to Jesus "wearing a linen cloth over his naked body" naturally suggests implications which Smith does not fail to infer.[29]

> Hostility has marked some of the initial reactions to Smith's publication because of his debunking attitude towards Christianity and his unpleasant suggestion that Jesus engaged in homosexual practices with his disciples.[30]

Many others cited rather prominently the homoerotic overtures of Smith's thesis in their objections to his overall work.[31] Another criticism, which holds more weight from a scholar's standpoint, was Smith's rejection of the form and redaction critical techniques preferred by the reviewer.[32]

Two scholars, embarassingly, found a flaw in Smith's use of what they considered too much documentation, as a ploy to confuse the reader.[33]

Many scholars felt that the Secret Mark fragments were a pastiche from the four gospels, some even suggesting that Mark's style is so simple to imitate the fragment must be a useless pseudepigraphon.[34]

In reaction to Clement's claim to perform initiation rites, some scholars simply dogmatized that Alexandrian Christians only used words like "initiation" and "mystery" in a figurative sense, therefore the letter must not be authentic.[35]

Finally, some reactions truly border on the petty. Two scholars held that Morton Smith didn't really "discover" the Secret Gospel of Mark at all. Because the letter only contains two *fragments* of it, Smith is described as dishonest in his subtitle "The Discovery and Interpretation of the Secret Gospel of Mark."[36] Worst of all is Danker, who complains that the Smith's first, non-technical book does not include the Greek text. "The designer of the jacket, as though fond of palimpsests, has obscured with the book title and the editor's name even the partial reproduction of Clement's letter," and that while there is another photo inside the book, "the publishers do not supply a magnifying glass with which to read it."[37] All this just to tell us that, after he and a companion had painstakingly transcribed the Greek text, Smith's transcription and translation are "substantially correct."[38] He deceptively omits the fact that Smith's Harvard edition includes large, easily legible photographic plates of the original manuscript, and alleges that Smith was "reluctant . . . to share the Greek text"[39] he had discovered.

Only one reviewer, Fitzmeyer, saw it worthwhile to point out that Morton Smith was bald. Whatever importance we may attach to the thickness of a scholar's hair, it seems that detached scholarly criticism fails when certain tenets of faith—even "enlightened" liberal faith—are called into question.

Is the Ink Still Wet? The Question of a Forgery

Inevitably a document which is so controvertial as Secret Mark will be accused of being a forgery. This is precisely what happened in 1975 when Quentin Quesnell published his lengthy paper "The Mar Saba Clementine: A Question of Evidence" in the *Catholic Biblical Quarterly*. In this article he brings to bear a host of objections to Smith's treatment of the document.

Foremost is the lack of the physical manuscript. Smith left the manuscript in the tower at Mar Saba in 1958 and had been working with his set of photographs ever since. Quesnell regards this as a neglect of Smith's scholarly duties.[40] Perhaps those duties might be assumed to include the theft of the volume *à la* Sinaiticus or the Jung Codex. In fact, even Smith's publication of photographic plates of the ms. are considered substandard by Quesnell. They "do not include the margins and edges of the pages," they "are only black and white," and are in Quesnell's eyes marred by "numerous discrepancies in shading, in wrinkles and dips in the paper."[41]

Quesnell calls into question all of Smith's efforts to date the manuscript to the eighteenth century. Although Smith consulted many paleographic experts, Quesnell feels this information to be useless as compared to a chemical analysis of the ink, and a "microscopic examination of the writing."[42]

Then he asks the "unavoidable next question"[43]: was the letter of Clement a modern forgery? He remarks that Smith "tells a story on himself that could make clear the kind of motivation that might stir a serious scholar even apart from any long-concealed spirit of fun."[44] Pointing out Smith's interest in how scholars tend to fit newly-discovered evidence into their previously-held sacrosanct interpretive paradigms,[45] and how Smith requested scholars in his longer treatise to keep him abreast of their research,[46] Quesnell asks if it might not be that a certain modern forger who shall not be named might have "found himself moved to concoct some 'evidence' in order to set up a controlled experiment?"[47]

Quesnell raises still more objections, and representative of them is his claim that the mass of documentation Smith brought to bear in *Clement of Alexandria and a Secret Gospel of Mark* is really a ploy to distract the reader. "It is hard to believe that this material is included as a serious contribution to scholarly investigation," Quesnell suggests.[48] In fact, he insinuates that its function is really to "deepen the darkness."[49]

Quesnell did not feel that scholarly discussion could "reasonably continue" until all these issues—and more—were resolved.[50]

Smith's answer to the accusation of forgery was published in the next volume of the *Catholic Biblical Quarterly*. Humorously he advised his detractor that "one should not suppose a text spurious simply because one dislikes what it says."[51]

"Not at all," was Quesnell's reply. "I find it quite harmless."[52]

Quesnell's arguments were still echoed in 1983 by Per Beskow, who wrote that Smith "can only present some mediocre photographs, which do not even cover the entire margins of the manuscript."[53] While the photographic plates in the Harvard volume do not extend to the margins due to the cropping of the publishers,[54] Smith's photographs are printed elsewhere and do include the margins of the pages. Furthermore, they are quite in-focus and cannot be described as mediocre.

The Popular Response

The religious right was particularly displeased with the new Secret Gospel of Mark. Even without the magical interpretation of earliest Christianity Smith promulgated in his two books, the discovery of another apocryphal gospel only spells trouble for conservative theologians and apologists. What information about Secret Mark made it past the blockade into the evangelical press? There was Ronald J. Sider's quick review in *Christianity Today*:

> Unfounded . . . wildly speculative . . . pockmarked with irresponsible inferences . . . highly speculative . . . operates with the presupposition that Jesus could not have been *the* incarnate Son of God filled with *the* Holy Spirit . . . simply absurd! . . . unacceptable . . . highly speculative . . . numerous other fundamental weaknesses . . . highly speculative . . . irresponsible . . . will not fool the careful reader.[55]

Evangelical scholarship has since treated Secret Mark as it tradition-ally has any other non-canonical text: as a peculiar but ultimately unimportant document which would be spiritually dangerous to take seriously.

Secret Mark and Da Avabhasa's Initiation to Ecstasy

Perhaps the strangest chapter in Secret Mark's long history was its appropriation by the Free Daist Communion, a California-based Eastern religious group led by American-born guru Da Avabhasa (formerly known as Franklin Jones, Da Free John, and Da Kalki). In 1982, The Dawn Horse Press, the voice of this interesting sect, republished Smith's Harper and Row volume, with a new foreword by Elaine Pagels and an added postscript by Smith himself.

In 1991, I made contact with this publisher in order to ascertain why they were interested in Secret Mark. I was answered by Saniel Bonder, Da Avabhasa's official biographer and a main spokesman for the Commununion.

> Heart-Master Da Avabhasa is Himself a great Spiritual "Transmitter" or "Baptizer" of the highest type. And this is the key to understanding both His interest in, and The Dawn Horse Press's publication of, Smith's *Secret Gospel.*

> What Smith discovered, in the fragment of the letter by Clement of Alexandria, is—to Heart-Master Da—an apparent ancient confirmation that Jesus too was a Spirit-Baptizer who initiated disciples into the authentic Spiritual and Yogic process, by night and in circumstances of sacred privacy. This is the single reason why Heart-Master Da was so interested in the story. As it happened, Morton Smith's contract with a previous publisher had expired, and so he was happy to arrange for us to publish the book.[56]

Because of the general compatibility of Smith's interpretation of the historical Jesus and the practices of the Da Free John community, the group's leader was inclined to promulgate Smith's theory. It is difficult to judge the precise degree of ritual identity which exists between Master Da and Jesus the magician. Some identity, however, is explicit, as revealed in Bonder's official biography of Master Da:

> Over the course of Heart-Master Da's Teaching years, His devotees explored all manner of emotional-sexual possibilities, including celibacy, promiscuity, heterosexuality, homosexuality, monogamy, polygamy, polyandy, and many different kinds of living arrangements between intimate partners and among groups of devotees in our various communities.[57]

The parallel between the Daist community during this time and the libertine Christian rituals described by Smith is made stronger by the spiritual leader's intimate involvement with this thorough exploration of the group's sexuality. "Heart-Master Da never withheld Himself from participation in the play of our experiments with us . . ."[58] Georg Feuerstein has published an interview with an anonymous devotee of Master Da who describes a party during which the Master borrowed his wife in order to free him of egotistical jealousy.[59] Like the Carpocratians of eighteen-hundred years ago, and the Corinthian Christians of a century earlier still, the devotees of the Daist Communion sought to come to terms with and conquer their sexual obstacles to ultimate liberation not by merely denying the natural urges, but by immersing themselves in them.

For many years Da Avabhasa himself was surrounded by an "inner-most circle" of nine female devotees, which was dismantled in 1986 after the Community and the Master himself had been through trying experiences.[60] In 1988 Da Avabhasa formally declared four of these original nine longtime female devotees his "Kanyas," the significance of which is described well by Saniel Bonder:

> Kanyadana is an ancient traditional practice in India, wherein a chaste young woman . . . is given . . . to a Sat-Guru either in formal marriage, or as a consort, or simply as a serving initiate. Each kanya thus becomes

devoted ... in a manner that is unique among all His devotees. She serves the Sat-Guru Personally at all times and, in that unique context, at all times is the recipient of His very Personal Instructions, Blessings, and Regard.[61]

As a kanyadana "kumari," a young woman is necessarily "pure"—that is, chaste and self-transcending in her practice, but also Spiritually Awakened by her Guru, whether she is celibate or Yogically sexually active.[62]

The formation of the Da Avabhasa Gurukala Kanyadana Kumari Order should be seen against the background of sexual experimentation and confrontation through which the Master's community had passed in the decade before, and in light of the sexuality-affirming stance of the Daist Communion in general. *The Secret Gospel* presented a picture of Jesus as an initiator into ecstasy and a libertine bearing more than a little resemblance to the radical and challenging lessons of Master Da Avabhasa, in place long before 1982 when The Dawn Horse Press reissued the book.[63]

The Cultural Fringe and Secret Mark

Occasionally one still encounters brief references to Secret Mark in marginal or sensational literature. A simple but accurate account of its discovery was related in the 1982 British bestseller *Holy Blood, Holy Grail*. Written by three television documentary reporters, the book describes an actual French society called the Priory of Sion which seeks to restore the French monarchy to a particular family which, it seems, traces its blood-line back to Jesus himself. In the course of arguing that this could actually be the truth, the authors find it convenient to cite Secret Mark as an example of how the early church edited unwanted elements from its scriptures. "This missing fragment had not been lost. On the contrary, it had apparently been deliberately suppressed."[64]

A quick reference to Secret Mark is made in Elizabeth Clare Prophet's book on the supposed "lost years" of Jesus. She writes that discoveries such as Secret Mark "strongly suggest that early Christians possessed a larger, markedly more diverse body of writings and traditions on the life of Jesus that appears in what has been handed down to us in the New Testament."[65] However, the remainder of the book speculates about whether Jesus might have studied yoga in India, and has little to do with Secret Mark or Jesus the magician.

Where Are We Now? (Scholarly Interest from 1982 to the Present)

For scholars the problem remains unsettled. While even the most acid of reviews often ended with a statement to wit that a real conclusion would require an in-depth treatment of Smith's books, none was forthcoming. In 1982, Smith commented wryly on the rhetoric of the reviews which made work on the Secret Mark problem almost impossible in the 1970s:

> For example, Achtemeier's review, of which the pretendedly factual statements are often grossly inaccurate. Though worthless as criticism, it cannot confidently be described as "useless." It probably pleased Fitzmyer, who was then editor of *The Journal of Biblical Literature*, and thus may have helped Achtemeier get the secretaryship of the Society of Biblical Literature. That both names rhyme with "liar" is a curious coincidence.[66]

Some important Catholic scholars, including Achtemeier, Fitzmyer, Quesnell, Skehan and Brown, have tended to ignore Secret Mark or dismiss it as worthless. C. S. Mann's Anchor Bible commentary on Mark, published in 1986, represents the whole controversy as finished, a matter of "mere curiosity."[67] With the blessing of the Imprimatur behind him, John P. Meier advised in 1991 that Secret Mark, the Gospels of Thomas and Peter, the Egerton Gospel and all other non-canonical Jesus material were worthless and might simply be thrown "back into the sea."[68]

At the same time, there has been an increase in the number of scholars producing Secret Mark studies since 1982. That "Morton Smith seems quite alone in his view that the fragment is a piece of genuine Gospel material," as claimed in 1983 by Beskow, is manifestly false.[69] Smith's work in the early seventies was greeted with more-or-less positive reviews by a small number of important scholars including Helmut Koester, Cyril Richardson, George MacRae, and Hugh Trevor-Roper. Some scholars did not write reviews but openly expressed the notion that Smith's work was meritorious. When asked by the New York Times about Smith's interpretation of Jesus as a magician, Krister Stendhal tactfully replied, "I have much sympathy for that way of placing Jesus in the social setting of his time."[70]

While that sympathy does not remain particularly widespread, accepting Smith's magical Jesus has nothing to do with taking Secret Mark seriously. The two issues may be discussed separately: the argument for magical practices in early Christianity may certainly be made without reference to Secret Mark, and Secret Mark may be discussed as a text with no more magical implications than we find in canonical Mark.

In Thomas Talley's 1982 article on ancient liturgy, he describes his own attempt to physically examine the Secret Mark manuscript. As his is the last word on the physical artifact in question, it is fortuitous to quote him at length:

> Given the late date of the manuscript itself and the fact that Prof. Smith published photographs of it, it seemed rather beside the point that some scholars wished to dispute the very existence of a manuscript which no one but the editor had seen. My own attempts to see the manuscript in January of 1980 were frustrated, but as witnesses to its existence I can cite the Archimandrite Meliton of the Jerusalem Greek Patriarchate who, after the publication of Smith's work, found the volume at Mar Saba and removed it to the patriarchal library, and the patriarchal librarian, Father Kallistos, who told me that the manuscript (two folios) has been removed from the printed volume and is being repaired.[71]

Although one wishes this document were available for the examination of Western scholars, it is no longer reasonable to doubt the existence of the manuscript itself. That it represents an authentic tradition from Clement of Alexandria is disputed only by a handful of scholars and, as Talley also points out, the letter has itself been included in the standard edition of the Alexandrian father's writings since 1980.[72]

Taking on the pressing question of Secret Mark's textual relationship with the version of Mark in our New Testament, Helmut Koester has published two intriguing studies arguing that the development of Mark was an evolutionary process. First came the version of Mark known by Matthew and Luke, the proto-Mark or *Urmarkus* long known to scholars of the synoptic problem. After this original version of Mark was published, the expanded version used by the Alexandrian church in Christian mysteries was made (and from that, its gnosticized Carpocratian version). Soon afterward or simultaneously, a mostly expurgated version of Secret Mark was published widely and became canonical Mark.[73] The original *Urmarkus*, lacking anything not found in Matthew or Luke, went the way of the sayings source and was not preserved.

Koester's view has made some inroads. Hans-Martin Schenke adopts it with the modification that Carpocratian Mark predates the Secret Mark of the Alexandrian Church.[74] John Dominic Crossan developed a theory like Koester's in his *Four Other Gospels* (1985). Secret Mark has been included in the texts being translated as part of the Scholars Version project, and is described as an early gospel fragment in material that the Jesus Seminar has been making available to popular audiences. None of these treatments is significantly affected by one's assessment of the magical Jesus suggested by Smith.

Still, Jesus as magician is not a dead issue. John Dominic Crossan's very intriguing book on *The Historical Jesus* has an extended discussion of the topic. He argues that Jesus may indeed be understood as a magician. He rejects an artificial dichotomy between magic and religion, saying, "the prescriptive distinction that states that *we* practice religion but *they* practice magic should be seen for what it is, a political validation of the approved and the official against the unapproved and unofficial."[75]

Conclusion: Where No Secret Gospel Has Gone Before

Secret Mark's plight constitutes a warning to all scholars as to the dangers of allowing sentiments of faith to cloud or prevent critical examination of evidence. When seen in light of the massive literature which has been produced by the other major manuscript finds of our century, the Dead Sea Scrolls, Nag Hammadi codices, the comparative dearth of good studies on this piece in particular can only be explained as a stubborn refusal to deal with information which might challenge deeply-held personal convictions. In this regard, it is good to keep in mind an unofficial directive of the Jesus Seminar: "Beware of finding a Jesus entirely congenial to you."[76]

"It is my opinion," writes Hans Dieter Betz, "that Smith's book and the texts he discovered should be carefully and seriously studied. Criticizing Smith is not enough."[77] Certainly it is reasonable to concur. After twenty years of confusion, it must be time to set aside emotionalism and approach both this fragment and Morton Smith's assessment of the role of magic in early Christianity with objective and critical eyes. However that question is ultimately to be resolved, Secret Mark provides yet another fascinating window into the remarkable ritual diversity we may identify in the first phases of the development of Christianity.

Notes

1. Parker, "An Early Christian Cover-up?", 5.

2. Smith, "Monasteries and their Manuscripts."

3. Smith, *The Secret Gospel*, 12.

4. Smith, *Clement of Alexandria and a Secret Gospel according to Mark*, 1.

5. Smith, *The Secret Gospel*, 13–14.

6. Smith, *The Secret Gospel*, 24.

7. Smith, *The Secret Gospel*, 25.

8. Knox, "A New Gospel Ascribed to Mark."

9. Smith, "Monasteries and their Manuscripts."

10. Smith, "Hellenika Cheirographa en tei Monei tou Hagiou Sabba."

11. Smith, *The Secret Gospel*, 76.

12. Smith, *Jesus the Magician*, 3–4.

13. Smith, *The Secret Gospel*, 94.

14. Smith, *The Secret Gospel*, 113 note 1.

15. Smith, *The Secret Gospel*, 113–114.

16. Shenker, "A Scholar Infers Jesus Practiced Magic."

17. Skehan, review of Smith's work in *Catholic Historical Review*, 452.

18. Fitzmyer, "How to Exploit a Secret Gospel," 572.

19. Fitzmyer, "Mark's 'Secret Gospel?'", 65.

20. Achtemeier, review of Smith in *Journal of Biblical Literature*, 626.

21. Achtemeier, review of Smith in *Journal of Biblical Literature*, 626.

22. Beardslee, review of Smith in *Interpretation*, 234.

23. Parker, "An Early Christian Cover-Up?", 5.

24. Conzelmann, "Literaturbericht zu den Synoptischen Evangelien (Fortsetzung)", 321. (Translation from Schenke, "The Mystery of the Gospel of Mark," 70–71.)

25. Conzelmann, "Literaturbericht zu den Synoptischen Evangelien (Fortsetzung)", 23. (Translation from Schenke, "The Mystery of the Gospel of Mark," 70–71.)

26. Brown, "The Relation of 'The Secret Gospel of Mark' to the Fourth Gospel," 466 note 1.

27. Danker, review of Smith in *Dialog*, 316.

28. Merkel, "Auf den Spuren des Urmarkus?", 123. (Translation from Schenke, "The Mystery of the Gospel of Mark," 69.)

29. Musurillo, "Morton Smith's Secret Gospel," 328.

30. Brown, "The Relation of 'The Secret Gospel of Mark' to the Fourth Gospel," 466 note 1.

31. Including Fitzmeyer, "How to Exploit a Secret Gospel"; Parker, "An Early Christian Cover-Up?"; Skehan, review of Smith in *Catholic Historical Review* 60 (1974); Gibbs, review of Smith in *Theology Today* 30 (1974); Grant, "Morton Smith's Two Books"; Merkel, "Auf den Spuren des Urmarkus?"; Kummel, "Ein Jahrzehnt Jesusforchung"; and Beskow, *Strange Tales about Jesus*. Anitra Kolenkow's comments on this bias are salient: "We know that the gospel of John long has been known as possibly containing both gnostic and homosexual motifs. John may have been written at approximately the same time as Mark. What difference does it make to us if Jesus is not separated from a homosexual situation?" (Quoted from Kolenkow's response to Reginald Fuller, *Longer Mark*, 33).

32. Examples are Achtemeier, review of Smith in the *Journal of Biblical Literature* 93 (1974); MacRae, "Yet Another Jesus"; Gibbs, review of Smith in *Theology Today* 30 (1974); and Fuller, *Longer Mark: Forgery, Interpolation, or Old Tradition?*

33. See the statements to this effect in Quesnell, "The Mar Saba Clementine," and Hobbs (response in Fuller, *Longer Mark: Forgery, Interpolation, or Old Tradition?*).

34. Such scholars included Pierson Parker, Edward Hobbs and Per Beskow.

35. See Bruce, *The 'Secret' Gospel of Mark*; Musurillo, "Morton Smith's Secret Gospel"; and Kummel, "Ein Jahrzehnt Jesusforschung."

36. Fitzmyer, "How to Exploit a Secret Gospel"; Gibbs, review of Smith in *Theology Today* 30 (1974).

37. Danker, review of Smith in *Dialog*, 316.

38. Danker, review of Smith in *Dialog*, 316.

39. Danker, review of Smith in *Dialog*, 316.

40. Quesnell, "The Mar Saba Clementine," 49.

41. Quesnell, "The Mar Saba Clementine," 50.

42. Quesnell, "The Mar Saba Clementine," 52.

43. Quesnell, "The Mar Saba Clementine," 53.

44. Quesnell, "The Mar Saba Clementine," 57.

45. Smith, *The Secret Gospel*, 25.

46. Smith, *Clement of Alexandria*, ix.

47. Quesnell, "The Mar Saba Clementine," 58.

48. Quesnell, "The Mar Saba Clementine," 61.

49. Quesnell, "The Mar Saba Clementine," 60 note 30.

50. Quesnell, "The Mar Saba Clementine," 48.

51. Smith, "On the Authenticity of the Mar Saba Letter of Clement," 196.

52. Quesnell, "A Reply to Morton Smith," 201.

53. Beskow, *Strange Tales about Jesus*, 101.

54. Smith, "On the Authenticity of the Mar Saba Letter of Clement," 196.

55. Sider, "Unfounded 'Secret'," 160.

56. Private correspondence with Saniel Bonder.

57. Bonder, *The Divine Emergence of the World-Teacher*, 234.

58. Bonder, *The Divine Emergence of the World-Teacher*, 235.

59. Feuerstein, *Holy Madness*, 90–92.

60. Feuerstein, *Holy Madness*, 94.

61. Bonder, *The Divine Emergence of the World-Teacher*, 287.

62. Bonder, *The Divine Emergence of the World-Teacher*, 288.

63. It is neccessary to stipulate that nothing in the above discussion of the Free Daist Communion should be read as derogatory. The purpose is simple description. Despite the controversy which has sometimes surrounded this movement, the author does not feel that its practices are in any way fraudulent or abusive. Scholars should consider the possibility that examination of contemporary religious movements such as the Da Avabhasa sect might be extraordinarily helpful in our understanding of the community dynamics of early libertine Christians such as the Carpocratians.

64. Baigent et al., *Holy Blood, Holy Grail*, 290.

65. Prophet, *The Lost Years of Jesus*, 9. Most interestingly, in her notes Prophet quotes a 1984 telephone interview with scholar Birger A. Pearson, in which he says that "many scholars, maybe even most, would now accept the authenticity of the Clement fragment, including what it said about the Secret Gospel of Mark" (434 note 16).

66. Smith, *The Secret Gospel* (1982 Dawn Horse edition), 150 note 7.

67. Mann, *Mark* (The Anchor Bible), 423.

68. Meier, *A Marginal Jew*, 140.

69. Beskow, *Strange Tales about Jesus*, 99. One wonders what a "genuine

piece of gospel material" might be. Are gospel additions such as the second ending of Mark (16.9–20) and the famous story of the adulterous woman (John 8.53–9.11) "genuine gospel material," even if we know they were not originally part of the gospels in which they are found?

70. Shenker, "Jesus: New Ideas about his Powers."

71. Talley, "Liturgical Time in the Ancient Church," 45.

72. Talley, "Liturgical Time in the Ancient Church," 45.

73. See Koester, "History and Development of Mark's Gospel," and *Ancient Christian Gospels.*

74. Schenke, "The Mystery of the Gospel of Mark," 76.

75. Crossan, *The Historical Jesus,* 310.

76. Funk et al., *The Five Gospels,* 5.

77. Fuller, *Longer Mark: Forgery, Interpolation, or Old Tradition?,* 18.

Bibliography

Achtemeier, Paul J. Review of Smith. *Journal of Biblical Literature* 93 (1974), 625–628.

Allegro, John M. *The Sacred Mushroom and the Cross.* New York: Doubleday, 1970.

Baigent, Michael, Richard Leigh and Henry Lincoln. *Holy Blood, Holy Grail.* New York: Delacorte, 1982.

Baigent, Michael, Richard Leigh. *The Dead Sea Scrolls Deception.* New York: Simon & Shuster, 1991.

Bauckham, Richard. "Salome the Sister of Jesus, Salome the Disciple of Jesus, and the Secret Gospel of Mark," *Novum Testamentum* 33 (1991), 245–275.

Beardslee, William A. Review of Smith. *Interpretation* 28 (1974), 234–36.

Beskow, Per. *Strange Tales about Jesus.* Philadelphia: Fortress, 1983.

Bonder, Saniel. *The Divine Emergence of the World-Teacher.* Clearlake, CA: Dawn Horse Press, 1990.

———. Private correspondence, 1991.

Brown, Raymond E. "The Relation of 'The Secret Gospel of Mark' to the Fourth Gospel," *Catholic Biblical Quarterly* 36 (1974), 466–85.

Bruce, F. F. *The 'Secret' Gospel of Mark.* London: Althone Press, 1974.

Bultmann, Rudolf. *Jesus Christ and Mythology.* New York: Scribner's, 1958.

Burkert, Walter. *Ancient Mystery Cults.* Cambridge, MA: Harvard University Press, 1987.

Conzelmann, Hans. "Literaturbericht zu den Synoptischen Evangelien (Fortsetzung)," *Theologische Rundschau* 43 (1978), 23f.

Crossan, John Dominic. *Four Other Gospels: Shadows on the Contours of Canon.* San Francisco: Harper & Row, 1985.

———. *The Cross that Spoke: The Origins of the Passion Narrative.* San Francisco: Harper & Row, 1988.

———. *The Historical Jesus: The Life of a Mediterranean Jewish Peasant.* San Francisco: HarperSanFrancisco, 1991.

Danker, Frederick W. Review of Smith. *Dialog* 13 (1974), 316.

Donfried, K. "New-Found Fragments of an Early Gospel," *Christian Century* 90 (1973), 759–60.

Feuerstein, Georg. *Holy Madness: The Shock Tactics and Radical Teachings of*

Crazy-Wise Adepts, Holy Fools, and Rascal Gurus. New York: Penguin Arkana, 1990.

Fitzmyer, Joseph A. "How to Exploit a Secret Gospel," *America* 128 (1973), 570–572.

———. Reply to Morton Smith in "Mark's 'Secret Gospel?'", *America* 129 (1973), 64–65.

Frend, W. "A New Jesus?" *New York Review of Books* 20 (1973), 34–35.

Fuller, R. *Longer Mark: Forgery, Interpolation, or Old Tradition?* (Center for Hermeneutical Studies, colloquy 18), edited by W. Wuellner. Berkeley, CA: Center for Hermeneutical Studies, 1975.

Funk, Robert W., Roy W. Hoover, and The Jesus Seminar. *The Five Gospels: The Search for the Authentic Words of Jesus.* New York: Macmillan, 1993.

Gibbons, J. Review of Smith. *Sign* 53 (September 1973), 48.

Gibbs, J. G. Review of Smith. *Theology Today* 30 (1974), 423–26.

Grant, Robert. "Morton Smith's Two Books," *Anglican Theological Review* 56 (1974), 58–65.

Greene, D. St. A. Review of Smith. *The National Observer* 12 (1973), 15.

Hanson, R. P. C. Review of Smith. *Journal of Theological Studies* 25 (1974), 513–21.

Hobbs, Edward C. Response to Reginald Fuller. In *Longer Mark: Forgery, Interpretation, or Old Tradition?*, edited by W. Wuellner, 19–25. Berkeley, CA: Center for Hermeneutical Studies, 1975.

Horst, P. van der. "Het 'Geheime Markusevangelie,'" *Nederlands Theologisch Tijdschrift* 33 (1979), 27–51.

Jaeger, Werner. *Early Christianity and Greek Paideia.* Cambridge, MA: Harvard University Press, 1961.

Johnson, M.D. Review of Smith. *The Lutheran Quarterly* 25 (1973), 426–27.

Johnson, S. "The Mystery of St. Mark," *History Today* 25 (1975), 89–97.

Kee, Howard Clark. Review of Smith. *Journal of the American Academy of Religion* 43 (1975), 326–29.

Knox, Sanka. "A New Gospel Ascribed to Mark," *The New York Times*, December 30, 1960, p. 1, 17.

———. "Expert Disputes 'Secret Gospel,'" *The New York Times*, December 31, 1960, p. 7.

Koester, Helmut. Review of Smith. *American Historical Review* 80 (1975),

620–622.

———. "History and Development of Mark's Gospel (From Mark to *Secret Mark* and 'Canonical' Mark)," in *Colloquy on New Testament Studies*, ed. Bruce Corley. Macon, GA: Mercer University Press, 1983.

———. *Ancient Christian Gospels*. Philadelphia: Trinity Press International, 1990.

Kolenkow, Anitra Bingham. Response to Reginald Fuller. In *Longer Mark: Forgery, Interpretation, or Old Tradition?*, edited by W. Wuellner, 33–34. Berkeley, CA: Center for Hermeneutical Studies, 1975.

Kümmel, Werner Georg. "Ein Jahrzehnt Jesusforschung (1965–1975)," *Theologische Rundschau* 40 (1975), 299–302.

Levin, Saul. "The Early History of Christianity, in Light of the 'Secret Gospel' of Mark," *Aufstieg und Niedergang der Römischem Welt* 2.25.6 (1988), 4270–4292.

MacRae, George. "Yet Another Jesus," *Commonweal* 99 (1974), 417–420.

Mack, Burton L. *A Myth of Innocence: Mark and Christian Origins*. Philadelphia: Fortess, 1988.

Mann, C. S. *Mark: A New Translation with Introduction and Commentary*. The Anchor Bible Series. New York: Doubleday, 1986.

Meier, John P. *A Marginal Jew: Rethinking the Historical Jesus*. Volume One. New York: Doubleday, 1991.

Merkel, Helmut. "Auf den Spuren des Urmarkus? Ein neuer Fund und seine Beurteilung," *Zeitschrift fuer Theologie und Kirche* 71 (1974), 123–144.

Metzger, Bruce M. "Literary Forgeries and Canonical Pseudepigrapha," *Journal of Biblical Literature* 91 (1972), 3–24.

Meyer, Marvin W., ed. *The Ancient Mysteries: A Sourcebook*. San Francisco: Harper & Row, 1987.

Mullins, Terence Y. "Papias and Clement and Mark's Two Gospels," *Vigiliae Christianae* 30 (1976), 189–92.

Musurillo, H. "Morton Smith's Secret Gospel," *Thought* 48 (1974), 327–331.

Osborn, Eric. "Clement of Alexandria: A Review of Research, 1958–1982," *The Second Century* 3 (1983), 219–244.

Pagels, Elaine. Foreword to the 1982 reprint of *The Secret Gospel*. Clearlake, CA: Dawn Horse Press, 1982.

Parker, Pierson. "An Early Christian Cover-Up?," *New York Times Book*

Review, July 22, 1973, p. 5.

————. "On Professor Morton Smith's Find at Mar Saba," *Anglican Theological Review* 56 (1974), 53–57.

Patterson, Stephen J. and Helmut Kuester. "The Secret Gospel of Mark," in Robert J. Miller, editor, *The Complete Gospels: Scholars Version*, Sonoma, CA: Polebridge Press, 1992, 402–405.

Petersen, N. Review of Smith. *Southern Humanities Review* 8 (1974), 525–531.

Prophet, Elizabeth Clare. *The Lost Years of Jesus: Documentary Evidence of Jesus' 17-Year Journey to the East*. Livingston, MT: Summit University Press, 1987.

Quesnell, Quentin. Review of Smith. *National Catholic Reporter*, Nov. 30, 1973.

————. "The Mar Saba Clementine: A Question of Evidence," *Catholic Biblical Quarterly* 37 (1975), 48–67.

————. "A Reply to Morton Smith," *Catholic Biblical Quarterly* 38 (1976), 200–203.

Reese, J. Review of Smith. *Catholic Biblical Quarterly* 36 (1974), 434–435.

Richardson, Cyril C. Review of Smith. *Theological Studies* 35 (1974), 571–77.

Schenke, Hans-Martin. "The Mystery of the Gospel of Mark," *The Second Century* 4 (1984), 65–82.

————. "The Function and Background of the Beloved Disciple in the Gospel of John," in *Nag Hammadi, Gnosticism, and Early Christianity*, Charles W. Hedrick and Robert Hodgson, Jr., eds. Peabody, MA: Hendrickson, 1986.

Schmidt, Daryl D. *The Gospel of Mark*. Scholars Version. Sonoma, CA: Polebridge Press, 1990.

Scroggs, Robin. Review of Smith. *Chicago Theological Seminary Register* 1974, 58.

Scroggs, Robin, and Kent I. Groff. "Baptism in Mark: Dying and Rising with Christ," *Journal of Biblical Literature* 92 (1973), 531–548.

Shenker, Israel. "A Scholar Infers Jesus Practiced Magic," *The New York Times*, May 23, 1973, p. 39.

————. "Jesus: New Ideas about His Powers," *The New York Times*, June 3, 1973, p. IV 12.

Sider, Ronald J. "Unfounded 'Secret,'" *Christianity Today* 18 (November 9,

1973), 160.

Skehan, Patrick W. Review of Smith 1973b. *Catholic Historical Review* 60 (1974), 451–53.

Smith, Morton. "Hellenika Cheirographa en tei Monei tou Hagiou Sabba," *Nea Sion* 52 (1960), 110–125, 245–256.

———. "Monasteries and their Manuscripts," *Archaeology* 13 (1960), 172–177.

———. *The Secret Gospel: The Discovery and Interpretation of the Secret Gospel According to Mark.* New York: Harper & Row, 1973.

———. *Clement of Alexandria and a Secret Gospel of Mark.* Cambridge, MA: Harvard University Press, 1973.

———. Reply to Joseph Fitzmeyer in "Mark's 'Secret Gospel?,'" *America* 129 (1973), 64–65.

———. "Merkel on the Longer Text of Mark," *Zeitschrift für Theologie und Kirche* 72 (1975), 133–150.

———. "On the Authenticity of the Mar Saba Letter of Clement," *Catholic Biblical Quarterly* 38 (1976), 196–199.

———. "A Rare Sense of προκοπτω and the Authenticity of the Letter of Clement of Alexandria," in *God's Christ and His People: Studies in Honor of Nils Alstrup Dahl*, edited by Jacob Jervell and Wayne A. Meeks. Oslo: Universitetsforlaget, 1977.

———. *Jesus the Magician.* New York: Harper & Row, 1978.

———. "Clement of Alexandria and Secret Mark: The Score at the End of the First Decade," *Harvard Theological Review* 75 (1982), 449–461.

———. Postscript to the 1982 reprint of *The Secret Gospel.* Clearlake, CA: Dawn Horse Press, 1982.

———. "Paul's Arguments as Evidence of the Christianity from which he Diverged," *Harvard Theological Review* 79 (1986), 254–60.

Stagg, F. Review of Smith. *Review and Expositor* 71 (1974), 108–110.

Talley, Thomas. "Liturgical Time in the Ancient Church: The State of Research," *Studia Liturgica* 14 (1982), 34–51.

Trevor-Roper, Hugh. "Gospel of Liberty," London *Sunday Times* (June 30, 1974), 15.

Trocmé, Étienne. "Trois critques au miroir de l'Evangile selon Marc," *Revue d'histoire et philosophie religieuses* 55 (1974), 289–295.

Wilson, Ian. *Jesus: The Evidence.* San Francisco: Harper & Row, 1984.

Wink, Walter. "Jesus as Magician," *Union Seminary Quarterly Review* 30 (1974), 3–14.

Yamauchi, Edwin M. "A Secret Gospel of Jesus as 'Magus?' A Review of Recent Works of Morton Smith," *Christian Scholars Review* 4 (1975), 238–251.

Author's note: The author would like to offer thanks to Saniel Bonder of the Mountain of Attention Sanctuary for his kind assistance in providing research materials and his willingness to share with me information pertaining to The Dawn Horse Press and *The Secret Gospel.* Further thanks are due to Dr. Jon Daniels of The Defiance College for his helpful insights into the subject matter of this study.

Knowledge, Reason, and Ethics:
A Neoplatonic Perspective

MICHAEL HORNUM

IN PREVIOUS ISSUES of *Alexandria* the problem of the possibility of objective knowledge has been touched upon in different ways by David Fideler[1] and Joscelyn Godwin.[2] Fideler bemoans the fact that modern philosophy has forsaken the idea that we can know things in themselves and accurately traces the current vogue of epistemological relativism to Kant's Transcendental Idealism. Godwin, on the other hand, promotes a relativist position that is professed to be one of Subjective Idealism or Mentalism ("the human mind constructs its own cosmos"), but which occasionally sounds more like the less extreme Kantian Idealism ("our only possible experiences are of our own mental states"). In either case, Godwin challenges the possibility of objective knowledge, that we can know things in themselves.

In this essay, I shall attempt to establish that objective knowledge is indeed possible, demonstrate that reasoning can be a method to obtain objective knowledge, and lay a rational foundation for ethical behavior. In the process I shall present critiques of Kantian/Neo-Kantian idealism, Subjective Idealism, and of epistemological relativism in general.

At the very outset, it must be pointed out that I have elsewhere supported the position that objective knowledge is not possible, at least in the case of God.[3] However, this has not been done so in the context of an epistemological relativism. It is not because objective knowledge in itself is impossible that we cannot know the One, but because the absolute infinity of the One—its transcendence of all distinctness that can permit delimitation—prevents all conscious experience of it, including knowledge. The mystical experience of

God is of a different order than thought and knowledge, and as such cannot be adequately communicated even to oneself, let alone to others. The root of my religious pluralism is therefore not the inadequacy of knowledge in itself, but its inadequacy before the Absolute. While the infinite cannot be grasped, anything bearing distinctness can be.

As Fideler[4] makes clear, the most widespread and pernicious form of epistemological relativism today is the offspring of Transcendental Idealism. Varieties of it can be found embodied in the most prominent philosophical schools of the "postmodern" age, from Husserl's "Transcendental Phenomenology"[5] to Quine's and Derrida's language-obsessed "Ontological Relativism"[6] and "Deconstructionism."[7] While, as Godwin[8] correctly asserts, it has shattered the arrogance of the old empiricist-positivist foundation of science, this relativism has become a serious blight at many levels of our society. It has had the effect of rendering all scholarly pursuits not quests for truth, but futile diversions for self-gratification, nothing except amusing little mind games. For if we cannot know anything except our individual or cultural conceptual or linguistic constructs, even the study of those constructs is in vain because we cannot truly know that there are such categories at all. In society as a whole, Kantian relativism has filtered into daily life. How often do we hear the expressions "your opinion is not my opinion" or "don't impose your values"? In a world with no objective knowledge, all is reduced to opinion and subjective "values." Is it any wonder that the practical results of such a state of affairs are the minority extremes of fundamentalist faith and amoral nihilism, with the vast majority living a life of intellectual paradox that seeks to "not impose values," but in so doing imposes *that* very value?

Immanuel Kant sought to mediate the philosophical impasse to which European thought had come in the latter part of the eighteenth century. On the one side was the rationalist tradition of Descartes and Leibniz, which argued that pure reason, without the input of sensation, could obtain knowledge of objective truth. On the other was the atomistic, skeptical empiricism of Hume, which maintained that all possible knowledge is of sense-objects, and that the mind is a blank slate on which sense data write their ensign through a flow of atoms in perception. Kant, initially attracted to the German idealist rationalism of Leibniz and Wolff, asserts that Hume's skepticism woke him out of a "dogmatic slumber," and began him along the road to his self-declared "Copernican Revolution" of philosophy. In his *Critique of Pure Reason*, Kant set forth his solution.[9] In agreement with Hume, Kant argued that sense data form the content of all knowledge. However, he rebelled against the idea that the fragmentary and momentary nature of sense-perception could of itself constitute the coherent picture we receive in our minds. The mind cannot, Kant asserted, be seen as a passive recipient of such data, but is rather the shaping, molding force that organizes those data into coherent wholes.

The mind accomplishes this task through the imposition of categories that already exist in the mind prior (*a priori*) to its reception of sense data. These categories are divided by Kant into the *a priori* intuitions of Space and Time, and the twelve *a priori* concepts (including Substance, Quality, Quantity, and Causation). Kant considers these categories as providing form to the chaotic content of the sense data. It is in fact the categories that provide the actual objects of knowledge, not the things encountered in sensation. We can never know what such objects are in themselves, only as they appear to us, or rather as we make them appear by reading them in terms of the *a priori* categories into which we fit them. This forms the basis for Kant's position that we can never know "things in themselves" (*noumena*), only things as they appear (*phenomena*).

At first sight these *a priori* categories imposed by the mind, which constitute the shape of our objects of knowledge, seem to resemble something akin to the Forms of Platonism, which exist prior to sensation and form the objects of knowledge in place of things perceived by the senses. However, such a similarity is, unfortunately as we shall see, only superficial. Kant's *a priori* categories are not objectively known things in themselves, for the mind is not merely their locus but their producer. They are activities or conditions of the mind. For example, the concepts are "moments of thought in judgement."[10] Hence, all knowledge is entirely subjective.

The main question with which Kant's epistemological subjectivism leaves us is that, if all our objects of knowledge are really reducible to mental constructs, precisely how does the mind accomplish the construction in the first place? The thinking process itself would seem to be the answer, hence the characterization of the *a priori* concepts as "moments" in thought activity. And since for Kant himself, and most subsequent Kantians, the thinking process is rooted in language, one may consider language as the constructing mechanism. Language can be seen as the essential foundation for thought because it permits the formation of general concepts not tied to sense objects, namely the *a priori* categories themselves. The current Transcendental Idealist position normally emphasizes the linguistic aspect of these categories, and argues that we cannot know anything beyond our own linguistic distinctions or the conceptual categories to which they refer.

The following small experiment may serve as an example of the fundamental problem with this typical Transcendental Idealist position.

Here is Horse: Here is Tree:
      O   O
Which one is this, Horse or Tree?
      O

The utility of the designations "Horse" and "Tree" and the mental pictures to which they correspond falls away if we do not prelinguistically and preconceptually grasp some measure of distinctness between them. Unless our minds grasp this distinctness, we are confronted only with uniformity, in the face of which we cannot meaningfully form a name or concept. The words and images simply will not stick. Our learning of words and the mental images they conjure up, our very retention of language itself, would be impossible in the face of such homogeneity. As in the example above, nothing could not be kept straight in our minds so that learning would take hold. Clearly, then, we must grasp distinctly different things prior to our constitution of names and concepts that go with them. An awareness of distinctly different things must lie at the foundation of language itself.

If we wish, as good Kantians, to avoid the conclusion that we can possess objective knowledge, at least as regards that measure of distinctness that makes possible language and its constructions, we must conclude that such distinctness is itself a set of prelinguistic *a priori* mental constructs. So, let us assume that this primal distinctness is produced by the mind without the aid of language, that it represents a series of non-acquired or innate mental constructs. How then does the mind produce these categories? As mind products, they must naturally be considered to be generated by thinking. However, as Plotinus[11] has shown repeatedly in his rejection of Mind as the One, the thinking process inevitably involves the duality of subject and object.

Just as we must grasp distinctness that differentiates things for language to be possible, we must also grasp it for thinking itself to be feasible. The mind that does not grasp such distinctness, but instead remains empty of it, will lose its mental objects in the face of uniformity and be left with nothing at all to think; and there can be no thinking process without something to think. Therefore, thinking cannot be the production method for this distinctness, because the thinking process would thereby be robbed of the thought objects required for its very existence. We would arrive at the self-contradictory conclusion that the mind produces the distinctness that differentiates things by a thinking process that itself already dictates the existence of such distinctness. To avoid such a conclusion, the Transcendental Idealist must prove that objectless thinking is possible and that such a mode of thinking is productive rather than purely receptive, like a bare wakefulness. It is doubtful that either can be indubitably demonstrated.

Consequently, that leaves us with the conclusion that, in our knowledge of the distinctness that permits differentiation, we either know unconstructed sense objects or unconstructed mental objects, in both instances things in themselves, and that this knowledge is therefore objective. The Kantian would object to objective knowledge of sense objects because of the momentary and fragmented nature of sense experience, and a Platonist would point to the ever-changing flux of the world of Becoming to which such objects belong. The conclusion must then follow, for the Kantian as for the Platonist, that we possess objective knowledge, and that it is of unconstructed mental objects, i.e. the Forms.

The pure subjectivist or Subjective Idealist would also contend that this distinctness we experience is itself mentally constituted. Indeed, the subjectivist would contend that not only must our knowledge be exclusively of mental constructs, but that nothing exists but mental constructs. This is essentially the position of another eighteenth-century philosopher, Bishop George Berkeley.[12] Starting with John Locke's position that sensation alone is the source of thought, and that the mind is nothing but matter, Berkeley counters that Locke's analysis cannot prove his conclusion, but rather demonstrates the opposite, that matter is nothing but mind. If all knowledge is of sensations and ideas derived from these sensations, there is no evidence that matter exists, just that the sensations and ideas it supposedly causes exist. In other words, there is no evidence that there is anything but bundles of sensations, in Berkeley's view mental conditions. Are these mental states then produced by us? Godwin[13] appears to think so; Berkeley's position we shall address later. If they are our constructs, the burden of proof falls to the subjectivist, like the Kantian, to identify some objectless, productive thinking process that creates what would otherwise be things in themselves. This is but one of the many severe philosophical problems that beset such a variety of Mentalism.

This sort of Mentalism fails to explain how, if "things" are nothing but mental constructs, why they are so difficult or even impossible to bend to our will. In addition, there is no logical reason why, if nothing exists aside from mental products, the mind forms distinctly different concepts at all. To say it just does so because it is part of its nature to do so begs the question. If the answer is that God or some Universal Mind compels us to do so, one has introduced another ultimate constructor of our objects, and our minds are not really constructing their world at all, but God is. If this is the case, in relation to our minds the objects are not mental constructs, but unconstructed things in themselves, accessible to objective knowledge. Also, the oft-used comparison with dreams rests upon the unproven assumption that we construct our dreams. Many cultures in fact believe that the dream world is not constituted by our minds but is another objective reality that we enter in sleep. At any rate, things in dreams, no matter how fantastic or bizarre, are always derived from things or combinations of things in the waking world; they are not produced from nothing. This dependence of dreams upon the "things" of the waking world shows that if dreams are to be used as an analogy for the waking world, our waking world construction cannot be *ex nihilo*, but must exhibit dependence upon things that are more than just our waking state mental activities.

Finally, there is the problem of solipsism, which Godwin[14] attempts to address. If his Mentalism is correct about the impossibility of objective knowledge, how can we know if there are other minds or if such minds really can construct their worlds or construct them in a fashion akin to ours? We cannot. To make God the source of the mental images held in common by various minds, as we have said above, opens the possibility for our minds to obtain objective knowledge, and this contradicts Godwin's basic conclusion that our minds are producing their worlds, unless, of course, God is the only mind and thus the only existent. This is the sort of Absolute Monism—the problems of which have been dealt with elsewhere[15]—that makes all individual knowledge or perspective, indeed all individuals themselves, illusory, and the contention that we each make our own worlds a vain one at the very outset. To avoid this problem, we are again left with a confirmation of the Platonic sort of idealism in which we know things that, while not "external" to our minds, are not created by them either, but exist independently of us. This would appear to be the direction that Berkeley himself should have taken since he holds that at least the mental conditions we call Nature are not produced by our minds, but by the mind of God. Berkeley's difference with Platonism would of course lie in his need to dematerialize the physical world altogether in order to avoid the problem of a mind/matter dualism in the midst of any knowledge rooted in sense-experience.

Epistemological relativism itself, whether arising from Transcendental Idealism or Mentalism, is philosophically unsound in two ways. First, it arises from a set of fallacious assumptions. Historically, the root of these types of subjectivism is the Cartesian dualism between mind and matter. This dualism has spawned a seemingly impossible impasse in which we cannot accept realism without first explaining how a spiritual mind can, as seems self-evident, have knowledge, which, if not of the corporeal, is at least rooted to some extent in a corporeal world. To skirt this difficulty, empiricists like Locke and Hume are prepared to dispense with a spiritual mind altogether and seek a materialistic monism. To avoid materialism and its attendant philosophical baggage, Berkeley, as we have seen, seeks to reduce material existence to a mental construct, while Kant attempts to make knowledge subjectively constituted. If objects of knowledge are composed of a different substance than the mind, it seems inexplicable how they can be apprehended. The Platonic position that knowledge is mental, not sensual, but objective nonetheless, is dismissed as another Cartesian bifurcation in which we are left trying to explain how sense-experience can serve as a vehicle for our spiritual mind to know the equally incorporeal Forms.

The Plotinian version of Platonism can, however, resolve the Cartesian impasse without resorting to materialism, monism, or subjectivism. The mind/matter problem is solved in the Plotinian continuum between mind, soul, and body, a continuum guaranteed by all three being progressive transformations of the absolutely Infinite. The corporeal is ultimately linked inseparably with the incorporeal like a "long life laid out at length, each part different from that which comes next in order, but the whole continuous with itself, but with one part differentiated from another, and the earlier not perishing in the later."[16] Such continuity assures that the spiritual mind of the soul* always has the Forms available to it because it guarantees that the soul not only lives its own proper life but also lives the life of the Nous, which, as the progressively transforming One, becomes it. But the soul's access, in its own proper life, to the noetic life is limited; its attention is focused elsewhere, namely in the Kosmos or Nature, its realm of activity. Nonetheless, the Kosmos serves as a stimulus via sense-perception for focusing the soul's attention upon a particular Form which is equally present to the sense-object and to the soul, and is grasped by the soul in its living the noetic life. The Plotinian continuum also assures that the stimulus itself can be received by the soul from sense-experience, not physically but spiritually, at a spiritual level which is entirely continuous with the physical, because the body, matter, *physis*—or whatever one terms the locus of sensation—not only lives its own life but also that of the soul, which becomes it in the same manner as the Nous becomes soul. The expansion of the soul's focus on the Forms and its full enjoyment of the noetic life available to it, of course, require more than merely sensory stimulus. That is where philosophy in its truest sense comes in.

The second downfall of epistemological relativism lies in its inherent logical self-contradiction. If we cannot know objective truth, how do we know that we cannot know? And how can we know that we cannot know that we cannot know? This line of questioning can extend on forever, for it represents a *regressus ad infinitum*. We can never know that epistemological relativism is true, or it would be made false by that knowledge. Therefore, taken to its logical conclusions, relativism, to avoid its own self-contradiction, must hold that we can neither know nor not know, nor know that we know or do not know, and so on for infinity. There cannot even be probability judgements because they would require an objective knowledge of the truth of probability, that we know that something is probable. Ultimately, the only noncontradictory conclusion of epistemological relativism is skepticism, a skepticism of the ancient Pyrrhic sort that should bring complete suspension of judgement and consequent silence. There-

---

* For the Neoplatonist it is the mind of the incorporeal soul, not the eternal Nous, that is of concern here, since it is the soul that receives the stimulus rooted in sensation.

fore, if relativists of the sort we are discussing are serious about their position they should fall mute; if they do not, this indicates that they are treating their relativism objectively, that their position is false, and that it should not be taken seriously by philosophers.

Should we then take seriously the silent skepticism of those of our opponents who remain true to their cause? Most certainly. For in his silence, the skeptic proclaims against the possibility of objective knowledge. To answer this challenge, we must turn to St. Augustine. Augustine, after shaken from the Manichean faith by Neoplatonism, turned skeptical, but in his profound skepticism found an answer to skepticism's challenge of objective knowledge, one which also, as expected, provides yet another, particularly stinging, refutation of relativism. If I doubt everything, asks Augustine,[17] is there anything of which I can be certain? Yes, I can be certain that I exist, for in order for me to question at all, I must exist ("*Si dubito, sum*"). But why should this not be incorrect? Because in order to be wrong, I must exist ("*Si fallor, sum*"). In the gravest doubt, we discover the unraveling of doubt. Augustine thereby refutes not only skepticism, but epistemological relativism. Such relativism is controverted because in the *dubito* I know that I am and that I must really be distinctly I if I am at all. Therefore, I know at least one unconstructed "thing in itself": my own distinct being.[18]

What then do we know objectively? First, the distinctness that underlies and permits both language and any conceptual thought rooted in language, a basic distinctness that cannot merely be a set of prelinguistic mental constructs produced by thought (because, if so, thought would lack the objects required for the thinking process itself). Second, we also objectively know abstract truths, like the truth of our existence known in the *dubito* or the truth of our ability to know things in themselves.

In the case of distinctness, we are confronted with two aspects: one distinctness that allows the differentiation of things, and another that grants the differentiation of events. Both must constitute essences, for what else is an essence but that which makes one thing or event different than another? Moreover, unless we wish to consider that the intrinsically unchanging nature of essences can abide the flux of time, this distinctness must be that of eternal Forms, the archetypes of all that is perceived in sense-perception. Sense-perception brings sight or sound or some other sensory experience through the nerves to the brain, but the sense object or event cannot be what is known. Instead, we should envision our minds as awakened through the sense experience to an immediate knowledge of the incorporeal, eternal essence that underlies and informs the sense object. (It might be objected that in the case of the experience of an occurrence, say harm or need, the harm or need clearly cannot be occurring to an unchanging archetype but to a temporal, physical creature, and that since we do not know the sense-perceived creature but its Form, we cannot know the harm or need that is occurring to it. However, it is the harm or need that we are knowing, not the thing harmed or the thing that needs; it is the essence of the event itself, that which makes the event distinct from other events and things. I do not have to not know that it is you that I harm or that I am in need in order to know harm or need as distinct from benefit, victory, or some other event.)

What is reason's role in my objective knowledge? Can the rational process provide access to such knowledge? It is clear from the discussion heretofore that our knowledge of essences does not primarily involve reasoning. In these cases it appears that objective knowledge represents a direct, intuitive grasp of unchanging, unconstructed realities that present themselves to our minds simultaneously with our perception of sense objects through our bodily organs. What then of abstract Forms, Forms not readily experienced in the stimulus of sense-perception, Forms like Existence, Good, Evil, Truth, and Falsehood?[19] Here it would appear that reason has a role. For when we come to the indubitable truth that we exist, we come to that knowledge through the rational method, the deduction that in order to doubt or be wrong we must exist. In fact, the truth uncovered in the *dubito* actually proves the validity of the rational method as a means to objective knowledge. Since we know indubitably that we exist, and we know this through reason, reason is undeniably demonstrated to attain objective knowledge.

But, says the critic, reason is always based upon an assumption that is not reached through the rational method. This is true of some forms of rational process but not all. Aristotelian syllogism or Stoic sentential logic both involve propositions, with certain assumed premises followed by deductions from those premises. For example, all cats are brown, Whiskers is a cat, therefore Whiskers is brown. The statement that all cats are brown is not demonstrated through reason, but is an assumption based upon perception; it is a given. There is, however, another rational process which does not involve assumptions, and this is Socratic/Platonic dialectic. In dialectic, which is the method Augustine uses for reaching the knowledge of his existence, the starting point is not a statement but a question. For example, in my doubting of everything, is there anything that I need not doubt? By a rational approach through questions, we never take a given as a starting point. Therefore, the critic is incorrect: unproven assumptions do not lie at the foundation of all logic. Dialectical reasoning, consequently, can aid us in reaching abstract Forms like Existence and Truth. Is this all? No, it also permits us to explore and come to know the relationships of those Forms directly intuited in the context of sense experience: Forms that, quite unlike the given of propositional logic, are not unproven assumptions but indubitable objects of knowledge. In addition, dialectic can serve to guide our actions by exploring the relationships of abstract Moral Forms and the relationships of those Forms to the Forms grasped in events.

Using Platonic dialectic, therefore, as a method with proven ability to reach objective knowledge, we can proceed with an attempt to lay an objective foundation for ethics through an exploration of Moral Forms. The most convenient manner in which to express dialectical argument is the dialogue. By virtue of this, I shall humbly spend the remainder of this essay in the venerable tradition of Plato and Plutarch. The two protagonists of the following dialogue I shall call Aristokles in honor of Plato himself and Arete in honor of Diotima, Amphiclea, Hypatia, and all of the virtuous women who have been guided by philosophy.

Aristokles: Good morning, Arete. I am rather surprised to see you sitting here along the Ilissos. Are you listening to the birds on this beautiful spring day?

Arete: Good morning, Aristokles. I am actually thinking about a rather unfortunate act that I witnessed yesterday.

Aristokles: Which was what?

Arete: I saw a hunter shoot down a dove, and this greatly troubled me. I have been trying to determine whether his action was evil.

Aristokles: Well, Arete, I think that we should begin by determining precisely what evil is. What is evil, Arete?

Arete: I am not exactly sure.

Aristokles: To be what it is, must not evil be different from all else?

Arete: Yes, it must be.

Aristokles: Accordingly, is not evil different from good?

Arete: Certainly.

Aristokles: Can you think of any way in which evil is similar to good?

Arete: No, I cannot.

Aristokles: Then, is not evil different from good in every way?

Arete: Undoubtedly.

Aristokles: And is not that which is different in every way from something the opposite of that from which it differs?

Arete: Yes.

Aristokles: And does not that which is the opposite of something possess nothing of that something of which it is the opposite?

Arete: So it would appear.

Aristokles: And does not possessing nothing of that particular something constitute the absence or awayness of that something?

Arete: No doubt.

Aristokles: Then, is not evil the absence or awayness of good?

Arete: Certainly.

Aristokles: And is not, therefore, an action which is evil that which is the absenting or taking away of good?

Arete: Of course, but how does this allow me to evaluate the hunter's killing of the dove?

Aristokles: Is not harm the taking away of some measure of good?

Arete: How so?

Aristokles: Is not harm the same thing as injury?

Arete: Yes.

Aristokles: And does not an injury constitute an impairment, a deterioration or worsening in quality, ability, or value?

Arete: No doubt.

Aristokles: And is not to be worse the same thing as to be less good?

Arete: Indeed.

Aristokles: Then, is not harm a loss of good?

Arete: Certainly.

Aristokles: And is not a harming action a taking away of good?

Arete: Yes.

Aristokles: Can we not then conclude that harm is the same as evil in being the absence or awayness of good, and that the harming action is identical with the evil action in being the taking away or absenting of good?

Arete: Of course.

Aristokles: And is not killing an act of harm?

Arete: How so?

Aristokles: Does not death constitute an impairment or deterioration in quality, ability, or value; in particular, a loss of all of these?

Arete: Yes.

Aristokles: Thus, is it not so that as harm is such an impairment, so death is the same?

Arete: Clearly.

Aristokles: Then, is not death a type of harm, and the act of bringing to death a type of harming?

Arete: Yes.

Aristokles: Can we not deduce that harm, including death, is the same as evil, and that harming, including killing, is identical with evil action?

Arete: Certainly.

Aristokles: Can we not but conclude as well that the hunter's killing the dove is an act of evil?

Arete: It seems that you have answered my question, Aristokles;

thank you.

Aristokles: But, Arete, is the act of harm really always an act of evil?

Arete: You have just proven that it is.

Aristokles: Have I? We have established that to ever cut off the leg of a horse would constitute an act of harm, have we not?

Arete: Yes.

Aristokles: But will not a gangrenous leg left in place cause blood poisoning and result in the horse's death?

Arete: Certainly.

Aristokles: So has not our act caused a loss of good in the sense that the horse can no longer run as well, but prevented a loss of good in the sense that the death of the horse would render the horse unable to do anything as well?

Arete: Indeed. This is most disconcerting. Are you are now telling me that harm need not be evil?

Aristokles: I am not certain that we should in fact consider our act in this case one of harm at all. Does not the net result of our action prevent the loss of greater good, and thereby provide greater good than we take?

Arete: I am not sure, Aristokles. How can you compare goods?

Aristokles: Is life prerequisite for walking or vice versa?

Arete: Obviously the former.

Aristokles: Then, is not the loss of life inclusive of both that proportion of good lost in a loss of life and also that proportion of good lost in the loss of a leg?

Arete: No doubt.

Aristokles: But the loss of a leg is not inclusive of the proportion of good lost in the loss of life as well as that lost in its own loss?

Arete: I would concur.

Aristokles: Accordingly, does not the loss of life necessarily involve a loss of a greater proportion of good than the loss of a leg?

Arete: Indeed.

Aristokles: And in preventing the loss of life, are we not preventing the loss of a greater good?

Arete: Yes.

Aristokles: And is not the preventing of the loss of life the same as providing life?

Arete: This is clearly so as well.

Aristokles: Thereby, do we not provide a greater good than that lost?

Arete: Certainly.

Aristokles: And is not, then, the net result of our action a giving rather than a taking of good, a benefit rather than a harm?

Arete: It must be so.

Aristokles: Must not evil then be that which remains a harm after weighing any good given, in other words, a net harm?

Arete: Indeed.

Aristokles: And to produce such a net result must not such weighing involve a qualitative comparison of that which is given and that which is taken away in order to determine which is more basic?

Arete: Yes, but what, then, are the most basic things that can be taken away?

Aristokles: Is not life required for pain or pleasure or for any activities and experiences at all?

Arete: Certainly.

Aristokles: And is not existence required for life, for example the existence of a species for the life of its members or existence as what you are for your life to be yours at all?

Arete: Definitely.

Aristokles: Are not, therefore, life and existence the most basic things that can be taken away?

Arete: No doubt.

Aristokles: Would not any removal of life or existence not done in order to provide the same or more basic of the two be a net harm, and therefore evil?

Arete: Of course.

Aristokles: And is the taking of the dove's life by the hunter required to provide life or existence for the hunter?

Arete: I am not sure.

Aristokles: Is the dove a predator, like the lion, that might attack the hunter in order to eat him?

Arete: No.

Aristokles: Then, does the dove threaten to take the life of the hunter through attack?

Arete: Clearly not.

Aristokles: So does the hunter need to take the dove's life to save his own?

Arete: No, it does not appear so. But what if the dove, like the locust, threatens to take the hunter's life by consuming the crop needed for the hunter's food?

Aristokles: Even if this were so, is there any need to kill the dove or the locust to stop such a threat, or will keeping the dove or locust away from the crop suffice?

Arete: Obviously the latter.

Aristokles: So, in this too, does the hunter need to take the dove's life to save his own?

Arete: No. He does not.

Aristokles: In what other way, then, may the taking of the dove's life provide life for the hunter?

Arete: I cannot think of any other ways except by eating the dove or by using its dead body for some other purpose.

Aristokles: In the life of humans other than the hunter, such as the Gymnosophists,[20] do we not experience an absence of eating and an absence of use of all that is killed, whether animal or plant?

Arete: Yes, indeed.

Aristokles: And is not a human life with an absence of eating the killed or an absence of use of the killed indicative of a superfluity of eating or using the killed for human life or existence?

Arete: Clearly so.

Aristokles: So is it not superfluous for the hunter to eat or to use in any way the dead dove so as to live or exist?

Arete: Yes.

Aristokles: And, as you have said, are not these the only other ways in which the taking of the dove's life may provide life for the hunter?

Arete: Certainly.

Aristokles: Then, again, is the taking of the dove's life by the hunter required to provide life or existence for the hunter?

Arete: No.

Aristokles: Is not the hunter's action, by consequence, a net harm, and therefore evil?

Arete: So it appears. However, even if the hunter need not take the life of the dove to sustain his life, does not the hunter, by killing and eating the dove, give life to those he would destroy in order to eat other things that are not killed?

Aristokles: How so?

Arete: Well, must he not cut down wild vegetation and destroy creatures living there to grow crops and must he not, when gathering wild foods, take sustenance from creatures that would otherwise eat such foods? By killing the dove, does he not give life to those creatures?

Aristokles: You make a valid point, Arete. However, when he grows crops or gathers wild foods does he not provide life as well?

Arete: What do you mean?

Aristokles: Does he not provide life for the crops and creatures that thrive in agricultural fields, and does he not, when he gathers wild foods, provide life for creatures that consume any creatures that die without such foods?

Arete: Yes.

Aristokles: Are we not then left with a series of balances of life taken with life given?

Arete: It is clearly so.

Aristokles: And does not such a state of balance cancel the life taken with that given?

Arete: Certainly.

Aristokles: And does this not leave us, by such cancellation, only with the question of the hunter's need to take life from the dove in order to live or exist?

Arete: It does.

Aristokles: But have we not already seen that this is not needed?

Arete: Yes.

Aristokles: Is not the hunter's action, then, a net harm, and therefore evil?

Arete: So it seems. However, by killing the dove, does not the hunter give life to the plants that the dove would eat? Or what if there is an overpopulation of doves? Will not the hunter, by killing the dove, provide life for another dove who cannot otherwise obtain needed sustenance?

Aristokles: Indeed, it is true that the lives of the plants are saved, and that, in the absence of enough life-sustaining resources for all, death of some is required for others to have life. But in so giving such life, does the hunter not also take life from those that need to eat the dove in order to live, I mean the fox or the cat, or, if the dove dies of illness, starvation or accident, the worms and mites?

Arete: Yes, but what if the hunter himself does not eat the dove and instead leaves it after the kill. Does he not then provide life for such creatures that need to eat the dove?

Aristokles: Certainly, but does he not then also take life from other creatures that would have eaten the dove at a later date of its death?

Arete: Yes.

Aristokles: So are we not, once again, left with a series of balances of life given with life taken?

Arete: Indeed.

Aristokles: And, as before, does not such a state of balance cancel the life given with that taken?

Arete: Definitely.

Aristokles: And does not such cancelling leave us only with the original question of the balance between what is taken from the dove and what is given the hunter?

Arete: This is clearly so.

Aristokles: And, once more, does the hunter require the death of the dove for the provision of his own life or existence?

Arete: No.

Aristokles: Therefore, yet again, is not the hunter's action a net harm, and thus evil?

Arete: Again, Aristokles, you appear to have answered my question. However, what about the limited character of our knowledge? How do we know that when we do not take the dove's life but rather preserve it, we are not actually taking away something more basic; for example, if the dove subsequently eats a plant which is the last of its species, thereby extinguishing its existence? Can we really be certain that such action is good or evil?

Aristokles: Is not the situation of which you speak a potential or possible situation?

Arete: Yes.

Aristokles: And when something is merely possible, is not its opposite also possible?

Arete: Certainly.

Aristokles: Is it not also possible, then, that the preservation of the dove's life will yield no such extinction, but might even result in the preservation of a species?

Arete: No doubt.

Aristokles: When taken together, do not such possibilities, accordingly, cancel each other out, just like positive and negative numbers added together equal nothingness?

Arete: I must concede that you are correct.

Aristokles: And does nothingness added to anything yield any effect or change?

Arete: No.

Aristokles: Therefore, can such a nothingness have any bearing or effect on the qualitative weighing of our action?

Arete: It cannot.

Aristokles: And does not the moral responsibility for the action shift from us, for whom the action is merely a possibility, to another, for whom the action is a certainty, namely, the one actually doing the deed, the dove in this instance?

Arete: So it seems.

Aristokles: And, moreover, can such a nothingness have any bearing or effect on the qualitative weighing of the action in question, namely the hunter's killing the dove?

Arete: Here too, it cannot.

Aristokles: And do we not then return only to a consideration of the hunter's action itself, in which the dove is certainly killed?

Arete: Yes.

Aristokles: Can we not thus be certain that the hunter's action is good or evil without regard to the possible consequences?

Arete: Indeed.

Aristokles: In sum, then, must we not conclude that the hunter's action, as one in which the net result is harm, is evil?

Arete: Yes, truly. Thank you for helping me, Aristokles.

Aristokles: You are thoroughly welcome, Arete. Χαῖρε.

Arete: Χαῖρε.

Notes

1. D. Fideler, "Introduction," *Alexandria* 1 (1991), 7–18.

2. J. Godwin, "Mentalism and the Cosmological Fallacy," *Alexandria* 2 (1993), 195–203.

3. M. Hornum, "A Plotinian Solution to a Vedantic Problem," *Alexandria* 1 (1991), 303–304; "The Availability of the One: An Interpretive Essay," *Alexandria* 2 (1993), 282.

4. Fideler, "Introduction," 12–13.

5. E. Husserl originally held a position not unlike the Platonic one. In his early work, such as *Logical Investigations* (1900), Husserl invited philosophical minds to return to "things in themselves." He developed a method for an intuitive investigation of essences, a "realist phenomenology" that sought to prepare consciousness for direct knowledge of objects as they are in themselves. Later, however, Husserl, in such works as *Ideas for a Pure Phenomenology* (1913) and *Cartesian Meditations* (1931), abandoned a realist position and concluded that phenomenological investigations are actually a vehicle for knowledge of objects constituted by consciousness, not objective entities. For a critique of this turn in Husserl's thought and a powerful attempt to restore phenomenology to a noumenology, see J. Seifert, *Back to "Things in Themselves": A Phenomenological Foundation for Classical Realism* (New York & London: Routledge & Kegan Paul, 1987).

6. W. V. Quine, in such works as *Word and Object* (1960) and *Ontological Relativity and Other Essays* (1969), has proposed the theory of "indeterminacy of translation" by which we can never know whether a foreign word means the same thing as the word we use to translate it into our language. This linguistic thesis may be contested from a purely linguistic perspective, but that is not my intention here. Its epistemological import lies in Quine's corollary thesis that because of such linguistic indeterminacy, different ways of interpreting being or "what there is" will be equally valid. We can never know other linguistic/cultural interpretations of reality except through our own interpretation or model. Hence, ontological issues of "things as they are in themselves" cannot be decided. Because we are limited in knowledge to our own linguistically or culturally defined world construct, and we cannot precisely comprehend the world constructs of other languages and cultures, we can never know whether one is correct and another is not. Quine's relativism, of course, rests upon the

Kantian position that language or some other constructing mechanism provides our only objects of knowledge. Without such a position, Quine's thesis possesses no epistemological relevance. If Kant was wrong and our knowledge is not limited to constructs, but must be of "things in themselves" for there to be any such constructs at all, then Quine's theory would at most merely relate to the problem of how different languages express the prelinguistically grasped reality, of which aspects of it they focus upon, and would not be of concern for actually knowing things as they are in themselves.

7. J. Derrida's Deconstructionism has, in one form or another, become very *chic* in the late twentieth century. Derrida's works include *Of Grammatology* (1967), and various readings of philosophers from a deconstructionist perspective. Derrida has gone Kant one better. Kant sought to take away from us a knowledge of "things in themselves," and replace it with a knowledge of mental constructs. Starting from the Kantian position that the objects of our knowledge are such constructs, Derrida seeks to remove any knowledge of even these constructs. He contends that our words and the concepts they denote have no conceptual purity, that their meanings are derived from the terms that are their opposites. Consequently, our constructs have no ultimate meanings, and cannot serve as adequate objects of knowledge any better than "things in themselves." As with those of Quine, such arguments and the further relativization of knowledge they entail rest entirely upon the edifice of the Kantian position that all we know are "things as we make them appear" through language, culture, constitutive thought, etc. Derrida's relativizing analysis of language, therefore, like Quine's, bears little relevance for the question of true knowledge, if language and linguistic thought are in fact rooted in a grasp of "things in themselves."

8. Godwin, "Mentalism and the Cosmological Fallacy," 197.

9. I. Kant, *Critique of Pure Reason*, published originally in 1781, and revised in 1787. An adequate English translation of this difficult work may be found in that of N. Kemp Smith (London, 1929).

10. I. Kant, *Critique of Pure Reason*, A69/B94, A70/B95.

11. Plotinus, *Enneads* 5.3.10.48–54, 5.3.12.47–50, 5.3.13.22–24; 5.6.5.1–5; 6.7.35.44–45, 6.7.39.20–24, 6.7.37–41; 6.8.16.26–27; 6.9.6.43–50. In *Enneads* 6.6.6.16–17 Plotinus also specifically refutes the idea that the mind creates its own objects.

12. G. Berkeley, *A Treatise Concerning the Principles of Human Knowledge* (1710).

13. Godwin "Mentalism and the Cosmological Fallacy," 197, 199–200, 201, for the world as a construct, projected by us, relative to the conditions of the producer, etc.

14. Godwin, "Mentalism and the Cosmological Fallacy," 197–199.

15. Hornum, "A Plotinian Solution to a Vedantic Problem," 298–300.

16. Plotinus, *Enneads* 5.2.2.27–30.

17. St. Augustine, *City of God* 11.26; see also *On the Trinity* 15.12.21.

18. Seifert, *Back to "Things in Themselves": A Phenomenological Foundation for Classical Realism*, 303–307; Hornum, "A Plotinian Solution to a Vedantic Problem," 299–300.

19. One can notice that I have included here among the Forms such negatives as Evil and Falsehood, which most ancient Platonists, except Amelius, were loath to include. I have done so because our knowledge of such things is as clear as that of positive abstract forms like Good and Truth. It may be objected, quite rightly, that in so doing I have opened myself up to criticisms that those who do evil are just as able to live noetically as the philosopher doing good, and that opposites such as good and evil within the Nous will destroy the unity of the Nous.

To answer the first charge it must be pointed out that if, as shall be demonstrated, evil is the absence of good and doing evil is therefore the absenting or taking away of good, then we can say that while both the Form Evil and the action evil are privative of good, the Form Evil is not entirely privative in that it gives to the things of this world that partake of it; but the evil action, lacking the donative nature of Form, is entirely privative. Therefore, the evil doer cannot reach the level of the Nous/Form like the doer of good, who, emulative of Form, always seeks to be giving. The doer of good can achieve such a state of giving even in the inevitable taking of life that occurs in this physical world, for example when breathing in microbes, because such a taking of life is not only balanced by its provision of life, but exceeded by the provision of existence that it brings. For if we cease to breathe not only do we die, but we lose an aspect of what makes us what we are because that which is required for our survival, like breathing, must be an essential part of our nature, otherwise it would not be required. And if we lose what we are, what defines us as us, we cease to exist at all.

To answer the second charge, the unity of the Nous will not be disturbed by the presence of opposing Forms any more than, as Plotinus states in *Enneads* 6.7.9–11, it is upset by the presence among the Forms of teeth, horns or claws, which are seemingly unnecessary for a life with none of the defense required here. All such Forms are necessary as parts of a balanced and harmonious richly varied whole, a self-sufficient complete living being.

20. I have used the ancient term Gymnosophists to allude to the Jains, the ascetic component of which, to this day, will not kill even plants for food or other uses, but subsist entirely off of only those plant products that are not uprooted. Concerning this matter, see C. Caillat, "Ahimsa," in *The Encyclopedia of Religion*, edited by M. Eliade (New York: Macmillan, 1987). Porphyry in *On Abstinence from Animal Flesh* also advocates not killing plants for food.

The Pythoness at Delphi
Vulci cup, fifth century B.C.E.

Delphi's Enduring Message: On the Need for Oracular Communications in Psychological Life

DIANNE SKAFTE

ALTHOUGH THE PYTHONESS AT DELPHI uttered her last proclamation 1500 years ago, we have never allowed her voice to fade from memory. Historians from the time of Herodotus to the present have deliberated upon the oracle's words, her methods, her mystery. Every worn stone and broken inscription from the temple site has been palmed over a thousand times in hopes of discovering new clues to the ancient wonder. The pythoness herself, throned upon a three-legged platform, eyes closed in ecstatic trance, has continued to inspire the images of poets, artists, and storytellers across the generations.

What is the basis of our enduring fascination with the oracle of Delphi? The most common answer, usually proposed as a way of dismissing the question, is that human beings have always longed to know the future, eagerly grasping at any potential source of precognition. We therefore search out divinatory knowledge in order to help allay the anxiety fostered by life's existential uncertainty. The Delphic shrine, it is argued, kindles hope of obtaining a glimpse of our own destinies.

While capturing one dimension of experience, this explanation fails on several counts. I would like first to review these failures and then offer a broader perspective that affirms the inherent importance of oracular communications for psychological life. I will confine most of my examples to Delphi because it is the most thoroughly researched of all oracle centers. We should remember, however, that famous oracles could also be found at Dodona, Claros, and Didyma in Greece; at the Oasis of Siwa in Libya; at Buto in Egypt; at Sardis in Asia; and in numerous other locations throughout the ancient world.

If obtaining a glimpse of humankind's future supplied the motivation for studying Delphic oracles, scholars would have shelved their
notebooks long ago. The pythoness (unlike the legendary sibyls)
showed little interest in forecasting global events or prophesying
about future epochs. Her pronouncements never ventured far from
their own cultural-historical setting. The Delphic responses that have
come down to us through legend reflect the preoccupations of a strife-
ridden era, often focusing on the war activities of local factions, the
colonization of foreign territories, or the rise and fall of somebody-or-
other's personal fortune.

We are told by Herodotus, for example, that the oracle denied
Laconia's request to conquer the territory of Arcadia but suggested
that it attempt to ravage neighboring Tegea instead. A suppliant
named Battus was instructed to sail without delay to Libya and destroy
the "savages wearing sheepskin cloaks" who tended their flocks there.
The Spartans were advised to select a young maiden from a well-born
family each year and sacrifice her upon the altar in order to end a
plague. The Lydian ruler, Croesus, was told that his military campaign against Persia would "destroy a mighty empire"—the empire
that fell proved to be his own, of course.[1] Though interesting from a
historical viewpoint, pronouncements such as these offer little inspiration to modern readers and tend to weary us with their ceaseless
themes of conquest and cruelty.

Our pleasure in studying ancient oracular responses is further
diminished by learning that only a fraction of them appear to be
authentic. Of the 535 Delphic oracles analyzed by the classicist Joseph
Fontenrose, only seventy-five were judged to be "historical."[2] Historical responses are those that were recorded at the time they were
given (often on tin plates) or were attested to by a writer living when
the response occurred. Fontenrose determined that most proclaimed
oracles were based on stories from previous ages, were intertwined
with folklore, or were made up for literary purposes. The practice of
fabricating prophecies after the fact or relocating oracles to more
convenient places in the historical record was common among ancient

chroniclers. Their intent was not to deceive, but to express the underlying divine meaning of secular events.

Granted that pronouncements from Delphi cannot shed much light on contemporary culture, it may be argued that the pythoness satisfied her devotees' longing to know the future, and that this fact alone makes her a subject worthy of study. But such reasoning is based upon a misconception. Fontenrose found that only two of seventy-five historical responses from Delphi offered clear predictions of the future. One of these told a male inquirer that his desire to have a child would indeed be fulfilled and that he should offer a lock of his hair on the altar in propitiation. The other response, recorded in late Roman times, predicts that the empress's newborn son would have "a glorious reign." Even among legendary oracles, predictions are not commonplace, occurring in only twenty percent of the cases.

It may surprise us that pilgrims to Delphi did not line up at the Omniscient's doorway and beg for glimpses of their futures. But most individuals in the classical world would have considered it impious to seek foreknowledge of events. They believed that humankind has its being within the matrix of Divine Being, and that personal destinies are not wholly ours to shape and control. The correct spiritual move, from their viewpoint, was to align oneself with the larger destiny and promote its intentions through right action. Then both personal and divine purposes would be served. The oracle provided a source of revelation and guidance for knowing the will of the Great Accomplishers—the gods.

Most petitioners came to Delphi for advice on how best to propitiate various deities, obtain blessings on their undertakings, or gain the right perspective on a problem. The majority of historical responses instructed suppliants on religious matters, particularly concerning the proper execution of ritual procedures. Other questions to the oracle concerned governmental matters and domestic life. Inscriptions from Delphi and Didyma tell us, for example, that the city of Erythrai should establish centers of worship for Aphrodite, Demeter and Kore, Dionysus, and another god whose name has disappeared; they indicate that the poet Philodamus has received the blessing of Apollo to publish a hymn that he wrote to Dionysus; a suppliant named Poseidonius is advised to worship the deities that his ancestors worshipped (a listing is provided) in order to best support the welfare of his family; and an athlete asking for success in the upcoming races is told that the divine patrons of athletics—Phoebus, Serapis, and Nemesis—will help him in his efforts if he prays to them.[3] Authenticated responses seem rather lackluster compared to the cunning verses from legendary sources. Yet the simpler directives are moving in their own way, for they reflect the concerns of a people who experienced the everyday world as infused with sacred meaning and intention.

If the pythoness offered no predictions for modern times and rarely cast the futures of her own suppliants, what meaning can we derive from her legacy? I would like to suggest that divinatory art in antiquity provided a *temenos* for archetypal spiritual yearnings. Among these are the yearning to be addressed by a numinous Other, the desire to expand consciousness beyond the boundaries of time and space, and the need to affirm one's personal unity with the matrix of All-That-Is. Oracle sites in the ancient world served psychological life by tending these needs within a framework of ritual mystery and beauty. Let us explore some of the ways in which oracular communications may speak to the psyche, using the Delphic example to observe how one institution successfully invoked their power.

Oracular Communications Bring Us into the Presence of Otherness

The personal self yearns to be addressed by something more comprehensive than itself. Sensing the constriction of its own boundaries, it longs to be met by a presence that will open new gates of potentiality. One may touch the beyond-self by falling in love, experiencing the wilderness, communing with dreams and visions, being transported by music or the arts, and many other means. Illness, defeat, and tragedy may also pay us a visitation and confer their terrible, sublime gifts upon the soul.

For citizens of the ancient world, the presence of otherness was never very far away. As the psychologist and Hellenistic scholar

Ginette Paris has pointed out, the Greeks experienced epiphanies in everyday life, perceiving in ordinary events the luminosity through which the divine signifies its presence. Paris noted that:

> One might sum up the psychological skills of a Greek this way: When a numinous event occurred, they asked, "Who is there? And what does that God or Goddess want of me?" When things were going badly in the life of a Greek, he or she would ask, "What divinity have I offended and how can I give him or her his due?"[4]

Within this rich cosmological framework, divinatory art offered an especially powerful means of accessing divine intention. Oracles (in which messages are delivered through a voice, usually human) and divinations (in which messages are conveyed by physical signs such as the behavior of animals, the movement of heavenly bodies, the pattern of thrown sticks, and so forth) were regarded as communications from the larger matrix of life. Suppliants must have felt immense satisfaction to receive messages from a meta-human source that addressed their personal concerns and issues. The Latin word for "address," *addrictiare*, originally carried the meaning of "making straight or right."[5] Oracular communications had the power to straighten out or make right those areas of psychic entanglement that individuals brought into the presence of Otherness.

We may understand more fully the impact of divinatory art on ancient petitioners by reviewing the operation of Delphi's great oracular institution. Since the historical/legendary record is full of uncertainties and inconsistencies, any synopsis of this subject is necessarily a construction based on selected information. The synopses that I will present in the next sections adhere as closely as possible to opinions offered by modern classical authorities. In referring to the Delphic priestess herself, however, I prefer the assignation of "pythoness" (used in translations of Herodotus) to the more common "pythia." The former term recalls the priestess's connection with the archaic she-serpent of Ge (Earth), whose shrine consecrated Delphi long before the temple of Apollo was built.

According to legend, the oracular site at Delphi was once a tract of wilderness. One day a goatherd followed his flock into the area as they grazed. He soon noticed that the animals were acting quite strangely, trembling and bleating, gamboling and leaping in a most peculiar manner. Drawing closer, the herder saw that his goats apparently had become intoxicated by inhaling vapors which were rising from a deep chasm in the earth. He bent over the chasm to get a better look and immediately fell into an ecstatic trance. When the herder's kinsfolk found him later, they were amazed to hear him uttering many wondrous things which gave them valuable knowledge about the past, present, and future. They rushed to the chasm and immediately were catapulted into the same exalted state of mind. Soon people from far and wide heard about the opening to the underworld and its mysterious powers. Crowds thronged the site, some of them falling or leaping into the crack. It was then decided that the area was too dangerous and should be blockaded from public access. Thereafter, one person alone would enter the *mania* of trance and bring back communications from the underworld. A woman of very pure character was chosen to become the intermediary between the powers of Earth and human beings. This is how the pythoness came to occupy her sacred office.[6]

The legend of Delphi's founding offers insight into the attitudes that suppliants probably brought with them when they approached the oracle. They did not regard the priestess merely as a consultant or a source of useful information. In their minds she provided connection with a force that was mysterious and wholly "other." The oracle-speaker (like the shaman of more ancient tradition) was revered for her ability to conjoin with a supernatural force and return unharmed, bringing back trails of wisdom for humankind.

Petitioners to the oracle prepared themselves for the encounter through prayer and ritual bathing in sacred waters. They may also have fasted for a period of time preceding their consultation. Upon reaching the temple they purchased a sacred barley cake from the Delphic priests and offered it to the gods upon an outside altar. Suppliants then proceeded to the inner hearth where the eternal flame burned. Here it was customary to sacrifice a goat or sheep as a way of thanking the gods for their willingness to assist them. With these rituals accomplished, petitioners were escorted to a room near the inner sanctuary where they would await their turn before the pythoness. Lots were drawn to determine the order in which they would have their sessions.

Pilgrims who entered into the temple were advised to "think pure thoughts and speak well-omened words."[7] While waiting in the darkened antechamber they sometimes smelled a haunting fragrance that defied description. Plutarch, who served as an officiating temple priest at Delphi for two decades in the first century C.E., commented upon this phenomenon:

> The room in which they seat those who would consult the god is filled, not frequently or with any regularity, but as it may chance from time to time, with a delightful fragrance coming on a current of air which bears it towards the worshippers, as if its source were in the holy of holies; and it is like the odour which the most exquisite and costly perfumes send forth.[8]

After waiting for a period of time, pilgrims were summoned individually to the holy inner chamber. They could not see the pythoness, but they knew that she was poised upon her tripod only a few yards away behind a curtain or thin wall. A priest or temple official now asked her the question which had been given to him in advance (verbally or in writing) by the petitioner. In all likelihood, the petitioner could hear her voice directly as it uttered the counsel of Apollo. No one was permitted to question or challenge the pythoness about her response, but sometimes it was acceptable to ask for a second message that would add clarification to the first.

When the session was over, the suppliant was escorted out of the chamber, blinking at the bright light of day and perhaps trembling with the import of what had happened. The prophetess may have spoken words that were simple and sensible, proffering no intriguing surprises. But the world itself seemed strangely altered after one emerged from her presence. It was for the sake of this deeper message—the one which could be conferred but not explained—that pilgrims across a thousand years made the journey to Delphi.

Oracular Art Lifts Consciousness Out of Time and Space

Divinatory communications issue from a place of experiencing where the past, present, and future coexist in the timeless presence of "now." It is as though all of time has been enfolded into one spacious moment that has no bounds. Everything that has occurred or will occur is contained there, as well as the infinite rings of possibility that life itself generates. Within this domain, distant events draw near, past sorrows tell their story, and future deeds imprint their images.

The ancient Greeks believed that "oracular space" belonged to the gods alone. Only by their grace could communications from the timeless expanse be received by human beings. On some occasions divine intention was communicated spontaneously through signs and prodigies. But it also spoke through those prophets, diviners, oracle-speakers, and individuals of inspiration who piously sought them. The psychological import of these messages cannot be overestimated. A single prophetic image could place a spin upon one's life that impacted many generations. Oracular responses of a simple advisory nature (the most common type found) also affected pilgrims deeply, for they opened up a wider area of sacred space around human concerns. Thus, consulting with the pythoness was an act of caring for the soul. As the psychotherapist Thomas Moore has observed, "The soul is at home when it participates in a sense of time that carries it beyond the limits of ordinary life."[9]

By what means did the pythoness of Delphi enter into a state of consciousness that allowed her to commune with the past, present, and future? Much has been written on this topic, most of it belonging to the realm of speculative imagination. Only fragmentary evidence from archaeological finds and eyewitness accounts are available to ground us factually. The following account summarizes features of the oracle's operation that have historical support.

A woman's preparation to serve as pythoness began the moment she was chosen. We do not know the means by which this selection took

place, but ancient sources make it clear that she had to possess a fine
personal character and belong to a respected family. From the classical
period onward, she was probably a woman who had reached midlife.
In *The Eumenides*, written around 458 B.C.E., Aeschylus describes the
pythoness as being forty years old; in one line of the play, she refers to
herself as "an old woman."[10] A museum in Naples has preserved an
amphora in which the pythoness is depicted with white hair,[11] and
Diodorus Siculus, writing around 40 B.C.E., stated that Delphic
priestesses were chosen only from among women over fifty years old.[12]

Once chosen, the pythoness took vows to live a life of purity. Her
spiritual and physical preparedness was continually renewed through
the practice of sacred rituals which had been passed down from the
earliest times. These probably involved fasting, purifications, bathing
in the "silvery eddies of the Castalian spring" (as Aeschylus described
it), and offering up sacrifices to the deities. Priestesses were required
to remain "pure," but whether this vow included celibacy is unknown.
It is likely that different prescriptions for sexual conduct prevailed at
different eras of Delphi's history.

Before entering the temple, the pythoness paid homage to the
deities who inhabited the temple site. We have a glimpse of what this
invocation may have been like from the opening scene of the *Eumenides*,
which was probably modeled on actual ritual practices of the time:

> First in my prayer of all the gods I reverence
> Earth [Ge], the first author of prophecy; Earth's daughter, then,
> Themis; who, legend tells us, next ruled this oracle;
> the third enthroned, succeeding by good-will, not force,
> Phoebe—herself another Titan child of Earth—
> In turn gave her prerogative, a birthday gift,
> Of her young namesake, Phoebus [Apollo].[13]

The priestess also saluted other divinities, including the nymphs of the
Corycian cave, Bromius [Dionysus], Poseidon, and finally "Zeus most
high, the Accomplisher." She closed with a prayer that Apollo would
guide her lips so that she could pronounce his truth.[14]

The pythoness made a burnt offering of laurel leaves and barley meal on a temple altar before entering the holy chamber. Because laurel is the heraldic emblem of Apollo, she possibly placed a few leaves of the plant in her mouth also. Some modern writers have speculated that the priestess chewed quantities of laurel in order to enter a trance state by biochemical means. But this practice is considered highly unlikely by other classicists, who point out that such an ingestion would probably have made her feel sick rather than inspired.

Because Apollo was the patron god of music, we can assume that the sounds of lyres, flutes, and other instruments were important during these rites. The musical style was probably restrained and dignified, for Plutarch noted that music played to Apollo was always "regulated and chaste" in contrast to Dionysian music, which was laden with emotion.[15]

The priestess now entered the most holy of chambers, the *adyton*. Seated on her tripod, a tall chair that resembled a covered bowl with three legs, she prepared to come under the spell of *enthousiasmos*— divine ecstasy. In one hand she held a branch of laurel. The other hand may have held a woolen cord that was attached to the sacred *omphalos*, the egg-shaped stone in Apollo's temple that marked Delphi as the center of the world. One illustration from the famous Vulci cup (fifth century B.C.E.) depicts the priestess holding a shallow bowl in her left hand. The bowl possibly contained a libation to pour into the Earth as an offering; or it might have played a role in divination procedures, since some questions put before the priestess appeared to be answered using a lot method.

Nearly all ancient legends about Delphi mention a crack or hole in the Earth below the priestess's feet from which vapors arose. Variously portrayed as seductive or repellent, mind-clearing or sense-sedating, these vapors were regarded as the divine *pneuma* (spirit/breath) that carried the oracle-speaker into trance. Because the shrine at Delphi was dedicated to Earth, emanations arising from the underworld were believed to confer special power. It remains an open question whether the mysterious chasm was a physical feature of the site or whether the image served as a metaphor for psychic connection with the depths. Archaeologists have found no trace of a chasm at the temple ruins, despite centuries of hopeful searching.

When the laurel branch in the priestess's hand began to shake, attendants knew that she had passed into a trance state and was ready to channel communications of the god. The priest then asked a question submitted by the petitioner. Some accounts reported that the pythoness's answer was intoned or sung in elegant hexameter verse. Other descriptions suggested that she responded in simple declarative statements. It is likely that two versions of some oracles might have been distributed, a simple one for the inquirer, and a more literary one for wider circulation. Plutarch noted that the responses given at Delphi in his day seemed artless compared to the sophisticated creations of centuries past.[16] This observation suggests that styles of oracle delivery changed over time.

How the priestess herself experienced her descent into trance, we will probably never know. Ancient commentators provided images and descriptions of her behavior during oracular sessions, but it is difficult to distinguish between those based on eyewitness observation and those based on fantasy or propaganda. Taken together, they send sharply contradictory messages. In the classical age, the pythoness was depicted as delivering oracles in a serene and self-possessed manner. References to her person carried the respectful tone afforded to individuals of dignity and importance. But beginning in the first century of the common era, a new tone prevailed. The priestess was now often portrayed as losing her wits as she became possessed by the god, shrieking dreadful sounds that only a committee of trained priests could interpret. She was described as tearing her hair, crashing into walls, and often falling insensibly to the ground as she struggled with the forces surging through her body. Two early church fathers, Origen and Chrysostom, added pornographic elements to their accounts. As the bride of Apollo sat upon her tripod with her legs spread apart, according to their vision, an evil spirit from the bowels of hell entered her vagina and filled her with madness, causing foam to gush from her mouth.[17] Perhaps these spectral images reflected the declining influence of divinatory art as well as the deteriorating position of women in late pagan and early Christian societies.

As we study the operation of Delphi's shrine, we notice a variety of conditions that supported the priestess's ability to enter "oracular consciousness" and perform her work. The oracle-speaker undoubtedly carried within her a sense of having been chosen, perhaps destined, to her vocation. Her daily life was permeated with spiritual presence through the agency of devotional ritual and prayer. She probably drew strength and inspiration from the ancient site itself, which connected her with a lineage of powerful feminine deities. Oracular sessions took place in a context of enchantment which engaged all the senses. The priestess bathed in cold waters, inhaled pungent incense, tasted bitter leaves, grasped a branch of laurel, and was lulled by celestial music. The tripod upon which she sat was an object of such intense meaning that even touching it could transport her into trance.

Additionally, the priestess must have derived confidence from the framework of institutional support that surrounded her work. She could surrender to an exalted state of *entheasmon* knowing that attendants protected her body, priests dealt with her petitioners, and the entire civilized world paid homage to her art. By allowing her consciousness to melt through the boundaries of time and space, the pythoness not only ministered to her suppliants, but affirmed for all generations the boundlessness of spirit.

Oracular Communications Unite Us with the Matrix of All-That-Is

Divinatory art is founded upon the principle that life unfolds within a unified matrix of existence. All elements of the matrix are connected to each other and to the whole. The matrix and its elements are not mute, but are constantly exuding communications about their nature, their intentions, their relatedness. The task of the diviner is to receive and interpret these communications with special clarity. "All teems with symbol," Plotinus observed in the third century C.E. "Wise persons are they who in any one thing can read another."[18]

The thousands of divination methods that have been employed across the ages are all based upon the principle of universal relatedness. The position of planetary bodies could be consulted to set a fortuitous marriage date because the marriage and the planets were believed to be linked together in an interactive relationship. The pitch and pattern of crow caws could direct a lost pilgrim back to the road because pleas for help could be answered by myriad voices, including those of birds. The shape of smoke ribbons rising from a suppliant's burnt offering could signal the approbation of a god because, in that sublime moment, the suppliant, the god, and the smoke all intersected to manifest a condition of blessedness. A Roman writer noted that holy women from the temple sought divine advice by walking into a field and picking up the first clod of earth that attracted their gaze; if its weight seemed light, they understood that the issue in question was favorably aspected; if the clod scarcely could be lifted, caution was advised.[19] No element of nature was considered too lowly to become a source of spiritual guidance. Dirt, entrails, and dung were revered along with the stars.

For most individuals in the ancient world, the matrix that bound all existence together was divine in nature. Some devotees conceptualized the matrix as a monadic unity, while others experienced it as a dazzling multiplicity. All of creation was seen as bearing its signature, and its voice was continually heard speaking through trees and birds, fish and animals, brooks and burning bushes. Human beings could become oracle-speakers because the divine presence itself yearned to find expression through them.

This view was expressed passionately by the fourth century C.E. philosopher Iamblichus, who wrote a treatise that sought to create a philosophical framework for understanding the "sacred arts." Iamblichus emphasized that oracles and divinations are possible only because the supernal force which permeates the universe desires to communicate itself through all of creation. By its very nature, this force "excites our faculty of understanding to a greater acuteness" so that we may enter into an increasingly profound relationship with it. Individuals who have a greater proclivity for receiving and expressing these communications are suited to become practitioners of the sacred arts. Fakers can easily be detected by the uninspiring nature of their pronouncements and the coarse (or evil) quality of their work. All divining power comes from the gods and involves a participation with their energies. Iamblichus summed up his position as follows:

If, indeed, we have stated these things rightly, the divining power of the gods is . . . present everywhere in entirety with those who are able to receive it. Not only does it shine from without, and fill all things, but it likewise permeates all the elements, occupies the earth, and air and fire and water, and leaves nothing destitute of itself, neither living beings nor things sustained from the realm of nature.[20]

Many great philosophers in the classical world regarded oracles and divinations as sacred. Socrates relied upon guidance from sources such as the oracle of Delphi, the flights and calls of birds, the chance meeting of particular persons, and the chance hearing of words in a crowd. He also received communications from an inner voice which he termed his *daimôn*. Xenophon, an associate of Socrates, noted that the philosopher often said, "The divinity has given me a sign." Socrates sometimes offered warning or advice to his associates based on the authority of his divine guidance. "And as a matter of fact," Xenophon noted, "those who listened to his warnings prospered, whilst those who turned a deaf ear to them repented afterwards."[21]

According to Xenophon, Socrates emphasized that individuals should never approach oracular sources with trivial subjects nor with questions that they could answer themselves after appropriate study. Imagine how profane it would be, the philosopher said, to seek the guidance of heaven on whether you should hire a expert coachman to drive your team of horses or to employ one who has never touched the reins! Yet some questions submitted to divination are no less absurd. Only those matters which are hidden from mortals should be brought to the gods for illumination. And there is no shortage of these, for the deepest aspects of life are beyond the grasp of reason.

Plato held oracular shrines in such high regard that he made them centerpieces of his imagined ideal cities. In the *Republic* and the *Laws*, he depicted leaders consulting the oracle for guidance on how to establish temples, conduct sacrifices, worship divine entities, and promote open channels of communication between human beings and the unseen world. Why should these concerns be given foremost attention? For Plato, spiritual reality was regarded as the undergirding of all material reality. It therefore followed that the first task of a community was to bring itself into a proper relationship with the sacred. The sacred could speak in many ways: through the inspiration of art and poetry, the transporting emotion of love, and the ecstatic celebrations of the divine mysteries. But in Plato's view, the oracle was an especially precious instrument for the communications of the divine.

When practiced in their highest forms, the oracular arts bestowed many gifts on citizens of the ancient world. They offered guidance, illuminated the past, conferred meaning on the present, cast images of the future, and revealed the underlying coherence of disparate events. But perhaps their greatest contribution was to open up a space of divine in-breathing which enabled the individual self to be once again filled with the *pneuma* of all creation.

Delphi's Enduring Message

In the year 362 C.E., the Roman emperor Julian the Apostate sent an emissary to Delphi. His purpose was to help revive the famous oracle, whose flame was almost extinct due to neglect and assault. Legend recounts that when the emissary asked what could be done to restore the great pagan shrine, he received a somber answer:

> Tell the king the fair-wrought house has fallen.
> No shelter has Apollo, nor sacred laurel leaves;
> The fountains now are silent, the voice is stilled.[22]

These words were reported to be the priestess's final proclamation. Three decades later, the last temple of Apollo was plundered and demolished by the Christian emperor Arcadius. The shrine at Delphi was destroyed with special thoroughness. Nearly all of the temple's interior structures, including the altars, the *adyton*, and the holy living quarters, were pounded into featureless rubble. The fair-wrought house had not only fallen but was mortally dismembered.

From a modern perspective, the loss of such an important spiritual shrine evokes pain. But how might the pythoness herself have made sense of Delphi's fate? Remembering that in Greek cosmology the ultimate creators, preservers, and disposers of all phenomena were the gods, she might have viewed the situation somewhat philosophically. The oracle may have reminded us that the deities are quite capable of taking care of their shrines when they wish to do so, as evidenced by many legends. When the Persians attacked Delphi in the fifth century, for example, Apollo not only caused huge boulders to roll down from the hillside and crush the enemy, but materialized a giant spirit-warrior who sent the invaders running in terror. Similar measures could easily have been employed to chase away a few Roman troops 700 years later. We can only conclude that the gods allowed—or perhaps even directed—Delphi's shrine to be destroyed at a particular point in history.

Imagination must guide us where no oracle is given, but it is not difficult to offer reasons why the Disposers might allow Delphi's curtain to fall. The temple's plush treasure-room, the increasingly costly fees that petitioners were asked to pay, the bloody animal sacrifices, the coterie of priests who padded around the grounds with little to do between ceremonies—perhaps the gods had grown weary of these forms and conventions. Even the pagan symbols of laurel and tripod, libation bowl and *omphalos*, may have lost much of their numinosity by the fourth century.

The office of pythoness probably offered diminishing satisfaction to the women who filled it. By Plutarch's time, the ideal priestess was one who could not read or write and knew little of the world beyond her courtyard walls. She was closely confined and allowed no concourse with strangers. Delivering an oracle in hexameter verse was probably out of the question for such an individual. Even if she were to grace her pronouncements with lyric art, its value would be lost on most of her petitioners, whose questions revolved primarily around money, property, political gain, and all of those issues that Socrates had deemed unworthy of the oracle's attention. The ancients believed that true divination occurred only when divine presence conjoined with human receptivity. Perhaps the oracular institutions of late antiquity no longer could inflame the spiritual passion of either gods or mortals.

As a final clue to why the Fates may have dismembered their shrine, we recall its mythological origins. Delphi's sanctuary belonged originally to Ge, the primordial creatrix and sustainer of life, whose earthly embrace had been worshipped for millennia. Delphi remained an oracle of the Earth even after Sun-Apollo took over as patron. It drew power from the materiality of rocks and caverns, roots and chasms, and all the deep places that sheltered soul. It opened a cleft into the mysteries of the underworld through the agency of dreams, visions, and chthonic encounters. Ge's mantic inspiration was available to anyone who could receive it. As we saw in the legend of the goatherd, people from all regions were drawn to the divine breath that issued freely from the Earth and filled them with exalted insight. Some pilgrims ecstatically relinquished their personal identity by casting themselves into the Primordium. Others returned to their villages and became poets or prophets. But then the decision was made to restrict universal access to this experience. Now, only certain individuals were given the right to speak for Earth. Regulated by officials and cut off from the pilgrims who thirsted for its counsel, Delphi's oracle became subject to increasing stricture. Perhaps the old shrines were destroyed so that individuals could rediscover their personal connection to Ge in fresh, new places.

Thus, Delphi's message for psychological life is inscribed in its rubble as well as its legend. Temples rise and fall, but oracular consciousness is imperishable. We will always reach out to sources of psychic vitality beyond the personal self, seeking a response that addresses the soul directly. Nor is the communication one-sided. Delphi's example suggests that life itself perpetually streams forth the many-splendored emblems of its nature and its desires. Oracular shrines in the ancient world served as holy receiving vessels for some of these messages. Although the old containers shattered long ago, their contents are ever present, urging us to answer them, voice to voice.

Notes

1. Reference to these oracles may be found in the following sources: the oracle to the Lacedaemonians: G. Rawlison, translator, *The History of Herodotus* (New York: Tudor Publishing Company, 1928), 23; the oracle to Battus: H. W. Park and D. E. W. Wormell, *The Delphic Oracle* (Oxford: Basil Blackwell, 1956), 75; the oracle to Athens: Joseph Fontenrose, *The Delphic Oracle* (Berkeley: University of California Press, 1978), 398; the oracle to Croesus: *The History of Herodotus*, 18.

2. Fontenrose, *The Delphic Oracle*. Fontenrose provides criteria of classifying oracles as "historical," "quasi-historical," "legendary," and "fictional," as well as for analyzing their content.

3. Fontenrose, *The Delphic Oracle*.

4. Ginette Paris, "Everyday Epiphanies: Lifestyles of the Gods and Goddesses," *Sphinx* 4 (1992), 62–75, 66.

5. *Oxford English Dictionary* (Oxford: Oxford University Press, 1971), s.v. "address."

6. Diodorus Siculus, *World History* 26.6.

7. Parke and Wormell, *The Delphic Oracle*, 33.

8. Plutarch, *The Obsolescence of Oracles* 495.

9. Thomas Moore, *Care of the Soul: A Guide for Cultivating Depth and Sacredness in Everyday Life* (New York: HarperCollins, 1992), 223.

10. Aeschylus, *The Eumenides*, translated by Philip Vellacott (Baltimore: Penguin Books, 1962), 47.

11. Robert Flaceliere, *Greek Oracles*, translated by D. Garman (London: Elek Books, 1965), 42.

12. Diodorus Siculus, *World History* 26.6.

13. Aeschylus, *The Eumenides*, 147.

14. For valuable reflections on the importance of Apollo, Dionysus, and the *omphalos* at Delphi, see David Fideler, "The Voice From the Center: The Oracle of Apollo and the Oracle of the Heart," *Gnosis* 5 (Fall 1987), 23–27.

15. Plutarch, *The E at Delphi*. No records have been found that mention music being played at the temple at Delphi, but Hoyle (see note 21) indicates that music played an important role at the oracular shrine at Didyma, whose operation resembled closely that of Delphi.

16. Plutarch, *The Oracles at Delphi No Longer Given in Verse*.

17. For a discussion of the relationship between virginity and oracular function see Giulia Sissa, *Greek Virginity*, translated by A. Goldhammer (Cambridge: Harvard University Press, 1990).

18. Plotinus, "Are the Stars Causes?," *Enneads* 2.3.7.

19. *Dio Chrysostom*, translated by J. W. Cohoon (Cambridge: Harvard University Press, 1950), 91.

20. Iamblichus of Chalcis, *On the Mysteries*, translated by Thomas Taylor and Alexander Wilder, edited by Stephan Ronan (London: Chthonios Books, 1989), 75 (*De mysteriis* 3.12).

21. Xenophon, *The Memorabilia or Recollections of Socrates*, translated by H. G. Dakyns (New York: Macmillan, 1897), 1.1.2–3.

22. Peter Hoyle, *Delphi* (London: Cassell and Company, 1967), 142.

Down Below My Monticello

Down below my Monticello
Is a grey-lit temple underground
Tall totem on the doorway mirror
and there stands a staghorned, baboon God

Down below my Monticello
On graphite-stone-black walls is writ
A hymn in painted gold inscription
A hymn Hermetic, a living myth

Down below my Monticello
Issues forth a vital stream
Where there was dreaming of Jefferson
Before Jefferson could ever dream

Down below my Monticello
If dreaming be my only gift
then some incurable mad-spot we all suffer
Each tiny point to light the Earth

Lyric by CHRISTOPHER REYNOLDS

Orfeo

When the world is only matter or energy
body or spirit,
where do the ancestors go?
The Gods?
The Soul?

We find them dwelling in our symptoms
in our sickness, in our addictions.

Weep for the Earth, Orfeo.
Orfeo, weep for the Earth.
For in such sorrow lies an awakening.

Orfeo, weep for the Earth.

Lyric by CHRISTOPHER REYNOLDS

Orpheus Playing the *Vihuela*
Woodcut from Luis Milan's *El Maestro*, 1536.

Off in the Distance the City is Burning

Off in the distance the city is burning
Confusion distracts the hearts of men
But here in the primeval forest clearing
Orpheus plays his mandolin

I sit round with beasts great and small
Enchanted by his magical call
The trees are dancing, bending they flow
Remember this song, this concord of all

Lyric on a Renaissance woodcut by DAVID FIDELER

Translator's Introduction

ANATOLIUS was a learned Christian of the third century B.C.E. Little is known of his life apart from the fact that he was born in Alexandria in Egypt, but became bishop of Laodicea, a coastal town in Syria (modern Latakia). He is probably to be identified with the Anatolius we hear of as one of the teachers of the eminent Neoplatonist Iamblichus. Equally little survives of his work. We know that he wrote on a vast number of scientific, philosophical, and religious topics, but the short treatise translated here is the only complete text of his we have (and even it may be an epitome of a longer work). The Greek text is available, edited by J. L. Heiberg, in *Annales internationales d'histoire, congrès de Paris 1900, 5e section, histoire de sciences* (Paris, 1901), pp. 427–41. Sections of it are also quoted by the anonymous compiler of *The Theology of Arithmetic*. This translation, the first into English, was originally published in the UK in the *Kairos Newsletter* for 1987/8. It is reprinted here with a few minor changes.

—ROBIN WATERFIELD

Anatolius: *On the Decad*

Translated by Robin Waterfield

THE NATURE OF THE DECAD and of the numbers within it provides and displays beauty in a great many respects, for those capable of using their minds for clear-sighted examination of such things. We will say as much as we can about each of the numbers. For now, we say this much in preface: that the Pythagoreans reduced all numbers to the ten, and that there is no number beyond ten, because once a whole decad is complete, all subsequent increase involves us returning to the monad;[1] moreover, because the decad is composed of a tetrad, the Pythagoreans revered the tetraktys above all.[2]

On the Monad

The monad is the first of all numbers. All numbers arise out of it, but it is subordinate to none of them. Hence it is called "matrix," because it is the matter of all the numbers, in the sense that if it did not exist, neither would any number exist.

It is indivisible and irreproachable; it does not depart from its own nature even when multiplied.[3] Moreover, even if not actually, yet in potential it is odd, even, even-odd, cube, square, etc.[4] It represents a point.[5]

The Pythagoreans called it "intellect," and likened it to the One, the intelligible God, the uncreated, the ideal Beauty, the ideal Good, especially since, among the virtues, they likened it to the wisdom of the One. For correct and appropriate action is one.

Moreover,[6] they regarded it as "being," "cause," "truth," "simple," "paradigm," "order," "concord," "what is equal among greater and lesser," "the mean in any interval," "moderation in plurality," "the instant now in past and future time."

Moreover, they regarded one as "container," "ship," "chariot," "friend," "life," "happiness." Furthermore, they said that in the middle of the four elements there lies a certain monadic fiery cube, whose central position they say Homer was aware of when he said: "As far below Hades as the heavens are higher than the Earth."[7] In this context, it looks as though the disciples of Empedocles and Parmenides and just about the majority of the sages of old followed the Pythagoreans and declared that the principle of the monad is situated in the middle in the manner of the Hearth, and keeps its location because of being equilibrated; and Euripides too, who was a disciple of Anaxagoras, mentions the Earth as follows: "Those among mortals who are wise consider you to be the Hearth."[8]

Moreover, the Pythagoreans say that the right-angled triangle too was formed by Pythagoras when he regarded the numbers in the triangle monad by monad.[9]

On the Dyad

The dyad is a source of number.[10] The first increase and change results in the dyad and in the doubling of the monad. It is the first of the series of even numbers, since adding dyad to dyad is equivalent to multiplying them: adding them and multiplying them have the same result, whereas in all other cases multiplication is greater than addition. It represents a line, which comes after a point.

It is analogous to matter and to everything perceptible. Among the virtues, they liken it to courage, for it has already made an advance. Hence too they used to call it "daring" and "impulse."

They also gave it the title of "opinion," because truth and falsity lie in opinion. And they called it "movement," "generation," "change," "division," "length," "multiplication," "addition," "kinship," "relativity," "the ratio in proportionality." For the relation of three numbers in three terms is the ratio in proportionality.[11]

On the Triad

The triad is the result of the monad coming together with the dyad. It is the first odd number. It is called perfect by some, because it is the first number to signify the totality—beginning, middle, and end. We exalt extraordinary events in terms of the triad, by calling people "thrice blessed," "thrice fortunate." Prayers and libations are performed three times. It is the first to represent beginning, middle, and end. It represents a plane figure, which comes after a point and a line. Triangles both reflect and are the first substantiation of being plane: for there are three types of triangle—equilateral, isosceles, and scalene. Moreover, there are three rectilinear angles—right, acute, and obtuse. And there are three parts of time—present, past, and future. Among the virtues, they likened it to moderation: for it is commensurability between excess and deficiency, rashness and cowardice. The triad is formed from the dyad and the monad or vice versa. It makes six by the addition of the monad, the dyad, and itself, and six is the first perfect number, properly speaking.

On the Tetrad

The tetrad is called "justice," since the square (i.e. the area) which is based on it is equal to the perimeter; for the perimeter of squares before it is greater than the area of the square, and the perimeter of squares after it is less than the area.[12]

It is the first square, and the first tetraktys among even numbers,[13] because the numbers from the monad up to the tetrad make ten, which is called a perfect number. It is the first number to represent solidity: the sequence is point, line, plane, solid (i.e. body). From the tetrad comes the game of playing with nuts to form the shape of a pyramid. Moreover, there are four elements, and four seasons which divide the year into four.

It is the first number which is even-times-even, and the first to contain the sesquitertian ratio[14] which belongs to the primary concord, the fourth. In its case everything is equal—area, angle, sides.[15]

There are four cardinal points—east, west, north, and south; there are four distinguishing points—ascendant, descendant, midheaven, and nadir. The primary winds are four.

Moreover, of the universe, some is intelligible, while the rest is perceptible, and for the intelligible part there is either science or dialectic, while for the perceptible part there is either belief or conjecture,[16] and these are four.

Some say that all things are organized by means of four—substance, shape, form, and principle.

Of all the numbers, the tetrad comprehends the principle of soul as well as that of corporeality: for they say that a living creature is ensouled in the same way that the whole universe is arranged, according to harmony. Perfect harmony seems to subsist in three concords: the fourth, which lies in the sesquitertian ratio; the fifth, in the sesquialter; and the octave, in double. Once there are the first four numbers—1, 2, 3, 4—then there is also the category of soul, which these numbers encompass in accordance with musical principle. For 4 is double 2 and 2 is double 1, and here is the octaval concord; 3 is one and a half times 2, a sesquialter, and so produces the fifth; and 4 is sesquitertian to 3, and here is the fourth. If the universe is composed out of soul and body in the number 4, then it is also true that all concords are perfected by it.

On the Pentad

The pentad is the first number to encompass the specific identity of all number, in the sense that it encompasses the first even number and the first odd number (the monad is not a number, even if it is odd). It arises by linear extension (i.e. addition) from the first numbers—even and odd, male and female. Hence, this is what it is called.[17] When it is added to itself, ten is the result because [. . .][18]

When it is squared, it always encompasses itself and terminates at itself: for 5 x 5 = 25. When it is cubed, it encompasses the square as a whole and terminates at itself: for 5 x 25 = 125.

Moreover, there are five solid figures with equal sides and equal angles—the tetrahedron (i.e. pyramid), octahedron, eicosahedron, cube, and dodecahedron. And Plato says that the first of these is the figure of fire, the second of air, the third of water, the fourth of earth, and the fifth of the universe.[19]

Moreover, not counting the sun and moon, there are five planets. Moreover, the familiar parallel circles on the globe are five—equator, two tropics, and the Arctic and Antarctic circles. There are five zones—two cold, two temperate, and one hot. There are five senses.

The square on base 5 is the first to be equal to two squares—the one on base 3 and the one on base 4. A tetrachord is said to consist of the first even and the first odd numbers.[20] Geometric concord is thought to fall under five.[21]

Moreover, since it is the result of adding 2 and 3, they used to call it "marriage."[22] Moreover, whatever you use to add up to 10, 5 is found to be the arithmetic mean—for example, 9 + 1, 8 + 2, 7 + 3, 6 + 4—add any of these pairs and you will always make 10, and 5 will be found to be the arithmetic mean, as the diagram shows.

On the Hexad

The hexad is the first perfect number: for it is counted by its own parts (1, 2, 3), which make 6: 1 x 6 = 6, 2 x 3 = 6, 3 x 2 = 6. Thus it is composed of its half, third, and sixth.

When squared, it includes itself, for 6 x 6 = 36; when cubed, it includes itself, but no longer the square: for 6 x 36 = 216, which includes 6, but not 36.

It arises out of the first even and first odd numbers, male and female, as a product and by multiplication; hence it is called "androgynous," and also "marriage" and "even-odd." It was called "marriage" because it is equal to its own parts, as has been shown, and because it is the function of marriage to make offspring similar to parents.

The harmonic mean is first formed by the hexad, when 8 is taken as the sesquitertian of 6, and 12 as the double: for by the same fraction 8 both exceeds and is exceeded by the extremes.[23] And the arithmetic mean is formed when 9 is taken as the sesquialter of 6, and 12 as the double: for by the same number, 3, 9 both exceeds one extreme and is exceeded by the other. Moreover, its parts (1, 2, 3) when taken together make a certain arithmetical proportion. Moreover, 6 also makes geometric proportion, with it as the mean, if we take its half, 3, and its double, 12: it becomes the geometric mean—3, 6, 12. Moreover, there are six extensions of solid bodies.[24] Moreover, 6 added to the first square, 4, makes ten.

On the Hebdomad

The hebdomad is the only number within the decad (apart from the monad) which neither generates nor is generated by another number within the decad; hence it is called by the Pythagoreans "virgin not born of mother." Of the other numbers within the decad, four is generated by the dyad and, along with the dyad again, generates eight; six is generated by the triad, but it does not generate a number within the decad; three and five are generators—three of six and nine, five of ten.

The sequence from the monad to seven makes 28, which is a perfect number—i.e. is equal to its own parts. The twenty-eight days of the moon are brought to completion in hebdomads.[25]

Starting with the monad and making a sequence by doubling, seven numbers yield 64, the first square which is also a cube: 1, 2, 4, 8, 16, 32, 64. Starting with the monad and making a sequence by trebling, seven numbers yield 729, which is a square and cube—the square of 27, the cube of 9—as follows: 1, 3, 9, 27, 81, 243, 729. In fact, seven always does this in such sequences: for instance, starting with 64, and doubling each time, yields the cube of 16.[26]

Moreover, the hebdomad consisting of the dimensions and the four limits makes manifest corporeality and organic life. The limits are point, line, plane, solid; the dimensions are length, breadth, depth.

Seven is said to be the number of the primary concord, the fourth (4:3), and of geometric proportion (1, 2, 4). It is also called "that which brings completion"; for seven-month children are viable. The hebdomad indicates crises in illnesses. Seven encompasses the sides around the right angle of the archetypal right-angled triangle; the length of one is 4, of the other 3.

There are seven planets. There are seven phases of the moon itself: it is crescent-shaped twice, halved twice, gibbous twice, and full once. The Great Bear has seven stars. Heraclitus says that it is a principle of the seasons that in the case of the moon the hebdomad is kept whole, while in the case of the Bears, the two constellations of immortal memory, it is divided.[27] There are seven Pleiades. The equinoxes and the solstices occur after seven months.[28]

That part of the soul which is different from the authoritative part[29] is divided into seven—into five senses, the faculty of speech, and the faculty of procreation.

Seven parts complete the body—head, neck, trunk, two arms, and two legs. There are seven internal organs—stomach, heart, lung, liver, spleen, and two kidneys. Herophilus[30] says that human intestines are twenty-one cubits long—i.e. three hebdomads. The head has seven channels—two eyes, two ears, two nostrils, and the mouth.

We see seven things—body, distance, shape, size, color, movement, and rest.

There are seven alterations of speech[31]—acute, grave, circumflex, aspirated, unaspirated, long, and short. There are seven movements—up, down, forward, backward, right, left, and circular. There are seven vowels—alpha, epsilon, eta, iota, omicron, upsilon, and omega. The lyre is seven-stringed. Terpander says this about the lyre:

> I turn away from four-toned song
> And sing new praises on the seven-stringed lyre.[32]

Plato in *Timaeus* composed the soul from seven numbers.[33] Straits usually ebb and flow seven times per day. Everything is fond of sevens.

Moreover, there are seven ages from infancy to old age—those of a baby, a child, an adolescent, a youth, a man, an elder, and an old man. And after seven years we change from being a baby to being a child, then from a child to an adolescent, and so on for the successive ages. Solon speaks as follows on this matter:

> A young child, still a baby, grows his first set of teeth and sheds them within seven years. By the time God has brought to completion his next seven years, the signs of youth have become apparent. In the third period, his chin sprouts a beard over his growing limbs and his skin loses its bloom. In the fourth of the hebdomads, everyone reaches a peak of strength, and here men show the signs of excellence. In the fifth, it is time for a man to think of marriage, and to look to the generation of children hereafter. In the sixth, a man's mind is mature in all respects, and he no longer desires to do reckless deeds as before. In the seventh hebdomad and in the eighth—for fourteen years in all—he excels with his mind and tongue. In the ninth, he still has power, but his tongue and intellect are too weak for great excellence. In the tenth, it is timely for whoever attains this age and completes it to die, as die he must.[34]

Hippocrates says:

> Seven are the seasons, which we call ages—child, boy, adolescent, youth, man, elder, old man. One is a child up to the shedding of teeth, until seven years; a boy up to puberty, until twice seven; an adolescent up to the growth of the beard, until three times seven; a youth up to the general growth of the body, until four times seven; a man up to one short of fifty years, until seven times seven; an elder up to 56 years, until seven times nine; from then on one is an old man.[35]

On the Ogdoad

The ogdoad is the first cube. It is called "safety" and "foundation." The seed of the ogdoad is the first even number. It is the sum of the monad, triad, and tetrad. The sequence from the monad to it adds up to 36, which is the time within which they say that seven-month children are formed.[36] The eighth sphere encompasses the whole—hence the saying "All is eight." Eratosthenes says that all the eight spheres of the universe revolve around the Earth. He speaks as follows:

"All these eight, with their eight spheres, revolve in a circle around the ninth, Earth."[37]

On the Ennad

The ennad[38] is the first square based on the first odd number, just as four is the first square based on the first even number. The sequence from the monad to it adds up to 45, which is the time within which they say that nine-month children begin to be formed. The eight spheres revolve around the ninth, Earth. It too is called "that which brings completion,"[39] since it completes nine-month children. Moreover, it is called perfect, because it is the product of three, which is a perfect number, taken three times. Homer says,[40] "All the nine stood up." Nine is also said to contain the principles of the concords—4, 3, and 2; the sesquitertian is 4:3, the sesquialter is 3:2, and the double is 4:2. It is the first number to be in a sesquioctaval ratio.[41]

On the Decad

The decad is potentially generated by even and odd: for ten is five times two. It is the perimeter and limit of all numbers: for they run their course by wheeling and turning around it as if it were a turning-point in a race. Moreover, it is the limit of the infinitude of numbers, because when we have counted from the monad up to it, we stop and say that eleven and twelve are next.

Moreover, twenty, the double of ten, is formed by adding twice the numbers from which ten is formed: for ten is formed by 1, 2, 3, 4, and twenty by twice 1, twice 2, twice 3, and twice 4, and subsequent decads are formed on the same principle.

The decad is called "power" and "all-fulfiller," because it limits all number by encompassing within itself the whole nature of even and odd, moving and unmoving, good and bad. And it is called "receptacle" because everything is contained within it.[42]

If the spaces occupied by a square whose area is 16 and an oblong whose area is 18 are levelled off, then a perimeter of hebdomads is found: the sides of the square and the oblong are respectively 4 and 6 (for 4 x 4 = 16 and 6 x 3 = 18), and 4 + 6 = 10.[43]

Moreover, it arises out of the tetraktys of the first numbers (1, 2, 3, and 4) combined.

Moreover, the decad generates the number 55,[44] which is full of beauty. For, in the first place, it is formed by doubling and trebling the systematic sequence of numbers—the doubles are 1, 2, 4, 8 (i.e. 15), the triples are 1, 3, 9, 27 (i.e. 40), and the addition of these makes 55. Plato also mentions these sequences in the passage on the generation of soul which begins, "He removed one portion from the whole," and so on.[45]

In the second place, while 55 is a construct of the decad, 385 is the addition of the squared decad; for if you square the successive numbers from the monad to the decad, and then add them up, you will get the aforementioned number, 385; and this is also 7 x 55.

In the third place, 55 is a triangular number.[46] In the fourth place, if you count the letters of the word "one," you will find by addition 55.[47] In the fifth place, if the hexad, the most fertile number, is squared, it produces 36, and this has seven factors, generated as follows: 18 taken twice, 12 taken three times, 9 taken four times, 6 taken 6 times, 4 taken nine times, three taken 12 times, and 2 taken eighteen times. There are seven numbers involved, and the sum is 55.[48]

In the sixth place, the sequence of the first five triangular numbers generates 55 (3, 6, 10, 15, and 21 make 55), and again, the sequence of the first five squares generates 55 (1, 4, 9, 16, and 25 make 55); and according to Plato the universe is generated out of triangle and square.[49] For he constructs three figures out of equilateral triangles— pyramid, octahedron and eicosahedron, which are the figures respectively of fire, air, and water—and the cube, the figure of earth, out of squares.

Notes

1. That is, 1–10 is primary, and 11–20, 21–30, etc., simply repeat the first decad. See the section on the decad.

2. The tetraktys is the first four numbers displayed as an equilateral triangle of evenly spaced dots, which add up to 10. Since it adds up to 10, it contains all the principles of the universe, according to the Pythagoreans (see also Theon of Smyrna, *Mathematics Useful for Reading Plato*, chapter 38), and was the chief Pythagorean symbol.

3. Because 1 x 1 = 1.

4. That is, all the Greek categories of number, for which see the glossary to my translation of *The Theology of Arithmetic* (abbreviated from here on as *ThA*).

5. As 2 does the line, 3 the triangle, and 4 the pyramid.

6. What follows occurs also in *ThA*. However, here and in other passages which are quoted in *ThA*, the text transmitted by the two manuscript traditions may differ somewhat. For the present purposes, I have translated Heiberg's text of Anatolius (apart from one or two slight changes), whether or not I think it better than that of *ThA*.

7. *Iliad* 8.16. Here and elsewhere in our tract, we glimpse the tendency to interpret Homer allegorically. The Greeks often conceived of the universe as concentric layers of the primary elements, from the densest at the center to the most rarefied at the outer rim. The Pythagoreans added the Hearth, a source of life, at the very center.

8. Empedocles, Parmenides, and Anaxagoras were Presocratic philosophers of the fifth century B.C.E. Anatolius' claim that they were Pythagoreans in this respect is highly implausible. Fragment 938 of the famous dramatist Euripides is quoted.

9. This is hard to understand. Perhaps it refers to the idea, found in *ThA*, that the Pythagorean triangle has *one* right angle, *two* other angles, sides *three*, *four* and *five* in length, and an area of *six*.

10. That is, like the monad, it is not an actual number. See *ThA* on the dyad.

11. This differs considerably from the equivalent text in *ThA*. I suppose Anatolius in this version means that three terms have two relations.

12. A square whose area is 16 has four sides whose sum is 16; smaller and larger squares differ as Anatolius claims.

13. I can't understand the qualification "among even numbers."

14. The sesquitertian is 4:3; the sesquialter, soon to be mentioned, is 3:2.

15. This sentence is incomprehensible; possibly the text is corrupt.

16. See Plato, *Republic* 506B–518B, 533E–534A.

17. "Male and female."

18. There follows a line of utterly corrupt text. In this place, *ThA* reads: "It is the mid-point of the decad" (see the diagrams a little later in our tract)— but this is sheer guesswork, if the compiler of *ThA* was faced with the same text as us.

19. *Timaeus* 53C–56C.

20. That is, a "conjunct" tetrachord—a sequence of four notes made out of one set of two notes and one set of three notes, where the last of the first set and the first of the last set are the same note.

21. This is hard to understand. Is he referring to the primary geometric proportion 1, 2, 4, whose extremes add up to 5?

22. Because two is female, three is male (likewise for all even and odd numbers).

23. As a matter of fact, however, the primary harmonic proportion was usually regarded as 3, 4, 6, not 6, 8, 12.

24. That is, the six directions—forward, backward, up, down, left, and right.

25. Seven-day periods.

26. The sequence is 64, 128, 256, 512, 1024, 2048, 4096. This last number is not only the cube of 16, but also the square of 64.

27. This is a spurious fragment (126A) of Heraclitus, the philosopher of the sixth/fifth centuries B.C.E. I'm not at all sure what the sentence means. Both Ursa Major and Ursa Minor could be said to have seven stars (strictly, Ursa Major has more, but the Plough, its brightest bit, has seven—even if one is double); so it is appropriate for them to appear in this context. Perhaps they are "constellations of immortal memory" because they are always visible, and since the Pole Star is part of Ursa Minor, it is a constant reminder; perhaps the hebdomad is said to be divided in their case simply because both constellations are similar in shape and consist of seven main stars—but there are two of them, so seven-ness is divided between them.

28. This is at best only approximately true, assuming that he is referring to

lunar months.

29. The authoritative part is the rational soul; the rest is the soul which informs the body.

30. Of Chalcedon, an eminent physician of the third century B.C.E.

31. That is, seven ways in which vowels can be sounded.

32. Terpander was a lyric poet of the seventh century B.C.E. This is his fragment 5.

33. *Timaeus* 35B–C.

34. Fragment 19 of the famous Athenian statesman and poet (seventh/sixth centuries B.C.E.).

35. Chapter 5 of the pseudo-Hippocratic *On Hebdomads*.

36. The Greek arithmologists were fascinated by the supposed fact that not only nine-month, but also seven-month children were viable (whereas eight-month children were supposed to be stillborn). Here Anatolius refers to the fact that seven-month children were thought to be fully, if minutely, formed in the womb by the end of the fifth hebdomad of days (35 days).

37. Eratosthenes of Cyrene was a scientific and literary polymath of the third century B.C.E. This is his fragment 17. The nine spheres are those of Earth, Sun, Moon, Mercury, Venus, Mars, Jupiter, Saturn, and the "fixed stars."

38. More usually "ennead."

39. As was the hebdomad too.

40. *Iliad* 7.161.

41. The ratio 9:8, which measures a major tone in music.

42. The Pythagoreans coined the word *dechas* ("receptacle") to be similar to *dekas* ("decad").

43. The Greek has required a little emendation to reach even this sense (such as it is!). Take a 4 x 4 square ABCD, and join on to it a 6 x 3 oblong ECFG. The dotted line "levels off" the two figures. The perimeter of the dotted figure consists of sides 6 and 1 in length (i.e. hebdomads). However, the importance of this is totally obscure to me.

44. Because $1 + 2 \ldots + 10 = 55$.

45. *Timaeus* 35B–C again.

46. In fact, it is the tenth triangular number.

47. Greek letters also did service as symbols for numbers; hence a system of gematria was inevitable. *Hen* ("one") adds up to 55.

48. Actually, the seven numbers mentioned add up to 54; the eighth factor is 1, of course, which makes the sum 55.

49. *Timaeus* 53C–56C again.

Two Letters of Marsilio Ficino

Qui musis abutuntur, non mel,
sed fel ab earum fonte reportant

**They who abuse the Muses bring back
from their fountain not honey but gall**

Marsilio Ficino to the distinguished citizen, Angelo Manetti:
greetings.

MY FRIEND, there are a number of writers, both Latin and Greek, who
compare to bees men who are totally devoted to study. For, like bees,
they gather here and there from many authors, as from flowers, and
store what they have gathered in the capacious hives of their memory.
They then let it ripen by reflection, to bring forth the mellifluous
liquid of learning and eloquence. If anyone should deny this comparison, which is made by the best authors, he would seem to me to deserve
to bring back gall rather than honey, even from the fount of the Muses.
I shall therefore subtract nothing at all from this simile, but rather add
to it.

You must have heard, my friend, that when bees suck from too many
wormwood flowers they very often produce honey which, when
swallowed, proves to be not sweet at all but bitter, almost like gall. We
know full well that something very similar often happens to gluttons
for study and devourers of books, who have neither measure nor
discrimination. Indeed, the more greedily they seem to drain the
sweet liquor of the Muses, the more bitterly do they take into their
heart I know not what! Perhaps this is what the Latin authors call bile,
the Greeks melancholy: a disease, as Aristotle shows, peculiar to men

195

absorbed by study. For this reason Solomon calls study a most onerous occupation; and he adds that the companion of knowledge is sorrow.

What therefore shall we say of Aristotle's remark: "The tree of knowledge indeed has bitter roots but the sweetest fruit"? We shall certainly grant this to Aristotle, but add that such a fruit is perhaps the peach, in which a bitter kernal lies within the sweetness.

What then? Should we denounce the Muses? Let us never think that the fount of celestial nectar and ambrosia pours forth bitter and deadly streams. Therefore, much as we praise the true use of the Muses, so we condemn their abuse. Who then makes the greatest abuse of the Muses? Surely one who heedlessly and importunately presses on their tracks; or one who impudently involves them with the common Venus; or who separates them from their lord Apollo. Ignorant little men do not attain knowledge when they grasp unwisely at wisdom herself. The Muses do not sing well when the wanton son of Venus molests them; either they are silent or they shriek. The chorus of the Muses does not dance becomingly, but limps and falters, whenever its lord Apollo is far away.

One who believes that he will perceive the sun's light without the sun's aid deservedly falls into darkness; he is not raised into light. So one who pursues this truth and that truth, separated from the highest truth, without doubt does not light upon truth but upon falsehood. No wonder that whoever searches for the nectar of heaven in the Stygian marsh deservedly drinks the genuine gall of opinion beneath the illusory honey of knowledge.

Omne tulit punctum, qui miscuit utile dulci

He who has blended the serious with the pleasing has satisfied everyone

Marsilio Ficino to Bernardo Bembo of Venice: greetings.

WHEN I CONSIDER the letters of my Aeneas, illustrious Bembo, I seem to be looking up at his mother Venus, joined with Jupiter. For at one moment our Aeneas pronounces weighty laws with Jupiter and at another he sings songs of love with Venus. Yet everywhere he appears full of light and everywhere benign. Should you enquire what connection there is between light and heavy qualities, the very nature of creation will directly reply: Beneath heaven, light and heavy elements are mixed, and flowers and leaves mingle with fruit. In the heavens, the swift are tempered by the slow and the fixed by the moving; also there is the greatest concord among the qualities when Mercury is in conjuction with Saturn, and Venus with Jupiter. He, then, who has blended the serious with the pleasing has satisfied everyone. Farewell and good fortune, my profitable and pleasing Aeneas!

Reprinted with permission from *The Letters of Marsilio Ficino*, volume 4, translated from the Latin by members of the Language Department of the School of Economic Science, London (London: Shepheard-Walwyn, 1988). See "Books in Brief" for ordering information.

Proclus's Hymn to the One

O, Transcendent of All! For what else is it lawful to call Thee?
How may I hymn Thee Who art exalted in all things?
How may speech hymn Thee? For Thou art expressible in no word.
Being alone Indescribable, since Thou giveth rise to all that is spoken.
How may thought grasp Thee? For Thou art apprehended in no
    mind.
Being alone Unknowable, since Thou giveth rise to all that is thought,
All Beings, both speaking and speechless, sing of Thee;
All Beings, both thinking and unthinking, honor Thee.
For the totality of desires and travails are for Thee;
All Beings worship Thee; To Thee all, sensing Thy tokens, offer a
    hymn of silence.
From Thee all things shine forth; Thou alone art dependent on
    nothing.
All rests in Thee, all rushes upon Thee;
Thou art the goal of all, being both one thing and all things,
Yet neither one nor all; many named, how shall I invoke Thee
Who art alone not to be defined? What Heaven-born mind
Shall penetrate Thy distant veil? Be gracious;
O, Transcendent of All! For what else is it lawful to call Thee?

Translated by MICHAEL HORNUM

Cosmologies

DANA WILDE

IN THE PAST FOUR HUNDRED YEARS we seem to have permanently cornered the problem of the one and the many. Science, not only a method of inquiring into but a guiding principle for understanding the nature of reality, has since the 1500s taught us to analyze details. "To analyze" means to break a subject down into its constituent parts and then describe how the parts work together. The emphasis is on the parts—the many. In this cosmology, the universe is many things adding up to one large thing.

This was not the cosmology of ancient philosophers and religious visionaries. Socrates, Buddha, Jesus, and Plotinus, for example, explained that the world only *seems* to be many things, but is in fact only one thing manifesting itself in a multiplicity of things. The One is first. This is most clearly explained by Plotinus, who demonstrates powerfully that the material world of ten thousand things is only the last stage of the overflowing of God, or the One, from a purely unified state into progressively more separate, less unified, and therefore more fragmentary and unreal states. The many things are simply a concatenation of appearances, or manifestations, of the single reality which gives rise to them. In a loose sense this single reality is also Jesus' Kingdom of Heaven, or Buddha's Nirvana.

When scientists shifted perspective in the Renaissance, deciding that reality adds up from individual objects rather than flows down from a great spiritual unity, they outlined a cosmology which has enabled us to take better care of our material lives. Science, indeed, has transformed human life. In the twentieth century we can survive lethal diseases, grow food in deserts, wipe out in a few minutes pains that in earlier ages would have lasted for days or a lifetime, and we make journeys in a few hours that before would have taken months.

But in taking better care of our material lives, something seems to have gone wrong. It is not hard for some of us to guess (or know) what it is. Now even some scientists are growing uneasy. A recent *Science News* article, for example, calls attention to the realization that cognitive psychology, while identifying numerous structures and parts of the brain's mental activity, has bypassed, in its concentration on the parts, its original inquiry: what is consciousness? If consciousness is the whole, and science is the analysis of parts, consciousness loses the attention of science.

In the past hundred years or more, most academic disciplines have sought to become scientific in their methods. Everything from molecular biology to literary criticism has taken to examining material parts in order to find out how they constitute the whole. Philosophy itself has become the study of how words mean—or even whether they mean anything at all—and religion has become in many parts of the world a complex social welfare system, with clergy as counsellors and comforters of the sick. Neither philosophy nor religion, in any general sense, concerns itself primarily with questions about reality or God. They concern themselves with individuals and their material needs.

The same is true of governments and ideologies; capitalism and communism are two sides of the same materialist coin. And nearly all institutions of moral instruction, from philosophy to literature to religion, have abdicated their responsibilities to define the parameters of good and bad human behavior in favor of objective scientific examination of material effects. The result of this abdication is a moral climate which envisions each individual as the creator and arbiter of his or her own ethical world, separate from all other worlds. It is the world of crack cocaine, automatic rifles, nuclear megatons, and money.

Science itself is not the evil satan of the materialist modern age. Science is a good thing: it provides the means for American troops to halt a horrible famine in Somalia. This is good. Socrates, Plotinus, and probably Buddha would approve of it.

But the problem is that feeding people is not the only good. The material world, according to the ancient teachers, is not the only world: people do not live by bread alone, but by the spirit too. In fact, the ancient teachers tell us, a human being's attention is best focused on matters of the spirit rather than matters of the world. The world is whole, one, in a spiritual sense, and it's fragmented and disparate in a physical sense. For this reason Jesus points us toward the Kingdom of Heaven; Plotinus toward the One. "All that is visible," suggests the *I Ching*, as interpreted by Richard Wilhelm, "must grow beyond itself, into the realm of the invisible" (Hexagram 51). The idea that spirit supersedes the material world has been common to most or all of humanity, in one form or another, for millennia.

But in the last four hundred years or so the scientific attitude, which focuses attention on material reality, has not provided spiritual guidance of any kind. Because the idea of "spirit" is essentially unavailable to scientific analysis, many scientists have both implicitly and explicitly denied its reality.

Science does not treat spirituality because, as we know from our own experience and from the great spiritual masters, spiritual activity is knowable only from the whole—by the one, not the many. Working back from the one, the real question is: what do we need to do to be spiritual, here in our incarnate life? Science does not tell us this. But Buddha, Socrates, Jesus, and Plotinus do tell us: they all, in speaking of our spiritual natures, speak first of our moral behavior. The foundation of a spiritual nature is a moral nature. A nature which is morally good is hard to analyze. Socrates never defined any of the virtues satisfactorily. Jesus speaks of the necessity of faith, in a moral sense.

This is why the *I Ching*, the Bible, the Platonic dialogues, the Vedas and the *Enneads* are literally about human conduct. The material world meets the spiritual world at the moral state of a human being. Plotinus describes the attention to heaven rather than earth as a moral act because it is attention to the inner being, the Soul—which has grown out of Mind, which has grown out of God.

Morality is the connecting-place of the physical world to the spiritual. The *I Ching* instructs us in this cosmic fact: "The superior man / Creates number and measure, / And examines the nature of virtue and correct conduct" (Hexagram 60). Number and measure are the foundations of the material world, and they are derived from the stars and planets; heaven and human nature meet at moral virtue.

Our spiritual disposition depends on our moral disposition. And our moral disposition is not our fulfillment of social duties, nor our perfunctory attention to religious ritual, but as the ancient teachers show over and over, our morality is our disposition toward the entire universe.

Because the scientific attitude has taken over our culture and sought (in some cases) to obliterate the idea of spirit, we are in a great moral crisis. Our problem now is not necessarily to create spiritual rites or churches or clans or study groups, but to reassemble our collective moral disposition. We are not merely a cloud of buzzing individuals, each doing his or her own thing, each person a tiny microcosm in him- or herself.

If this concatenation of human microcosms seems to us to be "real," it is because the scientific approach has taught us that the individual physical objects—in Hindu terms, *prakriti*—comprise reality. But we do not each invent our own personal moral and ethical systems. Morality derives from the needs of the whole. The whole, as all the ancient teachers repeat, is the spirit. If we keep our attention fixed on heaven—on the whole universe—our moral attitude will be shaped by the mountains, as the *I Ching*, again, suggests.

Feeding the starving in Somalia is a moral good, but perhaps we call it good because the vestiges of moral understanding remain in our minds despite science's insistence on the moral legitimacy of the material world. Feeding each other is good not simply because we have social responsibilities. It is good not simply because it agrees with the communist belief that all people should be clothed, fed, and socially enfranchised. Nor is it good because it agrees with the capitalist belief that all people should have the opportunity to clothe, feed, and enfranchise themselves.

It is good because we have the inner sense that our social responsibilities are linked with our moral responsibilities, and we know—from ancient teachings still lurking in our consciousness—that our moral selves are on the edge of the divine world, that the universe is all and one, interimmanent with itself, that we are all in all, and that our moral responsibility—our virtue—is to foster and return to that unity by our own dispositions, which are reflected in all our actions.

In *Enneads* 6.9 Plotinus says, "Things here are signs." These words teach us that the physical world has importance; we are right to study it, scientifically and otherwise. And because our physical needs are interrelated, we are right to minister to each other's physical needs. Science has helped us in this. But further, all that is visible must grow into the realm of the invisible. Science has hindered this growth by denying its possibility, and by denying our intuition that we are interrelated in spirit, and therefore morally.

If our cosmologies teach us that the physical world is all there is, and that our destiny is to continue to take things apart, then our moral natures similarly will come apart. But if our cosmologies teach us that the visible parts of the universe are signs of the invisible, spiritual reality, then we are at the edge of our moral nature, and the whole universe.

The Invisible College of the Rose Cross Fraternity
Theophilus Schweighardt, *Speculum Sophicum Rhodo-Stauroticum*, 1618.

The Invisible College

ANTHONY ROOLEY

THE CONCEPT of the Invisible College can, I'm sure, be traced back a long way, but it would take a person of much greater breadth of scholarship than mine. Someone like a Joscelyn Godwin would be well equipped to outline its history, perhaps. My task at this moment, however, is not that of writing a historical survey, but rather an individual statement of how the very concept is, for me, inspirational, and an introduction to how the College works in my own experience.

My first awareness of the Invisible College came in a conversation with Joscelyn Godwin and Todd Barton; it was taken up with immediate recognition by David Fideler and mentioned in his Introduction to *Alexandria 2*.

What the College is *not*:
    i) not a material building,
    ii) not in a fixed geographical location,
    iii) nor does it have professors (those that know), or students (those that are taught by those that know),
    iv) nor does it have a board of governors (at least who reside on this plane),
    v) nor a set of rules and regulations,
    vi) nor does it have a financial dimension—no profits or losses,
    vii) there is no syllabus, course of study, or examination.

What the College *is*:
    i) an exercise of the imagination,
    ii) a place of "self-examination,"
    iii) a sharing of enthusiasms with others who are receptive,

iv) the point where ancient knowledge is made present,

v) an awareness of silence and stillness in the continual program of self-education,

vi) a communion of equals wherever they may reside, whenever they might manifest themselves,

vii) a body where all who desire to join are welcome—there are no doors, so it is always open, but there are portals to show the way in.

* * *

The body moves slowly—even with the aid of Concorde it takes over three hours to get from London to New York—but the mind moves with phenomenal speed. I can exercise my thought such that in an instant I am both at my desk in my study in North Yorkshire, and with Joscelyn Godwin in his study in Earlville, New York. At the same moment I can recall an unforgettable car journey with Todd Barton as we drove the Pacific Highway from Portland to San Francisco eight years ago, and a breakfast meeting with David Fideler in an Ann Arbor hotel three years ago.

Thus the Invisible College is manifested: in one moment of focused thought the seminar begins and the imaginary discourse proceeds, limited only by the power of focus—for the inspiration is unbounded.

The notion of an unmanifest Temple of Knowledge works into one's daily life in curious ways. Walking the craggy coastal path on a gusty February day in North Cornwall, my thoughts were turned towards a conversation I had with Frances Yates (the great scholar of the history of ideas of the Renaissance, especially of Hermeticism) about Dowland as a hermetically aware composer, and particularly of Lucy, Countess of Bedford (his sometime patroness) and the obscure circle that surrounded her. Now I met Frances Yates only once, a short while before she died, and she was already in some pain. She did not find it easy to move about, for her legs caused her some considerable discomfort, but her mind moved with astonishing agility and grace.

The meeting I had with her on the Cornish coast was very much within the walls of the Invisible College. We leaped nimbly from boulder to terra firma, avoiding mud and water, and were joined by Lucy and Dowland. The dialogue which ensued continued from where we had left off at our physical meeting several years before, and was indeed inspirational. This communion, beyond time and place, actually occupies more of our awareness than we care to admit, and is coped with by being described as idle imaginings. But I recall Sir John Davis's poem, "Nosce teipsum—of Human Knowledge," where he describes the subtle organs of "Wit" and "Will" as the "maid-servants to the soul," that is, serving the Soul directly and faithfully. In turn, in a well-ordered mind, "Wit" and "Will" direct the "Fantasy," whose imaginings then become inspired and directed by the Soul.

The Jacobean Age was deeply connected to the work of the Invisible College, at least in the minds of the best patrons and artists. John Wilbey's great paean to darkness, "Draw on Sweet Night," tells us, in rich, passionate, six-part polyphony, that nighttime and darkness are the best hours for Hermetic inspiration: "I then shall have best time for my complaining."

Between great comforting billows of downy sleep, the mind may reflect with extraordinary clarity on subjects which melt away with light of day. Esoteric thoughts give way to exoteric action, and a beautiful balance between the two is perhaps what many of us strive for. The Invisible College exists, like the quintessential element "Ether" at the meeting point where the downward pointed triangle of unmanifest creation meets the upward poised triangle of manifest creations. The point where the pyramid seems to stop is where all the possibilities of potential creation wait. There the portals of the Invisible College are always open.

Last night, enjoying the soft sensuousness of lazy Somnus, I stirred and rolled to the left side and enjoyed calmly and with quiet relish the subject of membership of the Invisible College. I realized that it can only exist in the present, that there is no such time as past and future, and that I was as likely to meet with Marsilio Ficino as I was with any of my "living" colleagues. It struck me that were we to want to find a "patron saint" for the Invisible College, we could do little better than to choose Giordano Bruno, a man born perhaps 400 years before his time in terms of physical manifestation, yet whose work, ideals, concepts, and inspiration are eternally present. I enjoyed for a while the idea of Bruno as our symbol, but then considered that the Invisible College's archetypal image was probably most potently manifested in the god Hermes, whose caduceus with its intertwining opposites of optimist and pessimist gnosis hid the simpler truth of divine knowledge direct through revelation—the central wand around which the serpents coiled.

My body then grunted and snuffled, having had enough of leftsided deliberations and I heaved my somnolent frame over to the right side. The second "imparting" of the Invisible College for the night then unfolded. (Note: we cannot call them "lectures," not even "seminars," but an "imparting" seems to encapsulate the right atmosphere!) The topic had changed, to a consideration of an appropriate emblem for the Invisible College. The image which presented itself was simply the nearest we can come, graphically, to the "point," representing unmanifest creation. Somnus enjoyed mystifying my thoughts by playing games with all the figures of speech we use unconsciously, like "get to the point," "a point of view," "an appointment," "this is pointless," etc. So thus in sleep and waking college work ensued, and though at times rambling, circling, the point was not wholly lost—the observer enjoyed the play.

At last, when right-sidedness became wearisome, the body heaved and groaned, the pillows were pommelled and adjusted and the new attitude was prostrate, face up, centered, as though prepared for embalming or mummification, and ready for a long journey. The sensuous part of me enjoyed this position of eternal repose, and enjoyed the game of playing dead. Here I was joining all those who had gone before, out of choice—and I could see the point. Thus in an attitude of quiet contemplation, I was approached by a man of rather swarthy complexion, with something slightly beyond designer stubble on his chin. He was in a nervously excited state, using much movement of the hands to express his message. I thought at first he might be of Spanish origin, perhaps from the south, with a touch of gypsy in him. What he had to say and show me I do not pretend to understand, but I relay it now because it is typical of the barely comprehensible teaching that issues at times from that damned Invisible College!

As he approached me, he began to speak—in a deplorably broken English, rather like the English used in bad "B" movies twenty years ago!—"'ello, come wid mee! I show you somet'ing." He repeated this, several times over with the words arranged in various orders, as though he was trying to find the sequence of some magical incantation. In fact his comic exhortation was just that—he was replaying the role of Asclepius in breathing life and movement into statues, only I was that statue, the mummy, and I was being breathed into. It was a nice turn, though, that such serious work—for millennia branded as being the black magic of demons!—should be given a comic turn. The figure turned out to be my guide, and having got me to move I realized we were indeed at the southern tip of Spain, in fact just over the Straits of Gibraltar, the portal to the ancient world. We moved with some speed, with the urgency of his incoherent babble gathering momentum at the same time. By now we were at an Arabic city of some venerable age— I took it to be Fez—and he was urging me to enter one of the oldest mosques that had a truly magnificent prayer tower, capped with azure blue tiles on its dome. We almost ran up the internal spiral staircase, breathless but excited. My guide and I had become good friends by now, and I trusted him implicitly. It had become clear to me that he was a well-educated Arab of around the thirteenth century and he wanted to show me something of great importance to him.

We stepped out into the night air, a night of such blackness as Dowland so lovingly cried out for in his great hermetic prayer, "In darkness let me dwell." We were at the very top of the minaret and looking up to a sky which was of overwhelming beauty. Now how I wished I had taken my astronomy and cosmology classes more seriously at Invisible College First Grade! I was lost, bewildered, but the observer in me was quite calm as my guide took my hand and led me off the parapet into the night air, and upwards.

With effortlessness we moved high into the sky and began to get a long view of the scenery lit so clearly by starlight. There, to the left, was the imposing Rock of Gibraltar, surely one of the great natural wonders of the world so taken for granted for aeons. Stretching way north was the Costa del Sol, and the Balearics, all looking the worse for human wear and grubbily polluted. But worse was to come. As we continued our ascent, the great bay of the southern French coast curved in a sensuous manner, round the armpit where filthy Genoa nestles, down the west coast of Italy and terminating in the abused toe of that much abused nation. The physical light which darkly glowed revealed the most appalling morass of ignorance, brutality and self-interest—yet something more ancient glowed from beneath the present surface, the once noble Syracuse.

The tragedies which registered in the psychic light of night as the eye roved at the top end of the Adriatic were dreadful to behold, and the howls of pain (which have rung for centuries back) marked the desperate country of Albania. Islands of blissful innocence speckled the sea, like pearl drops hanging from the hem of Greece's garment, and with a thrill I heard a faint echo of the plangent songs Orpheus sang in the Thracian wilderness.

But more tattered than a venerable Turkish carpet was the Ephesian coastline, leading to a reviving Lebanon whose cypresses, even, had had enough of weeping, and on down past a brash and vulgar Tel Aviv, more recent (despite the oft-repeated exaggerated claims to antiquity—how can any man or nation claim the rights to any land?) than any of the many surviving remnants of various cultures.

But my attention, and that of my guide was dramatically drawn from this brilliant panoply which is the Mediterranean, by a glow from a great tower—it was the lighthouse of Pharos built around 280 B.C.E. by Ptolemy II, and one of the Seven Great Wonders of the ancient world. The beauty and awesome power of this inspired architecture quite drew the breath from this translucent and so recently reinvigorated body, such that the soul seemed to migrate upward in a gentle but faster-than-light movement to somewhere in the constellation Orion.

So ended another "imparting" at the Invisible College and Somnus became my mentor once more. And so continues the work of what is perhaps the only true universe-ity of the present time.

The Muse Euterpe
Tarocchi del Mantegna, fifteenth century.

Reviving the Academies of the Muses

DAVID FIDELER

MANY VOICES AGREE that there is an educational crisis in modern America. Academic testing documents the falling abilities and literacy of American students, while politicians clamor for reform so that we can "remain competitive in a global economy."

Most questions about education are phrased in terms of financial realities or test scores and are thereby designed from the start to avoid dealing with the important issues at stake. To *really* delve into the problems of education in the contemporary world would be an uncomfortable exercise for many, because the failings of the educational system provide one of the most perfect barometers of our shallow cultural beliefs and attitudes. To look too closely at the failings of higher education is a potentially dangerous, heretical enterprise, for it throws a penetrating light on the unspoken values of our materialistic age which underlie the ever-expanding machine of production and consumption.

The Cosmological Underpinnings of Education

Every civilization consciously or unconsciously bases its culture, art, and activities on some type of underlying cosmological framework. Call it a worldview, a worldview at its largest: a composite synthesis of all the ways we envision and relate to the universe. Let us call this "the underlying cosmological framework of culture and education," and let us grant—based on the study of human nature— that *the way we envision the world determines how we perceive the world.* Perhaps more importantly, how we envision the world literally

An earlier version of this article appeared in the Summer 1994 issue of *Gnosis* magazine under the title "Stranded in Flatland: A Critique of Education in Modern America."

determines the world we create. In this sense, we can see that our cultural and social world is to a very large extent the living image of our personal and collective cosmologies and mythologies. Reality is thus something of a malleable and magical construction, based on what we invoke. From this perspective, the skyline of a city, its layout and architecture, is the concrete reflection of the thoughts of its inhabitants, solidified over time; it is, however, essentially an idea.

One crucial aspect of any cosmology involves the question of *anthropology*; in other words, *What is the nature of humanity?* On the practical side, the belief that you are a totally pre-programmed machine, conditioned entirely by your upbringing, and that the greatest end of existence is to acquire the maximum level of material comfort, reinforces a particular experience of reality that will be different from someone who believes that the most important end of human existence is the realization of understanding, insight, and creativity. Thus the question "What is man?" always leads to a further question of *teleology*, from the Greek *telos* or "end": *What is the greatest end or goal of human existence?*

From a pragmatic standpoint, no one can maintain that cosmology, anthropology, and teleology are merely "abstract concepts." More than any other factors, the questions of "What is the structure of reality?", "What is the nature of humanity?", and "What should we strive for in life?" ultimately determine how we think about ourselves and others. They determine how we relate to others and to Nature. They determine how we experience reality, how we go about shaping the world, and what we specifically decide to do with our lives. In short, the assumptions that we carry in these areas, both individually and collectively, condition every sphere of life, including the sphere of higher education, that hallowed domain which supposedly enshrines the highest ideals of civilization and humankind.

Ascending Mount Helikon: Education as a Spiritual Journey

In ancient times, education was placed under the patronage of the Muses, the nine goddesses of inspiration who preside over the sciences, arts, and humanities: *Kleio* (History), *Euterpe* (Lyric Poetry), *Thaleia* (Comedy), *Melpomene* (Tragedy), *Terpsichore* (Lyric Poetry and Dance), *Erato* (Erotic Poetry), *Polymnia* (Storytelling), *Ourania* (Astronomy), and *Kalliope* (Heroic Epic and Eloquence). Our words *museum* and *music* are derived from the Greek word *Muse*. A museum or *mouseion* is a "place of the Muses," a place where the goddesses are invoked and their arts cultivated. Similarly, the goal of education in antiquity was to become "musical" in the largest sense: harmonious, graceful, balanced, cultured, and inspired.

Much of Greek culture was transmitted through poetry and storytelling, which was usually accompanied by music. According to ancient custom, the Muse was always invoked before a poet would recite or sing a sacred narrative. Appropriately enough, the Muses are said to be the offspring of Zeus and *Mnemosyne*, whose name literally means "Memory." Needless to say, scholars, poets, philosophers, and musicians rely heavily upon the faculty of *memoria* as a source of inspiration. And in antiquity Memory was also seen as a sacred, cosmic power, the faculty through which we "recollect" the primary realities of universal and human nature. That is why the Greeks referred to *truth* as *aletheia*, which means, literally, "not forgetting."

While the Muses can be invoked anywhere, certain mountains and groves are especially sacred to them. The Greek poet Hesiod was approached by the Muses while working as a shepherd on Mount Helikon; they conferred on him a scepter of laurel and breathed into him "a divine voice to celebrate the things that were and shall be." In his work thus inspired, the *Theogony*, Hesiod describes the Muses, "all of one mind," as spinning about the peak of the cosmic mountain, nine voices united in one song:

> There are their bright dancing-places and beautiful homes, and beside them the Graces and Desire live in delight. And they, uttering through

their lips a lovely voice, sing the laws of all and the goodly ways of the immortals, uttering their lovely voice.[1]

While the Greek mountains of Olympos, Helikon, and Parnassos were variously identified as the home of the Muses, what is being described here is an archetypal reality, the symbol of the World Mountain common to many traditions. The Cosmic Mountain is a polar, axial symbol located at the center of the world, depicting the levels and hierarchy of being. As we ascend from the miasma of the depths, at first the journey is arduous and painful; but as we progress, it becomes easier and more inviting. At the higher altitudes, the atmosphere is transformed; it becomes clearer, translucent, impregnated with light. We are led upward not in a spirit of conquest, but in a spirit of delight: the haunting choral harmonies of the Muses draw us skyward to their bright dancing places, and we are treated to ever more spectacular vistas along the way. Finally, at last, under the direct inspiration of the Muses, we join in their dance and encircle the pole of culture.

The upward ascent under the enchanting inspiration of the Muses is a spiritual journey of cultivation, education, and initiation. This is made clear by ancient Indo-European root *k^wel-* which means "to revolve, move around, sojurn, dwell."[2] Its basic form gives rise to the Latin *colere*, to till, cultivate, and inhabit, from which are derived the words *colony*, *cult*, *cultivate*, and *culture*. A suffixed form of *k^wel-* gives rise to the Greek *telos*, "completion of a cycle," which also means consummation, perfection, end, and result, while *teleos* means perfect and complete, and is the root of the word *initiation* (*teletê*). Other suffixed forms of *k^wel-* stand behind the Old English word for *wheel* and the Greek word *kuklos*, which means *circle* and *cycle*. Yet another suffixed form of *k^wel-* is the source of the Greek world *polos* or *pole*, the central axis of a sphere around which all things revolve.

By "going back to the roots of things," it is possible to see the powerful connections which exist between cultivation, culture, and the process of initiation, which denotes a form of personal "ripening" and becoming who you really are. True culture—the origins of which are traditionally ascribed to divine inspiration—encircles a central pole, which gives birth to the city or *polis*.[3] The words which spring from the Indo-European root *kʷel-* suggest that both culture and personal cultivation (education) encompass a cyclical dimension, something also suggested by the word *encyclopaideia*, which means "in the cycle of learning." True education, rather than something assimilated during four years of college, forms a cyclical process of cultivation and an authentic path of initiation which extends for a lifetime, and perhaps even beyond.

The Mythology of Education in a Hierarchical Universe

Up through the Renaissance, the universe was viewed as an organic, hierarchical structure stretched between the ideal extremes of spirit and matter. In addition to the linear, temporal dimension, reality is pictured as possessing a timeless vertical dimension. The anthropological aspect of this cosmology pictures humanity as a microcosm, the entire universe in miniature; humanity not only encapsulates spirit and matter, but is seen as the mediating principle between the two extremes. As the Renaissance philosopher Pico della Mirandola notes in his *Oration on the Dignity of Man*, humanity possesses an infinite freedom of choice, for it can fashion itself into whatever form it desires: man has the power to degenerate into the lower forms of life which are brutish, but he also possesses the power, out of the soul's judgement, to be reborn into the higher forms, which are divine.[4]

True education, I think, is implicitly based upon this traditional view of human nature which is rooted in a metaphysical vision of our place in the cosmos. From this perspective, the end or goal (*telos*) of education is the expansion of awareness and realization of the soul's innate potential; ultimately, this is the path of initiation (*teletê*). That is why, in practically every traditional allegory, the path of education is pictured in terms of an ascent—an ascent to the celestial domain of the Muses. The most famous is Plato's allegory of the prisoner in the cave who ascends from the shackles of opinion to ultimately gaze with true awareness upon the Sun, which symbolizes the source of Being, Beauty, and Goodness.[5] Nor is that the only example. Martianus

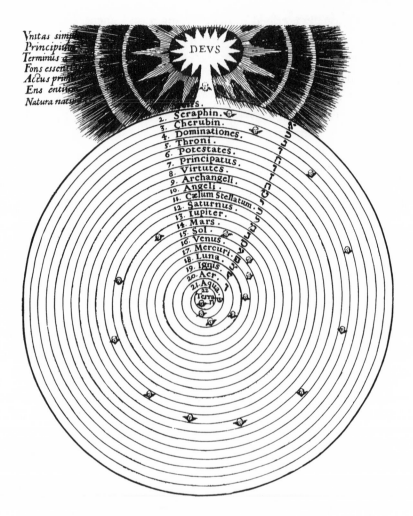

The Multidimensional Universe

This illustration from the works of the Renaissance Hermetic philosopher
Robert Fludd depicts the idea of a multidimensional, hierarchical universe,
and the various archetypes or intelligences which preside over the different
spheres of existence. While details may vary in different systems, the idea of
a multidimensional universe underlies every traditional conception of the
cosmos, whether pagan, Christian, Jewish, or Islamic.

Capella's fifth-century work on the Seven Liberal Arts, *The Marriage of Philology and Mercury*, is a fantastic allegory of Learning's heavenly ascent.[6] A similar allegory is Alan of Lille's *Anticlaudianus*; written in medieval times, it chronicles the celestial journey of Phronesis (Wisdom) and the ensuing perfection of man.[7] In all of these accounts, the end of education—and the end of humanity—is *the quest for authentic understanding*. Whether we speak of this process in classical terms as a "celestial ascent" or in contemporary terms as the cultivation of "psychological depth," the universe described is, in either case, clearly *multidimensional*.

The Mythology of "Education" in a Two-Dimensional World

Intimately associated with the hierarchical view of traditional cosmology is the notion that Nature is a *theophany*, a manifestation of the divine, the best possible image of divine reality within the confines of time and space.[8] With the Enlightenment, however, a linear, reductionistic, economically-driven, and materialistic view of the universe arose which, for most people, eclipsed the perennial vision of a multidimensional, hierarchical cosmos, in which the various levels of being are linked together by universal harmony and sympathy. All of a sudden, we were left stranded in Flatland.[9] And within the new, two-dimensional cosmos, Nature came to be seen not as an already perfect theophany, but as a "natural resource," ready to be "developed" and thereby improved by human technology. Traditional cosmology had always approached the transformation of nature through art and consciousness in an "alchemical" sense, which implied a corresponding transformation of both individual and culture; the new approach was dictated by exploitive, commercial motives.

The Enlightenment can been seen as a backlash against centuries of repression of free intellectual inquiry. Christianity appropriated the hierarchical universe of traditional cosmology, but it did so with a political agenda by proclaiming itself the sole custodian of universal truth. Under the auspices of the organized Church, the path of philosophical inquiry was replaced with theological dogmatism, and politically enforced belief triumphed over reason and knowledge. The modern era began when European intellectuals rebelled and demolished the dogmatic stranglehold of "theological certainty," but one evil was replaced with another. Freed of ecclesiastical constraint, science and technology broke loose, fueled by centuries of pent up, unrealized potential. But, because the new philosophy was largely relativistic, there was little left to guide the hand of science and technology, which became subservient to the interests of business and commerce and established itself as a new, materialistic faith. In the words of historian Theodore Roszak, "The study of the universe became a wholly secular pursuit, as deeply grounded in physical determinism as possible."[10] This two-dimensional philosophy of materialism had little use for the vertical dimension of value and meaning, and limited its sights to the Promethean manipulation of the natural world through technology. Thus, the guiding principles of science and commerce came to be dictated by entirely "pragmatic" concerns: "empiricism" on the one hand and "improving the bottom line on the other," a financial dictum which gave rise to the modern economic ethos of "unlimited growth."

Only against this historical backdrop is it possible to diagnose the ills of the modern educational system, which we can now see as synonymous with those of the modern world itself. The fact that education is in trouble should not surprise us, for if true education is rooted in a multidimensional view of reality, it simply cannot flourish—and perhaps even survive—in the current cosmological climate. Our culture, while often proclaiming high ideals, is essentially indifferent to beauty, art, education, and the spiritual dimensions of life. For example, politicians are fond of saying that we need to "raise the level of education so that we can remain globally competitive in a world economy," but what is really being said has nothing to do with true education—or the expansion of awareness—and everything to do with expanding economic interests. If we lived in a world that really did value education, the world itself would look and feel like a different place than it does today.

The most telling symptom of the breakdown of the educational system is the ever-accelerating transformation of our colleges and universities into trade and business schools. Most students don't go to college to expand their horizons or to get an education; they go to college to get a job. The anthropological assumption of our consumer culture is not that the individual is a spiritual entity with a unique relationship to the multiple levels of being; rather, the underlying view is that every individual is a potential cog in the economic machine of production and consumption. Students attend universities to be exposed to the latest techniques and technologies, but they are rarely encouraged to question their own lives or our cultural assumptions. Rather than presenting alternative models to the philosophy of materialism, universities regularly "sell out" to exclusively economic interests and thereby grant tacit approval to the two-dimensional cosmology of Flatland. Universities thus forsake their credibility as the custodians of education and, rather than questioning the integrity of the world we have created, become silent instruments of indoctrination and socialization for the economic machine. In the modern age, the myth of the celestial ascent is replaced by the favorite myth of American culture: climbing the corporate ladder. The pursuit of excellence, which formed the basis of Greek civilization, is replaced by the pursuit of higher sales, or a higher salary. And the realization of an individual's intrinsic humanity through art, creativity, and learning is replaced by yet another end: acquiring the external trappings of social status.

Reviving the Academies of the Muses

> No eye ever saw the sun without becoming sun-like, nor can a soul see beauty without becoming beautiful.
>
> —Plotinus

If the modern educational system is ultimately unsatisfying to both educators and students, what are the prospects of establishing a more integral perspective in which learning is once again recognized as a path of spiritual development? The key involves *mythology*, for as we observed at the beginning of this article, the way we envision the world determines the world we create. What we are ultimately facing is a crisis of the imagination. Indeed, as cultural therapist Thomas Moore is fond of pointing out, even the most subtle shift in imagination can have far-reaching effects. We need to realize that the mythology of Flatland is just one of *many* possible perspectives—and of those many perspectives it is one of the least satisfying. Our culture schizo-phrenically divorces spirituality from daily life, shunting into the separate sphere of "religion," which has itself in many instances become one-dimensional and uninspiring. However, spiritual, hu-manistic, and economic concerns are not intrinsically at odds with one another; indeed, the most satisfying results are usually obtained when we can unite the forces of creative inspiration with the hard work of serious discipline. In fact, our Western cultural heritage provides many examples of how the Academy can act as a catalyst for "spiritual development" without being transformed into the equivalent of a seminary. By returning to the archetypal root of the Academy, it might be possible to not only revivify and remythologize education, but also breathe new life into our wider culture.

The first places of education were sacred groves where the presence of divine inspiration and natural beauty were most clearly felt. These places later became the repositories of art and architecture which encapsulated the ideals of Greek culture, cultivation, and beauty. The Greek traveller Pausanias, for example, reports that there actually was a grove sacred to the Muses on Mount Helikon.[11] He visited it and describes its wonders in book 9 of his *Guide to Greece*. There he found statues of the nine Muses fashioned by famous sculptors. A bit further on, there was a bronze statue of Apollo wrestling with Hermes over the lyre. Portraits of poets and musicians abounded; they included a representation of Arion riding a dolphin and many others. Orpheus, too, was represented, surrounded by bronze and stone animals who listened to his song, and by his side stood Teletê, initiation personi-fied.

The first Greek philosophical school, founded by Pythgoras, was a religious guild dedicated to the Muses. This school is still famous for its philosophy of educating the whole person and its integration of scientific, spiritual, and artistic disciplines.[12]

Later, Plato's seminars were held in the grove Academus, a place sacred to the Muses, and the Academy, like the Pythagorean school, was formally incorporated as a *thiasos*, a religious brotherhood based on the worship of the Muses. The aims of the society were twofold: scientific research by the members in common and the transmission of learning through instruction.[13]

In Hellenistic times, the first international university, the Museum at Alexandria, was similarly dedicated to the goddesses of culture and inspiration. Through little heard of, there was even an archpriest of the Muses who presided over the confraternity of scholars assembled there;[14] presumably he reminded the scholars that they were engaged in a common spiritual enterprise, under the tutelage of the Muses, in which the all parts were united in a larger whole.

Another Academy worthy of being recalled is the Renaissance Platonic Academy which held its meetings at the Villa Careggi. Supported by Cosimo de Medici and centered around the Platonic translator and philosopher Marsilio Ficino, the Florentine Academy was but the first of a series of Renaissance academies. These groups are described by the *New Oxford Companion to Music* as

> special clubs or societies of like-minded individuals who banded together for the specific purpose of various forms of intellectual inquiry. . . . The first, the Accademia Platonica, appeared in Florence in 1470 and was devoted to speculative pursuits of all kinds: literature, drama, science and music. Similar clubs appeared throughout Italy, and by the mid 16th century they had begun to sponsor actual performances of music. Opera itself arose out of the activities of one such society—the *camerata* of Florence, who met in the salon of Count Giovanni de' Bardi in the latter part of the century.[15]

If the path of culture and cultivation is truly cyclical, then perhaps there is indeed hope; perhaps, out of stark necessity, the academies of the Muses will be reborn. The only way to obtain an education in the first place is to truly desire it; and while the quest for knowledge can be fertilized by a nurturing environment, knowledge itself is a prize that can only be won by the efforts of the individual. We may assimilate information, technique, and method, but knowledge, or *gnôsis*, is certainly more than these. Since teachers and professors cannot transmit knowledge, the very best they can do is act as helpful midwives—and serve as good examples.

When the fifth-century Christians removed the great statue of Athena from the Parthenon in Athens, the Neoplatonic philosopher Proclus had a dream that the Athenian Lady was coming to live with him.[16] Similarly, if universities are intent on becoming business schools, the Muses will seek out other homes, other temples. Organized systems like the Church, the economic machine, and academic administrations take on a lumbering life of their own and are usually oblivious to the effects—and needs—of the individual. As if by some type of providential compensation, however, individuals are alone capable of awareness, creativity, and insight, the very qualities the Muses most deeply treasure.

In our present age, the Muses call upon us to live our lives with integrity and devotion to their inspiring chorus of inspiration, which may entail "being in the world, but not of it." They invite us to adorn our lives with beauty, while living in a culture that sees beauty as "purely subjective" and irrelevant when weighed against the "objective world" of economic concerns. They encourage us to cultivate our sense of *taste* and appreciation, in a world where taste has been anesthetized in the quest for efficiency, mass production, and pursuit of the bottom line.

Above all, the Muses invite us to be creative and artistic in daily life and to form our own "academies" with like-minded souls. In their eyes, "a life well-lived is a work of art," and, despite the drought which blights the current cultural landscape, the Muses will provide unceasing inspiration to any soul who sincerely invokes their fertilizing streams.

Notes

1. Hesiod, Theogony 63–67, in H. G. Evelyn-White, editor and translator, Hesiod, *The Homeric Hymns* (Cambridge: Harvard University Press, 1914), 83.

2. The proto Indo-European language was spoken approximately 5,000 B.C.E. and is the original root language from which the Indo-European family of languages originated: Balto-Slavic, Germanic (including English), Celtic, Italic (Latin and other Romance languages), Albanian, Greek, Iranian (Persian), and Indic (Sanskrit, etc.). For more on $k^w el$- and other Indo-European roots, see the appendix in the third edition of *The American Heritage Dictionary of the English Language* (Boston: Houghton Mifflin, 1992).

3. While there is no valid etymological connection between *polos* (pole) and *polis* (city), the word play does nonetheless reflect a truth: in antiquity the polis always acted as the central pole of culture.

4. Giovanni Pico della Mirandola, *Oration on the Dignity of Man* 3–4. For a translation of this important work, see E. Cassirer, P. Kristeller, and J. Randall, editors, *The Renaissance Philosophy of Man* (Chicago: University of Chicago Press, 1948), 223–54.

5. Plato's allegory of the cave, which appears in his discussion of the theory of knowledge and education, appears in book 7 of the *Republic*.

6. See W. H. Stahl and R. Johnson, with E. L. Burge, translators, *Martianus Capella and the Seven Liberal Arts II: The Marriage of Philology and Mercury* (New York: Columbia University Press, 1977).

7. Alan of Lille, *Anticlaudianus, or The Good and Perfect Man*, translated by James Sheridan (Toronto: Pontifical Institute of Medieval Studies, 1973).

8 This idea is first set forth in Plato's cosmological dialogue the *Timaeus* but is a development of Pythagorean views concerning the nature of the divinely beautiful *kosmos*.

9. The term "Flatland" is taken from the title of the book by Edwin A. Abbot first published around 1880. In *Flatland* he describes the existence of a two-dimensional world and the beings who live there. The book deals with the multiple dimensions of space and how three-dimensional objects appear to the limited perceptions of the two-dimensional beings. See E. A. Abbott, *Flatland: A Romance of Many Dimensions* (New York: Penguin, 1987).

10. Theodore Roszak, *The Voice of the Earth: A Exploration of Ecopsychology* (New York: Simon and Schuster, 1992), 102.

11. Traces of it still exist and the temple of the Muses there provided a floor for the church of the Holy Trinity. See Peter Levi's translation of Pausanias, *Guide to Greece* (New York: Penguin, 1971), II, 369.

12. See K. S. Guthrie, compiler and translator, *The Pythagorean Sourcebook and Library* (Grand Rapids: Phanes Press, 1987).

13. John Walden, *The Universities of Ancient Greece* (New York: Scribners, 1909), 27–28.

14. John Walden, *The Universities of Ancient Greece*, 49. See also Edward Alexander Parsons, *The Library of Alexandria: Glory of the Hellenic World* (New York: Elsevier Press, 1952), 70.

15. Denis Arnold, editor, *The New Oxford Companion to Music* (New York: Oxford University Press, 1983), I, 451, s.v. "concert."

16. Marinus of Samaria, *The Life of Proclus or Concerning Happiness*, translated by K. S. Guthrie (Grand Rapids: Phanes Press, 1986), 47.

Plato, Athena, and Saint Katherine: The Education of the Philosopher

CHRISTINE RHONE

I. The Education of the Philosopher

For a generation that may well be bored with feminism, the old issue of women's education has been raised yet again, and this time has been heard round the world. Representatives of some 190 nations met in Cairo in September 1994 for the United Nations Conference on World Population to discuss the tidal wave of babies that seems ready to inundate the globe. It is estimated that the population of the Earth may almost double by 2050, something like an extra four billion people in less than sixty years. The conference was split on questions of birth control and abortion. But it was agreed that, of all the factors affecting population growth, the most important is the education of women. With the better economic and social status that education brings, educated women prefer having smaller families.

Nature does not always fulfill our predictions in the way we imagine. She is full of surprises. More predictable is the return of certain ideas in history. The idea of women's education has come back again and again, like a recurrent dream, a nightmare hound in humanity's sleep.

As far as I am aware, the earliest surviving written records that explicitly propose an educational program for women are the works of Plato, who repeats the idea in three of his dialogues.[1] He not only proposed that women be educated, he went much further and said that women should receive the very same education as men, a tough curriculum that included nude training in the gymnasium. This was still to be the rule even if the women students were old and ugly. "Lord, that's going to be a funny sight by present standards," exclaimed Glaucon when he and Socrates agreed on that rule.[2] Plato's

227

proposals on women's education put our United Nations Conference pronouncements in a humbling historical perspective: the philosopher was writing some twenty-four centuries ago.

On this point, Plato belongs to the rare historical category of radical equalists and has that in common with François Poulain de la Barre (1647–1723), who is mentioned by Simone de Beauvoir.[3] Poulain took a degree in theology in Paris and in 1680 became a Catholic priest. In the 1660s, when the works of the recently deceased René Descartes had been listed on the papal Index of Forbidden Books, Poulain attended a lecture given by a Cartesian philosopher and was changed forever.[4] To demonstrate the Cartesian method of rational deduction, Poulain wrote *The Equality of the Sexes*, an outstanding example of how Cartesian philosophy was applied with a revolutionary result.[5] Poulain argued that women are intellectually and physically capable of serving as heads of state, clergy, military officers, lawyers, and college professors, an educated class similar to Plato's Guardians, and that the key to women's advancement is education. He developed this theme in *De l'Éducation des dames pour la conduite de l'esprit dans les sciences et dans les moeurs* (1674). Poulain thought that his books would make a splash, but they were ignored in his day, and when Henri Piéron found a copy of Poulain's work in the Bibliothèque Nationale at the beginning of the twentieth century, no one had ever opened it before.[6] Poulain eventually left the priesthood, converted to Calvinism, and moved to Geneva, where he survived by giving language lessons, teaching the locals how to speak like the Parisians.[7]

Both Descartes and Plato were reacting to the sophists of their day and had a keen interest in Number. They agree that received opinion is of no value in the quest for knowledge. Plato compares opinion to the false perceptions of prisoners trapped in a cave who are watching a shadow show on the wall. Were these prisoners to leave the cave, they would be unable to distinguish real objects seen in the true light of day from the shadows in the dimness inside.[8] Descartes threw out the obscure arguments of scholasticism with their excessive dependence on ancient authorities (including Plato) and the received opinions of the world as hopelessly muddled, and looked for a touchstone of truth inside the individual through a method of systematic doubt.

Plato delayed discussing women's education in the *Republic* because he knew what a can of worms it would be. Socrates is goaded on to do so by his interlocutors, who refuse to accept his description of the ideal state until he has dealt with the question. Socrates answers, "You don't know what a hornet's nest you're stirring up by bringing up the subject. I deliberately avoided it before, because I saw all the trouble it would cause."[9] Socrates nevertheless concludes, through rational argument, that both genders should share the same physical and mental training. Poulain discarded any idea of female intellectual inferiority as part of received opinion, which had no place in Cartesian rationalism. However much Plato and Descartes may otherwise differ, it is noteworthy, especially bearing in mind how influential they have been, that the logical conclusion of both philosophers is one of radical equality in the area of women's education.

For Plato, however, the casting aside of received opinion is only a step on the way to full education, which was in fact a process of initiation to a vision of the form of the highest Good. From the lower steps of the educational program, which covered music, harmony, geometry, poetry, mathematics, physical education, and dialectics, the last step in the ladder takes the candidate beyond the borders of the intellectual realm to the realm of supra-individual knowledge, which the student must experience to become a philosopher and Guardian of Plato's ideal city-state.[10]

The kind of education generally encouraged at the United Nations Conference on World Population is aimed at raising the level of basic literacy and numeracy among Third World women—a noble aim, to be sure, but limited. The hound has jumped to our call again, not because she is dear to us, but because of fear: fear of a deluge of children. This education is not so much to teach women, or men for that matter, to discriminate opinion from truth, but rather to avoid motherly or material disaster. The aims are political and not philo-sophical, and thus will have limited results: some Third World women may learn to read and count and may gain some economic and political power. Gaining that kind of power may well be a necessary step, but it can never be more than one step on the way.

Humanity's problems are not political; they are philosophical. Until we awaken to that, political problems will have to be solved and resolved over and over again. As novelist Tom Robbins has aptly put it, in the quest for philosophy, politics is "simply a roadblock of stentorian baboons."[11] Until women's education is motivated by philosophy, rather than politics, the old hound will return to haunt our millenial sleep.

II. Athena the Immortal

Athena, goddess of philosophy and education, stood at the center of Plato's Magnesia. This was laid out according to the pattern of the heavens as a mirror image of the great clock of the stars. It represented heaven on earth. The whole territory was divided from the center into twelve equal parts, each part corresponding to a tribal area named after a zodiacal deity.[12] Each of the twelve tribal areas was further subdivided to create a correspondence with the 360 days of the year. While each of the twelve areas had its own identity and characteristics represented by symbolism used in temple pediments, statuary, and other art, there was implicit movement from zone to zone through rounds of festivals and song, and thus the ideal state resembled a gigantic wheel rotating round a fixed center.[13] It was a complete system, existing both physically and symbolically, encompassing time, space, music, art, dance, mathematics, politics, astronomy, religion, and philosophy. Everything that existed in it was related to the whole and had several levels of meaning. This pattern was widespread, not only in Greece, but throughout the ancient world.[14]

In the very center of the country, which represented the *axis mundi* or pole of the universe, there was to be a walled citadel with shrines to Hestia, Zeus, and Athena.[15] Hestia was the hearth, the eternal flame, unwavering in the storms of Olympian family quarrels. Zeus, the father of heaven, was here the patron of state. Athena, in the citadel of the acropolis, shared patronage of the state with Zeus and was its defendress.

Athena was immortality, the spirit, the Eternal Virgin. All of these were symbolized by her identity with the number seven. This number, according to the Pythagoreans, was itself the Eternal Virgin, because it is the only number in the first ten which neither breeds nor is generated. It is not generated as the product of the first ten numbers, as 6 is generated from 3 x 2. Nor can it produce one of these numbers, as 2 x 4 give birth to 8, or 2 x 5 breed 10. Only that which has never been born can be called eternal. Thus the number seven was applied to Athena, who jumped fully-armed and shouting out of Zeus's forehead, whose splitting headache was thus relieved. The design of Athena's first temple on the Athenian acropolis contained many symbolic references to the number seven in terms of its areas. Her esoteric number, calculated by adding the numerical values of the letters in her name (ἡ ᾿Αθηνᾶ) is 77. Athena thus stood for the eternal seven of spiritual creation at the hub of the wheel of civilization, symbolized by twelve, the numerical and symbolic matrix of all forms and structures.[16]

Athena's name is said by some to derive from Linear B words meaning "the immortal."[17] Others see in it a transposition of the name of Neith, the Egyptian goddess whose hieroglyph was a shield transfixed by arrows.[18] Plato is explicit about Athena's identity with Neith.[19] Herodotus declares that Athena's clothes and shield were inspired by the costume of Libyan women.[20] Neith probably began as the totemic deity of an Egyptian tribe, of which Herodotus says there were an original twelve.[21] Neith's domain was the city of Sais and its surrounding district, whose inhabitants felt a close affinity with the Athenians.[22]

Athena's Semitic relation was probably Anath, from whose name we get our word "anathema."[23] In Greece itself, Athena's ancestors are Gaia, the Earth Mother; her daughter Themis; and Dike.[24] Themis is the oracular power and wisdom of the Earth, established custom, and justice. Delphi was hers before it was Apollo's. Dike, the daughter of Themis, is the great wheel, the order of the universe.[25] The wheel of fate is identified with other goddesses as well: the Roman Fortuna, the Greek Nemesis, and later, the Christian St. Katherine. Athena is associated with the life- and death-dealing powers of the serpent-headed Gorgon, and with nocturnal, prophetic wisdom, whose bird is the owl.

Athena first taught the art and science of numbers, sacred to Pythagoreans and Platonists. Among her many inventions were the plow, the war-chariot, and the trumpet. She was patroness of the workshop and all the domestic arts, cooking, spinning, and weaving. She is often shown holding a lance in one hand and a spindle in the other. A new robe, woven and decorated by Athenian women, was offered to the statue of Athena Polias every fourth year at the festival of the Panathenaia.

The Athenaeum at Athens was sacred to Athena. It was a place open to professors of the liberal arts, where philosophers, poets, and rhetoricians could converse and teach. A similar institute by the same name was established by Hadrian in the first century C.E. for lectures and recitations by literary people.

III. Saint Katherine of Alexandria

In the Christian world, St. Katherine of Alexandria was long the symbolic figure for philosophical education, as Athena had been for the Greeks. In Plato's Magnesia Athena stood at the hub of the wheel of state with Hestia, the flame, and Zeus, the father. Although not central to Christianity, like Jesus and Mary, St. Katherine and her flaming wheel of martyrdom were nonetheless very important, especially in the Middle Ages, when she was highly revered, the object of long pilgrimages, and prayed to as one of the fourteen most helpful saints in heaven. In common with many temples of Athena, the shrines of St. Katherine tend to be sited on hilltops near sources of water: beacon hills looking out to sea, or mounds with a spring at their foot.

Saint Katherine was struck off the calendar of saints in 1969 by the Roman Catholics, who judged that her life had been apocryphal. Her story, however, may preserve some memory of the Neoplatonic philosopher Hypatia, a pagan who lived in fourth century Alexandria: the same time and place given for St. Katherine, and not far from Neith's city of Sais.[26] Hypatia, whose name means "the highest," was the daughter of Theon, the last known teacher of the Museum of Alexandria, who wrote on mathematics and astronomy. She had an excellent reputation as a teacher/philosopher and attracted students from afar, but nothing has survived of her writings on mathematics and astronomy, and there are few references to her by contemporaries.

Although there is some disagreement on details, we do know that Hypatia was attacked on the streets and murdered with such shocking brutality that it overshadows all the accounts of her life. Damascius points the finger of blame directly at Cyril, the Christian Patriarch of Alexandria, who had suppressed the churches of his Christian rivals and driven the Jews from the city. Scholars have dismissed Damascius's account, but most historians think that Cyril at least set the tone for the incident.[27]

Hypatia's fate dramatizes the death of the old Hellenistic world and the emergence of the new Christian era. With that shift, the figure of St. Katherine was superimposed over that of Athena to represent the idea of philosophical education.

St. Katherine is first named in the *Life of Paulus Junior* in the tenth century. Her story first appears in the *Menology* of Basileus, dated between 957–1027, and in the account of Simeon Metaphrastes, who died *circa* 956. These two versions were merged into one. Embellished over the centuries, the story has much in common with early martyr hagiographies. The daughter of an Egyptian king, Katherine, whose name means "the pure," was early trained in mathematics, letters, and philosophy. She became a Christian after having a vision of the Blessed Virgin. She grew up to be a stunning young woman of exceptional grace and wit. Emperor Maximianus then entered the scene and ordered everyone in Alexandria to make sacrifices to the pagan gods. She courageously went to meet the tyrant on the steps of the temple in order to protest. Infuriated, the Emperor demanded that she stop her Christian nonsense. In a series of brilliant debates, Katherine succeeded in converting to Christianity nearly everyone who heard her speak, including close members of the Emperor's entourage. As a last verbal resort, Maximianus summoned fifty philosophers to argue in favor of paganism, but all fifty were knocked down by Katherine's eloquence, who supported her arguments by citing Plato and the Books of the Sybils. The philosophers converted to Christianity on the spot and, for their betrayal, were instantly beheaded by Maximianus. The Emperor then tried to seduce Katherine. Having failed at this, he instructed his carpenters to concoct a horrific death device made of four hooked wheels. Into its center the young saint was cast. In divine reply, the hand of God struck the wheels with lightning and they burst into flame, sparing Katherine from being shredded. The Emperor finally succeeded in having her beheaded with a sword. From her severed arteries flowed not blood, but milk.

Angels arrived and flew what was left of her to the pink and grey peaks of the Sinai mountains, where Moses had received the Tablets of the Law. There the monks from the nearby monastery of the Burning Bush discovered her. The monastery was dedicated to St. Katherine in the ninth century and it became a high place of pilgrimage. From the entombed bones of the saint flowed oil that would cure any illness. The monastery has an unbroken tradition of icon painting and a great library that houses the Sinaitic Codex. St. Katherine's association with Sinai added the cult of a Christian saint to those of Moses and Mohammed on the holy mountain.

The story of St. Katherine was disseminated in the west by the Crusaders. Her feast on November 25th was celebrated with great splendor in the Christian world, especially in Venice, where there was trade with the Sinai monastery. The first place in Europe to claim a relic of St. Katherine was the city of Rouen, where Joan of Arc was later burnt at the stake.

The patroness of philosophers, teachers, lawyers, theologians, and preachers, St. Katherine was the constant theme of poetry, sermons, and painting. Her attributes are the palm, the Katherine Wheel, and the book. She is often depicted with instruments of geometry and a

The Martyrdom of Saint Katherine
Woodcut by Albrecht Dürer, *circa* 1498.

globe. The University of Paris was dedicated to her as well as many schools and convents. She was the tutelary saint of nuns and virgins generally. Her wheel made her the patroness of wheelwrights, potters, and mechanics. St. Katherine was associated with spinning, like Athena, and hence with spinsters or older, unmarried women. She was also the patroness of dressmakers and haberdashers.

Hundreds of churches, chapels, and holy wells in Europe are dedicated to her. In England, some of the best known sites are at Abbotsbury, a chapel on a conical hill overlooking the sea; Milton Abbas, the site of a vision by King Athelstan; Winchester Hill, with earthworks, a labyrinth, and a ruined chapel; and Guildford, on a pilgrimage route. St. Katherine's memory persists in secular England today, where many pubs are still named for The Catherine Wheel.

The very height of the cult of St. Katherine was around the time of Joan of Arc. Joan's guiding voices were those of St. Michael, St. Margaret, and St. Katherine of Alexandria, who had been divinely appointed as Joan's special advisor. Her voice told Joan where to find the sword that she needed to carry into battle, buried behind the altar in the pilgrimage chapel of Ste-Catherine-de-Fierbois. This was the said to be the sword of Charles Martel, who had freed France from the Saracens in 732.[28] It was widely believed to be endowed with magical powers. Joan was also an accomplished needlewoman and embroidered her war standard with angelic scenes.

The magic of St. Katherine continued to be a powerful source of spiritual inspiration until at least the mid-twentieth century, both in folklore observances and in religious mysticism. Every year, the young dressmakers of Paris, dressed in special green and yellow bonnets, used to make a procession to a certain statue of the saint as the patroness of spinners and spinsters. Therese Neumann of Konnersreuth, perhaps the greatest stigmatist of the twentieth century, who lived without food for several decades, experienced St. Katherine during her visionary episodes. She would see the saint defending the Christian faith against the philosophers, her beheading, and the angels taking her body to Mount Sinai.[29] Therese Neumann died in 1962, only a few years before St. Katherine was declared apocryphal.

IV. The Argo

Since Plato's time, education for women has become widespread in many parts of the world, but in others it is still a rarity. In some places education is founded upon religion, elsewhere on economic or political considerations, but in very few places is education, for women or anyone else, founded on philosophy.

The movements in education are continuous, the overall picture one of malaise. England clings to the shipwreck of its broken tradition, while America is awash with violence and materialism. Educational mini-centers are mushrooming under the eclectic umbrella of the New Age. Some people, in despair, are educating their children at home. For Western women, education is open wider than ever before, a lifeboat to the security of greater social power, while Third World women are targeted for reading and counting lessons to discourage excessive breeding.

As time ticks towards the new millenium, and we find ourselves adrift, we might consider taking a fresh look at what Plato proposed as the education of the philosopher. His foundation program was an intensive study of the laws of harmony, through music, poetry, astronomy, physical education, geometry, symbolic number, and philosophical tradition. This was followed by a lengthy period of practical experience and apprenticeship. The crowning phase was initiation to the highest form of knowledge, beyond the intellectual realm, to what Plato calls a vision of the form of the Good. Without this, says Socrates, the rest of our knowledge, however perfect, is useless.[30]

The education of the philosopher may be illustrated by the story of Athena and the ship Argo. Before Jason embarked on his journey, Athena, as patroness of philosophy and the practical arts, gave the just measures for building his ship and a sacred beam for its keel. The beam was of wood from the Oak of Dodona, the most ancient oracle site in

Greece, and it enabled the ship to speak.[31] She thus equipped him, in his quest for knowledge, with harmonic proportion and a core of tradition, to make his vessel sound and seaworthy. When Jason had completed his quest, Athena immortalized his ship by placing it in the sky, where it became the enormous south circumpolar constellation of Argo Navis, now divided into four modern ones: the Keel, the Sail, the Stern, and the Compass. In the first of these is Canopus, the second brightest star in the sky. From earliest times, it has been very important in celestial navigation for seafarers, and now is a reference in air and space navigation as well. This very star guided the pilgrims of the Middle Ages from Jerusalem to the monastery of Mount Sinai, for it indicated the south. They knew it as the Star of Saint Katherine. Through the many transformations of belief and opinion, the idea of philosophical education endures: St. Katherine's Star shines bright in the Argo, the sound ship designed by Athena.

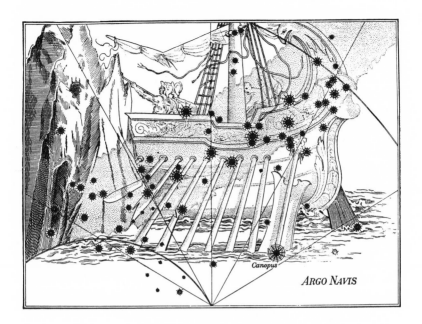

Canopus

ARGO NAVIS

The Constellation Argo Navis

Canopus, or Saint Katherine's Star, is the brightest star in the southern hemisphere. The ship was placed in the heavens by Athena, who had also guided the Argo's construction. (Bayer, *Uranometria*, 1603).

Notes

1. Plato, *Republic* 451C–457B; *Timaeus* 18C; *Laws* 805–806.

2. Plato, *Republic* 452B.

3. Simone de Beauvoir, *The Second Sex* (London: Penguin, 1987), 21, 22, 138, 164.

4. François Poulain de la Barre, *The Equality of the Two Sexes*, trans. and intro. by A. Daniel Frankforter and Paul J. Morman (Lewiston, NY: The Edwin Mellen Press, 1989), xiii.

5. François Poulain de la Barre, *The Equality of the Sexes*, trans. and intro. Desmond M. Clarke (Manchester: Manchester University Press, 1990), 2. This is the new English translation to replace that of 1677.

6. Poulain, *The Equality of the Sexes* (Clarke edition), 31.

7. Poulain, *The Equality of the Two Sexes* (Frankforter and Norman edition), xvi–xvii.

8. Plato, *Republic* 514–521B.

9. Plato, *Republic* 450B.

10. Plato, *Republic* 521C–540.

11. Tom Robbins, *Skinny Legs and All* (New York: Bantam, 1991), 460.

12. Plato, *Laws* 745.

13. Jean Richer, *Sacred Geography of the Ancient Greeks: Astrological Symbolism in Art, Architecture, and Landscape*, trans. Christine Rhone (Albany: State University of New York Press, 1994).

14. John Michell and Christine Rhone, *Twelve-Tribe Nations and the Science of Enchanting the Landscape* (Grand Rapids: Phanes Press, 1991).

15. Plato, *Laws* 745.

16. Michell and Rhone, *Twelve-Tribe Nations*, 85–86.

17. Richer, *Sacred Geography*, ch. 5, sec. 7.

18. Martin Bernal, *Black Athena* (London: Vintage, 1991), I, p. 51, for names of Athena and Neith.

19. Plato, *Timaeus* 21E.

20. Herodotus, *Histories* 189.

21. Herodotus, *Histories* 147–151.

22. Bernal, *Black Athena*, I, 51.

23. Bernal, *Black Athena*, I, 21.

24. Richer, *Sacred Geography*, ch. 5, sec. 4, discussing H. W. Parke's *A History of the Delphic Oracle* (Oxford: Oxford University Press, 1956), I, 8–9.

25. Jane Ellen Harrison, *Themis* (New York: University Books, 1966), 517, 527, 533.

26. A number of sources suggest the Athena–St. Katherine connection. See, for example, Anna Brownell Jameson, *Sacred and Legendary Art* (London, 1874), 475.

27. See the study on Hypatia and bibliography by Nancy Nietupski, "Hypatia of Alexandria: Mathematician, Astronomer, and Philosopher," *Alexandria* 2 (Grand Rapids: Phanes Press, 1993), 45–56.

28. Benedictine Fathers of Paris, *Vie des Saints et des Bienheureux selon l'ordre du calendrier avec l'historique des fêtes* (Paris: Editions Letouzey et Aré, 1954), XI, 869.

29. Rev. Alban Butler, *Lives of the Saints* (London: Virtue and Co., 1904), 298, on Therese Neumann.

30. Plato, *Republic* 505A.

31. Apollonius of Rhodes, *Argonautica* 1.524–527, 1.722–724.

The School of Wisdom

JANE LEADE

December 15, 1678: The School of Wisdom. A Transportation.

IN THE NIGHT after my first Sleep, I was consulting, whereunto the moving Star had brought us, and perceiving it still was in its circling motion (to shew that we had not yet arrived to the Center point, where we might mix with it, and cease from all further searching and Travel) I was longing now to be at rest in the Lord, both Internal and External. But it was replyed by the Holy Ghost, who hath God's secrets in readiness to reveal, that there could not be so quick a dispatch. For we were, said he, but newly entered upon the Borders of the unknown Land, where the Heavenly City doth stand, in which each one have reserved their allotted Mansion. And being cast into a Solitary and Mourning posture, because of this Word, that declared for a continual Warfare I was in some kind of Agony. In the sence hereof I Queried, now that the *Contraries* in Nature were agreed to walk in the narrow track of the Spirit unanimously. Upon which expostulation the Spirit did it reveal, that it was now the fittest Season to proceed forward in. For none could be capable of taking their degrees in order to a Seraphick Dignity, but those who had reconcile the striving Properties. Which from the outward Birth had made such a struggling. Which (being not only subdued, but made all willing) now must together launch into further Depths, as the Star above shall direct the *Measuring Line* in the Spirit's Hand: Which we are precisely to observe; and all will work to fetch up to God's rest.

Then after all this Opening and Spiritual Parly I was over-set, and cast as into a *Trance*, and had all my outward Senses drowned, and was brought by the Spirit into such a place, that was as the Scene of another

World. For the Ground where the Inhabitants moved, was as clear as Crystal, and the same above was the same below, all light and clear. The Spirit that brought me in, led me to do Obeyance to one, that was the *Princess* of the World. Who appeared great and full of Majesty, resembling the Face of a Woman, all cloathed as in waved Clouds. I was something abashed to come near her: but the Spirit annimated me. And She directed my Guide, to bring me into acquaintance with the residue, that did move there in distinct Figures. But they at first looked somewhat strange upon me, and shy: because I had no such clarified Body. Whereupon I did strive to make my Apology in way of Speech; but that did much displease. For it was advised, this was the *Magia School*; where all of Mortal Language was to be excluded. For all was understood by the operation of the Magia: here was no Speech, but all Power acted. Then one I was brought to, that had such a composure in his Countenance, as one might read profound Wisdom, signally resident upon him. I would have had them more free, and familiar with me, for I loved, and was much affected with them. But they saw, I was not versed in their high Method, and looked upon me as a stranger in their Region. And being very eager to ask them questions, what the denominated were? And who was the Soveraign Ruler here? And I was big with many Queries, but received a check, as being a young Novice, that did not understand the Magia-Rules. Then suddenly I was bound, and could move no way but no Hand touched me. And this was to let me know, what Soveraignty they could put forth. And then as suddenly as I was set free, and found my self at liberty.

Then heard I the Majestical Princess, that ruled all in that Sphear, say in a breath as soft as Air: *Do not despise the unlearned, that are not acquainted with this high Art. For this thing, time is allowed, for the fiting her out thereunto. But know, O Spirit, before thou goest from hence, that this is the one only thing, that is worthy to be learned, whereby Nature's Beast may be tamed, and to a Heavenly Figure renewed by the Magia-working Power.* Then brought I was into my Bodily Sense, where I was given to understand, what all this Transportation tended to. Which I was cautioned to remind, and lay up as a secret: and watch the turn of the Wheel, when *Sophia* should it once again move, to bring us to know and learn this high Mystery, which may the groaning Creation relieve.

—Jane Leade, *A Fountain of Gardens* (1700), vol. 3, 323–326.

Education in the New World Order: A Trialogue*

RALPH ABRAHAM, TERENCE MCKENNA,
AND RUPERT SHELDRAKE

RUPERT: Everybody agrees, even mainstream educationalists, that there's something wrong with the educational system we have today. Every society or civilization has an educational system of some kind. What would the educational system in the new world order look like?

I think it is of primary importance to recognize consciously that education is a form of initiation. Even in the present system, we have a training period and then we pass through a time of testing or trial. Some of us fail, others pass, and the passed ones become the initiates. At every level we have examinations, and each level of initiation is accompanied by impressive public graduation ceremonies. In this realm, the medieval hierarchy lives on, complete with robes, B.A., M.A., Ph.D., and so on. The initiates are like a secular priesthood qualified to run and order society. From their ranks are drawn our bureaucrats, scientists, technocrats, and intellectuals.

With certification of higher levels of education, people get better jobs, better employment opportunities, and more respect. For this reason, to the despair of educators throughout the world, most students passing through universities seem to have more interest in receiving degrees than real interest in the subjects they're studying. In the Third World, a B.A. or an M.A. changes a person's entire social status. In India, a person's marriage prospects and the size of dowry

* Reprinted with permission from Ralph Abraham, Terence McKenna, and Rupert Sheldrake, *Trialogues at the Edge of the West: Chaos, Creativity, and the Resacralization of the World* (Santa Fe: Bear & Company, 1992).

they can command depend on their degree.

In fact, modem education involves an initiation into the rationalist worldview. It elevates the intellect to a disembodied point of view in which everything is seen as if from the outside. Its slogan is objectivity. When schoolchildren are taught literature within this framework, the teacher does not read them great poems accompanied by the beating of a drum and the bringing in of magic and the realm of myth. Instead, the teacher tells them, "This poem was written by so-and-so who was born in so-and-so and influenced by so-and-so." Students learn facts about the poems rather than the poems themselves. This education system makes the supreme arbiter a kind of emotionless, detached, disembodied mind working through the medium of written language. It tests students solely in the written rather than the spoken mode.

The first step in this system is literacy. People must read and write so they can know what's in reports, official documents, newspapers, and books. This becomes more important than what they actually feel or experience. The great libraries are like temples, containing much more than any one of us could ever read or know about. The deeper one's initiation into the priesthood of the written word, the less the realm of personal experience counts for anything—except in the realm of private life, behind the diaphragm that separates the private person from the educated public persona.

An alternative educational model would still be based on initiation, but a broader kind not confined to the intellectual realm. Throughout the world, people realize that being initiated means taking on a new social role, and usually these roles are in some sense sacralized. There are guilds and castes of craftsmen—in India, the potter caste, the weaver caste, the priest caste, and so on—with their own traditions and skills passed from parents to children. Children are generally initiated into the skills of their parents. In our society, for example, most adults want to be initiated into the club of qualified drivers. They go through a learning period and pass a test, and then a new freedom opens up. There is real power with a magnetic pull and glamour to it. There are also initiations into skills like swimming and football, trades like plumbing, and the various professions.

Much of the present educational system could be transformed if we consciously recognized its initiatory quality. For example, medical students, in order to become doctors, are required to dissect a human corpse. To overcome their instinctive, deep-down revulsion to the array of dead bodies, as well as traditional taboos against interfering with corpses, students first entering the dissecting room presently adopt a highly detached and usually jocular attitude. In the new system, medical students would still dissect a human body, but they would prepare themselves with a meditation on death. As in some Tantric traditions where practitioners spend a night alone in a grave-yard, this would make explicit the initiatory quality of the solemn moment of confronting death.

Other trades and professions would have comparable initiatory elements. Computer modeling, for example, would be an important part of the initiation into mathematics. This would introduce the initiate to the mathematical landscape, which mathematicians don't talk much about. Rather than pretending that mathematics is only a rational system of numbers and symbols, the initiate would be exposed to the vivid visual imagination, which is where creative mathematicians realize the magic is.

Included in the new educational system would be rites of passage at puberty. These could happen at new-style summer camps where there would be a program involving a vision quest, for example, with at least twenty-four hours spent alone in the wilderness. Such camps already exist in places like northern Vancouver Island, mostly for Native American youth.

One kind of system that already has this initiatory quality is the workshop system. This is at present the principal model for an alternative educational system that could replace the present one. Workshops make the dynamics of people interacting as a group explicit, and they are based on learning through experience. They attract people who actually want to learn something with others, find some new insight, or make some new transition.

TERENCE: You put your finger on the fact that the initiatory ritual is the continuing thread from the archaic that can lead us into the future. The only thing I would add is that the education of the future should have a tremendous focus on history. The educational system currently in place has as its paradigm the teaching of physics—in other words, the conveying of an extremely abstract, mathematically based description of nature that leads to high engineering competence. In an ideal educational milieu, the science of archaeology might replace the science of physics as the place where the focus is put. With the revolution in data recovery ability that has occurred in archaeology in the last ten years, a kind of telescope into the past is being erected by the world archaeology community. To teach this in our schools would release us from the post-industrial notion of history as a kind of trendless fluctuation or class struggle or some other very dreary model of the human journey through time.

We've fallen into a sort of historical amnesia that has blunted the acuity of our political decision making. In reformed education, people must be taught that history is a system of interlocking resonances in which we are all imbedded. We must teach our children that they are going to be called upon to make decisions that will affect the state of life on this planet millennia in the future. Without some knowledge of history from the birth of the universe down to yesterday's headlines, we're not in a position to act in our own best interest. I define education broadly as the inculcation of attitudes that cause us to act generally in the interest of all.

RALPH: The workshop mode would be valuable to diffuse the curriculum with new dimensions of history, archaeology, and the revisioning of the past. There could be a different teacher every year, rather than a professor with tenure.

We've focused on higher education, and maybe when higher education is transformed, it will somehow change the whole educational system. I feel, however, that we haven't really addressed the main problems in the current system. The trouble is, we don't know exactly what they are.

Infusing the current educational system with a new spirit probably will not be sufficient. Who will be organizing all of this? Where is the department of administration, the administration building? Who's deciding which workshops will be offered, which teacher will conduct them, and so on? Will there be a new emphasis on a feminist revision of history? Will there be new interpretations of data from archaeology? Somebody must decide, whether it's the PTA or whatever, how many people are going to school. Everyone? A few? Those who wish? What rewards will be offered? These things are the nuts and bolts of running a school system. As the system evolves, or devolves, the path must be determined and put in place at the beginning.

In the current initiation system, there are two different processes: the initiation process and the accreditation process. This means that there is instruction and then there is a test. As a teacher, I've always hated the testing aspect. I am happy to teach people who want to learn from me. That is a role I can accept. Nevertheless, I must also write letters of recommendation or declare that a student has reached a certain level. Usually, I don't even know what level—using the grades of A, B, C, or whatever—the student has reached, and whatever I once thought the dividing line between the grades was, I'm no longer sure. I like the initiating and I don't like the testing. Yet if there is no testing, the educational system fails in its mission.

Spiritual, moral, and social values are consistent with initiation but not with testing. One of the things society asks education to do is produce people qualified for trades and professions. I think the heart of a school system's curriculum should transcend the trades, the professions, the basic skills. Where is the spiritual initiation? Where are the moral and ethical values? Where is the fabric of society, as it were? Where is this to be taught, if not in the schools? Did Plato's Academy have a final exam on Socrates's Philosophy 101?

Perhaps, in a new system, there would be a spiritual elite and professors of moral philosophy. Plato and Socrates would lead a workshop, or something like that. The administrators arranging the plumbing workshops and those arranging the spiritual workshops would be people with different qualifications.

Another thing that has crippled the modern university is the isolation of the specialties. Besides having workshops with one leader, we must have trialogue workshops to give the interplay of different specialties due time. I don't propose, as some have, that we completely replace courses in specialties with interdisciplinary courses. I think we need a partnership, like Mother Earth and Father Sky. There should be time for the specialties and equal time for the syncretists to free associate, to relate the subject matter of the entire educational experience to the progress and future of society and to the evolutionary challenges facing each generation.

The educational system of the new world order also needs the participation of the community in the determination of the curriculum. It needs to resist evolution that's too fast while not being too rigid to change. It needs to involve a partnership of the special and the general. It needs to relate to life, not only in terms of fixing the faucets but in terms of making everyday moral decisions about altruism and selflessness and synergy.

RUPERT: Obviously, the element lacking in what I've proposed is the spiritual dimension. I took for granted, based on the present system, that the educational system is essentially secular. If we think of a spiritually based system, there's a completely different realm of possibilities. Our problem is that if the education system were Christian, then Jews, Muslims, Hindus, Buddhists, and atheists would object. This is why secularism is an important feature of modern political ideology and why spiritual traditions and practices have no place in schools. The secular state by its very nature is desacralized. It's a rationalist concept.

For an entire society to have a spiritual dimension, one would need official state rituals like they have in Japan with the emperor and the Shinto religion and in Britain with the monarchy and the established church. The American model is entirely desacralized.

In America, the system would have to be a free-for-all. It would work something like this: Each student at age eighteen would be given books of fifty-five or so workshop vouchers, and the student would have to take fifty-five workshops over the next three years in order to become an initiated adult. There would have to be a minimum number taken in specific areas, like group dynamics, myths, history, philosophy, natural history, ecology, morality, and religion. To facilitate choice and logistics, there would be a computerized catalog of all the relevant programs offered at all recognized workshop centers.

RALPH: The graduating credential on finishing the use of the fifty-five vouchers would be the list of workshops completed at the point of initiation.

RUPERT: The whole process would start with a ceremonial induction into the pathway. Each workshop would itself have an initiatory pattern. The whole thing would culminate in some final test involving not only intellectual and practical skills but skills in groups as well. The final ceremony could also involve, as the Eleusinian mysteries, a psychedelic initiation, perhaps with mushrooms.

TERENCE: This would be the archaic return: a culmination of the educational process and the archaic mystery. Such ceremonies and sacraments were the original source of community. This concept follows very firmly in the steps of Aldous Huxley. In his last work, *Island*, he suggested annual ritualized encounters with psilocybin in a context of other radical forms of physical and mental therapy as a basis for a new form of education. As we reinvent Eleusis, we truly reinvent the wheel.

RALPH: This educational concept is actually a covert plan for the introduction of a new world religion through the religious aspects of initiation—and perhaps through visits to sacred sites. In the absence of an actual schoolhouse, there would be workshop centers all over the map. Workshops in religion, ethics, and so on would correspond to different established traditions as well as extinct, ancient traditions.

RUPERT: These workshops would be led by people from all traditions: Roman Catholic, Methodist, Islamic, Hindu, Tibetan Buddhist, and so on. If students wanted to know about Judaism, they wouldn't go to a professor of comparative religion, they would go to a workshop with a rabbi.

RALPH: The relationship between education and the job market would be clear in the classified ads: "Must have three W courses, two E courses, and one S course." As requirements of different industries become known, people seeking a particular profession would see to it that they took courses in the required subject areas.

RUPERT: This system could fulfill the needs of employers better than the present one.

RALPH: This vision becomes more satisfactory and plausible. What about the path that goes from here to there? How can we get rid of the entrenched system? The voters would have to have a plebiscite in order to vote on the opportunity to have a voucher system in the schools.

RUPERT: The system can simply be privatized. Vouchers would be valid at schools on an approved list drawn up by a new kind of educational board. The system would be pluralistic and extremely responsive to what people actually want and what students and parents are actually interested in. It would be decentralized and self-regulating.

TERENCE: This is school as business. Do we really want a marketplace of ideas?

RUPERT: It would be run not for profit, but through charitable trusts.

We also need to consider the reform of existing professions. Each branch of the present educational system already exists as a kind of guild of mathematicians or biochemists or engineers—with its own founding fathers, honored traditions, and so on. Each of these guilds needs to develop from within itself a vision of itself in the new world order. Groups of doctors or astronomers or geologists could get together in workshop gatherings in places like Esalen to discuss their original vision in becoming doctors. They would ask questions such as: What inspired us to study medicine? What is our present experience of the profession? What are the main limitations? What would a new vision of the healing profession be like? What could astronomy be for people today? How can the geologic profession reconnect with its patroness, Mother Earth?

RALPH: Even when the plebiscite is put on the ballot and passed, and when students are issued vouchers and the new structure simply begins, most teachers will still be ignorant of the meaning of ancient sites, the significance of stars, and the new vision of healing. Chances are they would continue teaching exactly as they teach today. While the new schools envision a new curriculum, the workshops would keep on teaching the old one.

What kind of miracle would get the whole system onto a new track? Particularly, how could the resacralization aspect that we are longing for ever happen?

RUPERT: You wouldn't just get a booklet of vouchers through the mail. When you start on your path, you would be entering a kind of apprenticeship. There would be an induction ceremony, which could be Christian, Jewish, Muslim, Buddhist, or secular. There would be plenty of scope for free enterprise in this area. You'd go through one of these ceremonies, calling in blessings on your journey. You'd get your book of vouchers as part of the ceremony. All of this would take place at a sacred place of your choosing.

RALPH: Setting up a system of initiation rites would be the key step for switching the whole system over.

RUPERT: This may become fairly easy as the importance of initiations and rites of passage for personal development becomes widely recognized.

RALPH: What about the five million young Americans who come of age for their first initiation this coming fall? Exactly how do we accommodate this number of students and produce thousands of new teachers to teach a quarter million workshops in a year?

RUPERT: Instead of an overnight change in the entire American system, I'm thinking of a pioneering experiment in a limited area.

RALPH: And it may slowly grow if it deserves to.

RUPERT: Things happen organically in society. We can't convert a system without some example of an alternative that actually works.

TERENCE: We need some concrete proof of concept demonstration.

RUPERT: The workshop system is already up and running as a concrete alternative. It exists in a pluralistic, free-market form, and it is self-sustaining. People go to workshops because they want to. Unfortunately, at present practically no one under thirty goes to workshops. It's a system of education entirely for the middle aged.

RALPH: What would be necessary to attract an eighteen-year-old to a workshop?

RUPERT: The fact is, a lot of teenagers don't know that this world of workshops exists. If they came to Esalen, for example, on an initiatory program, they would be initiated into an adult world, and new possibilities would open up to them.

Obviously, there would need to be a whole new breed of workshop leaders. Existing workshop centers would take on the new role of creating workshops to train and initiate workshop leaders.

RALPH: Somehow, standards would have to be maintained. It would have to be more than the popularity of a given workshop that guaranteed its continuous existence. Given the corruption that's a known mechanism in the downward spiral of societies, worse and worse workshops would become more and more popular because they would offer the valuation, the accreditation, and the initiation without the student actually doing anything other than sitting in a hot bath and meditating.

TERENCE: What you're implying is what you seek to avoid: a second overseeing entity that tests the workshop graduate.

RALPH: It could be that industries wouldn't employ somebody just for having graduated. They would insist on a prospective employee having gone to workshops from some of their favorite teachers or institutions. A bachelor's degree from Esalen could be worth more than a bachelor's degree from Stanford.

TERENCE: Corporations could post a list of courses that would enhance people's likelihood of being hired by them. Then students could chose for themselves which ones they would include as they formed their curriculum.

RALPH: This would be an intrinsic, self-organizational model. Maybe the corporations could just do their own testing.

RUPERT: This could start right away on a limited scale. Scholarships could be offered for, say, five workshop vouchers, with beginning and ending ceremonies for the whole thing. College students could do the workshops during their vacations. When they return to their college, they could tell their friends, who might then want to be initiated themselves. This would begin to establish a parallel system of education operating alongside the present one. If it becomes a sufficiently powerful attractor, it would have an enormous impact on schools and colleges. The traditional system's faults would become more and more apparent, because more and more people within it would have another take on what education could be like. Sooner or later, colleges would start offering workshop-type education themselves and eventually convert to the initiatory model.

RALPH: Present colleges could be persuaded to offer transfer credit for a set of five workshops in this program. Five workshops would count as one course. It would be like taking an extension course or a work/study program. In the summer, students could take workshops at five different workshop sites or just one, and they would get a college credit for it.

In sum, the new world system could actually begin with an educational program. We have to find a way to actually begin the pilot project. Since the adult education division is already functioning, we need to expand it into high school and college divisions. A few people presently coming of age, perhaps children of people who are already participants in adult workshops, could enthusiastically volunteer to be the first students of the new system. As this attractor grows and evolves and self-organizes, a bifurcation point will be reached, at which time a popular referendum could pass legislation for the fifty-five-coupon books. Existing universities and professional schools would then begin to accept workshops for transfer credit.

This system has to begin in an existing workshop center. Possibly it could be here at Esalen, since we're here dreaming this up. Assuming that corruption doesn't somehow annihilate the system as soon as it starts, it's a devious way of achieving the resacralization of the world.

The Teaching Mission of Socrates
IGNACIO L. GÖTZ

SOCRATES, says Jaeger, "is the greatest teacher in European history,"[1] and yet we do not know what he really taught, nor whether he had a theory of teaching method. He wrote nothing but a couple of poems, now lost. Certainly he was not trained to teach, and even though he obviously followed some kind of method, it was practiced rather than discussed.[2]

Socrates himself did not think he was a teacher, partly because he saw teaching as something very exalted, partly because being called a teacher implied at the time being paid for teaching,[3] and *that* Socrates never was. Also, claiming not to be a teacher, he could more honestly question those who made the claim or who charged for their efforts, and show how they fell short of the ideal. But he admitted that his questioning was, at times, annoying like a gadfly,[4] and that through his questioning he brought forth ideas as a midwife brings out an infant from the mother's womb.[5] Yet, these are descriptions, not theory. They possess what Ricoeur calls *symbolic* intentionality; that is, they may tell us what teaching is *like* (it is *like* disturbing questioning; it is *like* bringing forth ideas), but they do not tell us what teaching *is*, for its reality *an sich* eludes capture. When we call a helper in birthing "midwife," the word is, in a sense, transparent. But when we say *teaching is like midwifery*, the word is opaque but fruitful nonetheless. "The symbol invites," says Ricoeur. "I do not point the meaning, the symbol gives it; but what it gives is something for thought, something to think about."[6]

The truth about Socrates could never have been told directly. Therefore, Plato, Xenophon, Antisthenes, and Aischines of Sphettus constructed his life in story, the dialogue form being preferred because that is the way Socrates "taught."[7]

Socrates himself insisted he had never been anyone's teacher (*didaskalos*), but he added that he never refused to be engaged in conversation about serious and important matters.[8] His conversations, however, were construed to be teaching.[9] He said he never had pupils (*mathêtês*), only friends and associates (*hetairoi*) with whom he held converse. These were novel ways of speaking, designed to remove the speaker from the crowd of those who claimed to be teachers—mostly the early sophists. After his death these expressions were co-opted by the very people he had tried to disassociate himself from.[10]

The conversations took place in the gymnasium, on the banks of a river, at the *palaestra*, in the banquet hall, or at the home of friends. They were often charged with eroticism[11] or conducted in the midst of drinking and revelry protracted into the wee hours of the morning, for Socrates could outdrink them all.[12] In other words, they took place in a most unphilosophic atmosphere, and all the details given by Plato and Xenophon seem to lie below the high level of abstract thought in which philosophers are supposed to move and have their being.[13] And yet, how else except in such stories could the teacher that was Socrates have been "caught"?

Brief Biography

"The life of a great man," writes Taylor, "can never be a mere record of undisputed fact. Even when such facts are plentiful, the biographer's real business is with their interpretation."[14] That has been a problem with the life of Socrates: how to evaluate the various, often differing, interpretations of his life. Not merely that, but with the exception of Aristophanes's *Clouds*, which was produced in 423 (Socrates was forty-six years old), all documents about Socrates were written *after* his death. Aristophanes himself was some twenty-one years younger than Socrates, and Plato and Xenophon forty-one and forty-three years younger, respectively. They had not known Socrates before middle age, though they had access to many who had.

The bare facts of Socrates's life can be stated briefly. He was born

in 470/469 B.C.E. in Athens. His father, Sophroniscus, a friend of
Aristides, was a craftsman (*lithourgos*: sculptor or stonecutter) by trade,
hence the later legend that Socrates himself was a stonecutter. His
mother, Phainarete, had been married previously and had a son,
Patrokles, from her previous marriage. It seems that Socrates inherited enough money from them not to have to work at all during his
entire life, though he did not live in luxury, either.

As a teenager he became interested in the "scientific" theories of
Anaxagoras, and he may have joined the school of Archelaus, the
Athenian who succeeded Anaxagoras when the latter left Athens *circa*
450. He may even have been a leader of the school,[15] but his "scientific"
orientation does not seem to have altered his religious sensitivities.[16]

During this time Athens was at its zenith. This means that Socrates
saw the building of the Parthenon (447–432), including the forty-foot
high statue of Athena. Polygnotus the painter and Pheidias the
sculptor were active during this time, and so were the dramatists
Sophocles and Euripides, whose plays he must have witnessed.

He probably left the mainland only once, during a military expedi-
tion against Samos in 441, when he was twenty-eight years old. He was
an exceptionally brave soldier, as he demonstrated in the blockade of
Samos and at the siege of Potidaea (431–430) under Pericles. He was
also at the battle of Delium (424), where the Athenians were defeated,
and perhaps also at Amphipolis in 422. In fact, most of his adult life
transpired during the years of the Peloponnesian War (431–404) and
the consequent decline of Athens and its democracy.

He was in his late forties when he married Xanthippe around 420.
She seems to have been an affectionate woman, though later legends
made her out to be a shrew. With her he had three sons, Lamprokles,
who was a teenager when Socrates died, Sophroniscus, and Menexenus,
who was a mere infant at the time of the execution.

During these later years of his life his financial fortunes suffered, as
did those of many Athenians, due to the vicissitudes of the War. Still,
the fact that he served in the army as a *hoplites* indicates that he was no
pauper, for a certain income was needed to qualify for this rank. The

fact that he always went barefooted, therefore (with exceptions duly noted, as in *Symposium* 174A), had more to do with preference than with money. As Amipsias put it, he was "born to spite shoemakers."

When in his early thirties he formed a friendship with the young Alcibiades, probably only a teenager at the time, and at any rate some fifteen to twenty years younger than him. The association continued for many years and had its dramatic moments, as when Socrates defended the wounded Alcibiades at the battle of Delium. But the friendship eventually proved fatal. Alcibiades was rumored to have engaged in burlesque recreations of the Eleusinian Mysteries, something that a populace browbeaten and made more conservative by the reverses of war was not willing to tolerate. Then came the debacle against Syracuse, in which the Athenian fleet with Alcibiades in charge was defeated. Later Alcibiades turned traitor and began cooperating with Sparta against the motherland.

Athens fell to Sparta and Lysander in 404. The victors appointed a Commission of Thirty—among whom were Critias and Charmides, Socrates's cronies—to reorganize the government of Athens, but they botched things royally, and were quickly overthrown by a democratic revolt in 403; however, not before indicting Socrates for refusing to participate as ordered in the arrest and murder of Leon of Salamis (a disobedience punishable by death) and for criticizing their decrees mandating the execution of citizens. Socrates was reputed to have quipped that he had known no herdsman to pride himself for his skill in reducing the number of his sheep.[17]

To the new democrats there was a link between the traitor Alcibiades, the oligarchs Critias and Charmides, and Socrates. It did not matter that total amnesty had been declared for crimes committed before 403. Socrates was reindicted, this time for crimes not specified very clearly: for not worshipping the gods whom Athens worshipped, but introducing new and unfamiliar religious practices; and, further, for corrupting the young.[18] Anytus was the instigator, a sensible man who simply wanted to push Socrates to go into exile, as was customary after an indictment in order to avoid a trial. But Socrates did not leave;

therefore the trial took place. The prosecutor was Meletus, who seems to have been a religious fanatic.

For ordinary men such as the five hundred or so Athenians who made up the jury, there was more than a semblance of truth in the accusations. Hadn't Socrates been ridiculed by Aristophanes for his "new religious beliefs" and his denial of the supremacy of Zeus? Hadn't he been the "teacher" of Alcibiades, whose farces about the Mysteries had offended everybody? Weren't the accursed oligarchs, Critias and Charmides, Socrates's close friends?

Socrates was condemned to death in 399 and executed within a month of the sentence. His last days and hours were chronicled by Plato and Xenophon, neither of whom was present at the event: Plato was ill, and Xenophon was somewhere in Asia, but there is no reason to disbelieve their accounts. On their writings, principally, rests the evidence for the sanctification of Socrates.

Mysticism and the Maieutic Method

"Haven't you heard, you idiot, that I am the son of a midwife?"[19] Socrates was ribbing Theaetetus, but the jocular passage is the closest Socrates ever came to describing his *modus operandi*.

It is, of course, not at all clear that Phainarete, Socrates's mother, was a midwife.[20] She need not have been, for her name lends itself to the simile: "she who brings to light (*phainô*) virtue (*aretê*)." Moreover, in his farce, Aristophanes had made Strepsiades induce the miscarriage of a thought in one of Socrates's students by breaking into the "thought factory" supposedly run by Socrates.[21] Nothing more was needed to make the connection.

The passage in *Theaetetus* is fairly straightforward, but I want to draw attention to a couple of points generally neglected in the literature. Socrates points out that women become midwives only after they themselves have ceased bearing children. The reason is that helping at a birth is a skill that is not developed without experience: "human nature cannot know the mystery of an art without experience" (149C). The art is, of course, that of helping a woman give birth; or, in pedagogical terms, the art of letting others learn; that is, conceive and bring forth knowledge.

Midwives, adds Socrates, merely help in the delivery. Surely, it is part of their art to know when a woman is pregnant, when the pregnancy is advanced and the time of birth is at hand, and how to guide the fetus out into the world, and all this is difficult and requires experiential knowledge. But his own art, says Socrates, is more complicated. It is not just a matter of helping someone learn, for there are all kinds of knowledge, truthful and fallacious. His maieutic art, therefore, requires of him also to discriminate between truth and falsehood, and the success of the performance consists in examining whether the thought being brought forth is a phantom or a real thing imbued with life and truth (150C).

The maieutic method, therefore, is not neutral, a much craved state in the modern world. Neither is the method characterized simply by the production of ideas. What renders it distinctive, according to Socrates, is its power of discrimination—the ability of the teacher to let the young mind learn only the truth. One may quibble forever about the meaning of truth, but when one speaks of the Socratic method, truth, and the art of finding it, are intimately connected.

Intellectual midwifery, unlike the medical one, is not tolerant. Marcuse has drawn our attention to this meaning of tolerance. Tolerance does not mean the acceptance of absolutely every color and shade of opinion. The goal (*telos*) of tolerance is truth, and as truth begins to emerge, however weakly, tolerance ceases and commitment begins. Hence the need for a well developed art of discernment, for sensitivity toward the truth that is constantly being uncovered in the world and in human affairs.

Socrates also specifies as a characteristic of the maieutic art the ability to recognize the best midwife for each soul (151B). Not every teacher can teach every child, and part of being a sensitive, discriminating, and generous teacher is to place each soul in the care of the midwife best suited to help the young mind bring to term its own thoughts. We do this as a matter of course when it comes to taking care of our bodies: we look for the right physician, and to do this we ask the opinion of friends, of other doctors, and so forth, in an effort to place our bodies in the care of the best doctor; but we neglect to do this for our souls.[22]

Finally, Socrates places this commitment to the search for truth within the context of his "mission," his calling: clearly, he feels he is not permitted inwardly to acquiesce in falsehood or to deny the truth (151D). This means that the maieutic art is not something one can just learn through so-called "education" courses. It is not one more method one can add to one's repertory. Rather, it is a practice that flows out of one's calling to the life of a teacher, which therefore engages one's total being. It is so easy to see teaching as a mere job—another opportunity to make an honest buck. But clearly that was not the way Socrates construed it—even though he claimed he never taught; and perhaps he did so precisely to be able to emphasize his own commitment.

It is hard to know when Socrates began to look at his questioning as a *mission*. It may have had something to do with the answer of the Delphic oracle—that there was no one wiser than him—and his own "ironic" interpretation of this to mean that his wisdom consisted in not claiming to have "divine" knowledge.[23] This realization may have added a moral dimension to the quest for knowledge he had taken up in his youth: he may have felt morally compelled, "called," to help others come to a similar realization. Moreover, as he says in *Apology* 22–23, he worried that poets, politicians, and artisans alike knew many things, but were ignorant of the most important one, the care of their souls. He wanted to remedy this malady; he wanted to cure ignorance, but without substituting his own knowledge for it. He wanted to help the individual regenerate him- or herself, and he felt a moral calling to achieve this.

There is an element of mysticism involved in all this. Socrates, it is clear, had been initiated into the Orphic mysteries early in his life. Orphism was one of the common cults, but by the time he was an adult, it had degenerated, and Socrates may have moved away from its rites.

But his mystical inclination does not seem to have suffered; in fact, there is evidence that he continued to practice a kind of ecstatic contemplation, perhaps secularized,[24] which was acknowledged by others to be the source of much of his superior knowledge[25] as well as of his "strangeness" (*atopia*).[26] He himself referred to this (his "voices") in *Apology* 31D, where he termed it a "divine [or spiritual] sign" (*daimonion sêmeion*).

By the time he inquired after Charmides's soul, his mission seems to have been set. This was immediately after the battle of Potidaea (430–431), when he was in his late thirties, and after a long trance lasting some twenty-four hours, during which he stood quietly, under the careful watch of other soldiers in the camp.[27] Such experiences may have instilled in him a sense of calling to be a questioner, a perambulating teacher in a society that was not yet fully schooled. It appears, therefore, that a major part of his greatness as a teacher had to do with his having a sense of mission and not just with the use of a method or the following of a "profession." In this he was also inspired, it would seem, by a remarkable woman.

Diotima

Diotima, says Socrates in *Symposium* 201, taught him everything he knows about the art of love—by which he does *not* mean sex! The speech he delivers at Agathon's (at whose party he arrived late because of a trance during prayer on his way there)[28] is purportedly a report of her teachings, received from her when he was younger. There is no question here of his appropriating to himself a woman's teachings, of substituting his words for hers, as has so often been done: throughout his speech he makes it very clear that he is reporting *her words*.

Diotima is identified as a priestess from Mantinea, a city in Arcadia destroyed in 418 by the Spartans during the Peloponnesian War. She may have been a Pythagorean seer, much as the Pythia was Apollo's votary at Delphi, and Socrates may have come to know her through his involvement in Orphism: there were mutual influences and borrowings between these two mystical traditions. Many commentators consider her an invention of Plato's, and the speech a kind of *mythos*, though the reference to her having delayed the advent of plague for some ten years situates her historically and makes her existence difficult to deny.

I find it significant that the source of one of the most exalted utterances in the Western tradition—Socrates's discourse on love— should come from a woman seer, a woman who knows from experience what she is conveying, and who has intellectualized her experience to the point of distinguishing stages in the progressive initiation into the mysteries of love.[29] She also understands the need for a guide and the role this guide is to play—indeed, she models this role for Socrates by leading him, at least in conversation, through the various steps up to the vision of wondrous, absolute, everlasting beauty.[30] In Socrates's own words, she is his teacher, and if Socrates is "the greatest teacher in European history,"[31] what does this recognition make of her?

At the source of the pedagogical tradition of the West, when human concerns become more decidedly humanistic, there stands not just a man, but a woman, Diotima. Surely, it is Socrates who presents her insights to us, who does the questioning inspired by her, and who eventually loses his life for the integrity of his self. But the inspiring light, from the time he was young, came from a woman. This recognition of his indebtedness to her was repaid at his trial: politically, women were denied the vote in Athens; factually, no Athenian woman cast a vote for his death.

Conclusion

Socrates understood very well the Homeric injunction, "Excel always and stay ahead of your peers,"[32] but instead of taking it to mean bravery in battle or in sports, he understood it as the pursuit of inner superiority, the pursuit of virtue. Plato may have exaggerated his excellence and Aristophanes made fun of it, but in doing so he recognized it for what it was, and Socrates bore him no resentment for having made him the butt of his jokes.

The voice he heard was that of justice, not equality, and it seemed to him like the sweet sound of the flute in the ears of the mystic.[33] Heeding it, he prayed for inner beauty and for the inward balance that accords each talent and part of the soul its due, and which therefore is perfect justice. And also perfect happiness.[34] Therefore he was judged the wisest, the most just, and the best.[35]

Notes

1. Werner Jaeger, *Paideia: The Ideals of Greek Culture* (New York: Oxford University Press, 1945), II, 27.

2. Jaeger, *Paideia*, II, 62 ff.

3. Alfred E. Taylor, *Socrates* (Westport, CT: Greenwood Press, 1975), 53–54.

4. Plato, *Apology* 30B.

5. Plato, *Theaetetus* 149 ff., and 210B–C.

6. Paul Ricoeur, "Hermeneutics," in *The Philosophy of Paul Ricoeur*, edited by Charles E. Regan and David Stewart (Boston: Beacon Press, 1978), 37.

7. Jaeger, *Paideia*, II, 22; Gregory Vlastos, *Socrates, Ironist and Moral Philosopher* (Ithaca: Cornell University Press, 1991), 45.

8. Plato, *Apology* 33A; also 19D–E.

9. Xenophon, *Memorabilia* 1.2.31–38.

10. Jaeger, *Paideia*, II, 380 n. 142.

11. Plato, *Charmides* 153–154.

12. Plato, *Symposium* 223.

13. Jaeger, *Paideia*, II, 36.

14. Taylor, *Socrates*, 9.

15. Aristophanes, *Clouds* 94.

16. Vlastos, *Socrates*, ch. 6.

17. Xenophon, *Memorabilia* 1.2.32.

18. Taylor, *Socrates*, 113; Vlastos, *Socrates*, 293–297.

19. Plato, *Theaetetus* 149A.

20. Myles Burnyeat, "Socratic Midwifery, Platonic Inspiration," *Bulletin of the Institute of Classical Studies* 24 (1977), 7–15.

21. Aristophanes, *Clouds* 137–139.

22. Plato, *Protagoras* 313A–C.

23. Plato, *Apology* 21; Vlastos, *Socrates*, 3 ff., 82 ff., 236–239, 288–289.

24. Vlastos, *Socrates*, 79–80.

25. Plato, *Symposium* 175C–D.

26. Plato, *Symposium* 221D.

27. Plato, *Symposium* 220.

28. Plato, *Symposium* 175.

29. Plato, *Symposium* 209D.
30. Plato, *Symposium* 210D.
31. Jaeger, *Paideia*, II, 27.
32. Homer, *Iliad* 6.208 = 11.784.
33. Plato, *Crito* 54D.
34. Plato, *Phaedrus* 279C.
35. Plato, *Phaedo* 118.

A Note on Myth, the Mysteries, and Teaching in Plato's Republic

IGNACIO L. GÖTZ

IT IS GENERALLY AGREED that there are esoteric and mystical elements in Plato's work, and that the Academy was organized along the lines of a religious confraternity (*thiasos*), perhaps on the model of Pythagoras's school at Crotona. Here I want merely to highlight the religious character of the setting in which the discussion that is the *Republic* supposedly took place, and to draw from the practices of the initiation rites of the Mysteries in order to gain a deeper understanding of some comments on teaching Plato makes in the *Republic*.

I should begin by saying that I am using the Parable of the Cave in the *Republic* as a story, a *mythos* narrated by Plato to illustrate "the degrees in which our nature may be enlightened or unenlightened."[1] By using the Parable as a myth I do not mean to imply that Plato was a mythologist, a teller of stories, although in effect his picture of Socrates *is* a *mythos*.[2] Myth had begun to be downgraded by his time, a fact Plato acknowledges,[3] but he did not share in the rising skepticism (though he burned his tragedies and poems when he made Socrates's quest his own). For Plato, as Friedländer says, "*mythos* is opposed to *logos*, a 'story' in contrast to conceptual analysis,"[4] and the latter is preferable.[5] But the dialogue itself is a form of story and unmistakably bears the marks of narrative: in every dialogue we are told *a story about a conversation*. Further, many of the inquiries are conducted by way of a myth. In fact, Plato uses myths, first, as a more convenient form of exposition than conceptual analysis, and later as a way of saying what cannot be said any other way.[6] This is possible because myths, he says, are fiction mixed with truth[7]—they both reveal and conceal, as Heraclitus claimed Apollo did: "The lord whose oracle is at Delphi neither speaks nor conceals, but gives signs."[8] This is especially the case when the stories refer to illumination. Here, almost certainly, Plato has in mind the practices of the Mysteries.[9] Many descriptions convey this connection, such as the references to darkness and hollows in the ground,[10] the conception of the physical body as the soul's prison[11] immortalized in the pun *sôma sêma* ("body [is] tomb"), and the characterization of enlightenment as liberation.[12]

The context in which the *mythos* of the *Republic* is told was itself connected with the Mysteries. The year was 421 B.C.E. The Piraeus, Athens's seaport, was crowded, for many Athenians had walked down the five miles there for the celebrations in honor of the goddess Bendis, a Thracian version of Artemis. Bendis, like her counterparts throughout the ancient world, was a divinity associated with wildlife and fertility. Like Artemis, she was mistress of the beasts and patroness of birth and nurture.

Her cult in Athens was new, having begun perhaps only a few years earlier during the plague that scourged Athens between 430 and 429, but the worship was ancient, going back to the Mother Goddess rites of the Neolithic. After the advent of the Indo-Europeans, her rituals had become esoteric and mysterious, but now, with the waning of the Olympians, they were acquiring new prominence, as more people sought initiation in them.

The festival was generally open to all comers, and was considered preliminary to the formal ceremony open only to the initiates (*mystai*). While the festival took place during the day, the initiation was nocturnal. Flickering torches and lights were used, in contrast to the surrounding darkness, to symbolize the enlightenment that was to take place. For the initiates, the culmination of the festival was a "seeing" or "beholding" (*epopteia*)—a word that recurs often in Plato— which suffused them with incredible and deep-felt joy. Here, as Aristotle remarked, there was no learning *per se* (*ou mathein ti*), only an overwhelming and ineffable experience (*pathein*).[13]

Into this celebration Socrates had come, as he says,[14] to offer prayers to the Goddess and to see how the festival was conducted, since it was a new thing. He had enjoyed the procession, especially the contingent from Thrace, though he felt the Athenians had made a good showing. Now, in the late afternoon, he was beginning to walk back to Athens when he was detained by Polemarchos and his friends and invited to stay for the evening celebrations, which included a torch-race on horseback in honor of the Goddess. Socrates decided to stay, for many of his friends and young followers were there. There was, in other words, the right context for a conversation.

The conversation that ensued has been preserved in Plato's *Republic*. It was a wide-ranging discussion involving justice, talent, the state, art, education, and the afterlife. It must have lasted through the night, and we wonder if the conversants ever got to see the night revelries in honor of the Goddess.

However, one remark of Socrates acquires fresh meaning when placed in the context of a celebration of the Mysteries. It is a remark about teaching. Socrates, according to Plato, commented how teaching is

> an art whose aim would be to effect . . . the conversion [turning around] of the soul, in the readiest way; not to put the power of sight into the soul's eye, which already has it, but to ensure that, instead of looking in the wrong direction, it is turned the way it ought to be.[15]

Teaching, says Socrates (who claimed he never taught) is a pointing and a showing. It is a pointing in the right direction and a showing of "it" to the soul (*psyche*). The pointing is both verbal and performative. Teaching, in other words, tells, performs, shows.

Now, the Mysteries incorporated these same activities. There were recitations (*legomena*), performances (*dromena*), and showings (*deiknymena*).[16] The goal (*telos*) in both instances was not learning *per se*, but vision,[17] the sudden kindling of a "flame" in the soul.[18] In an ancient fragment reminiscent of the Parable of the Cave we read:

> At first there is wandering, and wearisome roaming, and fearful traveling through darkness with no end to be found. Then, just before the consummation (*telos*), there is every sort of terror, shuddering and

trembling and perspiring and being alarmed. But after this a marvelous light (*phos*) appears, and open places and meadows await, with voices and dances and the solemnities of sacred utterances and holy visions. In that place one walks about at will, now perfect and initiated (*memuemenos*) and free, and wearing a crown, one celebrates . . .[19]

It would seem most likely that the many metaphorical elements of the Parable of the Cave and the subsequent explanations were rooted in the experience of the mysteries,[20] the oldest of which were celebrations of the Goddess.

The Parable of the Cave is a story about enlightenment. Its culmination is the vision of the Sun,[21] but this is really the analogue for the vision of the Forms,[22] the sudden vision of unnameable reality[23] which, *like* a light flaring suddenly after a long search,[24] is the goal for the sake of which all manner of toils have been endured.[25] But the *conditio sine quâ non* of this enlightenment is conversion—literally, a turning around, or more precisely, being turned around (*periagôgê*). This is what is done to the lucky prisoner in the Cave who is set free, *forced* to stand up and *to turn his head* toward the fire light.[26] The implication is that turning around is effected by a guide, for guidance in such matters is required.[27] In fact, this is precisely what teaching is, as Socrates avers in the passage cited above. From the ritual turning of the Mysteries and the turning around to the fire light in the Cave, Plato constructs an image (*eikôn*) of conversion that characterizes the art of being a teacher.[28] The essential experience of teaching, therefore, appears to be one of converting; for the converting itself (helping one turn in the "right" direction) is a programmatic showing to which, perhaps, a discrete pointing may be added.

Notes

1. Plato, *Republic* 514.

2. Robert Scholes and Robert Kellogg, *The Nature of Narrative* (New York: Oxford University Press, 1966), 121.

3. Plato, *Phaedrus* 229B.

4. Paul Friedländer, *Plato* (New York: Pantheon, 1958), I, 172.

5. Richard Rorty, *Philosophy and the Mirror of Nature* (Princeton: Princeton University Press, 1979), 370.

6. Friedländer, *Plato*, I, 176–210.

7. Plato, *Republic* 377A.

8. Heraclitus, *Fragment* 93 [D].

9. Plato, *Symposium* 209E; Friedländer, *Plato*, I, 71–72.

10. Plato, *Phaedo* 111C.

11. Plato, *Phaedo* 67D.

12. Plato, *Phaedo* 114D ff.; *Republic* 515.

13. Marvin W. Meyer, ed., *The Ancient Mysteries: A Sourcebook* (New York: Harper & Row, 1987), 12; Plato, *Symposium* 211C.

14. Plato, *Republic* 327.

15. Plato, *Republic* 518.

16. Meyer, *Ancient Mysteries*, 10.

17. Plato, *Republic* 519.

18. Plato, *Letter* 7, 341C–D.

19. Meyer, *Ancient Mysteries*, 8–9.

20. Friedländer, *Plato*, I, 71 ff.

21. Plato, *Republic* 516.

22. Plato, *Republic* 517.

23. Plato, *Symposium* 210E ff.

24. Plato, *Letter* 7, 341C–D.

25. Plato, *Phaedo* 67B.

26. Plato, *Republic* 515.

27. Plato, *Letter* 7, 343E; Plato, *Symposium* 210A and 211B.

28. Werner Jaeger, *Paideia: The Ideals of Greek Culture* (New York: Oxford University Press, 1945), II, 295.

The Tarocchi del Mantegna:
An Overview of the Engravings

THE SO-CALLED TAROCCHI DEL MANTEGNA is an important document of the Western cosmological traditions, but is little-known except to historians of Renaissance art. In order to make the existence of these beautiful emblems more widely known, we are publishing Oliver Perrin's article on the Tarocchi of Mantegna, drawings of the complete set of engravings (facing), and photographic reproductions of selected plates in this volume of *Alexandria*.

The line drawings of the complete set reproduced here are taken from Henry René D'Allemagne, *Les Cartes a Jouer du Quatorzieme au Vingtieme Siecle* (2 vols., Paris, 1906). While these drawings are faithful to the actual engravings and provide a satisfactory overview of the entire series, they lack the rich detail of the originals.

The photographs that appear elsewhere in this issue are reproductions of the actual engravings from Arthur M. Hind, *Early Italian Engraving: A Critical Catalogue, with Reproduction of All Prints Described* (London, 1938), which includes the entire set. Another work containing photographic reproductions of the entire set of engravings is Paul Kristeller, *Die Tarocchi: zwei italienische Kupferstichfolgen aus dem xv. Jahrhundert* (Berlin: Graphische Gesellschaft, 1910).

—DAVID FIDELER

1. Beggar; 2. Servant; 3. Artisan; 4. Merchant; 5. Gentleman; 6. Knight;
7. Doge; 8. King; 9. Emperor; 10. Pope; 11. Calliope; 12. Urania

13. Terpsichore; 14. Erato; 15. Polyhymnia; 16. Thalia; 17. Melpomene;
18. Euterpe; 19. Clio; 20. Apollo; 21. Grammar; 22. Logic; 23. Rhetoric;
24. Geometry

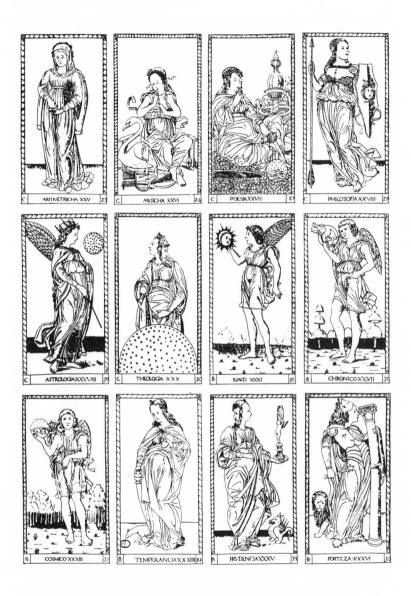

25. Arithmetic; 26. Music; 27. Poetry; 28. Philosophy; 29. Astrology;
30. Theology; 31. Genius of the Sun; 32. Genius of Time; 33. Genius of the
Cosmos; 34. Temperance; 35. Prudence; 36. Fortitude

37. Justice; 38. Charity; 39. Hope; 40. Faith; 41. Moon; 42. Mercury;
43. Venus; 44. Sun; 45. Mars; 46. Jupiter; 47. Saturn; 48. Eighth Sphere

49. Prime Mover; 50. First Cause

Reflections on the Tarocchi of Mantegna

OLIVER T. PERRIN

THE SO-CALLED TAROCCHI OF MANTEGNA is an excellent example of the enigmatic emblem tradition of the Renaissance. Within its seemingly obscure organization and symbolism, it lays out an ordered representation of the whole of Western cosmology as it was understood in the fifteenth century. This cosmology drew upon a rich, extensive ancestry of classical pagan symbolism which was synthesized with Christian doctrine. As we shall see, the way in which these images are organized as a system is no less important than their content and symbolic expression. The images of the Mantegna Tarocchi remind us of the Tarot and many common subjects of medieval and Renaissance art. In the Tarocchi, we see the Muses, the Virtues, and Vices, and we hear the haunting Music of the Spheres. Merchants, gentlemen, and beggars crowd shoulders with the Pope to utter the message of man. The lover of truth who pursues their secrets will not emerge unchanged.

The Tarocchi of Mantegna are a series of copper plate engravings dating from the mid-fifteenth century, probably within a few years of 1465.[1] It has been established for some time that they are not the work of Mantegna, but they continue to be known by this name, and I shall refer to them as such in this discussion. Though they could have been intended for some type of instructional game, it is clear that they do not constitute a set of tarocchi (which usually contain more than fifty cards), but they certainly resemble tarot cards in other ways. While guesses as to their place of origin range from Florence and Venice to Ferrara, it is most likely that the Mantegna series was produced in Ferrara.[2] These engravings were probably bound as a set in one volume; in fact, it is unlikely that they were ever used as "cards." No versions of the set exist today mounted as cards; however, there are several sets in book bindings that are as old as the engravings.[3]

There are fifty engravings in the set, of which two different versions were produced. Of these two versions, cards 1–10 of the earliest set are labeled E; in the later set, cards 1–10 are labeled S. For this reason, the two sets are referred to as the E and S series. Differences between these two sets are slight (though occasionally significant), and here they shall be considered together.[4] Albrecht Durer executed twenty drawings based on the E series. Michael Wolgemut also made reproductions from this series for a book that was to include assorted medieval allegories and copies of a Venetian edition of the Triumphs of Petrarch. This book, however, was never published.[5]

The importance of the Tarocchi of Mantegna becomes obvious when we realize that they were among the first of Italy's engraved works and that they captured the interest of artists of Albrecht Durer's caliber. One wonders where these illustrations came from; out of what mysterious background did they emerge?

The Art of Memory and Emblems as Points of Ingress into the Western Psyche

The fact that most of the Mantegna Tarocchi are found in book form is of great interest, for it suggests that they were never intended to be used as playing cards. Most of the popular speculation about the origins of the tarot is based, whether it is realized or not, upon the ideas of the Court de Gebelin, a French tarot enthusiast, who, in his *Monde Primitif* (1781), wrote that the tarot was an unrecognized book of ancient Egyptian wisdom. Inquiry of a more responsible sort has, in recent times, established that if any of the images from the tarot are of Egyptian origin, they were filtered through the complex of Classical as well as Hermetic and Neoplatonic doctrines to arrive as the stamped impressions we call the tarot today. This applies to the Tarocchi of Mantegna engravings as well. The fact that we find many of the extant impressions of the Mantegna series bound in books points more to the emblem books of the Renaissance than to the papyri of Egyptian sages. These emblem books, and indeed most of the art and literature of the time, were based firmly in the classical Greek and Roman tradition. If, however, we are inclined to judge de Gebelin harshly, we must remember that, several centuries before he put forth his ideas, Renaissance thinkers had already established the fashion of projecting the philosophy of the Greeks onto the mysterious remains of Egyptian civilization. The ubiquitous mania for attributing the origin of everything to the Egyptians was a common myopia in the Renaissance.

The Tarocchi series is hardly the only example of mysterious symbolism to confront those who pore through the images and texts of the Renaissance.[6] The fifteenth and sixteenth centuries in Europe, and indeed the many centuries before them, are well known for their passionate attempts to produce what A. M. Hind calls "epitomes of knowledge represented in pictorial form."[7] In many ways, the Renaissance was a culmination of such epitomizations and allegorical personifications, both pagan and Christian. The Renaissance scholar was a descendant of the medieval man of learning who would turn to his bestiary or his catalogs of flowers for a wealth of concepts expressed in an established pictorial form. To acquire an understanding of this tradition, we must review the strands of thought which flow and converge through history to the unique setting in which the Mantegna Tarocchi were produced.

Aristotle had stated in *De Anima* that we cannot contemplate or understand without an image in the mind's eye representing the thing considered. It was understood that the sensible form embodied the intelligible ideal.[8] The fodder of sense impressions gathered together in the imagination gives shape to concepts, allowing contemplation. This doctrine was given enormous authority when, in the thirteenth century, St. Thomas Aquinas incorporated it into his *Summa Theologica* and brought it more or less into the realm of the orthodox Christianity.[9] To meditate within the soul upon qualities of God or virtues and vices, one could allow the parade of concepts to flow through the mind as images. This ability to experience concepts and ideas as images that may be "sensed" in the eye of the mind, the *oculus imaginationis*, was seen as a manifestation in the microcosm (humanity) of the same "hierophany" (to borrow the term coined by Eliade) that exists in the world of nature.

From this perspective, the miracle of creation was seen as a "book" that could be "read." Moral explication and revelation in the world of creation through an informed perception of its parts and functions had always been a pastime of the medieval scholar who, as George Boas writes, "was accustomed to the idea that the whole world, of nature as well as of art, was a sort of rebus, the deciphering of which would produce not scientific laws as we use that term, but moral lessons."[10] Thus the eye of medieval man perceived the interiority of the soul as peopled with images, embodying the concepts with which he dealt; and without, in the external world of nature, the same rule could be applied. For him the heights of the mountains and the depths of streams, together with the qualities of flower and beast, spoke an eloquent language.

During the Renaissance, philosophies that had been placed on the back burner in favor of Aristotle (as interpreted by the scholastics) began to reemerge. Thanks to the translations of Marsilio Ficino, the Neoplatonic ideas of Plotinus gained currency once more, and his interpretation of Egyptian hieroglyphs was widely accepted. In the *Enneads* he writes that:

> the wise of Egypt . . . indicated the truth where, in their effort towards philosophical statement, they left aside the writing-forms that take in the detail of words and sentences . . . and drew pictures instead, engraving in the temple-inscriptions a separate image for every separate item.[11]

With the circumstances so well disposed towards the epitomization of knowledge in the form of images, it is not suprising that when a manuscript of Horapollo's *Hieroglyphica* was discovered in the early part of the fifteenth century, it was a seed that fell on fertile ground. This book, said to be by an Alexandrian Egyptian of the second or fourth century C.E., claims to lay bare the secret meanings of the Egyptian hieroglyphs.[12] What it did in fact accomplish, regardless of the historical truth of its assertions, was to confirm and perpetuate the

Renaissance view that hieroglyphs had been used by the Egyptians to embody sacred knowledge in cryptic images. Such images served the dual function of hiding their meaning from the profane and expressing profound ideas in a way that could not be accomplished by words alone. This was in keeping with the Egyptomania that swept through the learned circles of Europe during the Renaissance, which greatly influenced such things as Hermeticism, emblem books, and alchemy.

All of these elements must now be considered in the light of "The Art of Memory." Said to have been invented by the Greek poet Simonides, this art had originally been used by classical orators for recalling the subject matter of their speeches.[13] The primary classical sources for the Art were Cicero,[14] the pseudo-Ciceronean *Ad Herrenium*,[15] and Quintillian.[16] It was taken up in late antiquity and the middle ages as a tool of the clergy for preaching and as a technique for meditation. The foundation of the art was imaginal, for the image embodied the concepts one wished to remember or meditate upon. Emotionally striking images representing a subject would be fabricated and set in their *loci*, their place. This *loci* could be a room in an imaginary building,[17] a position on a rigorously memorized grid,[18] or a rung on an allegorical ladder.[19] Metrodorus of Scepsis was even said to have placed his images in a zodiacal system, as Giordano Bruno was later to recommend with great enthusiasm.[20] The emotionally striking nature of the image—figures covered in blood or engaged in comic acts—served to insure that the image would be remembered, while the spatial orientation of the images within a memory structure lent order to the concepts. Buildings could be memorized from experience or simply created in the imagination as an organizational system. Carruthers has argued convincingly that medieval culture was based on memory and that these memorial arts formed the foundation of education.[21] While space prohibits a further examination of this topic, the art of memory and the Renaissance emphasis on imaginal knowledge must be kept in mind as of great importance when considering the origins of the Tarocchi of Mantegna.[22]

This established, we begin to see the atmosphere in which the Tarocchi of Mantegna was conceived and executed. If all of creation—

both the soul of man and the outside world of things and events—was an emblem itself, what better way to represent it than in a set of "hieroglyphic" images? With the rise of the art of engraving in the mid-fifteenth century, all of these elements had found the perfect vehicle.

The Engravings

As we come to examine the specific symbolism of the plates, we must remember above all else that, at the time of this *tarocchi*'s production, every pagan system, classical philosophy, and gentile science was seen as prefiguring the coming of Christ. This trend was all-pervasive and may be clearly seen in the well-known doctrine of the *prisca theologia*,[23] in which the prophetic voices of the past were pressed into service as foreshadowing the incarnation of the Logos. This tendency is almost certainly reflected in the Tarocchi of Mantegna as well.

The fifty cards are broken down and arranged into five groups of ten cards each. The five divisions are as follows:

> Group E or S
> **The States of Man**
> 1. Misero (Beggar)
> 2. Fameio (Serving man)
> 3. Artixan (Artisan)
> 4. Merchadante (Merchant)
> 5. Zintilomo (Gentleman)
> 6. Chavalier (Knight)
> 7. Doxe (Doge)
> 8. Re (King)
> 9. Imperator (Emperor)
> 10. Papa (Pope)
>
> Group D
> **The Muses and Apollo**
> 11. Caliope (Calliope)

12. Urania
13. Terpsicore (Terpsichore)
14. Erato
15. Polimnia (Polyhymnia)
16. Talia (Thalia)
17. Melpomene
18. Euterpe
19. Clio
20. Apollo

Group C
The Liberal Arts and Sciences
21. Grammatica (Grammar)
22. Loica (Logic)
23. Rhetorica (Rhetoric)
24. Geometria (Geometry)
25. Aritmetricha (Arithmetic)
26. Musicha (Music)
27. Poesia (Poetry)
28. Philosofia (Philosophy)
29. Astrologia (Astrology)
30. Theologia (Theology)

Group B
The Genii and Virtues[24]
31. Iliaco (Genius of Light)
32. Chronico (Genius of Time)
33. Cosmico (Genius of the Cosmos)
34. Temperancia (Temperance)
35. Prudencia (Prudence)
36. Forteza (Fortitude)
37. Iusticia (Justice)
38. Charita (Charity)
39. Speranza (Hope)
40. Fides (Faith)

Group A
Nine Firmaments and The First Cause[25]
41. Luna (Moon)
42. Mercurio (Mercury)
43. Venus
44. Sol (Sun)
45. Marte (Mars)
46. Iupiter (Jupiter)
47. Saturno (Saturn)
48. Octava Spera (Eighth Sphere)
49. Primo Mobile (Prime Mover)
50. Prima Causa (First Cause)

The preceding list numbered one through fifty and with letters from E to A make it clear that the flow of the series runs numerically from Misero to Prima Causa. And if one follows the sequence of letters, it runs from the Firmaments and First Cause to The States of Man. This dual direction of ascent and descent clearly has much in common with the firmly established medieval representations of ladders as allegories for the stages of the ascent to virtue; such figures are found in the illustrated manuscripts of Prudentius and in many of the works of Ramon Llull.[26] (See Figure 1.) All these appear to find their inspiration in Jacob's dream of the ladder.[27] This concept of ascent and descent is a common one in medieval and Renaissance allegory and underlies the organization the Tarocchi of Mantegna.

The plates themselves seem to be based on the rules that were gradually being established at the same time for playing card composition. They usually show one figure positioned more or less uniformly in the set in relation to the horizon line. With few exceptions the figures are of uniform size and proportion. While this could be seen as simply an aesthetic decision based on compositional requirements, it would be worthwhile to investigate the *Ars Memoria* rules for places and images as a basis for composition and design in these engravings.[28]

Figure 1

The Ladder of Ascent and Descent. From Ramon Llull's *Liber de ascensu et descensu intellectus* (edition of Valencia, 1512).

The plate titled "Prima Causa" or First Cause is all-encompassing and contains the rest of the series within itself. (See Figure 2.) The entire cosmology represented in the set is one of a hierarchically organized, unbroken Chain of Being. As Shephard notes, an important difference between the Tarocchi of Mantegna and other early tarot "decks" is that the Mantegna series is rigidly numbered and ordered, and therein lies a key to Renaissance cosmology.[29] The very idea of playing cards is based on hierarchy, and thus lends itself admirably to an exposition of a universe that was understood to be rigidly ordered. While this concept of order may seem strange to the modern reader in this day of relativism and chaos, as Mircea Eliade points out, in order to manifest sacred space, a central point of orientation is necessary, a "center of the world."[30] In traditional cosmology, all things fell into their natural place because all things could be related back to their creator and sustainer. The Mantegna Tarocchi is a manifestation of this cosmology, for within its design, the Prima Causa is the source from which all things come, and to which all things return. This plate provides us with a key to the structure of the entire series.[31]

The imagery of the engravings is arranged according to the medieval version of the standard Aristotelian/Ptolemaic conception of the universe that grudgingly held sway until the blows of the Copernican revolution eventually won the day. In this geocentric world view, the Earth is pictured at the center of the universe; it is surrounded by the concentric spheres of the elements and the "wandering stars" (the classical planets). The planetary spheres are surrounded by the fixed stars (the belt of the zodiac), which are in turn moved by the Primo Mobile. Thus, all rests within the bosom of the Prima Causa. Since the universe was seen as revealing God's order, all things in creation were thought to be inextricably tied to this order in a hierarchy that men spent their entire lives attempting to discover.[32] This is clearly what the engraving of the Prima Causa displays. We see the Earth surrounded by a series of concentric rings showing the sublunar spheres, as well as the eternal celestial spheres.

Within this structured hierarchy the rest of the emblems fall into

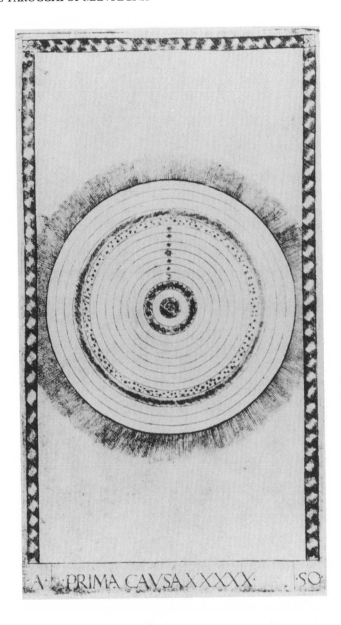

Figure 2
Prima Causa, Tarocchi del Mantegna

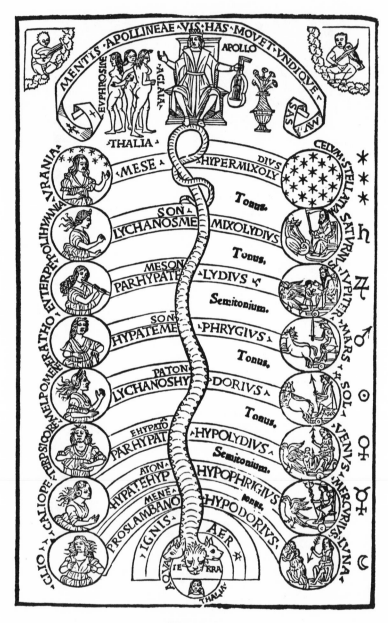

Figure 3
The Music of the Spheres from Gafurius's *Practica Musice*, 1496.

place. The States of Man appear as stages in an evolutionary process, as ways that man may manifest, and the strata of lessons with which he is confronted. Occupying the highest point in this group is the image of the Pope, who, as God's vicar on earth, was a leading force in both secular and ecclesiastical affairs.

Turning to group D, we see in the figure of Apollo a scarcely veiled Christ, the Logos principle that orders the heavens through the intermediary of the Muses, who govern the celestial spheres. Apollo is seated in a position reminiscent of manuscript illustrations portraying Christ seated with his feet upon the globe of the heavens and earth. In group D we see that each Muse possesses a globe, except for Thalia, who sits upon the earth in the same position reserved for her in a fifteenth-century plate from Gafurius's *Practica Musice* (1496), which depicts the music of the spheres.[33] (See Figure 3.)

Considerations of space prevent a detailed examination of each card, but perhaps a glance at two or three will shed some light on the types of symbolism reflected in the individual emblems. Rather than offering definitive explanations, these remarks are offered as suggestions for further inquiry.

Misero (Figure 4.)

This image of "The Beggar," which portrays an aged pilgrim leaning upon his staff, is suggestive of Psalm 23: "I fear no evil; for thou art with me; thy rod and thy staff, they comfort me."

Here we see man in his lowest possible condition. His desires, as represented by the two dogs, run wild, gnawing and worrying him. The dogs may also represent the condition of his body and worldly affairs; drawn, hungry, and afflicted by vermin, they plague Misero. Were it not for the staff that supports him, he would be unable to steady his gaze. A new covenant had been established between man and God with the coming of Christ, who proclaimed that "In me the laws are fulfilled." The lowest possible condition of man had been raised a rung with this covenant. The temple of Solomon had been the repository of the Ark of the first covenant and was representative of it in many ways. Perhaps our beggar stands in the ruins of the old

Figure 4
Misero, Tarocchi del Mantegna

Figure 5
Zintilomo, Tarocchi del Mantegna

covenant, the broken walls of the Temple of Solomon, raised by
Christ's love from humanity's previous state. It is God's grace, as
manifest in this second covenant, which sustains him, though the trees
before him bear no fruit.

Zintilomo (Figure 5.)

In the card "The Gentleman," our Beggar has come some distance.
He is well attired and now holds a falcon on his wrist, trained and ready
to soar through the skies in contemplation. He is standing, which
seems to suggest that he is in an active mode—we have not yet moved
to the seated contemplative figures of the Emperor or Pope. His
desires, his body, and spirit are well cared for, as evinced by the well
fed dogs restrained by his servant, who is gazing towards the earth.
Significantly, a servant now appears whose sole responsibility is to care
for what the dogs represent. Later in the group, when the gentleman
becomes a knight, this servant will become a page and gaze at the
heavens rather than at dogs and soil. Our gentleman is also wearing
spurs, which could be seen as representing the theme of restraint and
control, though perhaps they have a deeper meaning.

We must keep in mind that the multiple characters in the individual
plates represent parts of a single person or way of being. Moreover, it
would be unwise to view the images in the States of Man series as
representing the travails of a single individual; instead, we might view
them as a set of lessons for humanity as a whole, all or none of which
may be realized by a particular individual.

Temperancia (Figure 6.)

Let us now look to the Genii and the Virtues group, and to an
engraving that raises some interesting questions regarding the relationship between pagan and Christian elements in this series.

The plate "Temperance" represents one of the classic cardinal
virtues, usually shown in a group with Justice, Fortitude, and Prudence. This virtue is often represented with two vessels, the contents
of one being poured into the other. These are traditionally wine and
water, the wine being mixed with the water to temper it. This seems

Figure 6
Temperancia, Tarocchi del Mantegna

to be the meaning of the two vessels held by the figure in this plate. But what of the pig at her feet? What meaning could it have? Perhaps we will find a clue in the other depictions of the virtues.

Indeed, turning to the individual images of the virtues, we see that each virtue, without exception, has a beast at its feet. Traditionally, the virtues are often found paired with an antithetical vice. In the illustrated manuscripts of the *Psychomachia*, for example, we see virtues and vices locked in mortal combat; and in the stonework of cathedrals, victorious virtues stand atop the vanquished bodies of the vices to which they correspond.[34] In pairing the virtues with the vices, perhaps we see a hint of the fact that they cannot be considered separately; the one contains the other. One looked to the heart of a thing for its weakness. Following this tradition, the mirror of Temperance shows the beast its own face. In other words, when an individual gives way to the charms and wiles of generation, without the moderation of temperance, that individual succumbs to the charms of Circe, the sorceress who transformed Odysseus's men into swine.[35] Reason, in the form of Hermes, provided Odysseus with a drug which kept him from being transformed into a beast like his men. Renaissance philosopher Giordano Bruno refers to this theme when he remarks upon a "Circean enchantment put to the service of generation,"[36] and it is against the excesses of unrestrained impulse that Temperance arms us.

Reflecting further on this image, the two vessels with the water flowing between them suggests a deeper level of interpretation. Some Neoplatonic readers of Homer had seen Circe as a symbol of the cycle of *metensomatosis* or reincarnation.[37] From this perspective, the emblem of Temperance may represent a conflation of pagan and Christian themes, seeing that men are sent from one body to another based on the condition of their souls. In time this lady imparts wisdom, and the soul sees itself in her mirror. The pig is transformed into a man; or, if a soul degenerates, the man's soul manifests in the body of a pig, which suited it all along. According to this interpretation, Temperance is learned the hard way, in the peregrinations of incarnation.

Conclusion

It is very instructive to meditate upon the symbolism of the individual emblems, but we must not lose sight of the fact that the set of engravings consitutes a whole, which is far more than a mere collection of elements. In the series as a whole, we discern an attempt to organize the emblematic traditions of the Renaissance into a "book" that reflects the totality of the universe, but does not readily reveal its meaning. In order to understand the concepts embodied in the engravings, one had to bring a formidable education to them. The images, in turn, helped one to organize the knowledge that one already possessed, and helped to make new connections. In the process of absorbing and digesting the images and their meanings, they were made one's own.[38]

The emblem is a point of ingress to the living ideal, both in the collective and in the individual who attempts to embrace it. These emblems, in fact, point us to "such images as we may conceive to lie within the soul of the wise."[39] They also point toward a way in which knowledge is "stored" in the great thesaurus of memory, that realm in which the image precedes the word.[40]

Since the Renaissance, a great deal of territory has been lost in the realm of the imagination. Having become the stomping ground of advertisement-induced fantasy and the affect images of television networks, its landscape has grown cancerous and bleak. Couliano suggests that the imagination occupies its current degraded position in our culture as a result of the attacks of Catholics and Protestants in the Reformation and Counter-Reformation. Seemingly at odds, both groups agreed that the treasure house of the imagination had to be razed.[41] We stand today in the ruins of a once great garden. Amidst its dried up fountains and withered flowers stand the statues of the Muses, the great figures of the Liberal Arts, and the Virtues. Grammarians and pedants wrangle terminology, forgetting that "Though tight the net of words may bind, How surely Truth slips out!"[42] Perhaps by focusing our long-absent attention in this place, we may cause the garden to flourish once more.

Notes

1. A. M. Hind, *Early Italian Engraving: A Critical Catalogue, with Reproduction of All Prints Described* (New York, 1938), I, 225.

2. Hind, *Early Italian Engraving*, I, 225.

3. John Shephard, *The Tarot Trumps: Cosmos in Miniature* (Wellingborough, Northamptonshire: The Aquarian Press, 1985), 41.

4. For more information on the differences between the two sets, see Hind, *Early Italian Engraving*, I, 224–225. The two sets are clearly by two different engravers and seem to be separated in time by some years. In addition, there are small differences in the allegorical material employed to relate ideas.

5. Erwin Panofsky, *The Life and Art of Albrecht Durer* (Princeton: Princeton University Press, 1955), 31. The fact that plates from the Tarocchi of Mantegna were to be bound together with an illustrated edition of the Triumphs of Petrarch would seem to lend some support to Gertrude Moakley's hypothesis that the Tarot in general were to a great degree based on the Renaissance triumphal processions. See Gertrude Moakley, *The Tarot Cards Painted by Bonifacio Bembo* (New York: The New York Public Library, 1966).

6. See *The Hieroglyphica* of Pierio Valeriano, Alciati's *Emblemata*, and such densely populated works as Francesco Colonna's *Hypnerotomachia Poliphili*.

7. Hind, *Early Italian Engraving*, I, 222.

8. Aristotle, *De Anima* 3.8, in *The Complete Works of Aristotle*, edited by Jonathan Barnes (Princeton: Princeton University Press, 1984).

9. St. Thomas Aquinas, *Basic Writings of St. Thomas Aquinas*, edited by Anton C. Pegis (New York: Random House, 1945) I, I, question I, article 9.

10. Horapollo, *Hieroglyphica*, translated by George Boas (Princeton: Princeton University Press, 1993), 4.

11. Plotinus, *Enneads* 5.8.6 (MacKenna translation).

12. Horapollo, *Hieroglyphica*.

13. For information on the classical sources of the tradition of Simonides' invention of the art, as well as other interesting material, see Frances Yates, *The Art of Memory* (Chicago: University of Chicago Press, 1966), 27–30. This work by Yates is the primary English source for information on esoteric memory systems in particular and the Ars Memoria in general.

14. Cicero, *De Oratore*, translated by E. W. Sutton and H. Rackham

(London: Heinemann, 1942–1948).

15. pseudo-Cicero, *Ad Herrenium*, translated by H. Caplan (Cambridge: Harvard University Press, 1954). This work is included with the writings of Cicero in the Loeb Classical Library.

16. M. Fabius Quintillian, *Institutio oratoria*, translated by H. E. Butler (Cambridge: Harvard University Press, 1922); see also Yates, *The Art of Memory*, 1–26.

17. pseudo-Cicero, *Ad Herrenium* 3.20.33.

18. Mary Carruthers, *The Book of Memory* (Cambridge: Cambridge University Press, 1990), 249. This grid could be filled with ordered images or with letters, under which could be organized yet further grids. This use of letters carries over into Llull's system and remains of it may be seen today in acronyms.

19. See notes 26 and 27 below.

20. Yates, *The Art of Memory*, 19. Examples of Bruno's use of astrology in his memory systems abound in his works. An excellent example of this is his *Lo Spaccio de la Bestia Trionfante* available in an English translation: Giordano Bruno, *The Expulsion of the Triumphant Beast*, translated by Arthur D. Imerti (New Brunswick: Rutgers University Press, 1964).

21. Carruthers, *The Book of Memory*. Carruthers suggests that one of the basic assumptions in which the learning of the medieval era was grounded was that human learning was based in the memorative process. The medieval book was itself a servant to the memory, for its illustrations, colors, and letters were organized to train the memory of the individual who studied it.

22. For more on this see Yates, *The Art of Memory*, as well as the work of Carruthers already cited. The Art of Memory and related splinter systems go hand in hand with Western culture's love of allegory throughout much of history. The expression of exquisite and subtle philosophical and moral arguments in the form of allegorical memory systems was, up until the seventeenth century, much more the rule than the exception. Such works as the *Divine Comedy*, Brandt's *Ship of Fools*, *The Psychomachia* of Prudentius, and *The Romance of The Rose* are all arguably representative of different types of memory systems. For an interesting discussion of *The Romance of The Rose*, see Maxwell Luria, *A Reader's Guide to the Roman de la Rose* (Archon Books, 1982).

23. The idea that a secret tradition—an "ancient theology"—with Orphic

OLIVER PERRIN

origins had been passed down through antiquity, informing the great philosophers, was highly influential in the Renaissance. The notion that this tradition was "a Christianity before the coming of Christ," and that the words of the philosophers could be interpreted as prophesying Christ's arrival, was a common one. See Edgar Wind, *Pagan Mysteries in the Renaissance* (New York: Norton, 1968), 20–22.

24. For more information on the virtues see Adolf Katzenellenbogen, *Allegories of the Virtues and Vices in Medieval Art* (Toronto: University of Toronto Press, 1989).

25. For other memory images in this same tradition see the Memory theatre of Giulio Camillo (Yates, *The Art of Memory*, 129–159) and the planetary images in Giordano Bruno, *On the Composition of Signs, Images and Ideas*, translated by Charles Doria (New York: Willis, Locker & Owens, 1991).

26. For more on the ladder of virtue and its relationship to the manuscripts of Prudentius, see Katzenellenbogen, *Allegories of the Virtues and Vices in Medieval Art*, 22–26, and Helen Woodruff, *The Illustrated Manuscripts of Prudentius* (Cambridge: Harvard University Press, 1929). Mention of Llull's use of ladders is made in Yates, *The Art of Memory*, 179; see also Ramon Llull, *Doctor Illuminatus: A Ramon Llull Reader*, edited and translated by Anthony Bonner (Princeton: Princeton University Press, 1993), 241, 293.

27. Genesis 28:12. Jacob's dream of angels ascending and descending a ladder had been taken up into the Christian tradition at a fairly early date as an allegorical representation of several themes, among them that of the ascent to contemplative life and descent to the active life; the ladder of virtue and vice; and the ladder of creation on which the elements of the universe are placed in hierarchal order.

28. For information on medieval rules for places or *loci* that would lend themselves admirably to embodiment in playing cards, see Carruthers, *The Book of Memory*, 143–144.

29. Shephard, *The Tarot Trumps: Cosmos in Miniature*, 44.

30. Mircea Eliade, *The Sacred and The Profane: The Nature of Religion* (New York: Harcourt Brace Jovanovich, 1987), 22.

31. Shephard, *The Tarot Trumps: Cosmos in Miniature*, 44. Here Shephard is of a similar opinion.

32. For an amusing example of this hierarchy in action, see the tale of

Camillo's encounter with the lion and his dominance of it by way of superior "solar virtue" in Yates, *The Art of Memory*, 133–134.

33. Jean Seznec, *The Survival of the Pagan Gods* (Princeton: Princeton University Press, 1953), 9, 140–141.

34. Katzenellenbogen, *Allegories of The Virtues and Vices in Medieval Art*, 14.

35. Homer, *Odyssey*, book 10.

36. Giordano Bruno, *The Heroic Frenzies*, translated by Paul Eugene Memmo, Jr. (Chapel Hill: University of North Carolina Press, 1964), 60. In this passage Bruno is referring to women and their beauty and charms which influence men. It is interesting that Bruno is discussing Circe in a work devoted to revealing the meaning of a series of emblems.

37. Robert Lamberton, *Homer the Theologian* (Berkeley: University of California Press, 1986), 41–42, 115–118. Here Lamberton cites Porphyry as preserved by Stobaeus, on Circe as a universal force of *metensomatosis* and Hermes as the reason that allows the soul to escape this cycle.

38. For a dramatic example of this process see Carruthers, *The Book of Memory*, 179–182, where she relates Abelard's account of Heloise's taking of the veil.

39. Plotinus, *Enneads* 5.8.5.

40. Carruthers, *The Book of Memory*, 33. For another, somewhat later example of interior structures, see Teresa of Avila's *Interior Castle*, where structures of the soul are set forth. Useful material is to be found in Adam McLean, *The Alchemical Mandala* (Grand Rapids: Phanes Press, 1989), where he reintroduces alchemical diagrams and emblems as meditational devices. This book is of great use in suggesting contemplative approaches to this material.

41. Ioan P. Couliano, *Eros and Magic in the Renaissance* (Chicago: University of Chicago Press, 1987), 202–203, 222–223.

42. *The Tao*, translated by Charles H. Mackintosh (Theosophical Society of America, 1926), 21.

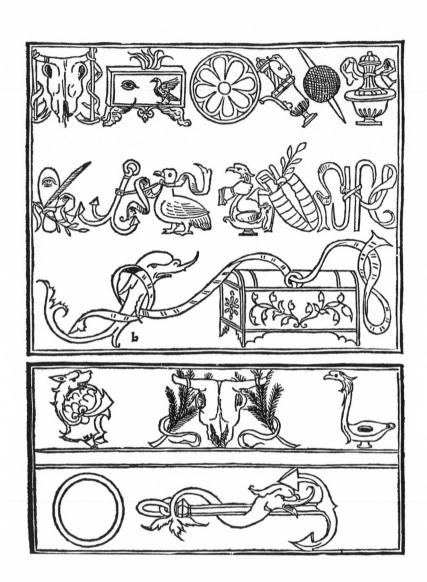

Emblematic "Hieroglyphs"
From the *Hypnerotomachia* or *Love-Dream of Poliphilo* (1499).

Speaking in Hieroglyphics

PETER LAMBORN WILSON

A KING who demanded of Paracelsus the secret of alchemy was told, "Surely your majesty realizes that it's your majesty who knows the secret of transmutation, not this humble physician. Kings don't merely change base metal to gold, but rather change *nothing* to gold—by granting licenses to banks to declare credit!" This demonstrates one of two possibilities: either that Paracelsus foretold the modern counterfeit state—or else, that the counterfeit state had already produced a Paracelsus, a critic able to explain it to itself.

The theory of hieroglyphs and emblems in Renaissance Hermeticism involved a *projective* semiotics rather than a mere *reflective* semiotics as practiced since de Saussure—not just the analysis of signs, but their deployment. Therefore the Church took an active interest in the moral purpose of this magical "linguistics," ostensibly because of the ambiguity of knowledge and power, but more deeply, to protect its own monopoly of interpretation. Now, the Spectacle can be analyzed as a Hermetic phenomenon (rather than Cartesian or Newtonian); and, as Couliano pointed out, advertising is a science of images in exactly the same way that certain aspects of Renaissance occultism comprised a science of images. My purpose in studying the hieroglyphs—not real Egyptian hieroglyphs but the Renaissance "misinterpretations" of the hieroglyphs—is to understand how this science works. First, because I want to disenchant myself. Second, because—who knows?—I may have a need for *reenchantment*.

Moreover, the hieroglyphs constitute a casebook study of "fortuitous mistranslation." By attempting to understand Egyptian writing through a series of filters—Islamic Hermeticism, Kabbalah, Gnosticism, Alexandrian Hermeticism—all masking the actual forgetting

and absence of the original meaning of that writing—the Renaissance
occultists constructed a new and brilliant meaning for the mysterious
glyphs—or, rather, a new *way* of meaning. They read the hieroglyphs
as emblems, visual codes which both concealed and revealed the
"essence" of a thing, in a manner both rational and intuitive, both
mediated (like allegory) and unmediated (as in the "unio mystica" of
the thing and its symbol). Of course, the "real" Egyptian hieroglyphs
cannot be analyzed or interpreted in this way; they cannot be "de-
coded" by magic. And yet the Renaissance sages were quite correct to
believe that Egypt—the very land of magic—would have embodied
magical ideas in its system of writing. The modern world finds
Renaissance hieroglyphology to be utterly useless because it was
based on *mistranslation*—but this objection itself is utterly pointless.
Any visual semiotic system with enough mystery and prestige would
have served the purposes of the Renaissance mages equally well—it
just happened to be Egyptian hieroglyphs. What they discovered with
this epistemological device, however, was of earth-shaking importance.

I first started wondering about the "false hieroglyphs" in Rome,
where I came across Piranesi's wonderful designs for faux-Egyptian
fireplaces, and above all the spooky little Emblematical church he
built for the Knights of Malta. As for the Emblem books, I've admired
Atalanta Fugiens for years. Now three new republications or translations of important works on Hermeticism* allow us to get back to the
origins of these artworks (which are already very late)—origins in the
Hermetic revival, in the original Hermetic flowering of Alexandria,
and in the strange history of the hieroglyphs. Of these books the most
fruitful proves to be *The Hieroglyphics of Horapollo*, which may have
been compiled as early as the fifth century C.E. Horapollo—if there
really was such a person—seems to have inherited a jumble of
Hermetic teaching along with some semi-accurate information on
the "real" hieroglyphs. But the whole package was accepted by
Europe in the fifteenth century as a true key to Egyptian wisdom,

---

* See last page for bibliography.

expressed in writing—not discursive but emblematic, in "natural not conventional signs" (to paraphrase the translator's preface). That is, signifier and signified were thought to be "mysteriously" identical or objectively linked by a series of codings so that—for ancient and learned Egyptians—to read a text (or even a single character) was to absorb the "wisdom" of that text directly, and to write a text was to deploy that wisdom in active mode, without the mediation between text and context which characterizes alphabetical writing or even spoken language.

The hieroglyphs are paradoxically both *legible* and *enigmatic*; that is, since they constitute a universal language not linked to any one particular language, they may potentially be deciphered by any reader at any time; and yet they are coded, "hermetic" and esoteric, and thus very nearly inaccessible. As Horapollo's first translator, Filippo Fasanini, put it:

> [The hieroglyphs] were enigmatic and symbolic engravings, which were much used in ancient times and preceding centuries, especially among Egyptian prophets and teachers of religion, who considered it unlawful to expose the mysteries of wisdom in ordinary writing to lay people, as we do. And if they judged something to be a worthy piece of knowledge, they represented it in plain drawings of animals and other things in such a way that it was not easy for anyone to guess. But if anyone had learned and studied thoroughly from Aristotle and others the properties of each thing, the particular nature and essence of each animal, he would at length, by putting together his conjectures about these symbols, grasp the enigma of the meaning and, because of this knowledge, be honored above the uninitiated crowd.[1]

Renaissance emphasis on the "elite" understanding of a code which appears *both open and closed* has little to do with mere snobbishness, but is rather a measure of the potential *power* of the glyphs. He who cracks the code can deploy the system, which expresses essences and thus involves magic power. He who sees the text, whether he understands it or not, will be influenced ("at a distance") by these essences. All kinds of writing are linked with magic, as we know—and in fact the *origin* of writing probably lies in magic (a theory mythologized in the "invention of writing" by Thoth Hermes)—but here, in Horapollo's hieroglyphs, the Renaissance perceived not the distant legendary traces of writing as magic, but a direct application of the principle, still surviving and retrievable in these fragments of the oldest and (in fact) *original* method of writing.

The theory of Plotinus on the hieroglyphs helped the Renaissance mages understand how much spiritual power depended on their success or failure at decipherment: in effect, the hieroglyphs present "Platonic archetypes" as direct objects of knowledge, an experience described by Plotinus as the life of the gods:

> It must not be thought that in the Intelligible World the gods and the blessed see propositions; everything expressed there is a beautiful image, such as one imagines to be in the soul of a wise man, images not drawn, but real. And therefore the Ancients said that real being is ideas and substances.

and

> It seems to me that the Egyptian sages, either working by right reasoning or spontaneously, when they desired to represent things through wisdom [*Sophia*], did not use letters descriptive of words and sentences, imitating the sounds and pronunciation of propositions, but drew pictures, and carved one picture for each thing in their temples, thus making manifest the description of that thing. Thus each picture was a kind of understanding and wisdom and substance and given all at once, and not discursive reasoning and deliberation.[2]

These ideas are enlarged upon in

> a gloss that Marsilio Ficino, the translator of Plotinus, wrote on the passage in which hieroglyphs were said to be Platonic ideas made visible.

The gloss runs: "The Egyptian priests, when they wished to signify divine things, did not use letters, but whole figures of plants, trees, and animals; for God doubtless has a knowledge of things which is not complex discursive thought about its subject, but is, as it were, the simple and steadfast form of it. Your thought of time, for instance, is manifold and mobile, maintaining that time is speedy and by a sort of revolution joins the beginning to the end. It teaches prudence, produces much, and destroys it again. The Egyptians comprehend this whole discourse in one stable image, painting a winged serpent, holding its tail in its mouth. Other things are represented in similar images, as Horus describes."[3]

In other words, the ability to read the hieroglyphs amounted to an auto-divinization, an existential participation in the creative cause/effect power of Ideas-as-images. This explains why the glyphs are sometimes described as a priestly or religious language, and sometimes as a magic language: one can use them either in god-like, god-directed contemplation and self-perfection, or else in the practice of magic. The magician, according to the *Greek Magical Papyri*, in truth is a god (in the sense of "mighty spirit" rather than "theological principle").

The hieroglyphs represent no spoken oral-aural language, but rather a visual imaginal language, a semiotics of signs that are seen. As Boas puts it:

The passage from intellectual to visual contemplation is perhaps made easier to understand by certain passages from Pico della Mirandola and Leone Ebreo. For most Neoplatonists sensible beauty was primarily visual and the eye was to sensible beauty what the intellect was to intelligible beauty. "What the eye is in corporeal things," says Pico, "that very thing is the mind in the realm of the spirit." So in Leone we find an eloquent passage in which the eye is to the microcosm what the sun is to the macrocosm. Vision, he maintains, has as its object the entire corporeal world, whereas the other senses perceive but parts of it. The medium of the other senses is one of the grosser elements, but vision has its medium in "the luminous spiritual transparency, that is the air illuminated by the light of heaven, which exceeds in beauty all other parts of the world, as the eye exceeds all other parts of the animal body."[4]

Now, it is true that we moderns have arrived at a critique of the "Empire of the Eye" and of the privileged primacy of sight, among all the senses, in the "discourse" of Western Civilization. Charles Fourier, who was himself a kind of Hermeticist (and much admired as such by certain Martinists, Illuminists, and Masons of his era), may perhaps claim the honor of first challenging the monarchy of the Eye with the democracy of the Nose. Most immediate of the senses, smell has none of the abstract alienating qualities of sight; moreover, the organizing principle of Fourier's cosmos is aroma, or rather the "aromal rays" which connect all things through a subtle but palpable *eros*, from stars to flowers. The rule of sight, which results in the visual tyranny of Bentham's Panopticon, must be overthrown by the orgiastic principle of aromas, which results in the utopia of the Phalanstery—the utopia of desire.

But we should recall that the Hermeticists were engaged in a struggle with two forces—Scholastic Theology, and emergent "modern science" (Bacon, Newton, Descartes)—which both agreed to exclude the entire *sensorium* as a valid epistemological means. For theology, faith takes precedence over any sense; for science, this absolute category is occupied by mathematics or symbolic logic. For theology and science, the "material bodily principle" is void of all significance except as a mechanism which exhibits the action of certain "laws"; it has no value in itself. The Hermeticists, although they adhered to Neoplatonism with its emanationist hierarchy of ontological values—the absolute and the contingent—nevertheless entertained a much higher estimation of material reality. This generalization can be bolstered by comparing the attitudes of Theology, Science, and Hermeticism toward the Earth itself, the emblematic embodiment of the bodily principle. For faith, the Earth was *fallen*— a locus of sin and the punishment for sin which is mortality. For science, Earth is "dead matter" to be measured by a detached intelligence which has transcended all contingency. But for Hermeticism Earth is a living being, a Goddess in effect—and is the indispensable locus of theophany, the shining-through of the Gods in Nature, in material becoming. Of the three paradigms, theology gave a negative accounting of Earth, revealing the depth of the "gnostic trace" which still informed its psychology of body-hatred. Science gave the Earth a neutral valuation, which allowed in effect the "conquest" of Nature in technology. Only Hermeticism gave the Earth a positive valuation. The exaltation of the sight, the "noblest" of the senses, arose from this positive valuation of the "world," even though the sense in question was seen as a link between the material level and the higher level of "essences" or archetypes.

The sphere of the glyphs and emblems occupies an in-between space, a liminal "isthmus" (as the Sufis call it) between the material and the divine spheres. This is the level of the *mundus imaginalis*, in Henry Corbin's phrase, the world of imagination or of images, which is both *immaterial and visual* (like a dream or vision). The glyph, looked at from this perspective, is a reflection of the imaginal sphere which can be seen even in this world, and can thus serve as a door to the highest level, the divine. However, like all symbols, the glyph points two ways: it also functions as a means of transmission from the god-world or realm of power, through the Images, "down" to the level of material sense. Once again, the glyph shows both a divine contemplative aspect, and an imaginal/magical aspect. For this reason, hieroglyphic knowledge could be expected to possess an active mode, in which manipulation of the language of "essences" would have an effect in the material world, both as source of knowledge and as source of power. Precisely because the world of the senses is not *primarily* the locus of sin nor mere "inanimate corpuscular material" in mechanical motion; precisely because the natural world is the living responsive matrix and theatre of the divine archetypes and essences; precisely for these reasons, magic was seen as a positive *praxis* leading to the harmony and mutual divinization of Nature and Culture—a program of no interest to theology or to science—but surely of some interest to us, here and now.

The glyph or image, therefore, is a visual package in which various levels of meaning have been packed, accordion-fashion, into an immediately-apprehensible sign. As Boas says, the emblems

> contained a set of meanings in layers. These layers had been distinguished early in Christian literature, one of the first discussions of which had been given by Clement of Alexandria. According to this Father, a hieroglyph might have a literal meaning, which is imitative, a figurative meaning (called by him "tropological"), and the allegorical meaning, which is "enigmatical." These distinctions were preserved throughout medieval and Renaissance discussions and in fact sometimes a fourth meaning was added, the anagogical. Thus the hieroglyphs of Horapollo were literally pictures of birds, beasts, and fish; allegorically, they meant certain gods and goddesses, certain times and seasons; tropologically, they might mean man's good and evil traits; anagogically, they conveyed such hidden messages as were expounded in the bestiaries.[5]

Some meditation on this structure will lead us to the process known in Islamic mysticism as *ta'wil* or "hermeneutic exegesis," in which a word, idea, or image is "traced back" through the layers of meaning to its "source." The glyphs, however, are not merely the passive objects of this hermeneutic, but are *also* the constituents of the very exegetical methodology itself. If individual hieroglyphic "words" reveal essences, we might say that the total field of operation of the glyphs and their interrelations constitutes a kind of "grammar" of essences. The glyphs teach the very process of their own decipherment. Taken together, they reveal a system of acquiring knowledge both about them and through them. The glyphs are an epistemological tool (or even "weapon") of great power; here one may legitimately speak of a *hieroglyphic science*. The fact that this science was not used successfully to decipher any actual real Egyptian inscriptions should not blind us to the genuine power of the science. In retrospect, we can see the arbitrary nature of the operation: virtually any set of signs could have been identified with any set of meanings (or "essences") with precisely the same result—provided only that the signs possessed *some* significance in the culture which deployed them. Horapollo already exhibits symptoms of this arbitrariness, giving the same sign two different meanings, or the same meaning a multitude of signs. In other words, what's important here is not *decoding* but *encoding*; not the decipherment of this or that emblem, but the *presence of the cipher*; above all, not Egyptian texts, but the power of the image. In Valeriano's commentary on the *Hieroglyphica* we read that "to speak in hieroglyphs [i.e. to deploy them rather than only interpret them] is nothing else than to lay open the nature of divine and human affairs."[6] The *reading* of the glyphs is the minor arcanum—the real science lies in their *composition*, or even in their creation, but above all in their *use*.

The *Hieroglyphica* can be studied from many points of view—art-historical, like Boas, or (like Iverson) as a chapter in the long-lost history of the real Egyptian hieroglyphs. For the moment, however, we're only interested in the cognitive structure: that is, the margin between the psychology and the ideology of the text. Whether consciously or unconsciously (it scarcely matters), Horapollo demonstrated a *mode of thinking*, a pattern for perception and cognition and expression, based on a complex of "structures" (the rebus, the enigma, the symbol, the allegory or "moral lesson," etc.) which may be applied to more than one set of actual contents or referents or specific meanings.

> When they wish to depict the Universe, they draw a serpent devouring its own tail, marked with variegated scales. By the scales they suggest the stars in the heavens. This beast is the heaviest of animals, as the earth is heaviest [of elements]. It is the smoothest, like water. And as each year it sheds its skin, it [represents] old age. But as each season of the year returns successively, it grows young again. But the fact that it uses its own body for food signifies that whatever things are generated in the world by Divine Providence are received back into it by [a gradual process of] diminution.[7]

In ideological terms we have here a typical Hermetic valuation of the "world" (the created universe, and the starry heavens) which exhibits none of the moral opprobrium of theology nor affectless neutrality of science. This is not the serpent of Genesis—nor of Linnaeus. As the earth resides at the attraction-point of cosmic gravity—and thus can be called "heavy"—so the snake must be "heavy" (by *essence*, not weight!) because it hugs the earth. The stars hug the earth too. In fact, Earth is the focus of cosmic *eros*—for the Hermeticists all follow Hesiod's theogony which posits Chaos, Eros, and Earth as the "first principles" of becoming. Water also hugs the earth, but introduces the image of waves (the snake imitates waves as it "undulates up and down while creeping along," as Valeriano explained in his gloss). The wave which disturbs the placidity of the primordial waters serves as a mythic image of the *clinamen* of Lucretius, the original "divigation" which gives rise to atomic matter. (And as Michel Serres points out in *Hermes*, the *clinamen* implies the "attractor," and thus the erotic nature of becoming.) The "world" grows old and sheds its skin but is then reborn: Nature is the paradoxical source of both mortality and immortality. Even "eternity" has a cyclic and material quality, represented by the serpent's autophagy; life is not a closed system, but depends on the "generosity of the divine," that is, the mysterious *antientropic principle* which (like Hesiod's Chaos) spontaneously gives rise to matter and attraction. And so on. The only aspect of all this which need concern us directly is that an image has been proposed which "contains" all this information, not as mere allegory (or not merely as allegory) but in a magical unified mode whereby the image *is* the information—provided one has the key, or can forge one out of wax and blank bits, like an old-fashioned burglar.)

Similarly, the year[8] "is" a woman, Isis, the Dog Star, the date-palm ("because the tree alone at each new moon sends forth a branch"); the hawk[9] (by a reverse process) "is" a god (Ares), the sun, the eye, or sight itself, sublime things *as well as* lowly things (because the hawk flies straight up and straight down), blood, victory. Here for the first time we note that—in this thought-way—an Image can represent two contradictory things. Symbols, originally the matching halves of a token (like a torn dollar bill), have two parts, and those parts can be dichotomous as well as harmonious. Benign and malign inversions can both take place. The hawk is also the soul[10] because it drinks only blood, and the soul also "is nourished" in blood—the blood is the life. The symbols themselves are double, and also redoubled. The hawk is the sun, and two hawks represent sexual intercourse (Ares and Aphrodite), because "they [the Egyptians] ascribe to the sun thirty sexual unions with a female."[11] But the same meaning is given to two crows, which are nocturnal rather than solar, and stand here for fidelity in love.

> To signify the only begotten, or birth, or a father, or the world, or man, they draw a scarab. The only begotten, because this animal is self-begotten, unborn of the female. For its birth takes place only in the following way. When the male wishes to have offspring, it takes some cow-dung and makes a round ball of it, very much in the shape of the world. Rolling it with its hind legs from east to west, it faces the east, so as to give it the shape of the world, for the world is borne from the east to the west. Then, burying this ball, it leaves it in the ground for twenty-eight days, during which time the moon traverses the twelve signs of the zodiac. Remaining here, the beetle is brought to birth. And on the twenty-ninth day, when it breaks the ball open, it rolls it into the water. For it considers this day to be the conjunction of the moon and the sun, as well as the birth of the world. When it is opened in the water, animals emerge which are beetles. It symbolizes birth for this very reason. And a father, because the beetle takes its birth from a father only. And the world, since its birth takes place in the shape of the world. And a man, since females do not exist among them. And there are three forms of beetle. The first, catlike, with rays coming from it, which they use as a symbol of the sun. For they say the male cat changes its pupils with the course of the sun. For they widen out towards morning at the rising of the god. And they become round like a ball at noon, and they appear somewhat faint as the sun is about to set. Wherefore in Heliopolis the statue of the god is in the form of a cat. And every beetle has thirty claws, because of the thirty days in the month, in which the sun, as it rises, runs its course. And the second kind of beetle is the two-horned and bull-shaped which is sacred to the moon, wherefore the Egyptian children say

that Taurus in heaven is the elevation of this goddess. Third, single-horned and *sui generis*, which they consider to be sacred to Hermes, is like the ibis.[12]

The scarab which thus clones itself gives birth without the mediation of the womb, just as the hieroglyph conveys meaning without the mediation of the discursive reason or the matrix of ordinary language. The glyph inserts itself directly into the understanding, like the beetle penetrating its solar ball, which is the "world," *materia prima*, the alchemical *hylê* —and also dung. The glyph is *self-born* (like the image of the bodhisattva in the lotus) rather than "only begotten" (*unigenitus* or *unicus*). The glyph divides and doubles, but it also *unifies*, and rests perfectly in itself, like an icon.

These mysteries receive some clarification in the emblem of the Vulture, which follows immediately.

WHAT THEY MEAN BY A VULTURE

When they mean a mother, or sight, or boundaries, or foreknowledge, or the year, or the heavens, or pity, or Athene, or Hera, or two drachmas, they draw a vulture. A mother, since there is no male in this species of animal. And they are born in this way: when the vulture hungers after conception, she opens her sexual organ to the North Wind and is covered by him for five days. During this period she takes neither food nor drink, yearning for child-bearing. But there is another species of vulture which conceives by the wind, the eggs of which serve only for food and are not fit for hatching. But when the vultures are impregnated by the wind, their eggs are fertile. The vulture stands for sight since of all other animals the vulture has the keenest vision. Then the sun is rising until it sets, it looks at it, and from the setting to the rising of the god, in that interval of time it provides food for its own use. It means boundaries, because when a war is about to break out, it limits the place in which the battle will occur, hovering over it for seven days. Foreknowledge, because of what has been said above and because it looks forward to the amount of corpses which the slaughter will provide it for food. For this reason the ancient kings sent out scouts to see what part of the battle-field the vultures were looking towards, whence they calculated who would be worsted. And the year, because in this animal's life there are divided the 365 days of the year during which the time of a year is fulfilled. For it gestates for 120 days, and feeds its young for the same number. And during the remaining 120, it takes care of itself, not in pregnancy nor in eating, but in preparing itself for another conception. And the remaining five days of the year, as I have already said, it consumes in intercourse with the wind. And pity, because it seems to some to be the very opposite of pity, since this animal destroys all things. But they were forced to say this, since in the 120 days in which it feeds its young, it does not fly, but busies itself about its nest and with food for its young. When it is at a loss to find food to prepare for its young, it cuts open its own thighs and allows its young to drink its blood, so that it may not lack food to give them. Athene and Hera, since it seems to the Egyptians that Athene rules over the upper hemisphere of heaven and Hera over the lower. Wherefore they hold it absurd that the heavens be male; female are the heavens. For the generation of the sun and the moon and the rest of the stars is accomplished in such a way that it is the work of the female. And the race of vultures, as was said above, is female only. Because of this, the Egyptians place the vulture as a crown on all female figures, wherefore the Egyptians extend the word to all goddesses—I abbreviate in order not to write about each in turn. Wishing to symbolize a mother, they draw a vulture, for the mother is a female animal. And the heavens, for they do not like to write the word "heaven" in the masculine, as I have said above, since their genesis is from Heaven. And two drachmas, because among the Egyptians, the monad is two lines, and the monad is the source of all number. It is logical therefore that when they wish to symbolize two drachmas they draw a vulture, since it seems to be a mother and a source, like the monad.[13]

This immeasurably rich emblem could be unpacked *ad infinitum*. Here is the feminine counterpart of the self-born scarab, the non-dual source of all meaning prior to linguistic elaboration and *reductio*, the self-generating womb, open to the wind, the spirit, the "holy spirit." But the dyadic principle appears here, the two-in-one (similar to the Taoist yin-yang disc), the very first stage of discrimination and separation: sight, the "abstract" sense, and *boundaries* or distinctions. The two-in-one is again paradoxical and seemingly contradictory: the vulture represents "pity, because it seems the very opposite of pity"— so hieroglyphs can work by opposites and masks as well as by the *coincidentia oppositorum* and the unveiling of essences. And here we are told (with what truth I know not nor greatly care) that for the ancient Egyptians the monad or original unity is represented by the figure of *two*!—as if the *archê*, the root of all things, generating all numbers but generated by itself alone, were already subject to the dyadic or dialectical principle.

The baboon "signifies" a wonderful set of items—the moon, the inhabited Earth, a priest, or anger, or a diver—but the most interesting is *"letters"* (i.e., the hieroglyphs themselves):

> letters, because here in Egypt a race of baboons exists who know their letters, in accordance with which, when a baboon was first cared for in a temple, the priest handed him a tablet and pen and ink. This was to attempt to find out whether he was of the race which knew its letters and whether he could write. Moreover, the animal is sacred to Hermes, the god of letters.[14]

The point here would seem to be that the glyph-system is so "natural" that even animals know it—so that animals are not only deployed as symbols in this system, but can also participate in it almost as creative partners with humans. Liturgical languages (like Hebrew or hiero-glyphics) are believed to exist outside the sphere of human relativity; they are not arbitrary, although they may be inaccessible (like glossolalia, or like undeciphered hieroglyphs). Such languages are used "cre-atively" by the gods, and can therefore be used *magically* by those humans who learn to reverse polarities, so to speak, and to use the language rather than merely receive it. Such a magical language is often ascribed to the birds or other animals—if only we had the key! (a favorite wish in fairy tales). The baboons, by bridging the gap between Nature and Culture, provide proof of this linguistic theory. While modern readers may reject the idea of a "divine origin" for anything so apparently arbitrary as language, I would prefer to see the baboon in the light of certain theories which emphasize the paralinguistic nature of language, its mysteriousness, its ludic quality, its "chaos" nature. The angry deep-diving moony purple-assed baboon—wise and tricky as Hermes—appeals to me greatly as an emblem of writing itself, and not just of hieroglyphics. Just as writing divides space into the archetypes, so the "clock" (or "calendar") divides time into segments as well—and the baboon is also the principle of the clock!

> Again, when they symbolize the two equinoxes, they draw the baboon, but seated. For in the two equinoxes of the year, it voids urine twelve times a day, once an hour. And it does the same thing during the two nights. Wherefore it is not illogical that on their water-clocks the Egyptians carve a seated baboon. And they make water drip from its penis, since, as has been said above, it indicates the twelve hours of the equinox... It is not without reason that they are pleased to do this, as they do other things, but also during the equinoxes the baboon, alone of all beasts, cries out each hour, twelve times a day.[15]

Leaving aside yet more wonders of the *Hieroglyphica* (which its translator, Boas, described as *banal*), we'll move on to a group involving the hieroglyphic theory more closely.

> SPEECH: To symbolize speech, they draw a tongue and a bloodshot eye. For the primary element of speech is the voice, the secondary the eyes. For words do not arise in the soul perfectly formed and changing with its changes, especially since other words are used for the soul among the Egyptians. And when they wish to symbolize speech differently, they draw a tongue placed above a hand: thus giving the primacy of speech-making to the tongue, and to the hand, which carries out the desires of the tongue, second place.[16]

> EGYPTIAN LETTERS: To denote Egyptian letters, or a sieve, or a scribe, or a limit, ink and a reed are drawn. Egyptian letters, for all writing is done

with these among the Egyptians. For they write with a reed and not with anything else. And a sieve, since the sieve first was used for making bread, being made from reeds. Accordingly, they show that everyone who eats should know his letters. But he who does not, should use another art. Wherefore education among them is called *Sbo*. Which being interpreted means "full nourishment." And a scribe, since he distinguishes between life and death. And a book among the scribes is called the *Holy Amber*, by means of which they decide the fate of a sick man lying down, whether he will live or not. This they judge from the position of the sick man. And a limit, since he who knows letters has come into a calm harbour of life, no longer wandering among life's evils.[17]

THE SACRED SCRIBE: Again, when they wish to indicate a sacred scribe, or a prophet, or an embalmer, or the spleen, or odour, or laughter, or sneezing, or rule, or a judge, they draw a dog. A scribe, since he who wishes to become an accomplished scribe must study many things and must bark continually and be fierce and show favours to none, just like dogs. And a prophet, because the dog looks intently beyond all other beasts upon the images of the gods, like a prophet. And an embalmer, since he looks upon the bodies which he has taken care of naked and dissected.[18]

Horapollo seems to imply that words "do not rise in the soul perfectly formed and changing with its changes," but that visual stimuli are needed to fecundate the soul with words, and to draw them forth into articulation. This idea might perhaps contradict the idea of the "divine" or natural origin of glyphs, but in fact can also be seen as complementing and extending that "magical" theory of language. We're working here toward a *modus operandi* for *using* ("speaking") the glyphs rather than only understanding them—hence the introduction of "the hand, which carries out the desires of the tongue," as an integral part of this emblem. Why is the eye *bloodshot*, however? We recall the complex *hawk-sun-eye-blood*, which would imply that blood here stands for the participation of "soul" or vital essence in the linguistic process. The bloodshot eye is the eye that sees "essences."

"Egyptian letters" (the hieroglyphs) form a gridwork or "sieve" pattern which is made up both of "limits" (boundaries, the crisscrossed reeds themselves) and of empty spaces. As in a Zen koan, the empty spaces turn out to be more vital than the gridwork (the pattern, the actual written "lines"), because the holes let through the nourishing flour—the sunlight—life itself—while the lines simply supply dialectical tension. The lines "fix," or, in an alchemical sense, "kill": the letter killeth. But without the letters, the "limits," there is no semantic content, no meaning, only the undifferentiated light. The scribe is a dog who has looked on unclean corpses (killed by the letter); hence he can discriminate like a judge, and knows the definition and limits of things, because he keeps his eyes on the *images* "of the gods," the hieroglyphs, the archetypes.

Have we read enough to begin to feel that the hieroglyphic science was in fact . . . semiotics? Or rather, that it might be a complex answer to the *problem* of semiotics, which (since the nineteenth century) has tried over and over again—without much success—to *reenchant itself*? In other words, semiotics for us was a process of demystification, a ridding-of-spooks of the attic of words and signs, actually a rather cruel "ethnic cleansing" of languages and sign-systems of all taint of Idealism.

In a sense it was a kind of baby/bathwater situation, reminiscent of Nietzsche's very mixed feelings about "truth" and its destructive effect on the existential fabric. We exorcized the poltergeist of language, and now it doesn't move anymore. We're looking at corpses. One way to "reenchant the landscape" leads very obviously toward spiritual fascism. But what we want is a materialist metalinguistics which would reintroduce "the marvelous" into discourse without the counterproductive authoritarianism of the Ideal. I believe the hieroglyphic science can be of some service in this project.

Remember that for the Hermeticists, the "moral" or *sophic* level or "layer" of the hieroglyph was the deepest and most central, the essence of the essence. We might accuse them here, above all, of arbitrariness, of packing imaginary contents into their imaginal sieves. True enough. But as the Renaissance mages compiled their catalogues of (real or imagined) glyphs and emblems, a landscape began to emerge and coalesce, a worldview, a topocosmic mandala. It actually bore some resemblance to the Alexandrian Hermetic ideal which was still embedded in Horapollo's text, and even deeper, to the social/ritual structures of ancient Egypt. But upon the framework of this emergent landscape the Renaissance Hermeticists superimposed (palimpsest-wise) a radical vision of the social—a utopia. The emblematical forest of the *Hypnerotomachia Poliphili*, saturated with the magic of eroticism—or the alchemical countryside of the proto-surrealist Michael Maier's *Atalanta Fugiens*—are emblem-complexes of a "revolutionary future," like the mindscapes of Hieronymus Bosch—or rather, emblems of revolutionary desire, mirrors of desire, images which we can use to criticize the "reactionary present" whether the images are "real" or only "imaginary." This explains the history of a "left wing" in Hermeticism: for example, Paracelsus, Bruno, the Boehmenite radicals (the Family of Love), certain trends in Rosicrucianism and Masonry, and—finally—Blake.

This history in turn helps us to understand why Hermeticism *lost* the paradigm-wars it fought with the Church, and then with science. Frances Yates has demonstrated that Hermeticism defined itself as "natural science" and that it pioneered a scientific method—but it could not defeat the Catholic mechanism of Descartes nor the Anglo-deism of Newton because its goals were to *change* reality rather than simply interpret it in a manner useful to the ruling classes. Subsequent to its defeat, Hermeticism was looted of its most usable bits, by Newton for instance (who smuggled "action at a distance" past the censors!)—and especially by political theorists. Like the king who threatened to jail Paracelsus if he didn't cough up the secret of alchemy, politicians (and bankers) went to Hermeticism for cheap parlor tricks (which any cyclotron can accomplish today!) and came away instead with something much more valuable—the science of Emblems, of Images.

The hieroglyphic science is a tool which can be used by anyone interested in the "occult" (i.e., non-physical) influences of images on the human "soul." The emblems contained what Walter Benjamin called the "utopian trace"; in fact, they constituted a veritable utopian code. Emblems thereby made "direct contact" with the unconscious, and because they contained "cryptic" encodings of potent cultural archetypes (myth, folklore, magic), they seemed able to influence the "mass" unconscious as well. The emblems of desire were desirable and could *channel desire*. In this context, an analysis of coins and banknotes becomes interesting—also of flags and national symbols—of propaganda and advertising—of "brainwashing"—of the commodity itself (with all its "metaphysical" shenanigans). In short, as Couliano pointed out, the Hermetic science didn't die and go away after all. It was secularized, stripped of its utopian content, disguised, and deployed by "Babylon" for its own purposes of *psychic hegemony*. The dystopia of the Image.

The whole hieroglyphic science is, as we have seen, an *erotic* science—and eros can manifest either as liberation or slavery, or as a complex mingling of the two states. Postmodern theory has tended to emphasize desire itself rather than the object of desire, which seems so ontologically slippery. But if we wish to "seize back" the hieroglyphic science from the minions of the counterfeit state (the state of pure simulation), then we may very well have to face the necessity of rethinking the problem of the *object*. We can grant that the object "drifts" (as in the layered and contradictory definitions of Horapollo) without necessarily denying the object. We can attempt a restoration of the utopian landscape of the hieroglyphs.

Meanwhile, of course, the "Blakean" tradition of Hermetic radicalism didn't die or disappear either. A "transmission" of inspiration in this field doesn't depend on a literal passing of the torch, because the torch itself is an imaginal emblem. Without falling into the *willed credulousness* of a Rimbaud (in his sonnet on the vowels)—a process of failed reenchantment which destroyed the whole Romantic movement—we can still ask ourselves what Hermeticism might offer us (here and now) as *liberating tactics*.

The Spectacle has trapped us in images, images of our desires, cut loose from every "material bodily principle" which might help us to realize those desires. Very simply, to understand the trap and free ourselves of it (a counter-gnostic move of "descent" into the body and away from the *pleroma* of images) we must be able to "read the hieroglyphs"—we need to master the hieroglyphic science as a weapon in the dialectical struggle for disenchantment. However, as we've seen, the hieroglyphs also suggest the possibility of a reenchantment through the playful and free deployment of a "magical" language, a poetics of the imaginal, of the utopia of desire, and of union with the object of desire. To accomplish this it may prove necessary not only to understand the hieroglyphs, but to use them. Not only to read—but also to *speak*.

Notes

1. Horapollo, *The Hieroglyphics of Horapollo*, translated by George Boas (Princeton: Princeton University Press, 1993), xviii.

2. Plotinus, *On the Intellectual Beauty* 5.8.5–6, in Horapollo, *The Hieroglyphics of Horapollo*, 8.

3. Horapollo, *The Hieroglyphics*, 14.

4. Horapollo, *The Hieroglyphics*, 9–10.

5. Horapollo, *The Hieroglyphics*, 22.

6. Horapollo, *The Hieroglyphics*, 25.

7. Horapollo, *The Hieroglyphics*, 43.

8. Horapollo, *The Hieroglyphics*, 44–45.

9. Horapollo, *The Hieroglyphics*, 45–46.

10. Horapollo, *The Hieroglyphics*, 46–47.

11. Horapollo, *The Hieroglyphics*, 47–48.

12. Horapollo, *The Hieroglyphics*, 48–49.

13. Horapollo, *The Hieroglyphics*, 49–51.

14. Horapollo, *The Hieroglyphics*, 53.

15. Horapollo, *The Hieroglyphics*, 55.

16. Horapollo, *The Hieroglyphics*, 59.

17. Horapollo, *The Hieroglyphics*, 62–63.

18. Horapollo, *The Hieroglyphics*, 63.

Bibliography

Couliano, Ioan P. *Eros and Magic in the Renaissance*. Chicago: University of Chicago Press, 1987.

Fowden, Garth. *The Egyptian Hermes: A Historical Approach to the Late Pagan Mind*. Princeton: Princeton University Press, 1993.

Iversen, Erik. *The Myth of Egypt and its Hieroglyphics*. Princeton: Princeton University Press, 1993.

Horapollo. *The Hieroglyphics of Horapollo*. Translated by George Boas. Princeton: Princeton University Press, 1993.

Maier, Michael. *Atalanta Fugiens: An Edition of the Emblems, Fugues, and Epigrams*. Edited and translated by Joscelyn Godwin. Magnum Opus Hermetic Sourceworks 22. Grand Rapids: Phanes Press, 1989.

Perez-Gomez, Alberto. *Polyphilo, or the Dark Forest Revisited: An Erotic Epiphany of Architecture*. Cambridge: MIT Press, 1992.

Three Exemplars of the Esoteric Tradition in the Renaissance

KAREN-CLAIRE VOSS

What is Esotericism?

In the popular mind, esotericism is identified with the occult, with that which is hidden and secret. For a variety of reasons, scholars of religion tend to think of esotericism primarily as it relates to one or another exoteric religious tradition; it is thought of as marginal, and therefore as being of little consequence.

To think of esotericism as something secret and hidden as opposed to something public and open is to overlook nuances connected with its original meaning: the word *esotericism* derives from the Greek word *esoteros*, meaning not "hidden," but "inner." Indeed, the worldviews and practices which it encompasses are not kept secret for their own sake; they are secret, but only in the sense that their meaning does not lie on the surface, but beneath, and is therefore not accessible to the casual observer. The "secrets" of esotericism yield to the hermeneutical efforts of empathetic scholars, as well as to those of its practitioners.

To think of esotericism only as it relates to the exoteric is to approach it negatively, and is of little help in reaching a full understanding. There is enough significant research to support the view that esotericism is a genuine religious tradition, possessing a *raison d'être*, coherence, and integrity of its own. Esotericism should not be thought of as marginal—since to term something marginal is to imply that it is trivial—but as liminal; as such, its generative function makes it worthy of serious consideration.

The articulation of the term "esotericism" to refer to a set of interrelated, identifiable phenomena did not occur until well into the nineteenth century, long after its first manifestations. Although its particular forms are immensely varied, they are related to one another by virtue of several common, invariable components that make the concept of an esoteric tradition coherent. The historian Antoine Faivre, whose work has helped further an understanding of esotericism in Europe and the project of establishing the study of esotericism as a legitimate specialization in the history of religions, has devised a taxonomy articulating the simultaneous presence of four "intrinsic" components or characteristics, which render esotericism identifiable. To summarize very briefly, the first is that of the doctrine of correspondences, which holds that all things in the universe are interrelated. The idea that there is a relationship between the microcosm and the macrocosm is part of this. Because of that interrelationship, every thing can, to a greater or lesser extent, influence, or be influenced by, every other thing. The second is that of "living Nature," meaning that Nature is dynamic, multivalent, multiform, and multilevel. Everything in Nature is a potentially epiphanic sign, whence is derived, for example, Henry Corbin's lyrical reference to the Sufi experience of Nature as "*une grande théophanie.*" The third characteristic pertains to a very precise form of imagination and mediation. All elements in the universe are interrelated by means of things which intrinsically possess a mediating character (i.e., by means of divinities like Hermes, so beloved of the alchemists), and what might be called "semi-divinities" (inasmuch as they have their being between two worlds and have access to both, like angels); or by means of things within which a mediating quality is thought to inhere, *or* which can be imbued with that quality, that is by being somehow pressed into the service of performing the function of mediation (e.g., images, mandalas, texts, rituals, etc.). The fourth component is called "transmutation," and entails progressively deepening gnosis linked to changes of being. The term "transmutation" is more precise than that of "transformation," since the latter "does not necessarily signify the passage from one plane to another, nor the modification of the subject in its very nature, i.e. ontologically."[2] Some years ago, Faivre wrote that esotericism is "both a way of life and an exercise of vision."[3]

This marriage between esoteric practice and theory is perhaps most apparent in the gnosis which is at the heart of esotericism. To be distinguished from the Gnosticism of the early centuries of our era, esoteric gnosis should be understood in a broad sense, thus meaning knowing and understanding as a way of spiritual development. This form of gnosis possesses a dual impetus which serves initially to turn us inward to probe the nature of the relation of the self to the divine; secondly, it moves us outward, to discover the nature of the relation of the self to the natural world. Here it should be noted that esotericism demonstrates a marked tendency towards individualism. Both the inward and the outward forms of gnosis entail a progressive acquisition of knowledge which corresponds to an initiatory process. In a sense, one can speak of initiatory stages, each stage having its own "guardian," as it were, who must be negotiated with before one can pass through to the next. Faivre comments that regardless of the term used to describe these guardians, they all "have something common in essence with the initiate, since otherwise the necessary relationships could not be established."[4] Thus, esoteric practice is highly personal and individual. Regardless of whether a practitioner is connected to a tradition or is independent, she necessarily forges her own path. The form under which she apprehends knowledge is greatly dependent on her own cultural, social, economic, political, spiritual, and personal experience. This individualism is also manifested in the tension which exists between persons working along esoteric lines and the established religious tradition (or traditions) which are part of their experience.

This article examines selected aspects in the thought of three exemplars of the esoteric tradition during the Renaissance: first, their respective theoretical formulations of cosmogony and causality (i.e., that which pertains to the movement outward); second, their understanding of the relation between human and divine (i.e., that which pertains to the movement inward). This essay also constitutes an exercise in comparative cultures and comparative worldviews, since two of these persons, Marsilio Ficino and Giordano Bruno, are well known, while the third, Domenico Scandella, remained entirely unknown until recently, when Inquisitorial records pertaining to his trial for heresy came to light.

Sources

Because none of Scandella's writings have survived, my analysis of his thought depends on a close reading of a recent book based on the Inquisitorial records pertaining to his trial which includes extensive quotes from his testimony.[4] The discussion of Bruno focuses primarily on the material in his *Cause, Principle and Unity*, which is considered his most important cosmological work. In the case of Ficino, I have relied upon Ficino's *The Book of Life*, a three-volume collection of his Letters, and P. O. Kristeller's commentary *The Philosophy of Marsilio Ficino*.[5]

I. Domenico Scandella

Our knowledge of Domenico Scandella is due entirely to a seren-dipitous discovery in 1962 by social historian Carlo Ginzburg, then at the University of Bologna. While carrying out archival research for another project, Ginzburg happened to notice a provocative descrip-tion of charges that had been brought against a man for asserting that "the world had its origin in putrefaction."[6] Privately resolving to return to the archives, Ginzburg noted the number of the trial, and in 1970 he was able to read the entire transcript. The fruits of that research are published in *The Cheese and the Worms: The Cosmos of a Sixteenth-Century Miller*.

Biographical information about Scandella is sparse. He was born in 1532 in the Italian town of Montereale, located in the hilly region known as the Friuli. We are told that "His name was Domenico Scandella, but he was called Menocchio," and although he had gained better than passing acquaintance with a number of different trades, his primary avocation was that of miller, attested to by his dress: he "wore the traditional miller's costume, a jacket, cloak, and a cap of white wool. Thus dressed in white he presented himself at his trial in 1584."[7]

Menocchio was married. Out of eleven children only seven survived. He managed to achieve a very respectable status in his village. In 1581 he became mayor of a district comprised of several villages besides Montereale, and at some point had administered the affairs of the village church. But what made Menocchio really extraordinary was that he knew how to "read, write, and add"; indeed, these were the very things which helped lead him into difficulty, since these rudimentary skills were found in combination with a keen intelligence, and perhaps even more importantly, with a temperament inclined to question authority.[8] Menocchio felt free to pick and choose his influences, without undue regard for their pedigree, and he exhibited this sense of freedom to a marked degree, saying whatever seemed to him to be right, expressing all of the ideas, which, as he eventually would tell his inquisitors, "come out of my own head."[9] While it's true that in a moment of weakness during his first trial, Menocchio told his questioners that he said what he did "because I was tempted, the evil spirit made me," he was usually prepared to take responsibility for his opinions, proudly insisting that they really came from his own "artful mind."[10] Besides his "artful mind," Menocchio's sources were a combination of books (secular and sacred) and the traditional "old religion" of the agrarian people. Both proved to be of great significance.

Menocchio's lack of formal education kept him ignorant for the most part of the Aristotelian and scholastic writings which were favored by the ecclesiastical establishment, but he was able to observe that composite through its effects; that is, as it was embodied by the Church through her clerical representatives. Menocchio dared to think for himself, and he resented the idea that the clergy were thought to be the only, or even the best interpreters of divine revelation. He was convinced this view was seriously mistaken; worse yet, he strongly suspected that it was politically motivated. With characteristic indiscretion, he voiced those suspicions. Ginzburg reports:

> Menocchio declared that he rejected all the sacraments, including baptism, as human inventions, as "merchandise," instruments of exploitation and oppression in the hands of the clergy: "I believe that the law and commandments of the Church are all a matter of business, and they [the clergy] make their living from this."[11]

Menocchio in fact had a great deal to say about the clergy's self-serving motives in administering each of the seven sacraments. He believed that more or less direct access to the divine could not be, nor should it be, the sole province of the princes of the Church, nor was it limited to Christians alone. Rather

> the majesty of God has given the Holy Spirit to all, to Christians, to heretics, to Turks, and to Jews; and he considers them all dear, and they are all saved in the same manner.[12]

He ran afoul of the Holy Office for the first time in 1583. Ginzburg explains that it was not so much Menocchio's blasphemous statements that outraged the authorities, but his insistence on talking about religion to anyone who would listen—"preaching and dogmatizing shamelessly," as one witness related:

> He will argue with anyone, and when he started to debate with me I said to him: "I am a shoemaker, and you a miller, and you are not an educated man, so what's the use of talking about it?"[13]

On the occasion of his first confrontation with the authorities, Menocchio was able to reassure the vicar general by swearing that he would refrain—forever—from disseminating his ideas, and so the matter was dropped. But the urge to proclaim what he felt to be right proved too much for him, and he resumed almost immediately. One of the villagers testified that

> no matter who his companion might be, he usually turns the conversation to matters concerning God, and always introduces some sort of heresy. And then he argues and shouts in defense of his opinion.[14]

Denunciation wasn't long in coming. There is some evidence that the one who turned him in was the village priest, whom Menocchio had angered long before. In any case, he was arrested on February 4, 1584, and subsequently sentenced to life imprisonment. Three years later, however, after a successful appeal, he was freed on the condition that he never again leave Montereale. Ginzburg states there were several other restrictions, too:

> He was expressly forbidden to speak of or to mention his dangerous ideas. He had to confess regularly, and wear over his clothing the *habitello* with the painted cross, the sign of his infamy.[15]

The first restriction was relaxed shortly and Menocchio was granted permission to travel wherever he needed in order to provide for his family, but ever the stubborn independent, he took it upon himself to violate the other conditions whenever he felt it necessary. All the while, the Holy Office was quietly pursuing another investigation into his affairs. In 1599, Menocchio was denounced once more, and arrested for what would prove to be the last time. This time, word of his case even travelled to the Vatican, where, as Ginzburg writes, the "supreme head of Catholicism, the pope himself, Clement VIII, was bending toward Menocchio, who had become a rotten member of Christ's body, to demand his death."

> In these very months, in Rome the trial against the former monk Giordano Bruno was drawing to a close. It's a coincidence that seems to symbolize the twofold battle being fought against both high and low in this period by the Catholic hierarchy in an effort to impose doctrines promulgated by the Council of Trent. This explains the persistence of the proceedings, which are otherwise incomprehensible, against the old miller.[16]

Menocchio was executed sometime between December 1600 and June 1601.

Cosmogony
Menocchio's ideas seem quite bewildering and we are handicapped by several difficulties. To begin with, since none of his writing has come down to us, we are not dealing with ideas organized in a text; instead, we must use the records of a trial. We are forced to take the

Inquisitor's word for what was said by the defendant. In addition, since Menocchio lacked formal training, his ideas not only *appear* to be unsystematic, they *are*. The elements of his cosmogonic story remind one of the spilled contents of a child's puzzle box: the problem is to try and make the pieces fit together so that they form a single picture. The difficulty soon becomes obvious as we find Menocchio caught up in inconsistencies and contradictions due only in part to the anxiety inherent in the circumstances. Nevertheless, it is possible to give a satisfactory overview of Menocchio's thinking.

From his reading and contemplation, Menocchio developed a cosmogony, an implicit causality (which included two distinct types), a surprisingly subtle account of the relation between human and divine, and a keen sense of what constitutes truly ethical behavior.

Genesis, according to Menocchio, occurred as follows:

> [In the beginning] all was chaos . . . and out of that bulk a mass formed—just as cheese is made out of milk—and worms appeared in it, and these were the angels. The most holy majesty decreed that these should be God and the angels, and among that number of angels, there was also God, he too having been created out of that mass at the same time . . .[17]

The chaos/God relation implied by this description is important. In response to a question posed by one of his examiners: "Could God have created the entire apparatus of the world himself [without chaos]," Menocchio answered with a decisive "No!" "I believe," he said, "that it is impossible to make anything without Matter, and even God could not have [done this]." There were other nuances as well. For example, "God receives his movement within the shifting of chaos," and thus "proceeds from imperfect to perfect." Moreover, "God *was eternal with chaos,* but did not know himself, nor was he alive, but later he became more aware of himself" (emphasis mine). Pressing for clarification, the examiners asked him: "Who moves the chaos?" And Menocchio responded: "It moves by itself."[18]

After studying all of Menocchio's references to "the most holy majesty" included in the text, as well as Ginzburg's comments about

the difficulties inherent in Menocchio's use of it, I am forced to agree
with Ginzburg when he says it is, after all, a "muddle"; Menocchio
used the term inconsistently. In one instance he identifies God with
the "most holy majesty"; and in another he says that it was "the spirit
of God who was from eternity."[19] To distinguish between them seems
not to have been a priority for Menocchio, since, in a certain sense,
each is but another aspect of a whole.

Here then, are the salient points of Menocchio's account:

1. God was co-eternal with chaos, but initially was neither alive
   nor self-conscious.
2. Chaos moves by itself.
3. God gets movement within chaos.
4. God could make nothing without Matter/Chaos.
5. God moves from imperfect to perfect.

Leaving aside for the time being Menocchio's point concerning the
necessity for the existence of matter, which moves us away from
cosmogony into the area of causality, there are important issues raised
by the other four which warrant particular attention.

The notion of God's co-eternality with chaos was not original to
Menocchio.[20] Genesis has been interpreted this way, although it is
problematic from the orthodox perspective since it opposes the view
of God as the sole source of everything. Such an interpretation
presents no problems for the historian of religion, but it certainly
presented problems for the miller.

The idea that God was initially neither alive nor self-conscious
suggests that he developed by degrees. Menocchio is thereby paving
the way for talking about an ontological continuum from which even
God was not exempt. Reality is a continuum of being in Menocchio's
view; the being of God develops in an analogous way: God developed
by degrees. This idea is underscored by the fifth point regarding God's
movement from imperfect to perfect.

The idea of God receiving movement from chaos in the third point
assumes that God's existence was dependent on chaos, for chaos was

the condition from which God emerged. Menocchio explains:

> God and the angels are of the same essence as chaos, but there is a
> difference in perfection, because the substance of God is more perfect
> than that of the Holy Spirit . . . and I say the same about Christ, who is
> of a lesser substance than that of God and that of the Holy Spirit.[21]

Thus, we have here the notion that God was an increasingly perfect
form which emerged from the substance which gave rise to everything. Since God and the angels differed in quality, but not in kind, it
is appropriate to call Menocchio's view monistic.

If we envision a continuum of perfection, beginning with the most
imperfect (chaos/cheese), which develops toward perfection (worms/
angels and God), we then move closer to the meaning of Menocchio's
startling myth of the beginnings, and his story about the selection of
God from among the angels becomes much more intelligible.

Causality

Although Menocchio's views on causality were not explicitly developed as part of a systematic account of motion or change in the
universe, there are nevertheless some important ideas on the matter
implied in the cosmogonic description quoted earlier. In keeping with
other mythic cosmogonies, all of this activity takes place before the
creation of the earth. When Menocchio speaks about the creation of
the earth, his account describes a creation which was informed by a
very different kind of causality, in contrast to the process-oriented
causality which informed the development of forms within chaos.[22]
We recall that the "most holy majesty" is quite distinct from the chaos,
and that the "decree" of this entity is analogous to a cause operating
on material unrelated to itself.

Menocchio explained that God possessed the will to create the
world as well as the power, and that along with knowledge, these
qualities "increased in him" as he moved toward perfection.[23] Having
conceived a desire to make the world, God then required tools with
which to do it. Just as a carpenter needs tools in order to make a

particular thing that he desires to make, so too did God require the necessary "tools" with which to make the world. Those tools were the angels. Ginzburg remarks that Menocchio thought of God as a lord, and everyone knew that lords did not do manual labor—they did not work with their hands, but left such things to others.[24] Ginzburg comments that Menocchio's choice of metaphors is not surprising, since to liken God's creative activity to that of a carpenter or a mason is hardly remarkable because the miller, like all of us, naturally tended to create God in his own image.[25] The angels were not created by God, nor did they emerge from him; rather, they emerged directly from chaos like God. There was a curious interdependence between God and the angels: "when they emerged [they] received will, intellect, and memory from God as he blessed them"; these same angels embodied the power needed for God to create the world in accordance with his will.[26]

Menocchio's metaphor of the carpenter clearly indicates his understanding of the creation of the world as a mechanical enterprise. The simultaneous presence of this kind of causality with a process-oriented one suggests that Menocchio was sophisticated enough to choose his metaphors deliberately in order to convey his understanding of a cosmos in which two different modes of causality are operating alongside one another.

The Relationship Between Human and Divine

The relationship between human and divine in Menocchio's thought can best be understood in terms of the continuum of being mentioned earlier. As noted, Menocchio did not use terms like "most Holy Majesty" and "spirit of God" in a consistent or systematic way. When considered together, however, it appears that Menocchio thought of both as God, or more precisely, as different aspects of God.

There is ontological continuity between the divine and the human, too. Menocchio equates the "most holy majesty" with God and "the spirit of God," the Holy Spirit (the second person of the Trinity) and the spirits of human beings.

We also find the suggestion that human beings are microcosmic reflections of God, though necessarily imperfect. Menocchio says that one difference between God and the "holy majesty which is the spirit of God" is that the former changes, developing in perfection, but the latter remains. Somewhat analogously he also states that "when the body dies the soul dies but the spirit remains."[27] Thus, in human beings, the body changes—it dies; the spirit, just as the "holy majesty," is that which endures.

Menocchio uses the old concept of spirit or *pneuma*, equating it on at least one occasion with "breath."[28] He is reported to have told a neighbor that "God is nothing else than a little breath," adding, "and whatever man imagines him to be."[29] Furthermore:

> Everything that can be seen is God . . . the sky, earth, sea, air, abyss, and hell, all is God . . . Air is God . . . We are Gods . . . the Holy Spirit is in everybody.[30]

Ginzburg argues that much of Menocchio's thought can be traced to an ancient oral tradition in which even the earth was considered sacred.[31] Menocchio asserts that God the Father is air, God the Holy Spirit is water, God the Son is earth, and "Fire is everywhere, just as God is."[32] Thus, Ginzburg's characterization of Menocchio as a stubborn materialist may seem attractive, but while Menocchio was indeed materialist, we must remember that his was a divinized matter, permeated by spirit. The boundaries we find in Menocchio's ontology are fluid, not fixed; permeable, not rigid. Concerning the relationship between chaos and God he says: "neither chaos without God nor God without chaos."[33] We have also seen that the relationship between God and the angels is one of interdependence. Finally, concerning the essential connection he sees between human and divine, he states: "When the body dies, the soul dies too. *But the spirit returns to God who gave it to us*" (my emphasis).[34]

A schematic of Menocchio's worldview would look like this:

HOLY MAJESTY / THE SPIRIT OF GOD = CHAOS / MATTER
GOD
ANGELS and the HOLY SPIRIT
CHRIST
HUMAN BEINGS
NATURAL WORLD

This is a model of a hierarchy of being that theoretically permits reciprocity between its formally separated levels. We shall see that Menocchio's ontology is such that it justifies locating his thought with the philosophy of Giordano Bruno and Marsilio Ficino.

II. Giordano Bruno

Giordano Bruno was born in 1548 in the ancient town of Nola, in Italy. Bruno began his education in Naples, where he attended public lectures and studied with a private tutor.[35] In 1565, when Bruno was seventeen, he entered the Dominican monastery in Naples, and was given the name Giordano.[36]

Bruno did not possess the philological propensities of someone like Pico della Mirandola, who was proficient in half a dozen languages, but he was gifted with elegance of style in his native Italian, and acquired a good command of Latin, which he learned early and well.[37] The young man naturally came to know the writings of Aristotle, and those of Thomas Aquinas, whom he once called "the light and honor of peripateticism."[38] Bruno's studies also encompassed an impressive breadth of secondary literature on Aristotle; he was intimately familiar with Plato's writings, and those of other Greek philosophers, including the Presocratics (among these, Pythagoras was most favored), as well as the work of poets like Lucretius.[39] He knew the writings of the Neoplatonists Plotinus, Proclus, and Porphyry, and he studied Arabian works in Latin translation.[40] Lastly, he did not neglect the work of more contemporary thinkers such as Copernicus, Tycho Brahe, Piccolomini, and Erasmus.[41]

Along the way, Bruno developed an intense and abiding interest in mnemonics, the art of memory, and his research in this area came to the attention of Pius V, himself a Dominican, who summoned him to Rome.[42] According to Dorothea Singer, aside from the pope's acceptance of the dedication of Bruno's *On the Ark of Noah*, now lost, Bruno's trip to Rome appears to have borne little fruit.[43] The fortuitous audience with Pius V could have been the beginning of an exceedingly helpful alliance; no doubt if Bruno had been a Ficino and not Bruno, it would have been. But nothing came of it. Bruno simply left Rome and resumed his life in Naples.

Almost immediately, a series of increasingly serious incidents occasioned by Bruno's unorthodox thoughts about the nature of reality—in combination with his lifelong inability to think before he spoke—began to arouse suspicions. Before long, Bruno discovered that a full-fledged campaign had been mounted against him, and that serious charges were about to be brought against him. Singer relates the tragicomic details:

> He managed to get to Rome to the headquarters of his order, but there he learned that a formidable indictment was being prepared against him in Naples, based on the discovery of an indiscreet attempt to conceal certain writings of Erasmus in the convent privy. Bruno determined to flee. Most unwisely, he shed his monastic habit, and thus debarred himself from hope of reconciliation with his superiors.[44]

Thus in 1576 the long years of exile began, and Bruno was never again to lead a settled existence. His wanderings took him through northern Italy; he crossed the Alps to Chambery, then, on to Geneva, and finally, to Lyons, Avignon, and Montpellier. Coming at last to Toulouse, he stayed there for twenty months and made friends. Bruno was given a chair at the University, where he taught astronomy and lectured on Aristotle. In 1581, he left Toulouse to go to Paris for two years. In 1583 he moved to England, after which there were further wanderings until he arrived in Venice.[45] In Venice, however, he angered the patron whom he had been tutoring and in whose house he had been living. As a result of his sponsor's denunciation, Bruno was taken from his bed and imprisoned.[46] Nine years later, on February 16, 1600, he was burned alive in the Square of the Flowers in Rome.

Similarities Between Menocchio and Bruno

Menocchio was from the low culture and lacked Bruno's formal education; however, there are a number of important similarities between Menocchio and Bruno. Temperamentally, they were very alike, and each thoroughly disdained pretense of any kind.

Menocchio used his vernacular Italian because he knew no Latin; besides, as he shrewdly observed, Latin functioned as a tool for oppression more often than not. Bruno, on the other hand, used both languages, but he reserved Italian for his dialogues and his poetry; a noteworthy fact, because he was thereby afforded an especially rich and lyrical medium with which to express his most deeply felt intuitions.[47]

What got Bruno into trouble with the Inquisition is another characteristic he shares with his less celebrated contemporary: a combination of learning with native intelligence and a naturally probing mind. Menocchio combined limited learning with a burning desire to move beyond the confines of the intellectual and religious framework he had inherited. Both men wanted to penetrate the given, to reach the very heart of the universe, and both of them asked startlingly similar questions about the nature of reality. It appears also that neither man, in contrast to Marsilio Ficino, was an especially artful politician. In the last analysis, each of them was far too compelled by his vision to bother with anticipating the possible consequences of communications to those around him, a fatal mistake considering the times in which each lived. Each paid the highest penalty for his vision of a material universe that was permeated with spirit, with the divine.

Before turning to a consideration of Bruno's ideas, it is important to point out that Bruno's ontology is implied in all his writing, no matter what the explicit topic is. Therefore we find each of the three foci of the discussion here—cosmogony, causality, and the relationship between human and divine—conflated within his worldview.

Cosmology

Thus far I have found nothing analogous to Genesis in Bruno's writings, and do not expect to find such an analog, since it would prove antithetical to Bruno's conception of the whole as a Unity "greater than which nothing can be conceived." This is one reason for the appearance of the term "cosmology" above rather than "cosmogony," for there is no place in Bruno's system for a myth of creation, or a divine maker or prime mover external to the stuff from which the world was made.[48] By the same token, since Bruno's Unity is either immobile or ceaselessly moving, depending on the vantage from which it is regarded, one cannot discuss Bruno's thoughts on how the universe *began*. Rather than an account of how the universe *began*, Bruno gives us an account of how it *proceeds*. The universe proceeds from a Unity, and in fact, he bases his entire system on the concept of this Unity, an "absolute unity" in which "we distinguish neither matter nor form," as one of his modern commentators puts it.[49]

Since Bruno's intended audience was steeped in the philosophy of Aristotle filtered through scholasticism, with which Bruno was thoroughly familiar, it was only natural for him to present his cosmological ideas using Aristotelian concepts. In so doing, he frequently had to redefine or refute those concepts, but he did use them. In the fifth and final dialogue from *Cause, Principle and Unity*, we find a statement clearly intended not only to address, but to refute wherever necessary, the philosophical positions which preceded it:

> The universe is then one, infinite, immobile. One, I say, is absolute possibility, one is act, one is form or soul, one is matter or body, one is being, one is the maximum, and the best. It is not capable of comprehension and therefore is endless and limitless, and to that extent infinite and indeterminable, and consequently immobile.[50]

Thus we encounter the conflation of categories I mentioned earlier. On account of the subtlety of Bruno's conception of this Unity from which everything proceeds we cannot talk about its "beginnings," but only its workings, and therefore are plunged directly into the heart of his thought.

This then is the unity on which Bruno's cosmology is based. However, since absolute unity is impossible for us to conceive, except in the most abstract terms, let alone talk about, because all distinctions are collapsed within it, Bruno is compelled to introduce a number of theoretical distinctions that serve as a kind of map. He begins by considering absolute Unity in terms of two aspects: implicative and explicative. In its implicative aspect, Unity is considered as it is in itself—there is no distinction between one element and another: "the manifold [is] implicated in the Unity."[51] "Act and potency are one and the same," wrote Bruno, and he quoted Scripture: "The darkness and the light are both alike to thee."[52] Then there is Unity in its second aspect, as "the manifold explicated in the universe," in Nature; that is, as it unfolds itself, and is apprehended by us.[53]

From this notion of absolute unity follows the immobility of the universe as a whole. Bruno argues that the universe does not move because, by definition, there is nothing besides itself to move to. Because it is infinite it is boundless; therefore there is no space that contains it. For this reason too, it does not move, since movement entails a space within which something moves. It does not undergo corruption or generation because there is nothing else for it to turn into.

In *The Heroic Frenzies*, Bruno uses the image of a wheel turning on its own axis to convey the same idea:

> the wheel turns upon itself, so that motion and rest concur, for the spherical motion of a body upon its own axis and its own center implies the rest and immobility associated with rectilinear motion; or one may say, there is a certain repose of the whole and a motion of its parts . . . [54]

Bruno considers matter and form to be identical, even, as he writes in *Cause, Principle and Unity*, "in nature, where forms vary to infinity and succeed one another . . . matter always remains identical.[55]

> Besides the fact that forms have no being without matter, in which they

are generated and into which they are resolved, it is out of her bosom that
they come forth and into it that they are gathered. Hence matter, which
always remains identical and fertile, ought to have the principal prerogative
of being recognized as the sole substantial principle, as that which is and
which forever remains. And forms, all of them together, are to be taken
only as varied dispositions of matter, which come and go, which cease and
renew themselves—so that they cannot, any of them, have the value of a
principle.[56]

Nature, seen through Bruno's eyes, is a theophanic mirror; the
macrocosm is revealed through the microcosm; the "explicate" reveals
the "implicate."[57] In verses which appear in the Prefatory Epistle,
Bruno extols the principle at the heart of his thought:

Cause, principle, eternal unity, on which all being, motion and life
depend: in length, in breadth, in depth your powers extend as far as
heaven and earth and hell may be—with sense, with reason, and with
spirit I've seen that reckoning, measure, and act can't comprehend the
force, the number and mass, which, with no end, pass all that's low or high
or set between.[58]

Causality

The central idea in Bruno's theory of causality is that of the World
Soul, or Intellect:

There is one intellect which gives being to everything, called by the
Pythagoreans and the *Timaeus* giver-of-forms: a soul and formal principle
which becomes and informs everything, called by the same thinkers the
fountain-of-forms: a single matter out of which everything is produced
and formed, called by everyone the receptacle of forms.[59]

This World Intellect or World Soul is the "universal efficient
cause," the divine energizing principle of Bruno's Unity, that which
"intrinsically contributes to the constitution of a thing and remains in
the effect."[60] Ordinary cause, on the other hand, is that which "con-

tributes to the production of things from outside and has its being outside the composition." Like Menocchio's cosmology, Bruno's cosmology distinguishes two modes of causality: Bruno was very concerned to draw a distinction between a maker who operates from outside a thing, working as he said "on the surface of matter"[61] and the "inner artificer" who works from within. Bruno sometimes calls this inner artificer the "universal efficient cause," or the "universal intellect"; it is "the first and principal faculty of the world-soul."[62]

Bruno uses the image of a tree to help illustrate his notion of the "inner artificer," which "works continuously in wholeness everywhere":

> We call it the inner craftsman, since it forms matter and shapes it from within, as from within the seed or root is sent forth and unfolded the trunk, from within the trunk are thrust out the branches, and from within the branches the formed twigs, and from within these the buds are unfurled, and there within are formed, shaped, and interwoven, like nerves, the leaves, flowers, and fruits. As from within, at certain times, the sap is recalled from the leaves and fruits to the twigs, from the twigs to the branches, from the branches to the trunk, and from the trunk to the root.[63]

In spite of the highly sophisticated philosophical vocabulary which affords a precise way to articulate even the most subtle ideas, Bruno, like Menocchio, has fallen back on an image to help convey understanding of his distinction between two kinds of causes. His use of an image is sufficiently important to justify a brief digression in order to consider some of its ramifications.

Paul Michel notes the difficulty Bruno had in communicating his vision, saying that he was "constrained to use the only available tools and terms" and that the chief difficulty lies in the fact that Bruno "is employing terms based on division to express unity, terms based on abstract logic to express a new sense of dialectical conflict and resolution."[64]

Michel's is a truthful enough observation, but one which can hardly be pressed into service as an explanation or justification for Bruno's extensive use of images, for, notwithstanding the limitations he experienced on account of the Aristotelian framework, he can hardly be considered to have been at a loss for words. To the contrary, Bruno's use of images was not simply by default; rather, it was utterly intentional. Like Menocchio, Bruno uses images and metaphors very deliberately, and as we have just seen, images even find their way into his cosmological discussions. There is in Bruno what Michel describes as

> an ever present underlying lyricism . . . A picture of the universe impressed on the souvenir of an obsessive dream looms on every page under the torn veil of appearances.[65]

Once more we encounter the idea of a theophanic world. The use of images was an integral part of Bruno's program; it was the basis of his magic, and of his work in mnemonics which had been so attractive to Pius V. Bruno's images mirrored the creative process of the universe; they gave form to the amorphous, just as an infinite profusion of forms poured forth from matter.

In fact, all of Bruno's works demonstrate, to a greater or lesser degree, his understanding of the function of images as powerful, magical "links" (to use Frances Yates's term) between the macrocosmic Unity and our microcosmic selves.[66] In the context of his philosophical system, these links did not bring about an ontological connection which had not previously existed, but rather, they helped us to remember what already *was*.

The Relationship Between Human and Divine (or That of the Parts to Each Other and to the Whole)

There is yet another significant congruence between Bruno and Menocchio. Menocchio's thought betrays influences from the old, pre-Christian belief in a divinized earth, while Bruno's magical writings are permeated with images and ideas which are the result of intimate familiarity with Hermetic philosophy and the Cabala.

Menocchio held that "God was everywhere, like a breath . . . all is God"; Bruno sees the divine Unity everywhere too, working throughout the cosmos, which is infinite. While Bruno generally refrains from using God-language, he makes it clear that this Unity is divine, that it is "the one whole everywhere, God, Universal Nature."[67] The cosmos of both Bruno and Menocchio, while conceived in materialistic terms, was nonetheless thoroughly divinized, magical, and alive.

In Bruno's universe everything is not the same as everything else; there is a qualitative difference between the One and the Many. But withal that universe constitutes a seamless whole, a continuum (somewhat reminiscent of Menocchio's in spite of being more refined) ranging from absolute Unity, pure being—in which act and potency are one—to the plethora of its manifestations.[68]

Bruno's doctrine that each thing possesses all being *in potentia*, although not in actuality, has significant implications for understanding the relation between human and divine. His view of an infinite material universe comprised of countless numbers of worlds has equally profound implications for understanding the relation between human beings and the rest of the universe. In *La cena de la ceneri*, for example, a work dealing with cosmology and philosophy, we find:

> We are instructed not to search for divinity removed from us, if we have it nearby, even ourselves; no less than the cultured of the other worlds need not search for it near us, having it near and inside themselves.[69]

This is a truly remarkable statement, coming as it did from the depths of an orthodoxy that upheld the bifurcation of human and divine.[70] It is also another example of the internal consistency which we find to such a degree in Bruno's system that his ontology has profound implications for his epistemology and for his ethics. The old ideas would have to crumble if one were to be faithful to this new paradigm. To think of the earth as being in the center of the universe is no longer acceptable, nor are the elegantly arrayed—though ultimately closed—spheres of Kepler sufficient.

Nor is that all. Concerning humanity's place in the cosmos, Bruno went even further than this, writing in *Cause, Principle and Unity* that:

> You do not come any nearer to proportion, likeness, union, and identity
> with the infinite by being a man than by being an ant.[71]

Thus it seems Man himself (and I use the pseudo-generic term
deliberately) would have to relinquish his cherished position as one
who was made uniquely in the image and likeness of God, as well as his
belief in himself as the being for whom all the fruits of the earth were
given.

Man would also have to relinquish his alleged moral and physical
superiority vis á vis Woman. For one thing, woman herself had been
redeemed indirectly from the onus that derived from her long association with matter, traditionally viewed as inferior and sinful, partly by
virtue of the fact that Bruno had in effect "redeemed" matter.

It seems that Bruno enjoyed women. Unlike Ficino, for example, he
was not celibate; far from it, he wrote that he had "never had a desire
to become a eunuch," and Michel comments that Bruno further
explained "that if, as regards the number of women, he had not rivalled
King Solomon, at least he had done his best."[72] However, some men
"enjoy" women, while secretly or openly considering them to be
inferior to themselves. Yet Bruno appears to have held an entirely
different view, for the fourth dialogue of *Cause, Principle and Unity* is
devoted to refuting the devaluation of matter in general, and of women
in particular. In an exceptionally biting passage in the first dialogue,
Bruno has one of the characters ask his listeners first, to "Consider a
little truth . . . Regard what men are and what women are," and then
to recite to themselves a list of qualities:

> Here error, *errore*, masculine; there, truth, *verita*, feminine. Here, defect,
> *defetto*, masculine; there, felicity, *felicita*, feminine. Here, the pedant
> Poliinnio; there, the muse Polinnia. To sum up, all the vices, defects, and
> crimes are masculine; and all the virtues, excellencies, and goodnesses are
> feminine. Hence, prudence, justice, fortitude, temperance, beauty,
> majesty, divinity, as they are named, as they are imagined, as they are

described, as they are painted: so they are feminine all.[73]

Bruno's thought is very much concerned with the relation of the parts to the whole. We've just seen how images were used as a means of connection. Now we will discover that Bruno's definition of absolute unity entails a revolutionary way of understanding the relation of particular things to the universe. He explains that:

> there is not a change which seeks another being, but a change which seeks another mode of being. And this is what makes the difference between the universe and the things of the universe. The former comprises all being and all modes of being. Through the latter each thing has all being but not all the modes of being.[74]

Thus, in Bruno's thought, just as in Menocchio's, we again see the organizing principles of esotericism.

III. Marsilio Ficino

Marsilio Ficino was born in 1433 in Figline, near Florence. His father was a physician, and his mother seems to have been a psychic of sorts, with an uncanny propensity for being able to foretell the future.[75] He studied philosophy and medicine at the University of Florence, and became interested in theology. As we would expect, Ficino knew his Latin, but took up the study of Greek when he was in his mid-twenties. He is perhaps best known for his translation of the Platonic dialogues, the first ever done in Latin. His major philosophical work, the eighteen-volume *Theologica Platonica*, was produced during the years 1469–1474. Ficino translated Porphyry, Proclus, and Plotinus, and wrote several commentaries.[76]

In 1462, Cosimo de Medici made a truly princely gesture: he gave Ficino the use of a villa at Careggi. Thomas Moore remarks that the real value of this "most practical gift was one of time and space."[77] Careggi became a vibrant center, a gathering place for the very best minds of the period. But possibly the most significant juncture of Ficino's career occurred a short while later, around 1460, when at

Cosimo's urgent request he left off the project of translating Plato's dialogues, in order to translate the newly available *Corpus Hermeticum* so that Cosimo could read these works before he died.[78] The task was completed in 1463.

Commenting on the significance of these events Mircea Eliade notes that

> both Cosimo and Ficino were thrilled by the discovery of a primordial revelation . . . the one disclosed in the Hermetical writings. Such an extravagant interest in Hermetism is . . . significant . . . it discloses the Renaissance man's longing for a "primordial revelation" which could include not only Moses and Cabbala but also Plato and, first and foremost, the mysterious religions of Egypt and Persia. It reveals also a profound dissatisfaction with the medieval theology and medieval conceptions of man and the universe.[79]

Eliade's assessment is apt, for we know that Ficino self-consciously located his philosophical and religious writings within the tradition of the *prisca theologia*, a tradition which had been broken centuries earlier, and that he had attempted to trace this tradition back in time, in order to reintroduce its tenets.[80] The Hermetic texts received their name from Hermes Trismegistus, a semi-divine figure who was said to have given the Egyptians their laws, and to have been the teacher of Pythagoras himself.[81] Ficino, like many of his contemporaries as well as thinkers before them, accepted the historical authority of Hermes Trismegistus. Paul Oskar Kristeller points out that Ficino's teachings were not simply intended to be the mere recapitulation of these earlier ones; rather, he understood himself to be rearticulating these doctrines at a higher level than before. Moreover, Ficino did not for a moment consider that what he was attempting was in conflict with Christian teaching. Kristeller writes:

> Along with and in accord with the Christian tradition . . . the Platonic tradition fulfills a mission necessary to the divine scheme of world history. As a follower and renewer of that tradition Ficino does not

hesitate to consider himself an instrument of divine providence.[82]

Ficino was acting as a conduit for Truth; in deliberately placing himself at the disposal of the divine will, he was trying "to bring back an ancient and divine truth to its eternal destination."[83] Indeed, in his role as one who continues the tradition of the *prisca theologia*, there is every indication that Ficino understood himself to be passing on spiritual wisdom that did not begin with Christianity, but preceded it.

As I mentioned earlier, Ficino had a far keener sense of political nuance than either Menocchio or Bruno, and therefore took great pains to avoid incurring ecclesiastical ire.[84] Nevertheless, it appears that in his role as a self-conscious carrier of the esoteric tradition, Ficino viewed the Christian revelation as a part of that tradition, but not as its culmination. It's even possible that, like Bruno, Ficino privately considered the more ancient wisdom to be purer, and therefore superior to Christian doctrine. This would help explain the fact that Ficino—in spite of himself—occasionally wavers in his resolve to appear orthodox.

Because of this, in order to understand what Ficino was all about, it is necessary first of all to see that he perceived himself a man with a divine mission. His sense of himself as midwife for the truth about the nature of the Real is what underlies all his writings; indeed, this is the meaning of his life. Like Socrates, Ficino seems never to have let an opportunity for embodied teaching escape; even his letters are pedagogical events.[85]

It has been pointed out that Ficino, together with other Renaissance thinkers, did not achieve great philosophical stature; his writings consisted for the most part of translation and commentary on the truly great thinkers that preceded him, especially Plato. Yet to ignore or to downplay the philosophical value of Ficino's writings (along with those of other Renaissance thinkers) is a mistake. Ficino managed to transform his generation—or, at least, he managed to profoundly affect the influential circle which gathered around him at the villa in Careggi. All of his associates became transfixed with the idea of the spiritual possibilities of the human being for achieving excellence.

Whether they understood the person to be made in the image of God, or illuminated by the reflected Light of the One, made little difference to the completeness of their transformation, and to their understanding of those possibilities.

Cosmogony

Ficinian hermeneutics views Genesis as a repository of hidden meaning; it contains teachings from the esoteric tradition about the significance of light. Light, and its corporeal manifestation, the sun, were themes that permeated Ficino's writings, as we see from the titles of his two works *De lumine* and *De sole*. Chapter 10 of *De sole* begins by asking, "What did God first create? Moses answers: light . . . rightly: for the light . . . is more like God than any other thing."[86]

Ficino placed the sun in the center of the universe, "not," as one modern writer tells us, "as a geometric focal point, but as an ever-present quality":

> In the Hermetic texts Ficino had read an intriguing description of God, one quoted many times in later literature: God is the center of a circle whose center is everywhere and whose circumference is nowhere.[87]

De sole also contains two chapters devoted to describing the analogical relationship between the Sun and God and between the Sun and the Trinity respectively. Ficino's eloquent praise of the sun's perfection, its capacity for illumination, and its relative proximity to the "Intelligible Light . . . the Light of Pure Intellect" is such that Ficino was suspected of being a perhaps too-close follower of Orpheus.[88] This is by no means the first time that we sense Ficino is a little more Hermetic than Christian.

Notwithstanding, Ficino concludes *De sole* with characteristic caution that "the Sun is very different from the Creator of the world, all heavenly things are by divine law related to the one Sun, lord and measure of the sky," as if to warn us, lest we think he is advocating sun worship.[89]

Frances Yates points out that for Ficino, partially under the influence of Dante (whom he greatly admired) and Thomas Aquinas, the function of mediation is central among the rest of the attributes associated with his symbolism of the sun.[90] The function of mediation is critically important since he conceives the universe as a series of spheres through which the soul makes its way. Though each of these spheres has its own character, one might say, and therefore may be distinguished from each other, they are essentially continuous. (Here one can see very plainly the tremendous influence that the Neoplatonic tradition had on Ficino's thought.) According to Kristeller:

> The old proposition that nature makes no leaps is . . . interpreted [in Ficino's system] to mean that contrasting entities in the world do not directly touch each other, but are bound together in a gradual sequence of intermediate members. The whole of Being is thus connected within itself, and the result is an ontological principle of universal continuity.[91]

Within this hierarchy of Being, Kristeller adds, the "most significant expression of this postulate of continuity is found in the important principle of mediation."[92] (When Ficino is not speaking symbolically, he attributes this function to the intellect or spirit.)

When we remember that Ficino emphasizes the primacy of the sun in the order of creation, and accords to the sun a central place in the cosmos, we see a profound convergence of metaphor, symbol, and ontology. The Ficinian symbol of the sun is very like the Tillichian understanding of symbol: Ficino's sun truly participates in the reality to which it points.[93] From its central position within the cosmos, the sun mediates between the numerous spheres and sub-spheres. What more appropriate symbol for explicating the idea of a system permeated by spirit could there be than that of a profoundly illuminating sun, whose light streams everywhere, and whose very warmth sustains life? Frances Yates explains:

> Ficino has intensified the continuity between hierarchies and spheres by introducing an almost astrological suggestion into the relationships between the hierarchies, which are said to "drink" the influences from

the Trinity . . . Ficino's natural or *spiritus* magic, aiming no higher than the planets and particularly at the Sun, would yet have an angelic continuation stretching out beyond and above it.[94]

It is the sun which, though not "an Image of the Original" is at least a "shadow" of it.[95] It is the Sun's light which either "instantaneously" illuminates "those natures which are already pure, harmonious, and celestial" or "warms first with light" those others "that are opaque and material"; it enlightens and purifies them "so that they can be illuminated" and finally can be "lifted by the Sun and made sublime."[96] Thus, all things can bask closer and closer in the reflected rays of the Intelligible light of the "Good in itself" which is God.[97]

It is this emphasis on solarity which makes Ficino's philosophy at once grand and forbiddingly austere. Unlike Bruno, who was very much of the earth, Ficino sought to transcend the material world and to live in the world of the pure and the perfect Spirit. While Bruno was familiar with many of Ficino's writings, and was influenced in certain ways by him, his, as Yates points out, was the voice of "a pure natural philosopher" who "seeks his divinity in the infinite worlds."[98] Ficino, on the other hand, remained a man of the cloth until his death. Partly by temperament and partly, I think, because he was physically unattractive, Ficino eschewed physical love. His letters demonstrate an affection bordering on love for many of his friends, but in spite of his exhortation to balance the body and the spirit, he seems never to have taken his own advice.[99] The predominance of solarity and all its associations indicates that Ficino prized above all the masculine principle. Ficino's solar spirit has been appropriately compared by Thomas Moore with Bachofen's tripartite typology of the development of solar consciousness. The first stage is "ruled by mother (earth) . . . and spirit is dominated by matter." The next stage is "Dionysian, an era of father-right . . . a phallic Sol forever seeking receptive matter in order to give it life." Lastly comes the Apollonian stage, in which the "phallic sun . . . is transformed into the immutable source of light," and foregoes any "idea of fecundation," or of "mixture with feminine matter." In this stage there is no longer "any bond with woman."

Moore observes that Dionysos and Apollo were "inseparable" in Ficino's view, and quotes Ficino himself:

> Heaven, the bridegroom of earth, does not touch her, as is commonly thought, nor does he embrace her; he regards (illuminates) her by the mere rays of his stars which are, as it were, his eyes; and in regarding her he fructifies her and so begets life.[100]

In spite of this eroticized prose, the predominance of Ficino's solar principle ultimately made for a dry, albeit dazzling, vision.

Causality and the Relation Between Human and Divine

Ficino's theory about causality maintains that it originates from out of a necessity arising from the nature of its source (i.e., God). Human beings similarly derive their existence by virtue of a necessity inhering as it were in the nature of God. Human existence is mediated through the Spheres of Being, and the First Cause allows mediation to take place between the different spheres, or levels of being. Thus mediation itself is a vehicle of causality throughout the universe. The explication of this process of mediation is critically important to Ficino, as we shall see.

Ficino's ontology was based upon a hierarchy of being with Pure Being/God as the source.[101] God first formed the world as an Idea, and then created it. Created things, however, are necessarily limited, and therefore the world and its creatures are not perfect reflections of that original Idea. However, to the extent that we *are* able, by means of our free will, to participate in the Idea as first conceived by God, we are reflections of it. Thus, once set in motion by God, the world is continued by virtue of the things in the world which strive to return to God, to become adequate reflections of God.[102] In one sense, it is correct to say that the Sun, together with its essential quality, light, performs a critical mediating function between higher and lower spheres of being by providing the illumination necessary for reflection of the higher by the lower. Ficino's concept of Sun/Soul is thus central to his theory of causality. Just as the Sun is said to illuminate otherwise dark, opaque matter, so too does Soul enliven what would otherwise be lifeless and inert. Soul is the force of everything that lives—it permeates everything— and we ourselves are therefore linked to what Ficino calls "the one that is simplest and good" by means of our own individual souls, which participate in the World Soul, or *anima mundi*.

On the macrocosmic level, the mediating term between the Idea and Matter is the *anima mundi*; on the level of the microcosm—and here the Earth and the person are each understood as a universe in miniature—the mediating term between Body and Intellect (Spirit) is the Soul.

The light of the Sun is but one example of the metaphorical descriptions which Ficino employed when describing the connection between the spheres, or explaining the way in which things are interrelated, or the way in which one thing affects another. Commenting on Ficino's use of a preexistent metaphorical tradition and his particular contributions to it, Kristeller observes that for Ficino

> The metaphor becomes a symbol when it is freed from its connection with thinking, transferred into reality, and, so to speak, "substantiated," . . . the relation of image and idea is transformed into a real relation between real objects.[103]

The possibility of an ontological connection between these spheres is an indication that Ficino took the Hermetic worldview quite seriously; there are numerous points of connection between Ficino's writings about the nature of mediation and the esoteric doctrine of interrelationship among all things. For example, as we consider Ficino's "substantiation" of metaphors, we move from a purely philosophical frame of reference into that of esotericism. Everything is related to everything else. All things can influence one another. The esoteric doctrine of correspondences, together with the idea of similitudes, are at the basis of Ficino's theories about the relationship among elements on the microcosmic level, as well as of his theories concerning the relation between the microcosm and the macrocosm.[104]

* * *

This article makes two implicit claims. The first is that Menocchio, Bruno, and Ficino were exemplars of a particular tradition which is designated by the term "esotericism." The second is simply that such a tradition existed.

Four components of esotericism were described. First, the doctrine of correspondences, which holds that all things in the universe are interrelated, that there is a relationship between the microcosm and the macrocosm, and that everything can be (though it need not be) influenced by every other thing. Second, the idea of living Nature, dynamic, multivalent, multiform, and multilevel. Third, the idea of imagination and mediation, which are the means of interrelation. Fourth, the idea of transmutation, which entails progressively deepening gnosis linked to ontological change.

Once we know where (and how) to look, we see that the history of religions contains countless manifestations of these four components. We also see that these are so numerous that the question of whether or not it is valid to speak of an esoteric tradition, even though that tradition is not articulated to the same extent as more organized forms of religiosity, no longer arises.

As for the claim that Bruno and Ficino and Menocchio constitute exemplars of the esoteric tradition, let us review some of the more salient features of their ideas.

To begin with, any difference between "high" or "low" culture fades into the background in light of our discovery of what Ginzburg called the "astonishing convergence" between Menocchio's views and those held by his more learned contemporaries. We've seen their views converge on several points: the origin of the world, the relation between divine and human, and the dynamics of the connections among soul, spirit, and body.

Bruno's materialistic cosmology enabled him to transcend the traditional separation between the celestial and terrestrial spheres. In place of a bifurcated universe, he substituted a Unity consisting of subtly interactive modes or aspects of the One. Logically speaking, the place of matter and form shifted within the Brunian framework, as did their relation to each other. But these were merely formal distinctions. Rather than positing their ontological separateness, Bruno emphasized their "implication" in Prime Matter, or Unity, and their "explication" in the world. The divine energizing principle of this Unity was the all-pervasive World Intellect or World Soul.

Bruno's conception mirrors Menocchio's notion of divinized matter, an instinctive and immediate notion arising from the experience of an agrarian people. The boundaries in Menocchio's ontology are permeable, interactive. Not for him is the rigid stratification of categories utilized by the scholastics:

> Everything that can be seen is God . . . the sky, earth, air, abyss, and hell, all is God . . . Air is God . . . We are Gods . . . the Holy Spirit is in everybody.

Surely this echoes Bruno's impassioned statements: "We are instructed not to search for divinity removed from us, if we have it nearby, even inside ourselves," and "You do not come any nearer to proportion, likeness, union, and identity with the infinite by being a man than by being an ant."

What of Ficino? His solar vision pushed him toward more arid vistas than either Bruno or Menocchio. Bruno's florid writings about heroic frenzy are more rooted in the earth and in the body than are Ficino's writings. His is the most systematic mind of the three thinkers we've discussed here. Still, he was also a mystic, and, as Frances Yates points out, a magician. The bent toward mysticism and magic was a kind of leaven, raising what could have been the solid mass of uninspired learning toward the symbols of light and sun. Ficino's vision—finer but not better—is also located along the continuum called the esoteric tradition.

Consider his focus on mediation, which runs like a *leitmotif* through all his writings. That focus implies a profound corrective to the traditional understanding of the universe. "No one ascends to God unless God himself has in some measure descended into him," he writes; and for Ficino, the divine *had* descended into the world. The divine permeates the world just as the light of the Sun illuminates even the darkest corner. Over and over we see Ficino, the physician of spirit and body, prescribe a course of treatment which will result in bringing the macrocosm and the microcosm together. Knowing the ontological dimension of Sun/Soul as he does, Ficino leads us to replicate the dynamic of the macrocosm within our own beings.

Ficino wrote that "Truth is the correspondence of the thing and the mind." Menocchio and Bruno and Ficino spent their lives trying to perfect their knowledge of the world, and to perfect the correspondence between their apprehension of the world and its real character. Each was very much an individual, but they held in common the way of esoteric gnosis. Since the world was but an outpouring of the One, the more perfectly they were able to apprehend its character, the more perfectly they resembled the divine principle of their existence. Their lives were spent turning the pages of the theophanic book that is the world.

Notes

1. Esotericism exhibits all the qualities one expects to find associated with other conditions of liminality. Esotericism therefore occasions a variety of artistic, cultural, and religious forms, continuing to enrich and sustain them long after their initial manifestation. In fact, the fate of esotericism within the agenda of the contemporary academy is markedly similar to the "general disregard of the liminal and marginal phenomena of social process and cultural dynamics" to which Victor Turner and Edith Turner refer in *Image and Pilgrimage in Christian Culture: Anthropological Perspectives* (New York: Columbia University Press, 1978), 251.

2. Antoine Faivre and Karen-Claire Voss, "Western Esotericism and the Science of Religions," forthcoming *Numen* 1995. For a full discussion of the components of esotericism, see Antoine Faivre, *Access to Western Esotericism* (New York: State University of New York Press, 1994), originally published as *Accès de l'Esotérisme Occidental* (Paris: Gallimard, 1986).

3. See Faivre, "Esotericism," in Lawrence E. Sullivan, editor, *Hidden Truths: Magic, Alchemy, and the Occult* (New York: Macmillan, 1987), 41.

4. Faivre, "Esotericism," 39.

5. Carlo Ginzburg, *The Cheese and the Worms: The Cosmos of a Sixteenth-Century Miller*, translated by John and Anne Tedeschi (Baltimore: The Johns Hopkins University Press, 1980); originally published as *Il formaggio e i vermi: Il cosmo di un mugnaio del '500* (Italy: Guilio Einaudi Editore, 1976). Giordano Bruno, *Cause, Principle and Unity*, translated by Jack Lindsay (Westport, CT: Greenwood Press, 1962). Marsilio Ficino, *The Book of Life (De vita triplici)*, translated by Charles Boer (Irving, TX: Spring Publications, 1980), henceforth referred to as *De vita*. *The Letters of Marsilio Ficino*, translated by Adrian Bertoluzzi and Clement Saleman (3 vols.; New York: Gingko Press, 1975, 1978, 1978), henceforth referred to as *Letters*. Paul Oskar Kristeller, *The Philosophy of Marsilio Ficino*, translated by Virginia Conant (Morningside Heights, NY: Columbia University Press, 1943).

6. Ginzburg, *The Cheese and the Worms*, xi.

7. Ginzburg, *The Cheese and the Worms*, 1.

8. Ginzburg, *The Cheese and the Worms*, 2.

9. Ginzburg, *The Cheese and the Worms*, 21.

10. Ginzburg, *The Cheese and the Worms*, 28.

11. Ginzburg, *The Cheese and the Worms*, 10.

12. Ginzburg, *The Cheese and the Worms*, 9–10.

13. Ginzburg, *The Cheese and the Worms*, 2.

14. Ginzburg, *The Cheese and the Worms*, 2–3.

15. Ginzburg, *The Cheese and the Worms*, 95. Menocchio had not been going to confession since he disliked the local priest.

16. Ginzburg, *The Cheese and the Worms*, 128.

17. Ginzburg, *The Cheese and the Worms*, 53.

18. Ginzburg, *The Cheese and the Worms*, 56.

19. Ginzburg, *The Cheese and the Worms*, 54.

20. See for example Jung's remark concerning Paracelsus and Dorn, in *Alchemical Studies* (Princeton: Princeton University Press, 1967), 236, and the discussion in Paul Henri Michel, *The Cosmology of Giordano Bruno* (Ithaca: Cornell University Press, 1973), 86–87.

21. Ginzburg, *The Cheese and the Worms*, 56.

22. In "From Chaos to Cosmos: An Analysis of the *Enuma Elish*," I discuss and compare two different modes of causality. The paper was presented at the National Meeting of the American Academy of Religion in Chicago in 1984.

23. Ginzburg, *The Cheese and the Worms*, 55. Cf. Jack Lindsay's description of Avicebron's distinction between God and God's will, in Bruno, *Cause, Principle and Unity*, 16.

24. Ginzburg, *The Cheese and the Worms*, 62.

25. Ginzburg, *The Cheese and the Worms*, 64.

26. Ginzburg, *The Cheese and the Worms*, 55.

27. Ginzburg, *The Cheese and the Worms*, 71.

28. Ginzburg, *The Cheese and the Worms*, 67, for the quoted material and for Ginzburg's discussion. See also the account of the tradition of spirit and breath in Proclus, *Elements of Theology: A Revised Text*, translated by E. R. Dodds (Oxford: Clarendon Press, 1933), 297. He writes: "The original meaning of *psyche*, as of the Latin *anima* is 'life-breath': our *psyche*, being air, 'holds us together,' as Anaximenes put it. Hence the close association in Greek thought of the notions of 'soul' and 'life': the word for 'alive' is *empsychos*, lit. 'ensouled.'"

29. Ginzburg, *The Cheese and the Worms*, 65.

30. Ginzburg, *The Cheese and the Worms*, 67.

31. Ginzburg, *The Cheese and the Worms*, xxiv, 20–21, 51, 58–61 and passim. If indeed Menocchio *was* linked to such an oral tradition—a highly plausible hypothesis—it might provide a possible explanation for his idea of the "most holy majesty" which existed before chaos, before "God" could be rooted in that tradition. I note that from antiquity, the goddess Diana had been a beloved favorite of the Italian witches, a principal figure in ritual practices which flourished in regions like the Friuli, and she is mentioned frequently in the Inquisitorial records of trials. A reference to the goddess Diana's appeal for advice to "the fathers of the Beginning, to the mothers, the spirits who were before the first spirit" appears in a curious work of the nineteenth century, purported to be a compilation of Italian rituals and incantations: Charles G. Leland, *Aradia, the Gospel of the Witches* (New York: Buckland Museum of Witchcraft and Magick, 1968). The idea of "spirits who were before the first" has connotations which are similar to those of Menocchio's "most holy majesty."

32. Ginzburg, *The Cheese and the Worms*, 105.

33. Ginzburg, *The Cheese and the Worms*, 54.

34. Ginzburg, *The Cheese and the Worms*, 72.

35. Dorothea W. Singer, *Giordano Bruno: His Life and Thought* (New York: Henry Schuman, 1950), 10.

36. Singer, *Giordano Bruno*. See also Michel, *The Cosmology of Giordano Bruno*, 13.

37. Singer, *Giordano Bruno*, 11.

38. Michel, *The Cosmology of Giordano Bruno*, 13.

39. Bruno read these works in Latin translation. Ficino produced many of the translations; for example, he wrote a commentary on Lucretius in 1457. See the "Translator's Introduction" to Ficino, *De vita*, vi. I note that Kristeller (*The Philosophy of Marsilio Ficino*, 13) tells us that Ficino's translations of Plato, for example, were of such excellent quality that scholars continued to use them until the nineteenth century.

40. Singer, *Giordano Bruno*, 11.

41. For a full discussion of the writers who were contemporaneous with Giordano Bruno, see Michel, *The Cosmology of Giordano Bruno*, 28–36.

42. The Dominicans did more than their share to enrich the memory tradition. See Frances A. Yates, *The Art of Memory* (Chicago: University of

Chicago Press, 1966), 108.

43. Singer, *Giordano Bruno*, 12.

44. Singer, *Giordano Bruno*, 13.

45. Here I am indebted to Michel, *The Cosmology of Giordano Bruno*, 13–15.

46. There is an account of the circumstances leading up to Bruno's arrest and his trial, including a summary of the extant documents pertaining to his trial, in Michel, *The Cosmology of Giordano Bruno*, 19–25. See also p. 25, n. 5 for a reference to an article by Benedetto Croce "in which he insinuates that the documents relating to the trial at Rome, missing since 1817, were deliberately destroyed."

47. For example, Bruno's *De gli eroici furori* (written in Italian between 1583 and 1585 in London) contains twenty-eight sonnets which are couched in the language of erotic love. They describe the journey of the soul as it seeks to be made one with the divine; each is introduced by an illustrative description of an image, or emblem, having a theme appropriate to the sonnet.

48. Bruno generally refrains from using god-language, but he makes it clear that this Unity is divine. See, for example, Michel, *The Cosmology of Giordano Bruno*, 77. See also Antoinette Mann Paterson, *The Infinite Worlds of Giordano Bruno* (Springfield, IL: Charles C. Thomas, 1970), 47–48, 131–132.

49. Michel, *The Cosmology of Giordano Bruno*, 79.

50. Bruno, *Cause, Principle and Unity*, 135.

51. Michel, *The Cosmology of Giordano Bruno*, 78.

52. Michel, *The Cosmology of Giordano Bruno*, 78.

53. Michel, *The Cosmology of Giordano Bruno*, 78.

54. I have quoted this passage (which is from Bruno's *De gli eroici furori*, already mentioned in n. 47, supra), as it appears in Paul Eugene Memmo, *Giordano Bruno's The Heroic Frenzies: A Translation with Introduction and Notes* (Chapel Hill, NC: University of North Carolina Press, 1964), 195. See Michel, *The Cosmology of Giordano Bruno*, 102, for Michel's discussion of the implications of Bruno's image of the wheel turning on its own axis.

55. Bruno, *Cause, Principle and Unity*, 102.

56. Bruno, *Cause, Principle and Unity*, 107.

57. The journal *Spring* has excerpted and translated passages from *La philosophie iranienne islamique aux XVII et XVIII siècles* (Paris: Buchet-Chastel, 1981), written by the late Islamicist Henry Corbin. While I have not seen this

work and lack the publication details for the issue in which this appeared, the excerpted material is so relevant that I quote from it here: "To see in each existent the one Being which causes it to be, to see in each luminous thing the light that reveals it, is the very notion of theophanic form (*mazhar elahi*) . . ." This is precisely the way in which Bruno experienced the world. Intense and passionate on the one hand, possessed of a sublime mystical bent on the other, Bruno seems to embody the mediating force that links heaven to earth. For a full discussion of "creation as theophany," see Henry Corbin, *Creative Imagination in the Sufism of Ibn'Arabi* (Princeton, NJ: Princeton University Press, 1969), 184–195.

58. Bruno, *Cause, Principle and Unity*, 55.

59. Bruno, *Cause, Principle and Unity*, 106.

60. Bruno, *Cause, Principle and Unity*, 80.

61. Bruno, *Cause, Principle and Unity*, 82.

62. Bruno, *Cause, Principle and Unity*, 81.

63. Bruno, *Cause, Principle and Unity*, 82.

64. Michel, *The Cosmology of Giordano Bruno*, 24.

65. Michel, *The Cosmology of Giordano Bruno*, 51.

66. Frances A. Yates, *Giordano Bruno and the Hermetic Tradition* (London: Routledge and Kegan Paul, 1964), 265.

67. Quoted from Bruno's *De immenso*, II, 12, as cited in and translated by Irving Louis Horowitz, *The Renaissance Philosophy of Giordano Bruno* (New York: Coleman-Ross, 1952), 72.

68. See Bruno, *Cause, Principle and Unity*, 112.

69. Cited by Paterson, *The Infinite Worlds of Giordano Bruno*, 20.

70. See, for example, Bruno, *The Expulsion of the Triumphant Beast*, translated by Arthur D. Imerti (New Brunswick: Rutgers University Press, 1964), 285, n. 16.

71. Bruno, *Cause, Principle and Unity*, 136.

72. Michel, *The Cosmology of Giordano Bruno*, 22. Cf. Memmo, *Giordano Bruno's The Heroic Frenzies*, 61–62.

73. Michel, *The Cosmology of Giordano Bruno*, 74–75.

74. Bruno, *Cause, Principle and Unity*, 138.

75. See Ficino, *De vita*, v.

76. Kristeller, *The Philosophy of Marsilio Ficino*, 17–18.

77. Thomas Moore, *The Planets Within: Marsilio Ficino's Astrological Psychology* (Great Barrington: Lindisfarne, 1990), 31.

78. This story is related by Mircea Eliade in *The Quest: History and Meaning in Religion* (Chicago: University of Chicago Press, 1969).

79. Eliade, *The Quest*, 38.

80. Kristeller, *The Philosophy of Marsilio Ficino*, 26 ff.

81. The immensely varied facets of this figure are explored in Antoine Faivre, ed., *Présence d'Hermes Trismégiste* (Paris: Albin Michel, 1988). See also Antoine Faivre, *The Eternal Hermes: From Greek God to Alchemical Magus* (Grand Rapids: Phanes Press, 1995).

82. Kristeller, *The Philosophy of Marsilio Ficino*, 27.

83. Kristeller, *The Philosophy of Marsilio Ficino*, 27.

84. For example, while discussing the use of images in *De vita*, Ficino repeatedly speaks of what "the ancients have said" concerning the benefits of images, as if to suggest that he himself would never countenance such views. See, for example, p. 145.

85. His letters reveal that never once did Ficino put pen to paper in a less than intentional fashion. See *Letters*, passim.

86. Arturo B. Fallico and Herman Shapiro, editors and translators, *Renaissance Philosophy* (2 vols. New York: Modern Library, 1967), I, 131–132. Along with Hermes, Ficino ranked Moses as a source of ancient wisdom. Cf. Yates, *Giordano Bruno and the Hermetic Tradition*, 152–153, where she discusses the analogous images from the *Asclepius*.

87. Moore, *The Planets Within*, 128.

88. Fallico and Shapiro, *Renaissance Philosophy*, I, 132. See D. P. Walker, *Spiritual and Demonic Magic from Ficino to Campanella* (Notre Dame: University of Notre Dame Press, 1975), 12–24, for a discussion about Ficino's preoccupation with the Sun.

89. Fallico and Shapiro, *Renaissance Philosophy*, I, 141.

90. Yates, *Giordano Bruno and the Hermetic Tradition*, 119–120.

91. Kristeller, *The Philosophy of Marsilio Ficino*, 99.

92. Kristeller, *The Philosophy of Marsilio Ficino*, 101.

93. Paul Tillich, *Dynamics of Faith* (New York: Harper and Row, 1957), 42.

94. Yates, *Giordano Bruno and the Hermetic Tradition*, 120.

95. Fallico and Shapiro, *Renaissance Philosophy*, I, 140.

96. Fallico and Shapiro, *Renaissance Philosophy*, I, 131.

97. Fallico and Shapiro, *Renaissance Philosophy*, I, 135.

98. Yates, *Giordano Bruno and the Hermetic Tradition*, 250.

99. See, for example, the letter "The way to happiness" in which wisdom is praised not only above riches, health, beauty, strength, nobility of birth, honors, power, and prudence, but also above the remaining classical cardinal virtues justice, fortitude, and temperance, as being alone good in itself. *Letters*, I, 4–6.

100. Moore, *The Planets Within*, 131–132.

101. For a fuller discussion see Kristeller, *The Philosophy of Marsilio Ficino*, 74–91 (Chapter 6, "Hierarchy of Being") and passim.

102. This reminds one of the movement described by Plotinus in *Enneads* 2.9.3. In a sense, the world, which is an effect, so to speak, of the "Principle of Being," "turns its gaze upon the One," that is, it strives to return to God.

103. Kristeller, *The Philosophy of Marsilio Ficino*, 94.

104. See Michel Foucault, *The Order of Things: An Archaeology of the Human Sciences* (New York: Pantheon Books, 1970), 17–25, for a discussion of the four similitudes; and pp. 25–30 for a discussion of the related doctrine of signatures. First published as *Les Mots et les choses* (Paris: Editions Gallimard, 1966).

Ships with Wings

REPORTS FROM OUR FILES

AND STRAIGHTAWAY they went aboard as the wind blew strong; and
they drew the sail down, and made it taught to both sheets; then Argo
was borne over the sea swiftly, even as a hawk soaring high through the
air commits to the breeze its outspread wings and is borne on swiftly,
nor swerves in its flight, poising in the clear sky with quiet pinions.

—Argonautica 2.930

From the Diaries of Jane Leade
February 9, 1678: A Transport

IN THE MORNING, after I was awaked from Sleep, upon a sudden I was
insensible of any sensibility as relating to a corporeal Being, and found
myself as without the clog of an Earthly Body, being very sprightly and
airy in a silent place, where some were beside myself, but I did not
know them by their Figures, except one, who went out, and came in
again: and there was no speaking one to another, but all did set in great
silence, and I my self with my Eye fixed forward.

And I did suddainly see at a pritty distance, where I was, a rich,
splenderous thing come down all engraven with Colours, the Ground
thereof being all of God. It was in the form of a large Ship with Wings,
I cannot say, whether more then four, which spred themselves out,
being like varnished Gold, it came down with the greatest swiftness as
imaginable. Upon which amazing sight, I asked some by me, do you
not see this wonderful sight? And they said no. But I saw my self, or
something like my self, leaping and dancing, and greatly rejoycing to

meet it. But when I came up to it, then it did as suddainly go up again, withdrawing out of all sight, unto the high Orb from whence it came. After which I found my self in my Body of sence, as knowing I had been ranging in my Spirit from it for a while, that I might behold this great thing.

—Jane Leade, *A Fountain of Gardens* (1700), vol. 3, 66–67

Apuleius in the Underworld:
A Footnote to Metamorphoses 11

JOHN CAREY

THE HIGH POINT of the eleventh book of Apuleius's *Metamorphoses* is undoubtedly the moment when the protagonist Lucius, who has suffered throughout most of the narrative in the form of an ass, miraculously regains his human appearance during a festival of Isis. What follows, although an anticlimax in merely narrative terms, has a vivid interest of its own: we are told how the grateful youth became a student of the mysteries of Isis, and was at last rewarded with enlightenment. The veiled passage in which he refers to this epiphany runs as follows:

> . . . Igitur audi, sed crede, quae vera sunt. Accessi confinium mortis et calcato Proserpinae limine per omnia vectus elementa remeavi, nocte media vidi solem candido coruscantem lumine, deos inferos et deos superos accessi coram et adoravi de proxumo. Ecce tibi rettuli, quae, quamvis audita, ignores tamen necesse est.

> "Listen then, but believe, for my account is true. I approached the boundary of death and treading on Proserpine's threshold, I was carried through all the elements, after which I returned. At dead of night I saw the sun flashing with bright effulgence. I approached close to the gods above and the gods below and worshipped them face to face. Behold, I have related things about which you must remain in ignorance, though you have heard them."[1]

Much has been written about these suggestive lines, and it is not my purpose to recapitulate all of the relevant scholarship here. Rather, I

371

take as my point of departure the views of J. Gwyn Griffiths, who in his exhaustive commentary on the eleventh book has repeatedly drawn attention to points in which Apuleius's account reflects native Egyptian tradition. In the case of the present passage Griffiths has argued for a connection between Lucius's revelation and ancient Egyptian doctrines of the afterlife, particularly the descriptions of the sun god's nocturnal journey through the underworld which are found in certain funerary treatises.[2] Further evidence of such a connection is furnished by the rituals which follow the epiphany, in which Lucius successively dons twelve cloaks,[3] then appears to the populace wearing a radiate crown and holding a torch.[4] Not only do I find Griffiths's position persuasive, but I believe that it can be taken further: the purpose of this note is to suggest that in hinting at the mysteries of Isis Apuleius was actually paraphrasing an Egyptian text.[5]

Themes similar to those which we glimpse in Apuleius's cryptic description can be found in many Egyptian funerary writings. Thus we find the following at the beginning of a spell in the *Book of the Dead*:

> Secrets of the nether world, mysteries of the god's domain: seeing the disk when he sets in life in the west and is adored by the gods and the blessed in the nether world. . . . As for every blessed one for whom this roll is used, his soul goes forth with men and gods; it goes forth by day in any form it wishes to assume. It is not kept away from any gate of the west in going in or out. It prevails among the gods of the nether world, for it is one who cannot be repelled. These gods surround it and recognize it. Then it exists like one of them. . . . It knows what befalls it in the light; it exists as a blameless soul.[6]

The similarities here are suggestive; but a closer parallel can be found. One of the most important and widely disseminated accounts of the sun's night journey was the work known as the *Amduat*, first written *circa* 1500 B.C.E. Not too long thereafter an abridged version was produced, and this proved extremely popular: it has been found carved in several tombs, and there are a great many papyrus copies. In summarizing the original *Amduat*, the reviser abstracted the names and magic words which it was most useful for the deceased to know, omitting descriptive passages and speeches placed in the mouths of supernatural beings; but he also added sections at the beginning and the end.[7] Here are the lines which appear as the conclusion of the shorter version:

> The beginning is light,
> the end is primeval darkness.
> The sun's path westward,
> the secret schemes which this god achieves.
>
> The chosen clues, the secret writing of the underworld,
> which is not known by anyone save the chosen.
> Thus is that image made,
> in the secrecy of the underworld,
> invisible, imperceptible!
>
> Whoever knows these secret images is well provided for, is an initiate.
> Always he goes in and out of the underworld,
> always he speaks to the Living Ones,
> as has been proved true, millions of times![8]

Nearly everything in Apuleius's description is here as well: the statement that only the initiate can understand the secrets being discussed, the journey into and out of the underworld, the privilege of communing with the gods, the assertion of truth. The only significant omission is the lack of any direct reference to the sun's night journey—but this is of course the subject of the *Amduat* as a whole.

On the strength of these correspondences I propose that the mysteries into which Apuleius was initiated retained strong links with the pharaonic past, and that the abridged version of the *Amduat* was one of the scriptures from which he was instructed. The wonders which he experienced are, indeed, closed to us; but I think that he may have told us a little more than he intended.[9]

Notes

1. Apuleius of Madauros, *The Isis-Book (Metamorphoses, Book XI)*, edited and translated by J. Gwyn Griffiths (Leiden: E. J. Brill, 1975), 98–99.

2. Comments in Apuleius, *The Isis-Book*, 292–308. See especially the discussion of the sun seen at midnight on page 303: "This remarkable phenomenon is presented, on the first level, as something bizarre. Yet it admirably suits the situation in the *Book of Amduat*, where the sun-god is depicted as voyaging through the twelve hours of the night in the Osirian underworld. This, in fact, is the crucial point in determining the exact Egyptian context. . . ." Similar arguments may be found in the work of earlier scholars: thus Willi Wittmann, *Das Isisbuch des Apuleius* (Stuttgart: W. Kohlhammer, 1938), 111–19; and R. Reitzenstein, "Zum Asclepius des Pseudo-Apuleius," *Archiv für Religionswissenschaft* 7 (1904) 393–411: 406–8.

3. *The Isis-Book*, 98–99; on p. 309 Griffiths points out the evident link between the twelve cloaks and the twelve underworld regions traversed by the sun god. Cf. Wittmann, *Isisbuch*, 114; Reitzenstein, "Zum Asclepius," 408.

4. *The Isis-Book*, 100–101. On p. 315 Griffiths comments that "in this cult the initiate can be identified with none other than Osiris, but here, after a ceremony which depicts the visit of the sun-god to the Osirian realm of the dead, the triumph over the dead is fittingly symbolized by an Osiris-figure with solar attributes. An identification with the god is therefore present."

5. It is noteworthy that Apuleius mentions books in hieroglyphic script which were kept in Isis's shrine, and describes a priest reading from them to his disciples (Griffiths, *The Isis-Book*, 96–97). On p. 285 Griffiths observes that "Apuleius begins the *Metam.* with a description of an Egyptian papyrus roll, and there is every reason to believe that he was acquainted with papyri in which various Egyptian scripts were used."

6. *The Book of the Dead or Going Forth by Day*, translated by Thomas George Allen (Chicago: University of Chicago Press, 1974), 22. I have slightly adjusted Allen's punctuation and capitalization in order to make this excerpt read more smoothly.

7. On the wider use of such passages, which he calls "preliminary and terminal rubrics," see Allen, *Book of the Dead*, 2.

8. Erik Hornung, editor and translator, *Das Amduat: Die Schrift des*

verborgenen Raumes, Teil III: Die Kurzfassung, Nachträge (Wiesbaden: Otto Harassowitz, 1967), 35. I have translated Hornung's German; he gives the hieroglyphic text of the passage in question on pp. 25–26.

9. For more on the survival into late antiquity (and beyond) of the doctrines of the *Amduat*, see my article "The Sun's Night Journey: A Pharaonic Image in Medieval Ireland," forthcoming in the *Journal of the Warburg and Courtauld Institutes* 57 (1994).

To Hestia

Hestia, thou who tends the holy house
Of lord Apollo, Pythian, shooting far,
Thou having hair that drips with silky oil,
Approach this house and enter, of one mind
With all-wise Zeus; and for my song grant grace.

Homeric Hymn 24
Translated by BRUCE MACLENNAN

To Hestia

Thou, Hestia, in ev'ry lofty home
Of deathless Gods and folk who walk the Earth,
Hath gained a seat eternal, honor grand;
Thy prize is fair and noble; lacking thee,
Feast not we mortals, if both first and last
We offer not sweet wine to Hestia.

Thou, Argus-slaying Zeus's and Maia's son,
Gods' herald, giving goods, with rod of gold—
Be kind, you two, and help us, awed and fond.
Inhabit this fair house as mutual friends;
For you, who know the noble deeds of folk
Who walk the earth, sustain their wit and youth.
Hail, Kronos's child, and Hermes with the rod!
I will remember you and one more song.

Homeric Hymn 29
Translated by BRUCE MACLENNAN

To Earth, Mother of All

Of Gaia sing I, Mother firm of all,
The eldest one, who feedeth life on Earth,
Whichever walk on land or swim the seas,
Or fly; sustaineth she each from her wealth.
Through thee the folk are blest in child and fruit,
O Queen, who giveth and reclaimeth life
Of mortals; rich whoe'er it pleaseth thee
To honor; all abundance is for them;
Their fertile land is fruitful; through the fields
Their flocks do thrive; their house is filled with goods.
They rule well-ordered states with women fair,
And ample wealth and riches follow them;
Their sons exult with youthful merriment;
Their daughters play in dances flower-strewn
With happy heart, and skip through fields abloom.
Such givest thou, holy rich divinity.

So hail, God-Mother, Starry Heaven's Wife;
Repay my song with pleasing sustenance!
Of thee I'm minded—and another song.

Homeric Hymn 30
Translated by BRUCE MACLENNAN

The Eighth Sphere
Tarocchi del Mantegna, fifteenth century.

Astronomy, Contemplation, and the Objects of Celestial Desire: Notes from a Cosmological Journal

DAVID FIDELER

FOR COUNTLESS HOURS behind closed doors, a young man has been grinding and polishing a magic crystal, carefully following the time-tested stages of an alchemical procedure. Transformed from its raw state, this crystal, soon to be perfected, will allow him to transcend the boundaries of time and space. Once properly mounted and positioned, by gazing into the crystal he will be able to view events that occurred in the distant past.

This story is not the stuff of fantasy, unless our lives are somehow the stuff of imagination made real. The young man has been grinding a parabolic curve into a glass mirror. Once the mirror is mounted in the telescope he is building, he will be able to view distant galaxies whose light has been traveling through space for countless millenia. Through the light-gathering power of the mirror, his vision will take on a transcendent quality, enabling him to look millions of years backward in time.

Gazing simply at the Andromeda galaxy, which can be seen with the naked eye on a dark night, we can see the combined glow of some 300 billion suns. As galaxies go, Andromeda is quite near, a mere 2.2 million light years away. Yet, despite its distance, once visual contact is made, we are in physical touch with Andromeda as its two million-year-old photons tumble into our eyes. Even by *thinking* about the Andromeda galaxy, we are somehow in touch with it. In this sense, beyond its empirical dimension, astronomy is an imaginal activity, and the mind's attempt to grapple with universal realities.

Contemplation "in Theory and Practice"

> The sense of wonder is the mark of the philosopher. Philosophy
> indeed has no other origin.
>
> —Socrates

This essay is an attempt to revive the ancient dialogue between the act of observing the heavens and the act of philosophical speculation. Out of this discussion, astronomy emerges as an ideal metaphor that can literally "carry us across" (*metapherein*) to deeper ways of seeing and reflecting. The desire to observe the heavens in wonder and the root impulse toward philosophical contemplation are one and the same. This identity is reflected in the ancient Greek word *theôria*, which means "to visually look at," yet also denotes the act of intellectual contemplation. *Theôria*, from which we obtain the word theory, signifies the act of observing, regardless of whether we observe with our eyes or reflect with our minds. The early Greek philosophers valorized the contemplative life, the *bios theôrêtikos*, above all others; and in antiquity the contemplation of the heavenly sphere was an integral part of the philosophical enterprise.

The sense of wonder and astonishment that our ancestors felt when they looked at the sky is an essential aspect of human nature. Because the stars change so slowly in terms of human lifetimes, we can experience essentially the same view of the heavens that the ancient Greeks did 2,500 years ago, if we can get away from our light-polluted cities. And as we partake of the sight, we transcend the barriers of time and resonate with all those before us who gazed at the sky in wonder. With our telescopes we can see deeper and farther, but I doubt if our fundamental capacity for wonder has similarly increased. If anything, our belief in progress and current preoccupation with technology has in many ways diverted us from the fundamental experience of observing; astronomy has gained precision, but we have also lost the ability to see the night sky from our major cities. Many people are superficially impressed by the ever-changing wonders of technology, but

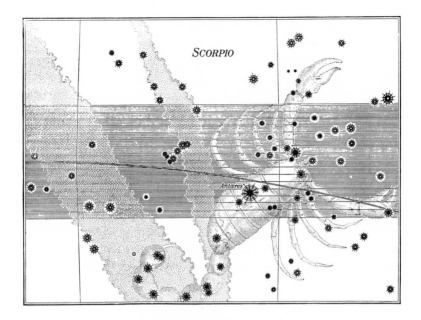

The Constellation Scorpio
From Johann Bayer's *Uranometria*, 1603.

others ask if we, as a result of technology, have lost our deeper imaginative faculties and the ability to resound with the music of the spheres. For some, however, astronomy is as much an imaginative experience as it is the literal act of viewing objects in the night sky. In other words, observational astronomy is not only a rational, scientific activity, but it is an imaginal practice that feeds and inspires the soul. Archetypal psychologists tell us that imagination is the primary activity of the soul, and since time immemorial, imagination has peopled the heavens with enchanted images: constellations of gods, fabulous beasts, and mythic figures. Psyche or soul is clearly implicated in astronomy for, as the philosopher Novalis reminds us, "the seat of the soul is where the inner and the outer world meet. Where they overlap, it is in every point of the overlap."[1] Wherever we find imagination, there too is soul.

Reflecting on the Mysteries of Insight

As humans, we are ably equipped to see with our physical eyes, but of all the creatures who tread the earth, we are the only species endowed with the faculty of *insight*, the inner faculty of contemplative reflection. While many other types of creatures experience and delight in the beauty and harmonies of nature, which they themselves reflect, it is only we humans, endowed with the faculty of mind, who can consciously reflect upon the nature of beauty and harmony.

Of all the physical sciences, astronomy is by nature the most philosophical and contemplative. It is also the most visual. Astronomy is based upon the observation of light, and the Latin term *contemplation* literally means "to observe." Of all the physical senses, vision is traditionally the most spiritual, and the language of vision is also the language of contemplation: we experience "insight," "illumination," and "reflect on" the nature of things. Our thoughts are "observations." People have "bright ideas" and, in understanding, I can "see" another person's point. A person with great ideas is a "man of vision." Significantly, the words *idea*, *wisdom*, and *vision* all originate from a common Indo-European root which means "to see."[2] An idea is an *insight*, an inner flash of illumination, that can result in wisdom; some ideas enable us to revise or literally "revision" our perceptions of things, thus allowing us to see things in a new light. Finally, it is worth noting that the Latin word for mirror, *speculum*, is the source of the term "speculation": seeing in a reflective or contemplative fashion. To speculate is thus to reflect on images, either through the mirror of a telescope gathering celestial light, or through the faculty of imaginal insight.

Visiting Urania's Heavenly Temple

> Mortal as I am, I know that I am born for a day. But when I follow at my pleasure the serried multitude of the stars in their circular course, my feet no longer touch the earth.
>
> —Ptolemy

It's a beautiful, starry night, and the moon will not be rising until

Observatory in Alexandria, Egypt
From Camille Flammarion, *Les Etoiles.*

shortly before dawn—the perfect opportunity to view some nebulae and take in the sight of distant galaxies. Since the glare of my neighbor's overhead security light washes out the more delicate objects hidden in the depths of the night sky, it's time to head to the country. Astronomical observing is always a good excuse to get out of the city, and I'm looking forward to being surrounded by the choir of stars above and the chorus of crickets below. After carefully loading my telescope into the car, I'm off, headed for the observatory.

It's a twenty minute drive to the Veen Observatory, owned and operated by the Grand Rapids Amateur Astronomical Association. I'm now thirty-three, which means that my first visit to the observatory was some twenty-five years ago. Since then, much has changed. As Grand Rapids continues to sprawl outward, what was once meadow, forest, and farmland is now populated by office buildings, strip malls, and supermarkets. I can still hear the crickets and cicadas once I pass a certain point in the drive, but it takes much longer to reach that point. The once dark skies at the observatory are gradually being eroded by the encroachment of suburbia. In ten years, the situation will be much worse. The two-lane road leading out of the city will be expanded to four lanes, far past where it is today. Not far from the observatory, housing subdivisions have started to spring up. I'm now driving down a wooded, country road, but on my left stands a row of uniform two-storey houses where, but months ago, nothing had stood before. The vinyl-sided structures, their driveways and treeless yards, are starkly illuminated by a chain of mercury vapor lights reaching off into the distance.

Minutes later, I reach my destination, and turn down Kissing Rock Road, the gravel road that leads to the observatory. My highbeams light upon a giant, six-foot boulder which has been spraypainted vivid, phosphorescent colors. There must be a story behind the giant boulder that has given the road its name. I can't tell you what it is—perhaps the local teenagers could—but the Kissing Rock is always a reassuring landmark. Not far ahead, the headlights catch a little white star rising above a mailbox, a silent hieroglyph signaling the drive to the observatory.

The observatory with its two domes, lecture room, and library is located atop a hill that broadly overlooks the Grand River Valley; navigating the road to the summit is the last leg of my pilgrimage. Turning off the main road, a closed gate crosses the drive, and a nearby sign warns me that the observatory is a private facility reserved for members only, except on public visitors' nights. Surrounded by trees, the hum of the engine, and the sounds of a summer night in the country, I get out of the car and open the gate. Back in the car, I switch off the headlights and prepare to inch my way to the top of the hill, guided only by the parking lights. There might be other observers atop the hill, and a blast from the headlights would ruin their night vision.

There is always a sense of excitement in passing the ritual threshold and making the ascent to the temple of Urania, the heavenly Muse who presides over the science of astronomy. It is a slow, steep ascent through the tunnel of trees as I strain forward and try to stay on the road under the feeble illumination of the parking lights. The driveway stretches up the hillside in serpentine coils that seem indeterminately long; and despite having made the trip many times, it's always hard to predict when the road will finally end. Moments later, though, the trees open up, revealing a spray of stars against a velvety black sky. The two domes of the observatory immediately come into view, silhouetted against the starry heavens. A faint red glow near the door of the observatory indicates that I am not alone. After parking the car and getting my bearings, I can see that one of the domes is open, staring skyward, a silent locus of contemplative activity. Down at ground level, two figures are hovering around a portable telescope set up on the lawn, and the big Dobsonian reflector, part of the observatory complex, is also in use.

* * *

If the heavens inspire awe and wonder, there is also something awe-inspiring about observatories, which seem to physically incarnate humanity's wonder about the universe. Visiting the observatory as a child was an event charged with excitement, and even though I have now repeated the trip many times, there is still a feeling of magic whenever the domes come into view on that lonely hilltop. Removed from the flow of daily life, the observatory is a special structure, like a temple, which reveals something deep and instrinsic about human nature. From this perspective, observatories embody a sense of the sacred, for they are set apart and sanctified for the sole purpose of contemplating the heavens.

Speaking historically, we know that the first astronomers were priests, and the first observatories were temples. The Latin word *templum* literally means "a place set aside for observing the heavens," and the act of observing the heavens from the temple gave rise to the word *contemplation*.

The word *temple* comes from the prehistoric Indo-European root *tem-*, which means "to cut."[3] A temple is a sacred space, a place of retreat that is literally "cut out" from busy demands of everyday existence. The Greek word *temenos*—the sacred precinct in which a sanctuary is located—originates from the same root as *templum*. The Latin word *religio* means to "relink," and the ritual performed in a temple is a religious act, designed to relink us to the universe and ensure that the proper balance is maintained between humanity and the cosmos. From this perspective, observational astronomy is also a "religious" activity, for it is a contemplative act that relinks us with the universe and the mysterious depths of our own being. As Henry Corbin notes in his book *Temple and Contemplation*,

> It is significant that the Latin word *templum* originally meant a vast space, open on all sides, from which one could survey the whole surrounding landscape as far as the horizon. This is what it means to *contemplate*: to "set one's sights on" Heaven from the *temple* that defines the field of vision. ... The term was actually used above all to designate the field of Heaven, the expanse of the open Heaven where the flight of birds could be observed and interpreted. ... The *temple* is the place, the organ, of vision.[4]

By "going back to the roots of things," the relationship between

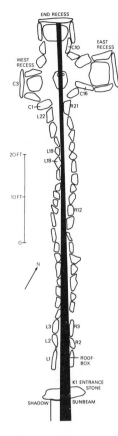

Megalithic Mound at New Grange in Ireland, *circa* 3000 B.C.E.

ABOVE: Entrance stone to the mound.

LEFT: The path of the sun's beam at sunrise on the winter solstice, the shortest day of the year. From Martin Brennan, *The Stones of Time: Calendars, Sundials, and Stone Chambers of Ancient Ireland* (Rochester: Inner Traditions, 1994).

astronomy and contemplation displays a lucid clarity. Since the first temples were open places for observing the heavens, it is not surprising, as sacred architecture developed, that many temples were oriented toward celestial bodies. *Orientation* means "to face the east" or the orient—to face the rising sun or some other heavenly object. Sir Norman Lockyer, one of the first astroarchaeologists, discovered that some Egyptian temples were oriented toward the rising or setting sun on a special day of the year. On the feast day of the temple god, and only on that day, the sun would send a flash of light down a long, narrow corridor, where it would finally enter the holy of holies, illuminating the cult statue of the divinity.[5] Similarly, the five thousand-year-old mound at New Grange in Ireland is oriented toward the rising sun on the winter solstice (December 21), the shortest day of the year.[6] On that morning, a shaft of light penetrates a long tunnel and illuminates the back wall of the innermost chamber. Thus, at the turning point of the year, the sun plants its fertilizing seed deep within womb of the Earth, initiating the return of life in the spring.

If space permitted, dozens of other aligned sites could be listed from all around the world, ranging from Stonehenge to Greek temples to Native American medicine wheels to Central American pyramids. In all such cases, scientific knowledge has been united with the practical, magical act of maintaining harmony between human life and the larger life of the cosmos. As humans, we still have the need to channel the fertilizing energies of the cosmos into our everyday lives through science, art, and the imagination. In the past, this ritualized activity of maintaining balance between the heavens and the earth constituted the science of priestcraft and the art of magic. In the words of the Renaissance philosopher Pico della Mirandola, "as a farmer weds his elms to vines, even so does the magus wed earth to heaven."[7]

Astronomy, Wonder, and the Beginning of Philosophy

In the beginning, philosophy and religion were one and the same. As Socrates said, wonder is the beginning of all philosophy, and gazing up into the depths of the night sky, far from the light pollution of our cities, is one of the most awe-inspiring activities that anyone can engage in. On my last observing trip up north to the pristine skies of Sleeping Bear Dunes National Park on the shores of Lake Michigan, there were no man-made light sources to degrade the awesome wonder of the night sky. On that clear, moonless night, thousands of stars pulsated in the Milky Way as if alive. As the boundaries separating heaven and earth melted away, the star stream shone three-dimensional with white clottings and dark riffs, bright enough to illuminate the ground and the trees with a faint, phosphorescent glow. The ancients called it *Galaxias kuklos*, the Circle of Milk, but it was also the road that led to the home of the gods. Alternately, the Milky Way was envisioned as the meeting-place of souls. Thinking back on that night, I am reminded of the ancient Orphic formula, buried with initiates, to vouchsafe an unmolested passage into the afterlife. It reads,

> I am a child of earth
> and starry heaven,
> but my race is of heaven.[8]

Are we creatures of earth who have emerged from the oceans of becoming to gaze upward in rapt contemplation at the starry heavens? Or are we heavenly creatures by nature, consigned for only a period to walk upon the bottom of the sky? In a mystical sense, the Orphics stressed the celestial nature of humanity, which, through forgetfulness of its true nature, has descended into the sorrowful cycle of Birth and Becoming. Conversely, for the poet Keats, our physical existence is not merely a vale of tears; he calls the world "the vale of soul-making." These words imply an almost alchemical orientation. Everything that lives has soul, but in the human realm, great souls are made and not born. The deepening of psychological life requires care, nurturing, and the gentle heat of alchemical attention; we pass through periods of darkness, fire, separation, conjunction, and distillation in the never-ending process of refining the prime matter. From a mythological perspective, scientific theories of evolution are alchemical too. Our roots reach down deep into the mineral, vegetable, and animal layers, but humanity at its highest—as alchemical artisan and contemplator of divine beauty—is truly "the crowning of nature." There is nothing more miraculous than the incarnational embodiment of the *lumen naturae*, the light of nature, in our human form. As we contemplate the light of the heavens, the light of Mind reflects the light of the stars. Light reflects light. However, according to the Sufi poet Shabistari (fourteenth century), there is only *one* light:

> "I" and "you" are but the lattices
> In the niches of a lamp,
> through which the One Light shines.

"I" and "you" are the veil
Between heaven and earth;
Lift this veil and you will see
No longer the bond of sects and creeds.

When "I" and "you" do not exist,
What is mosque, what is synagogue?
What is the Temple of Fire?[9]

According to the One Light Theory, our imagined act of observing the stars is based upon the illusion of duality. In reality, at its very core, the universe is just one thing. From this perspective of nondualism, ego-consciousness is a mirage, for we are not separate from the universe; we are aspects of the One Thing that is the universe. Consequently, when we appear to be observing the stars, in reality the universe is observing itself. Or, "there is just observing." Or, "all is Mind." This is what the Buddhists are getting at when they say

First there is a mountain.
Then there is no mountain.
Then there is.

It is this underlying unity of all things that allows the Zen master archer to repeatedly hit the center of the target, even when blind-folded.

Early Greek Philosophy and the Valorization of Contemplation

> If we pursue the heavenly way and live in our kindred star, then we will philosophize, living truly, busied with the most profound and marvellous speculations, beholding the beauty in the soul immutably related to truth, viewing the rule of the gods with joy, gaining perpetual delight and additional insight from contemplating, and experiencing pure pleasure absolutely unmingled with any pain or sorrow.
>
> —Iamblichus, *The Exhortation to Philosophy*, fourth century C.E.

> We do not ask for what useful purpose the birds do sing, for song is their pleasure since they were created for singing. Similarly, we ought not to ask why the human mind troubles to fathom the secrets of the heavens. . . . The diversity of the phenomena of Nature is so great, and the treasures hidden in the heavens so rich, precisely in order that the human mind shall never be lacking in fresh nourishment.
>
> —Johannes Kepler, *Mysterium Cosmographicum*, 1596

In early Greek philosophy, the contemplative faculty that experiences beauty, wonder, and awe is identified as the flower, the highest part of human nature. For the early Greek philosopher Anaxagoras (*c.* 500–*c.* 428 B.C.E.), contemplation is the true end of human nature. When he was asked why anyone should wish to have been born rather than not, he answered, "In order to contemplate the heaven and the structure of the world-order as a whole."[10] In another account, when Anaxagoras was accused of ignoring the affairs of his native land, he said "I am greatly concerned with my fatherland," and pointed toward the heavens.[11] The medieval writer Bernardus Silvestris tells a similar story about the Greek philosopher Empedocles (*c.* 493–*c.* 433 B.C.E.). When asked why he was alive, Empedocles replied, "That I may behold the stars; take away the firmament, and I will be nothing."[12]

As Werner Jaeger notes

> The most notable feature in the character of the first philosophers ... is their intellectual devotion to knowledge, their absorption in studying Existence for its own sake. Their singlemindedness was admired and yet considered paradoxical by the later Greeks, and doubtless by their contemporaries too. Their scholarly disregard for the things which others held important—money, honour, even home and family—their apparent forgetfulness of their own interests, and their indifference to popular enthusiasms, begot many famous anecdotes.[13]

One such story was told about Thales, the sixth century B.C.E. philosopher, astronomer, and mathematician. One evening Thales was contemplating the stars when, distracted by the pursuit, he tumbled down a well. Thales was chastised by a beautiful Thracian maid who witnessed the mishap for ignoring the things at his feet and having his head up in the clouds. Such are the dangers of the contemplative life, and as Socrates warns, "Anyone who gives his life to philosophy is open to such mockery."[14]

Criticisms like those of the Thracian girl are sometimes aimed at celestial observers today. As astronomer Robert Burnham writes, "it sometimes happens, perhaps because of the very real aesthetic appeal of astronomy and the almost incomprehensible vastness of the Universe, that the more solidly practical and duller mentalities tend to see the study as 'an escape from reality.' "[15] Burnham, however, goes on to call this view "one of the most thoroughly lopsided views ever propounded" and notes, in a truly philosophical spirit, that

> only the most myopic minds could identify "reality" solely with the doings of man on this planet. Contemporary civilization, whatever its advantages and achievements, is characterized by many features which are, to put it very mildly, disquieting; to turn from this increasingly artificial and strangely alien world is to escape from *unreality*; to return to the timeless world of the mountains, the sea, the forest, and the stars is to return to sanity and truth.[16]

From this perspective, perhaps we need the therapeutic benefits of observational astronomy even more than the ancients, who suffered far less estrangement from the beauties and wonders of the natural world.

The valorization of the contemplative life runs throughout the entire history of Greek philosophy. Pythagoras (*c.* 570–*c.* 496 B.C.E.), the first man to call himself a *philosopher* or lover of wisdom, said that there were three main motivations of human behavior: the desire for wealth, the desire for honor, and the desire for knowledge. As Iamblichus writes in his book *On the Pythagorean Life*, Pythagoras

> likened the entrance of men into the present life to the progression of a crowd to some public spectacle. There assemble men of all descriptions and views. One hastens to sell his wares for money and gain; another exhibits his bodily strength for renown; but the most liberal assemble to observe the landscape, the beautiful works of art, the specimens of valor, and the customary literary productions. Some are influenced by the desire of riches and luxury; others, by the love of power and dominion, or by insane ambition for glory. But the purest and most genuine character is that of the man who devotes himself to the contemplation of the most beautiful things, and he may properly be called a philosopher.[17]

Moreover, the most beautiful thing to contemplate is the cosmos, for

> Pythagoras adds that the survey of the whole heaven, and of the stars that revolve therein, is indeed beautiful, where we consider their order, which is derived from participation in the first and intelligible essence.[18]

This contemplative tradition is carried forward by Plato, who in the *Timaeus* writes:

> As concerning the most sovereign form of soul in us we must conceive that heaven has given it to each man as a guiding genius—that part which we say dwells in the summit of our body and lifts us from earth toward

our celestial affinity, like a plant whose roots are not in the earth, but in the heavens.[19]

Thus, in mythical terms, the contemplative faculty, rooted in the head, pulls the body upward and draws our attention toward heavenly concerns. Continuing, Plato writes:

> Now if a man is engrossed in appetites and ambitions and spends all his pains upon these, all his thoughts must need be mortal and, so far as that is possible, he cannot fall short of becoming mortal altogether, since he has nourished the growth of his mortality.[20]

On the other hand, in the Platonic version of contemplative soul-making, if a person's

> heart has been set on the love of learning and true wisdom and he has exercised that part of himself above all, he is surely bound to have thoughts immortal and divine, if he shall lay hold upon the truth, nor can he fail to possess immortality in the fullest measure that human nature admits; and because he is always devoutly cherishing the divine part and maintaining the guardian genius that dwells with him in good estate, he must needs be happy above all.[21]

Thus, human happiness and contemplation are intimately linked in the Greek philosophical tradition. Through contemplating that which is timeless, beautiful, and immortal, we partake of beauty, immortality, and true happiness or fulfillment. And in this sense, contemplation is transformative.

Plato's program of philosophical soul-making constitutes both a theory of education and a type of *psychotherapy*, for it is also a "care of the soul." In this therapeutic process, the contemplation of the heavens plays a central part for, as he writes,

> there is but one way of caring for anything, namely to give it the nourishment and motions proper to it. The motions akin to the divine

part in us are the thoughts and revolutions of the universe; these, therefore, every man should follow, and correcting those circuits in the head that were deranged at birth, by learning to know the harmonies and revolutions of the *cosmos*, he should bring the intelligent part, according to its pristine nature, into the likeness of that which intelligence discerns, and thereby win the fulfillment of the best life set by the gods before mankind, both for this present time and for the time to come.[22]

The influence of these Pythagorean and Platonic ideas regarding the role of contemplation are so far-reaching that they define a pivotal conception of human excellence in the Western tradition. Central to this notion is the understanding that true knowledge is both transcendental—larger than the individual—and divinizing, leading to the completion of Nature. If we can understand principles that are truly universal and timeless, some part of the soul partakes of the universal and timeless, for only like can know like. In this realization—and in the contemplation of universal reality, beauty, and harmony—lies an important dimension of human fulfillment. Thus Aristotle wrote:

We ought not to obey those who tell us that a man should think a man's thoughts, and a mortal the thoughts of a mortal. On the contrary, we should endeavor as far as possible to become immortal, and to do all that we can to live in accordance with what is highest in us.[23]

While ancient Greek mythology pictured the gods and goddesses in anthropomorphic terms, the early philosophers saw humanity in theomorphic terms.[24] In other words, human nature, at its best and highest, reflects the light of divine reality.

Aristotle sums up the entire Greek tradition regarding contemplation when he argues at length in the *Nicomachean Ethics* that "Perfect happiness (*eudaimonia*) is a contemplative activity."[25] Here the term "happiness" is somewhat misleading, because *eudaimonia* is not an emotional state but an *activity*. As Martha Nussbaum points out, it is more accurate to translate *eudaimonia* as "human flourishing."[26] In this way, we can see that approaching the universe with a sense of awe,

wonder, and serious reflection, allows us to live "the flourishing life."
The flourishing life, in turn, provides for the deepest realization of
human nature, and the deepest appreciation of the universe.

Ironically, while Aristotle identified contemplation with the flourishing life, it was with Aristotle himself that philosophy began to close
itself off from the numinosity of the universe and the deep experience
of Being. For Socrates, philosophy entailed the practice of "the
examined life" through inquiry and dialectic; philosophy itself was
envisioned as a way of *praxis*, a path of transformation. To embark
upon this path, it was necessary to enter into dialogue, both with other
humans and with the nature of existence itself. Plato, following in the
footsteps of Socrates, presented his thought not in the form of
doctrinal expositions, but as *dialogues*. For Plato, the cultivation of
intellect and discursive reason is not an end in itself, but a means to an
end. Intellect is not to be discarded, but the ultimate goal for Plato is
the direct, experiential knowledge of Being, which lies *beyond* limited
intellectual definition. For Socrates and Plato, philosophy is a trans-
formational activity in which feeling and reason are not antagonistic;
philosophy itself is pictured in an "erotic" context as the *desire* for
beauty. Eros, feeling, desire, wonder, awe, beauty, and aesthetics are
all implicated in the historical roots of the Western philosophical
tradition. Pythagoras, the first to call himself a philosopher, was also
the first to call the universe a *kosmos* on account of its *beauty*. Philosophy begins with wonder and with a deep perception of the "aesthetic
fitness" of the universe.

With Aristotle, however, philosophy takes another turn. Aristotle
was enticed by the idea of intellectual certainty and the "enforceable
demonstrations" of mathematical logic and syllogistic reason. Consequently, in the words of Robert Cushman, Aristotle "was impatient
with dialogue and preferred the declarative treatise."[27] The sense of
wonder that we can tangibly feel in the greatest early philosophers is
replaced with the quest for mathematical certitude and
"verificationism." The intellect, rather than "pointing toward" ultimate reality in a Zen sense, becomes mistaken as the goal in itself. In
the Aristotelian approach, contemplation thus loses its emotional

engagement with the living universe and retreats into the abstractions of the intellect; *theoria* is reduced to "theory." As philosopher Stephen Rowe observes in his book *Rediscovering the West*, it is with Aristotle (and not Descartes) that the Western philosophical tradition began its trajectory toward self-referential alienation. Rowe suggests that Aristotle's demand for logical, deductive demonstration has ultimately

> led to the elevation of intellectual/cognitive knowledge over all others, and to the fragmentation and specialization of knowledge, to an "intellectualist bias." As a result, the greatness of our tradition, philosophy as "the love of wisdom" (*philo-sophia*), is hardly visible as an option today.[28]

In a similar vein, Kierkegaard wrote that "It is the misfortune of our age that it has too much knowledge, that it has forgotten what it means to exist,"[29] while Heidegger concluded that philosophers would be better off asking how to experience Being rather than how to know Being.[30]

In a time when contemporary physics speaks of such concepts as "the uncertainty principle," the observer as "participator" in the creation of reality, and asserts (in the words of Niels Bohr) that "A great truth is a truth whose opposite is also a great truth," the faith in reason as the *only* valid key to reality has been severely shaken. Yet, the criticism of abstract, mathematical reasoning—what William Blake called "Satan's Mathematick Holiness"—is not a recent one. For example, the dry, intellectual abstraction resulting from the Aristotelian approach must have been a major factor in leading many Hellenistic philosophers to conclude that

> a precise, logically rigorous argument that is not well suited to the needs of its hearers, an argument that is simply and entirely academic and unable to engage its audience in a practical way, is to that extent a *defective philosophical argument*.[31]

Cicero criticizes the Greek Stoics in precisely this vein when he writes

> Their narrow little syllogistic arguments prick their hearers like pins.
> Even if they assent intellectually, they are in no way changed in their
> hearts, but they go away in the same condition in which they came. The
> subject matter is perhaps true and certainly important; but the arguments
> treat it in too petty a manner, and not as it deserves.[32]

From this perspective, contemplation, whether practiced in astronomy, philosophy, or science, must be a transformative experience.
Contemplation is a creative act, for, in the act of seeing, the worldview
that we carry determines the type of universe we allow ourselves to see.
But the primordial act of seeing the universe, conversely, must
innately carry within the potential to transform the observer and
expand our conceptual limitations. The practice of contemplation is
thus a twofold creative act that allows us to both imagine and revision
our place in the universe simultaneously.

Seeing with an Imaginal Eye

> As a man is, So he Sees. As the Eye is Formed, such are its Powers.
> You certainly Mistake when you say Visions of Fancy are not to be
> Found in This World. To Me This World is One continued Vision
> of Fantasy or Imagination.
>
> —William Blake

If, since the time of Aristotle, philosophy has fallen prey to the self-
recursive loop of closed, discursive reasoning, one of the many factors
left out of the equation is the cognitive faculty of the imagination, the
faculty of imaginal insight. Throughout the history of the Western
world, there has existed a subterranean philosophy of the imagination
that has resurfaced at various times and places. In this tradition,
images, myths, and symbols embody active forms of imaginal cognition which, like sprouting seeds, can unfold their meaning in the fertile
ground of the soul. Iamblichus sums up much of this tradition when

he writes that "Things more excellent than every image are expressed through images."[33] Or, as Plotinus explains, in the realm of pure Being, "each manifestation of knowledge and wisdom is a distinct image, an object in itself, an immediate unity, not an aggregate of discursive reasoning and detailed willing."[34] Reasoning comes later, as the wisdom and knowledge held within the image comes to be articulated.

If the Aristotelian perspective "harnesses the power of nature" by standing outside of nature, the imaginal perspective participates in the infinite fertility of Nature itself. However, because the imaginal faculty of the soul possesses its own organic grammar which differs from the "enforceable demonstrations" of Aristotelian logic, over the past 2,500 years there has been a tacit, ongoing warfare between the world of spirit (or reason) and the world of soul (or imagination). If the Western philosophical tradition has been predominately one-sided in its focus on abstract reason, it has achieved this onesidedness by systematically devaluing the very images that could embody deeper ways of seeing. Thales, the first of the Presocratics, was a scientist, mathematician, and astronomer, yet he could simultaneously assert that "all things are full of gods"; since then, it has become far more difficult for individuals in the Western world to balance the rational and imaginal modes of cognition. Philosophy asks what we *think* about the universe, but not how we *imagine* it, and thus ignores the fact that even its own supposedly dispassionate, intellectual approach is governed by the unexamined fantasy of the heroic ego. However, if the contemplative sense of wonder is more imaginal than intellectual, the faculty of imaginal seeing warrants attention in the context of observational astronomy. That is because the speculum of consciousness is twofold: on the one hand, our telescopes objectively gather the light of distant images; on the other hand, the universe that we psychologically perceive is an active, imaginal envisioning, an activity of soul.

Sir William Herschel wrote that astronomical "Seeing is in some respect an art, which must be learnt," while Edwin Hubble affirmed that "Observations always involve theory." In observational astronomy, theory and *theôria* intrinsically go together. In the ephemeral world of ancient photons, where astronomers use techniques like "averted vision" to increase their seeing power,* having a prior idea of what you are looking for often enables you to see it in the first place. Because they were forced to depend on visual observations alone, earlier astronomers could rarely be sure about what they were looking at. Today, thanks to deeper knowledge, when I observe the ghostly, edge on galaxy NGC 4565 in Coma Bernices, cut in half by a subtle dust lane, I can truly "envision" far more than earlier astronomers, even though we've shared the same physical view.

In the art of astronomical observing, prior knowledge greatly enhances the experience. As astronomy writers Terence Dickinson and Alan Dyer note, "the more you know about what you are seeing, the more beautiful and meaningful it becomes."[35] The human eye cannot match the light-gathering power of time-exposure photography, but time-exposure photography cannot match the experience of actually *seeing* galaxies that are hundreds of millions of light years away. Visual astronomy is very much an imaginal activity: a contemplative practice in which our accumulated knowledge (the prior study of photographs, distances, scales, relationships) flows outward *through* the sense of vision to meet the incoming photons head on. Put another way, it's exciting to observe a fine globular cluster, but it's an entirely different experience to view it with the understanding that you are seeing one million stars in a sphere 200 light years across, located 16,000 light years away in a particular sector of our own Milky Way Galaxy. A multidimensional cognitive perspective "gives depth" to the visual field. In the words of William Blake, this is "a seeing not with but through the eyes,"[36] while Plotinus speaks of "an eye filled with its vision, a seeing that bears its image with it."[37] This imaginal seeing is not fantasy in the derogatory sense of the term, but a way of peering deeper, a way of "seeing through" the literalisms of the visible world to achieve a greater vision of reality. Through an expanded sense of

---

* In the technique of "averted vision," by looking off to the side of a faint luminosity, the object is aligned with the more sensitive receptor cells around the periphery of the retina.

A Globular Cluster
Omega Centauri, one of the nearest globular clusters to the Earth, contains
an estimated one millon individual stars. From *Burnham's Celestial Handbook*.

vision, we can, in the words of Plotinus, awaken to a "another way of seeing, which everyone has but few use."[38]

Contemplation and the Mirror of Nature

In the beginning was the cosmic Unity. From the primordial Unity came all that is. From the ancient myths of the Cosmic Egg, through the generating Monad of the Pythagoreans and the emanating One of the Neoplatonists, reaching forward to the cherished "big bang" of modern cosmology, the underlying pattern of cosmogenesis remains the same: the One gives birth to the Many.

In mystical terms, by re-collecting the divine sparks of creation and returning them to the Source through the practice of contemplation, the universe is restored to completeness, multiplicity is returned to unity. Through the contemplative act, the Golden Age is restored through a cognitive *metanoia*, a "re-turning of consciousness" to gaze at its source. In mythological terms, nature is only "fallen" because our own perception is clouded, a Hermetic idea that was also given currency by Paul when he implied that "the fall of humanity brings nature in its train, and consequently nature can be regenerated with humanity's help."[39] With the regeneration of humanity, "the creation itself will be set free from its bondage to decay and obtain the glorious liberty of the children of God."[40] According to the mythology of alchemy, spirit is hidden in matter, but longs to return to its glorious state; the return to the source, and the flowering of matter into spirit, is made possible through the process of evolution. Understood from an alchemical perspective, all of Nature and matter is alive and animated, and all metals, hidden deep within the bowels of the earth, are slowly ripening toward gold. The practice of alchemy is a form of spiritual and imaginal midwifery through which the natural process is made conscious and slowly nursed along. All humans transform matter into light or spirit through the digestion of food, for food is transformed into mind and the activity of contemplation; but the alchemist is especially concerned with the nature and stages of this process, and is thus allowed to participate more fully in the Great Work of Nature. However, as Françoise Bonardel points out, the

Reflecting on Nature's Mirror
Detail from frontispiece, Johann Bercher's
Psychosophia oder Seelen-Weisheit (Lauenburg, 1707).

alchemist does not stand outside Nature in a Faustian or Promethean
stance of objectification for purposes of exploitation:

> Nature in reality is not a thing for the mind to meditate on in order to
> extract its laws and so increase its mastery over the created world. It is the
> divine Mirror thanks to which the reflective possibility of catching a
> glimpse of itself is offered to each mind that sincerely renounces the
> inevitably violent appropriation of such an "object." The invocation of
> Nature as sole mistress of the Work, which punctuates all the treatises on
> alchemy, was therefore not a concession to a naturalism whose collusion
> with scientism was only to increase in the course of history . . .[41]

The Hermetic philosopher does not stand outside Nature, for such objectification leads to a cosmology of alienation and anxiety, reflected thoughout the fabric of modern life. Rather, in the alchemical universe, humanity is a microcosmic reflection of the heavens, an idea encapsulated in the Hermetic dictum "As above, so below." In the words of the church father Origen, "The sun and the moon are within you, and also the stars." Or, as Carl Sagan puts it, "We are star-stuff." From the Hermetic perspective and that of modern physics, Nature is the mirror through which the invisible is made visible. Going further, humanity itself is the Mirror of Nature. Through self-reflection in a Hermetic context, contemplation of our inner depths and the outer mysteries of the phenomenal world are part of the same, speculative enterprise. There is no radical break between man and nature, between the inner and outer worlds. Through the *speculum* or mirror of humanity, Nature becomes self-aware. We are made out of the stuff of stars, and through the contemplative practice of observational astronomy, the stars themselves become conscious, reflected in the Mirror of Mind. As Theodore Roszak writes, "The systems we see around us in nature are the cosmologically given archetypes of what rises to articulate self-awareness in us as 'thoughts.' We think because, in some sense that blends the literal and the figurative, the universe 'thinks.'"[42]

Paradoxically, as contemporary academic philosophy continues its movement away from traditional human concerns—for example, inquiry into the nature of love, beauty, and happiness—to ponder such questions as whether computers can be said to think, modern, scientific cosmology is becoming more Hermetic, more traditional. Nothing seems more metaphysical than the discoveries of modern physics, and many scientists are entertaining teleological ideas like the Anthropic Cosmological Principle—the notion that there is an inherent predisposition toward conscious life in the universal fabric—and the Gaia Hypothesis, the idea that the biosphere itself is an interconnected, self-regulating organism. In the Renaissance, it was thought that human beings actively participate in the divine, ongoing creation of the world through the creative imagination. Today, evolutionary cosmologists influenced by the holistic theory of self-organizing systems assert that evolution is not deterministic but inherently *creative* and unpredictable. The creed of scientific determinism, which held that life is a meaningless, cosmic accident, is being replaced by the perspective that "there are creative forces at work in matter that encourage it to develop life"[43] and a growing awareness that "our presence in the universe represents a *fundamental* rather than an *incidental* feature of existence."[44] The cosmos is beginning to look less and less like the wind-up mechanistic model of Newtonian physics, and more like a slowly evolving, creative organism. The word *create* itself has profound organic implications, for it is related to the word "cereal" or wheat, and comes from the Indo-European root *ker-*, which means "to grow."[45] Standing close to the Renaissance perspective, some suggest that the human imagination is itself a creative outgrowth of the universe—our imaginal nature is not separate from the universe, but a voice or expression of universal nature. Modern cosmology seems to be moving toward a renewed vision of the *anima mundi* or World Soul and the idea that our intrinsic drives toward understanding, creativity, philosophy, science, speculation, art and myth are *objective* expressions of the cosmic organism. When we dream, perhaps the earth and the stars are dreaming through us.

Eros and the Objects of Celestial Desire

> [The Soul is] eager to penetrate the object of contemplation, and it seeks the vision that comes by observation.
>
> —Plotinus, *Enneads* 3.8.6

The innate, mystical desire to return phenomena to their source through contemplation underlies the scientific study of cosmology. There is an "erotic" drive that compels philosophers, mystics, and scientists to wonder about the ultimate source of things. The empyreal sphere of the burning stars kindles a fire of celestial desire to understand and experience, in the deepest possible way, the Source and mystery of all that is. Speaking of the poet John Keats, Andrés

Rodrígues writes that "The imagination reflects an ardor, a fire which corresponds to 'empyreal' in its Greek root *empurios*, 'in fire.'"[46] If our cosmologists, like our poets, were not enflamed by a burning passion, it is unlikely that they would spend so much energy studying the mysteries of the expanding universe or constructing Grand Universal Theories. The mystical desire to grasp the ineffable Source is as much alive in scientific thought as it is in religious speculation. The scientific desire to understand the beginning of all things is essentially a religious drive to *reconnect* (*religio*) with the Source of all Being. Simply gazing in wonder at the mysterious depths of the night sky reflects a contemplative movement to reconnect with the seedbed of our own becoming.

1. *Plato: Eros, Recollection, and Philosophy*

The theory of an innate, erotic drive toward understanding is first clearly outlined in the writings of Plato. And in long course of the Platonic tradition that follows, the topics of *beauty*, *vision*, and *eros* are so inextricably interwoven that it is impossible to speak of one without speaking of the others.

In Plato's *Phaedrus*, Socrates presents a myth to explain the divine madness of love. Before birth, each soul that took on human form followed in the train of the gods. There, in the winged, cosmic procession, each soul glimpsed beauty and true knowledge to varying degress, feeding upon the vision like ambrosia and nectar. Due to forgetfulness, however, the soul grows heavy; it loses its wings and sinks down toward the earth in a state of amnesia. We are all thus born in varying states of forgetfulness.

When we fall in love, the vision of the beloved incites a form of divine madness. Eros is the desire to possess the beauty of the beloved, and in this condition "the whole soul throbs and palpitates." The effluence of beauty moistens the hard, atrophied roots of the soul's feathers, which again begin to swell and sprout. This causes an itching and feverish sensation like the cutting of teeth. When the beloved is near, the sensation of beauty moistens the follicles of the feathers; this soothes the discomfort and fills the soul with joy. But when separated from the beloved, the follicles start to harden and close up; they prick the soul, and throb painfully like pulsating arteries.

Socrates explains that the beauty of the beloved reminds the soul of its true, winged nature; the soul is reminded of the beauty that it gazed upon in the heavenly realms before being dragged down into a state of forgetfulness. Love is a reawakening to our essential, winged nature. We long to recover our essential nature, but, in the experience of love, often do not see what is really happening. There is a well known tendency to fall down and worship the beloved as the ultimate source of the lover's experience, rather than see the beloved as a catalyst of transformation; and in the misplaced concreteness of this perception, there exists the danger of not viewing the soul's awakening within a larger context. This does not imply that the beloved should be viewed merely as the reminder of a higher reality.[47] The suggestion is that an individual love, beautiful in itself, can also awaken us to greater realities. Love is a noble end in itself, but also the means to greater ends.

Eros leads beyond itself. For Plato, the experience of love is the beginning of the soul's awakening and education. Eros is the desire for beauty, and love reminds us of the beauty and knowledge of ultimate reality that lies *within* the soul. The word *education* means literally "to lead out," and in the Platonic tradition the mind is not a *tabula rasa* or blank slate to be filled up with facts and figures. Rather, philosophy is a "leading out" and articulation of the wisdom and knowledge that inherently exists within. Ultimately, Socrates defines the philosopher as "a lover of beauty, or one with a musical or loving nature."[48] Of all souls born into human life, the true philosopher—"the true musician and lover of beauty"—possesses the greatest share of recollection and remembrance, for such a soul has "seen the most" in its prenatal existence. Thus the soul of the philosopher holds the highest rank thanks not to superior intellect, but due to its greater capacity for *vision* and its ability to "see through" the literalisms of experience.

In the *Symposium*, Plato further describes how the path of love can return the philosopher to authentic knowledge, the contemplative vision of universal Beauty, which is the vision of Being itself. Socrates describes how he was initiated into the mysteries of love by Diotima, a wise and prophetic priestess. In the famous "ladder of love" speech, Socrates relates her teachings. In the philosopher's erotic awakening, he first falls in love with a particular body. Next, he realizes that beauty is not limited to one particular form, but belongs to many. From the beauty of bodies he advances to gaze upon the beauty of the soul and the fair order of human conduct. The philosopher is next led to contemplate the beauty of knowledge and scientific understanding, and from this he is led to the ultimate vision and "final secret," the vision of pure Beauty in itself. This Beauty is "the final object of all those previous toils" and is "ever-existent and neither comes to be nor perishes."[49] In coming to know the very essence of beauty (reflected in all levels of existence), "a man finds it truly worthwhile to live."[50] Thus the path of Eros leads from the outer vision of physical beauty toward the inner vision of contemplative insight.

In the *Symposium*, Eros himself is described as a great *daimôn*, a mediating spirit between the mortal and immortal levels of being. Love is mythically described as the offspring of Fullness (Poros) and Poverty (Peneia), and consequently partakes of both. Love possesses a fullness and richness of being, but is simultaneously a desire for that which it lacks. The lover, painfully aware of his emptiness, desires to possess the beauty of the beloved; the philosopher, keenly aware of his lack of wisdom, desires the wisdom that eludes him. Love and philosophy are seen as an *identical* movement toward knowledge, wisdom, and the experience of Being. In this sense, says Diotima, even Eros is a philosopher, "a lover of wisdom," because he too exists between wisdom and ignorance.[51] Love and philosophy are revealed not as the idealized destinations of one's quest, but as the arduous journey itself. Philosophy is revealed as the practice of eros: the desire for the Good, or that which is best.

2. *Plotinus: Eros and the Vision of Mystical Insight*

In the Neoplatonic tradition, Plato's insights about love are taken to the cosmological level. Love exists in the human soul and leads us to knowledge and the contemplation of reality, but Eros is also a cosmic force—a magnetic desire—through which the entire universe yearns to return to its source. Human love is described as part of this larger cosmic movement.

Rooted in the tradition of Plato, who described the ultimate source of reality as "beyond Being" itself (and therefore ineffable), Plotinus (204–270 C.E.) envisioned the source of the universe as the ungraspable One. The One is the Unthinkable Emptiness that lies behind all Form and Being. Because it is limitless and perfect, the One creatively overflows out of its infinite abundance; infinite Emptiness thus gives birth to Form. The Neoplatonists called the world of Form *Nous*, "Mind" or Intelligence, which they identified as the first level of Real Being. The Neoplatonic Nous is like the Christian Logos, the first "emanation" or "image" of the wholly Transcendent: "In the beginning was the Logos, and the Logos was God." However, in this cosmology we are not dealing with a planning and thinking divinity who stands outside of the universe and draws up a plan. Nous or Logos is the spontaneous, unpremeditated, spilling forth of the One. This overflowing is not something that happened in the past; it is an eternal event (and simultaneously outside of time). The universe is *constantly* arising from the unlimited power of the Void; in the words of the Jewish tradition it is a *creatio ex nihilo*, but one that is eternally unfolding. Behind the veil of manifest phenomena perpetually stands the pregnant emptiness of the One.

Plotinus describes Nous as Real Being; Intellect; an "image of the One" (insofar as the One can be imaged at all); the source of all Form; one God and all gods at once; the timeless repository of all universal principles; and the act of "vision" which is the simultaneous act of thinker, thought, and object of thought conjoined. The Intelligence of the universe is not the thought of an external God, but is subject and object united in a thinking that thinks itself. It is everything that exists; every thought, form, and process; the living image of the Void; Being (*ontos*) in the literal sense of "That Which Is."

In the same way that the One overflows and gives birth to Nous, Intelligence overflows and gives birth to Soul. This Soul is the living Soul of the Universe, the *anima mundi*, and Nature is its offspring.

Thus, Nature is the image of Soul, Soul is the image of Intelligence, and Intelligence is the image of the One. Ultimately, Nature is the image of the Void, but a beautiful and finely articulated image at that.

In Plotinus and the later Neoplatonists, everything desires to return to the One via the erotic desire for the Source which leads to inquiry and contemplation. The keywords here are the familiar Platonic trinity of Beauty, Vision, and Eros. Planted within the nature of all existence, varying only in degree, is the seed of longing for the Objects of Celestial Desire.

The highest movement toward the Source takes place in the upper reaches of the transcendent Soul. (These spatial metaphors, says Plotinus, are inadequate but unavoidable, owing to the limited nature of discursive language.) As he explains in his essay "On Love," the Soul is Aphrodite, who gives birth to Eros through the faculty of her vision. Looking back at Intellect, Soul "brings forth Eros through whom it continues to look at him." Love is "the eye of the desirer" and "by its power what loves is enabled to see the loved thing."[52] Thus, through contemplation, "the Soul conceived and brought forth an offspring worthy of itself and the vision."[53] Looking back at its source, "there is a strenuous activity of contemplation in the Soul . . . and Eros is born, the Love which is an eye filled with its vision, a seeing that bears its image with it."[54]

Plotinus' emphasis on *vision* as the ideal metaphor of transcendent insight is a major theme in his important writing on "Nature, Contemplation, and the One." There he argues that "all things are striving after Contemplation, looking to Vision as their one end"—not only humans, but even animals, the life principle in plants, "and the Earth that produces these."[55] For Plotinus, contemplation is a supremely creative act, and Nature is productive precisely because it is contemplative: "creation is the outcome of a contemplation which never becomes anything else, which never does anything else, but creates by simply being a contemplation."[56]

Contemplation is a direct act of *seeing* that is far more immediate than verbal description; thus, while the Sage employs discursive reason to explain this act to others, "in relation to himself he is

Vision."[57] Similarly, all the forms of true Being "spring from vision and are a vision."[58] The world of Nous, as a living unity composed of subject and object united through contemplation, is described as "a Seeing that lives."[59] "Contemplation and its object constitute a living thing, a Life, two inextricably one."[60] Intelligence or Nous is "a Seeing, and a Seeing which itself sees,"[61] and in the Intelligible world "the gods see, each singly and all as one."[62] This "Seeing that lives," which is a thinking, is the reflection of Intelligence in the void, and is synonymous with life, for "Every life is some form of thought, but of a dwindling clearness like the degrees of life itself."[63]

It is the task of the philosopher to awaken to this type of seeing which every person has, but which few people use.[64] This seeing is a transformative "re-turning" to the Source of Being that implies a corresponding revisioning of one's *own* being, a reassimilation to the objects of desire. In the words of Plotinus, "No eye ever saw the sun without becoming sun-like, nor can a soul see beauty without becoming beautiful. You must become first of all godlike and all beautiful if you intend to see God and beauty."[65] Or, as he explains in another passsage, "All that one sees as a spectacle is still external; one must bring the vision within and see no longer in that mode of separation but as we know ourselves; thus a man filled with a god—possessed by Apollo or by one of the Muses—need no longer look outside for his vision of the divine being; it is but finding the strength to see divinity within."[66]

3. Proclus: Singing Sunflowers and the Circle of Cosmic Love

The greatest of the later Neoplatonists was Proclus (412–485 C.E.), and he was one of the last to lecture at the Platonic Academy in Athens before the school was closed down in 529 by an edict of Justinian, which outlawed the teaching of pagan philosophy.[67] A deeply religious individual, and the greatest scholastic philosopher of antiquity, Proclus united a profound mysticism with the reasoning of Aristotelian logic to articulate a systematic theology of the cosmic process and the mystical return to the One.

In his *Elements of Theology*,[68] Proclus argued that every effect *remains* in its cause (by virtue of its similarity to the cause); it *departs* from its cause (by virtue of its difference from the cause); and strives to *return* to its cause (because everything strives to return to its source of perfection). By returning to the cause, the effect is perfected, and it can even be said to desire its return. This threefold pattern of remaining (*monê*), proceeding (*proodos*), and returning (*epistropê*) underlies the entire structure of the cosmic hierarchy, linking every level of reality together in one continuous chain.[69]

The entire living universe, reaching from the Intelligible World to the physical cosmos, is thus united in one magnificent circuit, animated by the motive power of love, the erotic desire of each level to return to its own immediate cause. As Proclus writes, "every kind of love is the cause of the return of all things toward the divine Beauty, since it is always the intermediary between that which returns and the goal of the return which is desired by the effect."[70]

If Proclus was more rigorous, systematic, and perhaps hairsplitting than Plotinus, he was also more inclined toward mystic ritual, an activity that Plotinus avoided. As is well known, Proclus advocated the use of theurgic ritual as a means by which the soul of the philosopher may return to the level of the gods. All natural phenomena reflect traces of divine, transcendent reality, and specific forms of ritualized devotion allow the soul to ascend the rays of cosmic sympathy suspended from the heavens. Through *theourgia* ("divine work"), which taps into the celestial current of the ensouled universe, it is possible to bypass reason and directly elevate the soul to the experience of transcendental realities. In the Renaissance, Marsilio Ficino practiced a similar form of sympathetic magic when, through the means of love coupled with musical performance, he attuned himself "with the rays of the heavenly *spiritus*" given off by the planets. Describing the underlying theory of theurgy (and his own theurgic practice), Ficino wrote that:

> Our *spiritus* is in conformity with the rays of the heavenly *spiritus*, which penetrates everything either secretly or obviously. It shows a far greater

kinship when we have strong desire for that life and are seeking a benefit
that is consistent with it, and thus transfer our own *spiritus* into its rays
by means of love, particularly if we make use of song and light and the
perfume appropriate to the deity like the hymns that Orpheus consecrated
to the cosmic deities . . . For the *spiritus*, once it has been it has been made
more akin to the deity by emotional disposition, song, perfume, and light,
draws a richer influence from it.[71]

In the erotic, magical cosmos of both Proclus and Ficino, where the
various levels of reality are bound together through hidden sympa-
thies, marvelous feats of natural magic become possible through
cultivation of desire and the imagination, which are themselves
aspects of the larger cosmic life. Describing how the divine circuit of
cosmic life permeates all levels of being, Proclus explains how even
sunflowers pray, by tracking the physical sun. That is because

> all things pray and compose hymns to the leaders of their respective
> orders; but some, intellectually, and others rationally; some in a natural,
> and others after a sensible manner. Hence the sunflower, as far as it is
> able, moves in a circular dance towards the sun; so that if any one could
> hear the pulsation made by its circuit in the air, he would perceive
> something composed by a sound of this kind, in honour of its king, such
> as a plant is capable of framing.[72]

In one sense, the praying, contemplative flower is but one stage in
the divine circulation of light. The energy of the sun fuels the life of
all creatures, and the light incarnated in the flower attempts to return
to its source by tracking the sun. At a higher level, the same phototropic relationship also exists between the flower of the human soul and
the intelligible light of the One, the transcendent source of all reality.
Based on a statement of the *Chaldean Oracles* that "there is a certain
Intelligible which you must perceive by the flower of your mind,"[73]
Proclus suggested that there is an essential unity of our being, "the
flower of the soul," that is the highest aspect of our nature:

For just as we possess [universal] Mind only because of our [individual] mind, so we possess the One, the Source of all knowledge, only because of the unity or, as it were, the flower of our existence which connects us the most with the Divine.[74]

In other words, the human soul is able to experience a direct relationship with the One—the transcendental source of the cosmos—by virtue of the divine unity that exists at "the center of our whole being and all its numerous powers."[75] This flower of our innermost being— "the fire-brand of the soul"[76]—"is alone able to bring us to the Absolutely Transcendent of all things."[77]

Seen in perspective, the role of theurgy in later Neoplatonism might best be viewed as a Western analog to the symbolic, tantric dimension of the Eastern traditions, with their magic and ritual practices. Alternately, we need not look so far afield. Great cathedrals are designed to accomplish a theurgic transformation, in which light, color, incense, and choral harmonies combine to transport individuals to an awareness of angelic realities.

4. *Aphrodite's Companions: The Flowering of Vision in Renaissance Florence*

If Proclus represented the circle of cosmic love by the rigorously defined logical categories of remaining, proceeding, and returning, the Florentine Platonist Marsilio Ficino (1433–1499) found a more fertile image for the circle of love in the dance of the three Graces, the handmaidens of Aphrodite. Originally, the Graces were flower goddesses, associated with the beauty and pleasures of spring. In Greece they had been known as *Thalia* (Blooming), *Aglaia* (Splendor), and *Euphrosyne* (Joy). In the Renaissance, they took on the titles of *Pulchritudo* (Beauty), *Amor* (Love), and *Voluptas* (Pleasure). According to the first-century writer Seneca, the three Graces represent the power of giving, accepting, and returning thanks. For Ficino, they symbolize the circle of divine love and the conversion of the soul back to its source. As he writes:

This divine beauty has generated love, that is, a desire for itself, in all things. Since if God attracts the World to Himself, and the World is attracted, there exists a certain continuous attraction (beginning from God, emanating to the World, and returning at last to God) which returns again, as if in a kind of circle, to the same place whence it issued. And so one and the same circle from God to the World and from the World to God is called by three names. Inasmuch as it begins in God and attracts to Him, it is called Beauty; inasmuch as emanating to the World it captivates it, it is called Love; inasmuch as returning to its author it joins His work to Him, it is called Pleasure. Love, therefore, beginning from Beauty, ends in Pleasure.[78]

For Ficino, contemplation is an inherently pleasurable activity. Reflecting on the beauty of nature and observing the wonders of the heavens may have few "practical" benefits, but these activities, motivated by love, result in genuine *pleasure*. The end of the contemplative life is not the acquisition of worldly power and status (which often implies the exploitation of individuals and the natural world), but the cultivation of beauty, love, and pleasure in every sphere of life. According to Plotinus, contemplation is the source of all creativity, and the end of the contemplative life, inspired by eros, is pleasure and creative fertility. Rather than exploitation, the goal of the contemplative life is *appreciation*. When we realize that modern industrial society is based upon the fantasy of unlimited growth (and the exploitation that follows), it becomes obvious that a worldview based on the values of appreciation, creative fulfillment, and compassion would radically transform the world as we know it.

Neoplatonic Metaphors and the Language of Contemporary Cosmology

> The Universe is built upon a plan the profound symmetry of which is somehow present in the inner structure of our intellect.
>
> —Paul Valéry

When Plotinus used the term "emanation" to describe the procession of all reality from the transcendental One, he was careful to point out that he was using a spatial metaphor to describe a logical structure of Being that is beyond both space and time. For Plotinus, the One gives birth to all that is, but it does not physically emanate the universe in space or time.

Oddly enough, contemporary scientific cosmology has once again become emanationist. We now know that the universe is expanding in every direction and that galaxies are condensations of primordial energy. According to the canon of contemporary cosmology, all evidence suggests that everything in the universe emerged from a primordial "singularity," the fireball of the big bang. The word *universe* means "to turn around one thing," and all of contemporary cosmology orbits around the idea of the primordial singularity of the First Cause, which some have likened to a black hole in reverse. Many observers have pointed out that the idea of the big bang is intrinsically mythological, like the ancient stories of the Cosmic Egg. Even the term *big bang* was coined by astronomer Fred Hoyle in derision of the concept. But just because the big bang is a myth doesn't mean that it didn't happen. Perhaps the myths have been right all along.

The most remarkable thing about contemporary cosmology is its doctrine that everything has come from *nothing*.* Or, if the universe did come from something, that "something" was a point of infinite

---

* According to contemporary physics, the quantum vacuum is constantly boiling with virtual particles. In the vacuum genesis thesis of Edward Tryon, the universe itself is pictured as a fluctuation in the quantum vacuum. In this scenario, the enormous energy in the universe is cancelled out by the opposing force of gravitational attraction. If correct, the universe has zero net energy and is a quantum fluctuation that has emerged from *nothing*. The parallels between this theory and "the void" of Plotinus' "One," which is "no thing," are remarkable.

density occupying zero volume. Medieval theologians have been ridiculed for arguing about how many angels can dance on the head of a pin, but if you can obtain 20 billion observable galaxies from something the size of a photon, the idea of an infinite number of angels on a pinhead becomes more tenable. Writing in the current issue of *Scientific American*, one leading cosmologist suggests that it might be possible to create a universe in a laboratory from a tiny amount of compressed matter, and that our own universe might have originated from a physicist-hacker's experiment.[79] Others suggest that there are an infinite number of universes outside of our own, and that each black hole gives birth to another universe.

Perhaps in time the existence of black holes will give rise to a new theory of *post mortem* existence: when a living system collapses in on itself and "dies," the singularity of death opens out into another universe of life. A similar idea was expressed by the Greek philosopher Heraclitus when he wrote that "The immortal becomes mortal, the mortal immortal, each living in the other's death and dying in the other's life." If we start to die as soon as we are born, perhaps we start to live when we appear to die. According to some cosmological theories, at this very moment we are living within the center of a dead star: the infinitely collapsed singularity of a black hole which has, through cosmic reciprocity, infinitely expanded outward to form our universe.* If reality itself is a dreaming in the Void, the distinctions between the living and the dead may be artificial, as many traditions have taught.

In its own way, modern physics has deconstructed the idea of materialism. If matter is ultimately energy, and one substance can be turned into another, the most important characteristic of any thing is the underlying *pattern* that provides its unique form. All of a sudden, the Platonic theory of Forms is reestablished, and we discover ourselves inhabiting the universe that Plato described in the *Timaeus*: reality is the offspring of Form married with the Receptacle of time,

---

* Roger Penrose and Stephen Hawking showed thirty years ago that the equations describing the big bang are the same equations, reversed in time, describing the collapse of a black hole.

space, and becoming. If the universe has come from nothing and possesses zero net energy, the Neoplatonic notion that reality is a "Thought" hardly seems farfetched.

Plato maintained that "time is a moving image of eternity, which revolves according to Number."[80] Put another way, that which is beyond space and time is played out *as* space and time. From this perspective, the idea of a big bang is congenial with Neoplatonic cosmology. Plotinus's structure of The One : Intelligence : Soul : Nature may exist beyond space-time, but there is no reason that the structure itself should not be articulated within space and time. For example, every flower comes from the singularity of a seed. The seed is articulated into the pattern of life which, like Proclus's praying sunflower, looks back toward the sun. In this looking back at the Source, the being of the flower experiences completion, ripening, and fertility. In the contemplative act, the flower becomes productive and gives birth to new seeds and new lives. Like the flower strewing its seeds, perhaps the cosmic Imagination, when contemplating the ineffable Source, gives birth to infinite worlds, to infinite universes. As John Gribbin notes, one dramatic implication of modern cosmology is that "many, perhaps all the black holes that form in our own Universe may be the seeds of new universes."[81]

Interestingly, Proclus's threefold logical scheme of remaining, proceeding, and returning to the Source fits quite well with the contemporary model of the big bang:

1. Remaining. Despite the fact that the big bang occurred 15 billion years ago, we nonetheless abide within the singularity. We are not ultimately separated from the source of the cosmos because it *is* our source and we have something in common with it. Because space-time curves in on itself, some cosmologists have suggested that, for all intents and purposes, our universe itself exists within a black hole.

2. Proceeding. The source expands, moving outward, and receives articulation in the matrix of space-time, which is created through the act of procession itself.

3. Returning. We spiritually return to the source when we contemplate the beauty of nature, wonder in awe at the limitless depths of the cosmos, and investigate the source of all things. On the material level, we may also one day return to the source. According to astronomers, if there is a sufficient amount of hidden mass in the universe known as dark matter, the universe will eventually stop expanding outward and contract upon itself, to form a black hole. After the interval of many billions of years, the universe will collapse upon itself in a "big crunch" to form another singularity, thus literally consummating the mystical marriage of Alpha and Omega, the Beginning and End of creation. From the end of one universe another cosmos may arise, once again expanding from the core of the Cosmic Egg. According to this model, over tens of billions of years the universe may alternately expand and contract like the beating of a heart. In meditation, the contemplative becomes unified with the cosmos, in part by watching the rhythm of his or her breath. Now it seems as though we may live in a "breathing universe" that exhales and inhales over millenia, only to exhale again. The ancient Hermetic philosophers, who based their cosmological symbolism on the faculty of *analogia* or proportional thinking, surely would have delighted in this pneumatic congruence of macrocosm and microcosm.

Planets also illustrate the cycle of remaining, proceeding, and returning. Like a ball twirled around on a string, each planet desires to fly outward from the center. Yet, simultaneously, each planet is pulled inward toward the source. Caught between the simultaneous tensions of expansion and contraction—proceeding and returning— each planetary wanderer abides in its own set place, dancing round between the poles of dispersion and unification. As Proclus suggested, the three tendencies are simultaneously at work on every level of reality. In the physical universe, the path of return is associated with the phenomenon of gravity, which pulls things together and allows for the emergence of higher, more complex states (galaxies, solar systems, humans, etc.). If the big crunch theorists are correct, the force of gravity will physically return all phenomena to their source: the primordial seed. In the spiritual universe, the path of return is contemplative, a phototropic movement toward insight and illumination.

In their orbits around the sun, the planets are moved by an aspiration toward their source. Yet, in the same way that the planets aspire toward the sun, every star—dispersing the gifts of Being and Life—both yearns for and reflects an even higher reality. This may account for the belief of Origen, the Alexandrian theologian, who asserted that the sun, moon, and stars form a choir, hymning and praying to the First Cause. If we possessed the sensitivity to hear the sound given off by Proclus's dancing sunflower, we'd also be able to hear the songs of the stars.

*　*　*

Perhaps the greatest cosmological question is how we can know anything at all. As Einstein said, "The most incomprehensible thing about the universe is that it is comprehensible."[82] Technologists and empiricists sidestep the question by focusing on pragmatic, utilitarian results: as long as they can *use* the principles of physics, it doesn't matter how they know them. But sidestepping the question is not a way of addressing it. The problem with the empiricist approach is that the human mind possesses an uncanny, Promethean ability to directly intuit the principles of physics which can *later* be tested experimentally. As I have noted before in these pages, Einstein's theory of relativity predicted the curvature of space before it was later verified by astronomers. Moreover, it's unlikely that atomic fission could ever have been achieved by empirical experimentation alone. In some way that transcends scientific understanding (because we cannot stand outside of cognition), our human intelligence is very intimately related with the Intelligence or laws of the universe. Because of the similarity, it is possible for like to know like. As Plato said, education is an external articulation of the knowledge that we innately possess within. Learning is "recollection," and experimentation with the things of sense is an important part of the learning process. But the desire for knowledge—and the design of every experiment—is some-thing which arises from within the mind itself. Like musical improvi-sation, which makes use of external instruments, scientific experimen-tation is a creative activity of the soul.

Following the Pythagoreans, Plato suggested that, aside from Exist-ence itself, the two ultimate principles of the universe are Sameness and Difference.[83] Following the path of Sameness, Novalis wrote that "I am you."[84] Following the path of Difference, he wrote "One is alone with whomever, whatever one loves."[85] In some sense, we are able to know the universe because we are *identical* with the universe; in another sense, we can know other things because we are *different* from them. Sameness and Difference exist not only as cosmic principles; they make human knowledge possible. Perhaps this is what Empedocles was getting at when he said that the universe is governed by the dual principles of Love (Sameness/Unity) and Strife (Difference/Duality). According to the Platonic tradition, true learning originates from an ongoing dialectic between Sameness and Difference—between the *a priori* and *a posteriori* ways of knowing—in the context of philosophical and scientific inquiry.

The word *science* means "to know," but comes from an Indo-European root that literally means "to cut" or "to split." The same root gives birth to the word *schism*. The scientific method literally cuts reality up into little parts for the purpose of controlled experimenta-tion. While scientific theory is rooted in the mysterious *a priori* ways of knowing—itself rooted in our innate connection with the uni-verse—scientific *method* is based upon *a posteriori* experimentation.

When the scientific method becomes falsely identified as the single path to authentic knowledge, then the belief system of *scientism* is born. Rooted in an obsessive, controlling vision of the observer standing apart from the world, scientism is based on the reductionistic premise that the scientific method is the *only* way to certain knowl-edge. In this chauvinistic perspective, one authentic but limited pathway to human understanding claims for itself the *whole* of reality. Moreover, in the wake of scientism, other modalities of human knowing are politely encouraged to atrophy, for if such pursuits as poetry, art, and music are "not scientific," how can they be said to possess any real value?

The scientific method is perfectly valid in its own domain. However, the problem with science is that it slices up reality and never tells us what anything really *is*—the *Ding an sich* or "thing in itself" is sacrificed to abstraction. Science describes aspects of phenomena, but cannot lead us to experiential knowledge. For example, we could jot down all the known properties of light on a piece of paper, which certainly would tell us something about it. But the only way to grasp what light really *is* is to experience it firsthand. Gnosis, like beauty, love, and art, is experiential. Similarly, if we could mathematically describe every process in the universe in the course of one unified equation, it would hardly "explain" what the universe is. Nor would such an equation tell us whether our existence has any meaning. The error of scientism thus originates with a reasonable proposition, from which it draws an unwarranted conclusion:

1) The experimental, scientific method does not encompass questions of meaning.

2) Therefore, the universe is itself meaningless.

Based upon the pragmatic achievements of applied technology, the faith of scientism has gained many converts and has significantly contributed to the narrow, one-dimensional view of reality that permeates the official world of business, technology, and economics. But true scientists are more than technocrats, they are *philosophers* and cosmologists interested in a greater vision of reality. Our increasing scientific knowledge about the universe does not diminish the sense of wonder, but *increases* it, as long at it can be communicated in a living fashion. In a Platonic sense, scientific knowledge can point toward a greater, experiential connection with the universe and the mysteries of being.

Science means "to cut," but the root of the words *wisdom, vision,* and *idea* means "to see." In this sense, *philosophia* is a way of "seeing the bigger picture" through luminous ideas which unify our experience of reality. Scientific method is fine as far as it goes, but the need for a more inclusive cosmology has never been more keenly felt than in the present time, characterized as it is by cultural fragmentation and a split between the worlds of "fact" and "value." A true cosmology is more than just a description of scientific laws. It is a living harmonic *vision*— a contemplative *seeing*—of how all the parts fit together into a larger whole.

One of the remarkable parallels between Greek philosophical thought and contemporary cosmology centers around the question of *harmonic symmetry.* The Pythagoreans were fascinated with the perfect symmetry of the 6:8::9:12 "harmonic proportion" which underlies the structure of the musical scale. Modern physicists are fascinated by the fact that the forces of nature reflect "broken symmetries." It is thought that these broken symmetries emerged from some type of perfect symmetry that existed at the beginning of the universe. In this sense, perhaps music is a reflection of the primordial cosmic symmetry; as the Pythagoreans suggested, our human music reflects the extraterrestrial "music of the spheres."

"Supersymmetry," writes astronomer Timothy Ferris, "portrays this ultimate perfection as a hyperdimensional universe, of which our poor imperfect universe is but a paltry shadow."[86] Such a model is virtually identical with the cosmology sketched by Plato in the *Timaeus.* In Plato's myth, the World Soul consists of Sameness and Difference woven together through the perfect, symmetrical ratios of musical harmony. The physical universe is an "imperfect" reflection of the higher universe, but it is the best possible image of the hyperdimensional universe in the more extended regions of time and space. Plato maintained that the human soul contains a "memory" of the higher world, the imprint of which allows us to have genuine knowledge. Timothy Ferris closely mirrors this understanding when he suggests that the universe is comprehensible because it is defective—that because it forsook the perfection of nonbeing for the welter of being, it is possible for us to exist, and to perceive the jumbled, blemished reality, and to test it against the ghostly specter of the primordial symmetry thought to have preceded it.[87]

If we can "test" the imperfect physical universe against something more perfect, we must contain a reflection of the higher perfection within. Such a view closely parallels the idea of Proclus that we are able to directly and non-verbally experience the nature of the One because the unified "flower of the soul" is cast in its image. As in the Gnostic myths, we may be able to intuitively grasp the universal symmetry that existed before the big bang—the rending of the Pleroma—because the soul itself contains a divine but slumbering spark of that perfect symmetry. Thomas Aquinas wrote that three things are needed for beauty: wholeness, harmony, and radiance. According to the Platonists, when we observe the beauties and symmetries of nature, they excite a feeling of kinship with the primordial symmetry which has left its imprint within the soul. When we look at the stars, we experience a sensation of identity.

Scientific cosmology is by no means a futile pursuit; over the last seventy years it has opened infinite vistas of beauty and wonder. But Plato, Plotinus, and Proclus describe another kind of direct knowledge which doesn't involve intellectual separation from the living universe. This is the experiential knowledge engendered by the contemplative act—an essential act of Vision in which the beauties of the cosmos act as windows for the radiance of the primordial Beauty. Through this act, which returns things to their Source, the broken symmetries of nature are both healed and revealed as images of a higher Beauty and Intelligence. Ignited by wonder, Eros, and the fires of celestial desire, the soul looks back to the Source, contemplates the mysteries of Being, and that which lies Beyond. This contemplative movement may be initiated by any manifestation of beauty that calls to us, including the beauty of the night sky, which excites a starry-eyed longing for greater understanding. Appropriately enough, this magnetic pull of the heavens is reflected in the source of the word *desire*—the Latin *desiderare*—which literally means "of the stars."

In the Wake of a Cosmological Revolution

> A single lifetime, even though entirely devoted to the sky, would not be enough for the investigation of so vast a subject . . . And so this knowledge will be unfolded only through long successive ages. There will come a time when our descendants will be amazed that we did not know things that are so plain to them . . . Many discoveries are reserved for ages still to come, when memory of us will have been effaced. Our universe is a sorry little affair unless it has in it something for every age to investigate . . . Nature does not reveal her mysteries once and for all.
>
> —Seneca, *Natural Questions*
> First century C.E.

We are clearly standing in the wake of a cosmological revolution. The third century B.C.E. philosopher Aristarchus of Samos suggested that the earth orbits the sun, but it was less than five hundred years ago that the heliocentric revolution was inaugurated by Copernicus. Using an instrument less powerful than the telescopes now sold in department stores, Galileo made his first observations of the heavens in 1609. The doorway of telescopic astronomy had opened, at least a crack. But it was a large enough crack to forever shatter the Aristotelian view that the planets were made of a quintessential element more pure than fire. Looking at the moon, Galileo saw a world ravaged by craters, and when he turned his sights to the Milky Way, the telescope revealed countless stars.

In 1771, French comet-hunter Charles Messier pubished a list of 103 glowing nebulosities in the night sky. These are the well known "Messier objects" like "M31" (the Whirlpool Galaxy), much loved by backyard astronomers. But Messier had not set out to systematically catalog the heavens; he had the more prosaic intent of recording those objects that might be mistaken for comets. Ironically, while he was the discoverer of several comets, Messier is only now remembered for the deep sky showpieces that bear his name.

The first systematic catalog of deep sky objects was made in the late 1700s by the astronomer (and musician to the royal court) Sir William Herschel, who was knighted for the discovery of the planet Uranus. While his contemporaries focused on planetary observations, Herschel, together with the help of his faithful sister Caroline, undertook a systematic survey of the entire sky and cataloged over 2,500 deep sky objects that we now know are hundreds, thousands, or millions of light years away. The problem was that neither Messier nor Herschel could be exactly sure about what they were looking at. Herschel correctly supposed that the great nebula in Andromeda was actually "the united luster of millions of stars," but was unable to prove it; when observed with the human eye, distant galaxies look like soft glows even through the largest telescopes. It is possible to get an idea of their outer shape and even see some internal structure, but individual stars can only be resolved with time exposure astrophotography.

Herschel and company were thus left uncertain as to the precise nature of the luminous nebulae, even though some of them displayed a distinctive spiral structure. The French mathematician Pierre-Simon de Laplace suggested that the "spiral nebulae" were condensing clouds of luminous gas and dust, solar systems in the making, while others, like the philosopher Immanuel Kant, suggested that they were "island universes" composed of myriad stars. The debate raged on throughout the nineteenth century and was only definitively settled when, in 1924, astronomer Edwin Hubble announced his proof that the "nebula" in Andromeda was over a million light years away and therefore a distant "island universe"—a "galaxy" like our own Milky Way. As Robert Burnham observes, "If nothing else had happened in this century, the final identification of the spirals as external galaxies was sufficient to alter our whole conception of the large-scale features of the Universe."[88] Shortly thereafter, in 1929, Hubble announced a correlation between the distance of galaxies and the redshift in their spectra, an indication that the universe itself is expanding. With these discoveries, we had entered the modern age; ten years later, in 1939,

Niels Bohr and John Archibald Wheeler developed the theory of nuclear fission.

*　*　*

As the ancient philosophers realized, we live in a state of forgetfulness. It's amazing how much we take for granted: who we are, what we are, where we live, our unique place in history.

Today, in the Promethean myth of modernity, the human mind divorces itself from the world and stands outside Nature, looking at the world as something "other." The Cartesian split gives rise to the exploitation of Nature, the birth of technology, and a vicious circle of alienation: technology leads us to live in an ever more abstract, conceptual world, cut off from the experiential presence of Being. This conceptual alienation leads to the creation of more technology and the cycle becomes self-perpetuating.

*　*　*

The alarm goes off in the morning and it's time to catch my flight at the airport. I turn on the lights, then switch on the heat. The coffee maker with its built-in timer stands nearby, ready to offer me a freshly brewed cup. After a hot shower, I blow dry my hair. Throwing my bags in the car, I set off down the road, roll up the electric windows, and turn on the radio. On the way to the airport I pass the shopping district. There are hundreds of stores, stretching for miles, and the only way to reach them is by automobile. At this hour, the vast parking lots are empty and the malls look like deserted movie sets, bleakly illuminated by the nauseating glow of sodium vapor lights. Reaching the airport, I park the car, enter through electric doors, and pass through a metal detector. Once my bags have passed inspection by an X-ray machine, I am allowed to enter the jet, a structure of metal and plastic that flies through the air. As we head down the runway and the speed mounts, I momentarily reflect upon my mortality and hope that the airplane's computers are more reliable than the one I have at home.

The point of the description is simple: *none* of this was here a lifetime ago. We've become so habituated to life in the technopolis that we unconsciously mistake the artificial world of our own creation with reality itself. In the minds of many people, the very idea of Nature has vanished. Instead, with the colorless affect of clinical detachment, we speak of "the environment."

Ironically, the power of technology, which can lead to alienation from nature, has allowed us to more deeply appreciate our place in the universal fabric. Over the last seventy years, we have come to realize in an almost tangible way the intuitions of those earlier thinkers who claimed that we inhabit an infinite, living universe. Epicurus, for example, wrote in the third century B.C.E. that "There are an infinite number of worlds both like and unlike this world of ours."[89] And when Giordano Bruno tried to convince Pope Clement VIII in the Renaissance that God "is glorified not in one, but in countless suns; not in a single earth, but in a thousand, I say, in an infinity of worlds,"[90] he was rewarded by being burnt at the stake. But now, given what we know about the universe, any other conclusion is untenable.

All of the stars that we can see are inhabitants of our own Milky Way Galaxy, which is estimated to house over 100 billion stars and easily some 10 billion planets. But beyond our Milky Way, the number of galaxies is virtually limitless. The six-volume *Catalogue of Galaxies and Clusters of Galaxies* lists nearly 15 million galaxies that have been photographed from Earth. However, by using electronic chips which are more sensitive than film emulsions, at least 20 billion galaxies can be detected in a full sky survey. Based on the fact that we don't have perfect vision due to the vicissitudes of time and space, astronomers estimate that there must be at least 100 billion galaxies in our universe, each containing on average 100 billion stars.

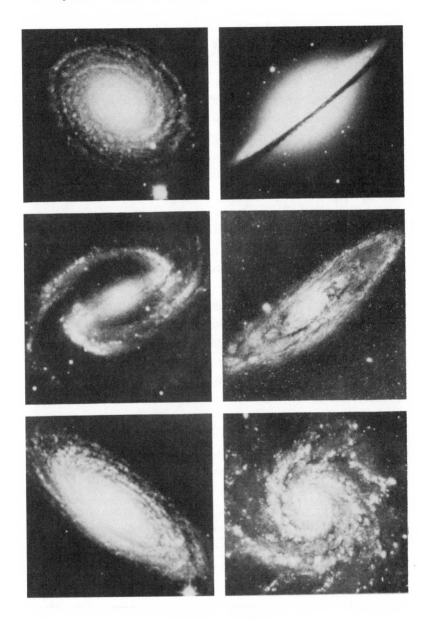

A Variety of Galaxies
From *Burnham's Celestial Handbook*.

Nature Regained: Modern Cosmology and the Reenchantment of the Universe

The universal perception of all traditional peoples is that the world itself is alive and animated. The loss of the vision of the living universe marks the beginning of the modern era, but throughout the history of the Western world the idea of the living universe has been influential. Pythagoras called the universe a *kosmos* ("ornament," "adornment") because "it is perfect, and 'adorned' with infinite beauty and living beings."[91] *Kosmos*, the root of the word "cosmetic," means to be "adorned with beauty." Similarly, Plato described the *kosmos* as "a visible living creature" and calls the universe "a perceptible god, image of the intelligible, greatest and best, most beautiful and most perfect."[92] Significantly, Plato offers this description in the *Timaeus*, the writing where he introduced the idea of the *anima mundi* or World Soul into Western philosophical discourse. In Plato's cosmological myth, this living World Soul is numerically proportioned according to the ratios of musical harmony, for it is the harmonic principles of relation and resonance that sympathetically link the many parts of creation together into a living whole. Aristotle thought it reasonable to suggest that the stars were alive and "endowed with activity,"[93] while the church father Origen maintained that the sun, moon, and stars are engaged in prayer.[94] For the Neoplatonist Plotinus, *everything* that possesses form participates in soul or life to some degree. The cosmos is the manifestation of One Life, and Plotinus described the soul of the universe as resembling a net, stretched out in the sea of time and space:

> The Cosmos is like a net which takes all its life, as far as it ever stretches, from being wet in the water; it is at the mercy of the sea which spreads out, taking the net with it just so far as it will go, for no mesh of it can strain beyond its set place: the Soul is of so far-reaching a nature—a thing unbounded—as to embrace the entire body of the All in one extension; so far as the universe extends, there soul is; and if the universe had no existence, the extent of soul would be the same; it is eternally what it is.[95]

A thousand years later in the Renaissance, one of the greatest defenders of the ensouled, living universe, was the philosopher Marsilio Ficino. Ficino asserted that the entire universe is alive in his *Commentary on Plato's Symposium on Love*,[96] and wrote in his *Three Books on Life* that "There is nothing to be found in this whole living world so deformed that Soul does not attend it, that a gift of soul is not in it."[97] Thus during the historical period, up through the seventeenth century, the idea of the living universe reigned supreme for many hundreds of years. But the living universe was not just an idea; it was something that people *experienced*. In the living universe, our bodies, emotions, thoughts, dreams, and higher insights are all integral aspects of the larger Cosmic Life in which we participate. The phenomenon of magic—the power to influence reality through imagination and desire—owes its existence to the World Soul, which links everything together into a seamless whole. All works of art (itself a magical practice) likewise incarnate and channel the energies of *anima mundi*. Thanks to the soul of the universe, the outer world moves the inner and the inner world moves the outer. In some way that is more than metaphorical, Nature herself is *sympathetic*.

Since the time of Descartes, Locke, and Hume, there has been a well-known tendency to place all psychic reality inside people, leaving an alienated, disenchanted outer world of dead matter for our disembodied intellects to ponder, manipulate, and exploit.[98] Because this approach to reality is reductionistic and denies essential aspects of our nature, there have been many types of reactions against this perspective, both conscious and unconscious.

Ideas and fantasies are powerful entities. Fantasies like those of progress, utilitarianism, and imperialism influence the way that we perceive and relate to both the world and other people. Since many of our modern crises originate from the quite recent perception that the universe is dead, perhaps we need to revive the vision of a living universe, a perspective that is supported in many ways by the findings of modern cosmology.

While the Greeks spoke of the stars as immortal and unchanging in their circular dance, we no longer think of celestial phenomena exhibiting the pristine, mathematical perfection associated with ancient ideas of cosmic piety; even the stars partake of genesis and becoming. But if modern cosmology has dealt a blow to the literal notion of eternal perfection existing somewhere "up there," it simultaneously describes a universe far more organic and alive than anything the Greeks could have imagined. We now speak of the "birth, life, and death of stars," and can see that spiral galaxies are beautifully spun, moving, pulsating, evolving, and mutating entities—celestial flowers or starfish—containing billions of individual cells. Our life, and all life on Earth, is a condensation of the celestial life, and we are creatures of light who feed and live off the light of our sun. It is clear that we are living in an evolutionary universe, but it is uncertain what is guiding this process; the beauty of Nature, however, on both a terrestrial and astronomical scale, confirms that we inhabit a *cosmos*, a cosmos in the way the ancient Greeks used the word: a universe informed by order, pattern, and beauty (value).

It is now all but impossible to avoid the conclusion that the universe is alive in another sense. I am speaking of the lives and minds on other worlds, who also experience the beauty of the universe and wonder about their place in the *schêma* or pattern of things. As one astronomer writes,

> an important feature of our modern cosmology is that it makes the existence of other inhabited worlds not only credible, but some would argue, virtually certain. Two things have helped to bring this about. We have discovered that in our own Galaxy there are about 100 billion stars, and that there are hundreds of millions of other galaxies within range of our telescopes. Also we now understand, at least in outline, how the solar system was formed together with the sun, and we can see no apparent reason why the same thing should not have happened around other similar stars. It seems possible that in our own Galaxy alone, there may be as many as a billion planets rather like the Earth. To say the least, it appears unlikely that our Earth is the only one to support life.[99]

A far more simple argument is offered by the fourth century B.C.E. philosopher Metrodorus. He wrote that

To consider the earth as the only populated world in infinite space is as absurd as to assert that in an entire field sown with millet only one grain will grow.[100]

Everything that we can now see and know about the universe suggests that the cosmos is teeming with life, and that, consequently, our lives here must now be seen in some type of cosmic or universal context. "The question of extraterrestrial life," as astronomer Timothy Ferris notes, "is also a way of examining ourselves and our relationship to the rest of nature."[101] There are more stars, and possibly more planets, than there are grains of sand on the earth. The photographs of our beautiful, blue planet taken from space have helped to give rise to a new perspective of "planetary consciousness": it is no longer possible to think solely in terms of personal or national self-interest. As the saying goes, we must now "think globally." The next step is that we need to think *universally*, and place our existence within some type of larger, cosmic context. I would suggest that this is the ultimate "cosmopolitan perspective" and one that is now unavoidable for the realization of our intrinsic humanity, the understanding of our truly universal nature, the realization that we are children of the universe. Thus modern cosmology, which reestablishes the idea of the living universe, enables us to relink and reintegrate ourselves with the fabric of the universe in a way that is deeply religious, but different from "religion" as it is commonly known.

"The religious question," as I envision it, is not whether "God" exists, but whether there is some form of Intelligence and meaning that pervades the universal fabric. The Pythagorean approach sidesteps the question of theism by pointing toward the wonderful beauty and order of the universe, the recognition of which arouses a sense of awe, wonder, desire, and meaning in the human spirit. This approach, which also underlies the Logos cosmology of antiquity, identifies Intelligence with the principle of order and harmony shining in the mirror of Nature. The question of meaning is affirmed by the beauty of the cosmos and the beauty of human nature. In a strictly deterministic universe, the existence of beauty would be irrelevant and detract from utilitarian efficiency; similarly, if the whole purpose of life were merely survival, there would be no need for myth, art, or music. A deterministic universe would not call for humans when organisms akin to robots would clearly suffice.

The outcome of "the cosmological question"—whether or not the universe is alive—depends solely on the perspectives of scale and context. Novalis wrote, "Man is a Sun and his senses are planets."[102] If we can regard our senses as being distinct from us, then we can also regard the planets as being separate from the sun. But if we take a more inclusive perspective, it is obvious that the senses are integral to any animal, and that the Sun and the planets comprise one holistic system. From this perspective, the planets are the "organs" of the solar system and the Sun is its heart.

The question is, "Where do we draw the dividing line?" If life can arise as quickly from matter as it did on Earth—the scientifically acceptable theory of "spontaneous generation"—how can we assert that matter is dead and inert?[103] Similarly, if a galaxy of 100 billion stars contains, at any one time, ten thousand living worlds, how can we claim that the galaxy itself is not alive? If a galaxy is silently humming with the thoughts of beings who wonder about the meaning of existence, how can we say that the galaxy is itself unconscious? Just as the skeletal system provides a solid foundation for our more complex life processes but in itself does not think, galaxies, stars, and planets should not be hastily dismissed as dead and unintelligent when they are inhabited by intelligent life. Interestingly, if we could view a time exposure of the solar system as it moves through space over decades, it traces out a pattern that looks like a jellyfish with a long tail, trailing the pathways of planetary spirals. Like our own lives, the universe itself is not a thing, but an *event*, unfolding like a flower.

Similarly, the question of theism involves the question of perspective. The Greeks were able to see the cosmos as divine and ensouled without having to postulate the existence of a separate, personal creator God standing outside the universe. In Neoplatonism, beyond the finite-infinite world of Intelligence and Form lies the transcendent yet omnipresent void of the One, paralleling the Zen realization that

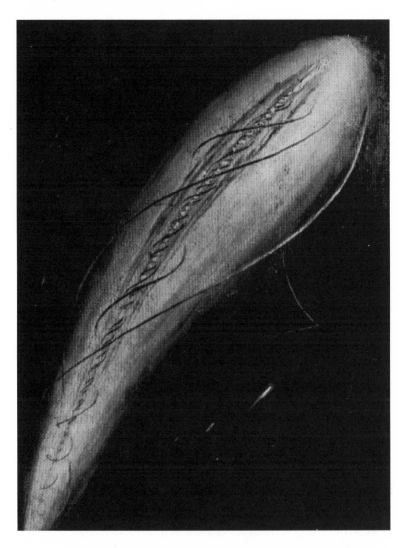

"The Long Body of the Solar System"

The Sun, and hence the entire solar system, is moving through space toward the constellation Lyra at 12.5 miles per second. This painting shows what the entire solar system would look like in an eighty-year "moment of perception," as it trails its planetary spirals in organic harmony. From Rodney Collin, *The Theory of Celestial Influence* (London: Vincent Stuart, 1954).

"behind Form is Emptiness" and that even "Emptiness is mysteriously Full." The paradox of existence is that it is both entirely Empty and entirely Full. Another paradox of existence is that, on the one hand, the universe is intrinsically evolutionary and genuinely creative; on the other hand, the nature of our existence and all the beauty that surrounds us must have been, in some real but nonmaterial sense, intrinsically present yet unarticulated in the void at the beginning of the universe. In this sense, it seems legitimate to say that "In the beginning was the Logos" and "The Logos was God." In some paradoxical way that transcends language, all the future possibilities must potentially exist in the beginning, perhaps even in a sense of "predestination"; but simultaneously, there is creative freedom. Put another way, perhaps we achieve the greatest level of personal freedom when we work as co-creators, working in harmony with the universe, each in our own unique way. Thus the idea of the living universe points toward a cosmic humanism. This perspective advocates a society based on cooperation rather than exploitation, and a view of human nature in which "contemplation"—defined in the absolutely widest sense of creative exploration and enjoyment—results in *eudaimonia*, "happiness," or "living the flourishing life."

We are the inhabitants of the Earth, a beautiful and fragile world, delicately poised in the alchemy of creation; it is our task to therapeutically care for her through compassion, art, and the practice of presence. If we can care for the Earth in this way, we will also be caring for the best part of ourselves. Yet, in addition to being *humans*, a word that literally means "Earth-dwellers,"[104] we are also children of the universe; and if we would like to meet the extraterrestrials face to face, we need only to look at ourselves. Similarly, if we would like to contact life on other worlds, the only way to achieve immediate results is to sit in silence and experience our innate connection, not only with life on Earth, but with the living cosmos as a whole. For every time we gaze at the stars with a sense of wonder, we participate in a larger community of souls that extends throughout the universe.

Notes

1. Novalis, *Pollen and Fragments*, translated by Charles Passage; in Robert Bly, *News of the Universe: Poems of Twofold Consciousness* (San Francisco: Sierra Club Books, 1980), 48.

2. See *weid-* in the Appendix of Indo-European Roots, *American Heritage Dictionary of the English Language*, third edition (Boston: Houghton Mifflin, 1992), 2131.

3. Appendix of Indo-European Roots, *American Heritage Dictionary*, 2129.

4. Henry Corbin, "The *Imago Templi* in Confrontation with Secular Norms," in *Temple and Contemplation* (London: KPI, 1986), 386.

5. Norman Lockyer, *The Dawn of Astronomy* (London, 1894). Lockyer discovered that the great temple of Amon-Ra at Karnac was exactly oriented toward the setting sun on the summer solstice, the longest day of the year.

6. See Martin Brennan, *The Stones of Time: Calendars, Sundials, and Stone Chambers of Ancient Ireland* (Rochester: Inner Traditions, 1994).

7. Pico della Mirandola, "Oration on the Dignity of Man," in Ernst Cassirer, *The Renaissance Philosophy of Man* (Chicago: University of Chicago Press, 1948), 249.

8. R. C. Hogart, translator, *The Hymns of Orpheus* (Grand Rapids: Phanes Press, 1993), 33.

9. Shabistari, *The Secret Rose Garden*, translated by Florence Lederer (Grand Rapids: Phanes Press, 1987), 64–65.

10. Aristotle, *Eudemian Ethics* 1.5.1216A, in John Robinson, *An Introduction to Early Greek Philosophy* (Boston: Houghton Mifflin, 1968), 191.

11. Diogenes Laertius, *Lives of the Eminent Philosophers* 2.7.

12. Bernardus Silvestris, *Cosmographia*, twelfth century; quoted in Norman Davidson, *Sky Phenomena: A Guide to Naked-Eye Observation of the Stars* (Hudson: Lindisfarne Press, 1993), 122.

13. Werner Jaeger, *Paideia: The Ideals of Greek Culture* (New York: Oxford University Press, 1965), I, 153.

14. Plato, *Theaetetus* 174B.

15. Robert Burnham, Jr., *Burnham's Celestial Handbook: An Observer's Guide to the Universe Beyond the Solar System* (New York: Dover, 1978), I, 6.

16. Burnham, *Burnham's Celestial Handbook*, I, 6.

17. Iamblichus, *The Life of Pythagoras* 12, in Kenneth Sylvan Guthrie, translator and compiler, *The Pythagorean Sourcebook and Library: An Anthology of Ancient Writings Which Relate to Pythagoras and Pythagorean Philosophy* (Grand Rapids: Phanes Press, 1987), 70.

18. Iamblichus, *Life of Pythagoras* 12.

19. Plato, *Timaeus* 90A; F. M. Cornford, translator, *Plato's Timaeus* (Indianapolis: Bobbs-Merrill, 1959).

20. Plato, *Timaeus* 90B (Cornford translation).

21. Plato, *Timaeus* 90B–C (Cornford translation).

22. Plato, *Timaeus* 90C–D (Cornford translation).

23. Aristotle, *Nicomachean Ethics* 1177 b 32; translated by John Robinson, *An Introduction to Early Greek Philosophy* (Boston: Houghton Mifflin, 1968), 60.

24. Cf. John Rist, *Eros and Psyche: Studies in Plato, Plotinus, and Origen* (Toronto: University of Toronto Press, 1964), 16–17.

25. Aristotle, *Nicomachean Ethics* 1178 b 5. The *Nicomachean Ethics*, book 10, chapters 7–8, are devoted to arguments that contemplation (*theôria*) represents the highest form of happiness. Aristotle's ultimate conclusion is that the philosopher is the happiest man and "the dearest to the gods."

26. Martha Nussbaum, *The Therapy of Desire: Theory and Practice in Hellenistic Ethics* (Princeton: Princeton University Press, 1994), 15, n. 5.

27. Robert E. Cushman, *Therapeia: Plato's Conception of Philosophy* (Chapel Hill: University of North Carolina Press, 1958), xvii.

28. Stephen C. Rowe, *Rediscovering the West: An Inquiry into Nothingness and Relatedness* (Albany: State University of New York Press, 1994), 90.

29. Søren Kierkegaard, *Concluding Unscientific Postscript* (Princeton: Princeton University Press, 1941), 240.

30. For one attempt to recover the living experience of Being in contemporary life, see Ralph Harper, *On Presence: Variations and Reflections* (Philadelphia: Trinity Press International, 1991).

31. Nusbaum, *The Therapy of Desire*, 15.

32. Cicerco, *De Finibus* 4.7 (Quoted in Nussbaum, *The Therapy of Desire*, 15–16).

33. Iamblichus, *On the Mysteries* 1.21. Ralph Waldo Emerson quotes this

passage, from Thomas Taylor's translation, in his essay on "The Poet" in *The Works of Ralph Waldo Emerson* (New York: Charles C. Bigelow, no date), I, 246.

34. Plotinus, "On the Intellectual Beauty," *Enneads* 5.8.6. Unless otherwise noted, I am using Plotinus, *The Enneads*, translated by Stephen MacKenna (Burdett: Larson Publications, 1992).

35. Terence Dickinson and Alan Dyer, *The Backyard Astronomer's Guide* (Camden: Camden House, 1993), 43.

36. "This Life's dim Windows of the Soul / Distorts the Heavens from Pole to Pole / And leads you to Believe a Lie / When you see with not thro the eye." William Blake, *The Everlasting Gospel* 97–100, in David V. Erdman, editor, *The Complete Poetry and Prose of William Blake* (New York: Doubleday, 1988), 520.

37. Plotinus, "On Love," *Enneads* 3.5.3.

38. Plotinus, "On Beauty," *Enneads* 1.6.8 (Armstrong translation).

39. Antoine Faivre, "Ancient and Medieval Sources of Modern Esoteric Movements," summarizing Romans 8.19–22, in Antoine Faivre and Jacob Needleman, editors, *Modern Esoteric Spirituality* (New York: Crossroad, 1992), 6.

40. Paul, Romans 8.21.

41. Françoise Bonardel, "Alchemical Esotericism and the Hermeneutics of Culture," in Faivre and Needleman, *Modern Esoteric Spirituality*, 79–80.

42. Theodore Roszak, *The Voice of the Earth: An Exploration of Ecopsychology* (New York: Simon and Schuster, 1992), 171.

43. Paul Davies, *The Cosmic Blueprint: New Discoveries in Nature's Creative Ability to Order the Universe* (New York: Simon and Schuster, 1989), 202.

44. Davies, *The Cosmic Blueprint*, 203.

45. See *ker-²* in the Appendix of Indo-European Roots, *American Heritage Dictionary*, 2108.

46. Andrés Rodrígues, *Book of the Heart: The Poetics, Letters, and Life of John Keats* (Hudson: Lindisfarne Press, 1993), 53.

47. This interpretation is supported by A. H. Armstrong in his article on "The Divine Enhancement of Earthly Beauties: The Hellenic and Platonic Tradition" in Read and Armstrong, *On Beauty* (Dallas: Spring Publications, 1987). Armstrong notes that "Hierarchical superiority in the Neoplatonists

does not mean greater remoteness" and stresses the immediate presence of the intelligible cosmos. In this sense, particular beauties function as windows, admitting the light of the transcendent Beauty.

48. Plato, *Phaedrus* 248D.

49. Plato, *Symposium* 210E.

50. Plato, *Symposium* 211D.

51. Plato, *Symposium* 204B.

52. Plotinus, "On Love," *Enneads* 3.5.2.

53. Plotinus, "On Love," *Enneads* 3.5.5.

54. Plotinus, "On Love," *Enneads* 3.5.5.

55. Plotinus, "Nature, Contemplation, and the One," *Enneads* 3.8.1.

56. Plotinus, "Nature, Contemplation, and the One," *Enneads* 3.8.3.

57. Plotinus, "Nature, Contemplation, and the One," *Enneads* 3.8.6.

58. Plotinus, "Nature, Contemplation, and the One," *Enneads* 3.8.7.

59. Plotinus, "Nature, Contemplation, and the One," *Enneads* 3.8.8.

60. Plotinus, "Nature, Contemplation, and the One," *Enneads* 3.8.8.

61. Plotinus, "Nature, Contemplation, and the One," *Enneads* 3.8.11.

62. Plotinus, "On Intellectual Beauty," *Enneads* 5.8.10.

63. Plotinus, "Nature, Contemplation, and the One," *Enneads* 3.8.8.

64. Plotinus, "On Beauty," *Enneads* 1.6.8.

65. Plotinus, "On Beauty," *Enneads* 1.6.9 (Armstrong translation).

66. Plotinus, "On the Intellectual Beauty," *Enneads* 5.8.10.

67. The legislation was not aimed at pagans alone. According to the *Oxford Classical Dictionary*, "Justinian drastically reinforced the penal laws against pagans, Jews, and [Christian] heretics."

68. See Proclus, *The Elements of Theology*, translation and commentary by E. R. Dodds (Oxford: Oxford University Press, 1993).

69. For a good discussion of "the circular path of the effect," see Laurence Rosán, *The Philosophy of Proclus: The Final Phase of Ancient Thought* (New York: Cosmos, 1949), 74–76.

70. Proclus, *Commentary on the Alcibiades*, col. 356, 15–17 (quoted in Rosán, *The Philosophy of Proclus*, 206). In an etymological word play, Proclus derives the Greek *kalon* (beauty) from *kalein* (to call). Thus the effect of divine beauty is to "call to itself what exists and thinks," to "captivate" and "enchant." See Werner Beirewaltes, "The Love of Beauty and the Love of God" in A. H.

Armstrong, editor, *Classical Mediterranean Spirituality: Egyptian, Greek, Roman* (New York: Crossroad, 1986), 307.

71. Marsilio Ficino, *Commentarium in Plotinum* 38. Translated by John Warden in John Warden, editor, *Orpheus: The Metamorphoses of a Myth* (Toronto: University of Toronto Press, 1982), 95.

72. Proclus, *On the Sacred Art*, translated by Thomas Taylor in his 1792 edition of *The Mystical Hymns of Orpheus* (Los Angeles: Philosophical Research Society, 1981), 75–76.

73. Fragment 1 in Ruth Majercik, *The Chaldean Oracles: Text, Translation, and Commentary* (Leiden: E. J. Brill, 1989). See also Hans Lewy, *The Chaldean Oracles and Theurgy* (Paris: Études Augustiniennes, 1978), 165ff.

74. Proclus, *Commentary on Alcibiades*, col. 519, 17–24; in Rosan, *The Philosophy of Proclus*, 215.

75. Proclus, *The Chaldean Philosophy* 4; in Rosan, *The Philosophy of Proclus*, 215.

76. A term used in Proclus' *Platonic Theology*. See Rosan, *The Philosophy of Proclus*, 216, note 160.

77. Proclus, *The Chaldean Philosophy* 4; in Rosan, *The Philosophy of Proclus*, 215.

78. Marsilio Ficino, *De Amore* 2.2. Marsilio Ficino, *Commentary on Plato's Symposium on Love*, translated by Sears Jayne (Dallas: Spring Publications, 1985), 46.

79. Andrei Linde, "The Self-Reproducing Inflationary Universe," *Scientific American* (November 1994), 53. Alan Guth first proposed this in 1987.

80. Plato, *Timaeus* 37D.

81. John Gribbin, "Is the Universe Alive?", *New Scientist* (January 15, 1994), 38–40.

82. Albert Einstein, quoted in Ferris, *Coming of Age in the Milky Way*, 385.

83. Plato, *Timaeus* 35ff.

84. Novalis, *Pollen and Fragments*, 55 (Versluis translation).

85. Novalis, *Pollen and Fragments*, 57 (Versluis translation).

86. Ferris, *Coming of Age in the Milky Way*, 334.

87. Ferris, *Coming of Age in the Milky Way*, 386.

88. Robert Burnham, *Burnham's Celestial Handbook*, I, 7.

89. Epicurus, *Letter to Herodotus*, in Whitney J. Oates, editor, *The Stoic and*

Epicurean Philosophers: The Complete Extant Writings of Epicurus, Epictetus, Lucretius, and Marcus Aurelius (New York: Random House, 1940), 5.

90. Giordano Burno, quoted in Allen G. Debus, *Man and Nature in the Renaissance* (London: Cambridge University Press, 1978), 87.

91. Anonymous, *The Life of Pythagoras Preserved by Photius* 15; in Guthrie, *The Pythagorean Sourcebook and Library*, 139.

92. Plato, *Timaeus* 92C.

93. Aristotle, *On the Heavens* 2.12.292a.

94. Origen, *Contra Celsum* 5.11. Translated by Henry Chadwick (Cambridge: Cambridge University Press, 1980), 272.

95. Plotinus, "Problems of the Soul," *Enneads* 4.3.9.

96. Marsilio Ficino, *Commentary on Plato's Symposium on Love* 6.3.

97. Marsilio Ficino, *Three Books on Life* 3.1. Translated by Carol Kaske and John Clark (Binghamton: Medieval and Renaissance Texts and Studies, 1989), 245.

98. See the important paper by James Hillman, "Anima Mundi: The Return of the Soul to the World," *Spring* 1982, 71–93. Hillman argues that "Ecology movements, futurism, feminism, urbanism, protest and disarmament, personal individuation cannot alone save the world from the catastrophe inherent in our very idea of the world. They require a cosmological vision that saves the phenomenon 'world' itself, a move in soul that goes beyond measures of expediency to the archetypal source of our world's continuing peril: the fateful neglect, the repression, of the *anima mundi*."

99. Hanbury Brown, *Man and the Stars* (Oxford: Oxford University Press, 1978), 165–66.

100. Aetius, *Opinions of the Philosophers* 1.5.4.

101. Ferris, *Coming of Age in the Milky Way*, 369.

102. Novalis, *Pollen and Fragments*, 71 (Versluis translation).

103. According to contemporary estimates, the Earth condensed out of dust and gas some 4.6 billion years ago, and life took hold approximately 4 billion years ago. As Marsilio Ficino asks, "Who will deny that the elements earth and water are alive, since they give life to the creatures born from them?" (*Commentary on Plato's Symposim on Love* 6.3).

104. See *dhghem-* (Earth) in Appendix of Indo-European Roots, *American Heritage Dictionary*, 2102.

Exploring the Universe: Two Suggestions for Further Reading

In theory:

Timothy Ferris, *Coming of Age in the Milky Way* (New York: William Morrow, 1988). Now available in paperback, Ferris's *Coming of Age in the Milky Way* is a well-crafted history of cosmological discovery full of good quotes and cogent observations. Ferris combines excellent writing with a wealth of information in this landmark work which traces the history of scientific discovery from antiquity up to the latest cosmological theories.

In practice:

Terence Dickinson and Alan Dyer, *The Backyard Astronomer's Guide* (Camden: Camden House, 1993). This complete guide to observational astronomy discusses all popular telescope types, equipment, star atlases, finding your way around the sky, observing deep sky objects, and much more. With its wealth of illustrations and wide-ranging coverage, this is probably the best one-volume introduction to observational astronomy currently available. The book contains annotated bibliographies, addresses of suppliers and astronomical organizations, and other useful resources.

Book Reviews

Daimonic Reality: A Field Guide to the Otherworld by Patrick Harpur. New York: Viking Arkana, 1994. Cloth, 330 pp., $29.95.

Reviewed by John Michell.

PATRICK HARPUR'S last book, *Mercurius*, was an alchemical treatise with an account of the Great Work performed in a modern English village. This one naturally follows. As an alchemical adept whose profession is literature, he is inevitably committed to the highest quest of all, for transpersonal redemption, the symbols of which include the restoration of the Grail, the re-creation of the Temple, and the enthronement of God on earth. This is most dangerous ground, a minefield littered with the exploded remains of cranks, tyrants, and idealists from all periods of history. This author strolls through it with ease and good humor. He is a writer of great art and learning, but these are never obtrusive. Everything is made simple. Readers are not asked to accept any new belief or go beyond the range of their own observations and reason. "Daimonic Reality" is the title of this book, but in fact it is about reality as a whole. Nothing so comprehensive has been attempted since the Middle Ages, and its depth of insight harks back to the ancient sages. What I'm trying to say is that this is a seriously important book.

Between ultimate reality and corporeal existence is the realm of (as the Greeks put it) *daimons*. That is a mental concept which is no more literally true than any other image of reality. In practice, however, it has claims to being the most useful image that the mind can adopt as the basis for coming to terms with the life we have to experience. It is sanctioned by traditional wisdom, and underlies all ancient codes of religion, philosophy, and government. Its greatest recommendation is that, as the framework-pattern for a balanced, all-inclusive mentality and worldview, it actually works.

To illustrate the effects of daimonic influence, Harpur displays witches and monsters, UFOs and ghostly lights, visions, dreams, apparitions, alien abductions, mass panics, phantom creatures, fairy relics . . . and so on through the range of traditional and modern phantasmagoria which, in one form or another, are inseparable from human existence. Modern science keeps aloof from such things; modern medicine holds them in suspicion; modern religion is dead against them. But daimonic reality outlasts all man-made institutions and inevitably brings down any system that rejects or ignores it. Apparently, therefore, it is more truly real, and provides firmer ground for a realistic worldview, than any physical product of nature or any creation of the human mind.

The reality which Harpur describes is the same as that which Charles Fort depicted throughout his four great books. In this field Fort is forever paramount, but he was content with the universe as a self-contained, unicellular organism, whereas Harpur seeks transcendence. He follows Jung into discussions of the anima, soul, spirit, the subtle body and that of bone and flesh, their interrelations and their relevance to the concept of daimonic reality. The thinking here is alchemical; but Harpur's alchemy is not the easy, pleasant sort that appeals to the New Age. There is anguish in it, and constant paradoxes arise. True to his subject, he is resolved neither to classify nor to explain; as he writes, "Rigorous classification and explanation, admirable in themselves, will always tend to do violence to daimonic reality, either by forcing it into the straightjacket of a single perspective or, worse, by denying it altogether (scientism) or demonizing it (official Christendom)." Yet no rational discourse on any subject can proceed without at least temporary classifications, and even the phrase "daimonic reality," if repeatedly applied to every type and case of mysterious phenomenon, moves imperceptibly from being a substitute to standing for the explanation itself. By the same process "mass hysteria" became an explanation rather than a description, so did "poltergeist," and Rupert Sheldrake's "morphogenetic field" is heading the same way.

You must of course call it *something*—the ether, the Prima Materia, the subtle body of Gaia, the Holy Spirit, the daimonic realm—but all these names attract literalisms (e.g., Reich's attempt at bottling "orgone energy"), and these in turn misrepresent the very nature of the medium that the names were meant to describe. Even its actual existence can not definitely be affirmed. Confucius made this plain in speaking about the Kwei Shun. These correspond to the Greek daimons and are behind all movements and appearances in this world. So Confucius taught, in accordance with tradition, and one thing he said about the Kwei Shun was that, though incorporal, they are by no means immaterial. Harpur makes the same point in drawing attention to the physical though ever enigmatic evidence for UFOs, yetis, fairies, and other daimonic effects. When asked the obvious question, whether the Kwei Shun really exist, Confucius replied that it is best to act as though they do.

It is a brave step for an English writer of modern, secular education to enter this realm of the Mysteries where, if he puts a foot wrong, he will be guilty of impiety and radically misleading his generation. Fortunately for him and us, Patrick Harpur knows enough, understands enough, and is humble enough to have passed the test of his ambitions. His book is addressed to all readers, from schoolchildren to college professors. On the simplest level it is a compendium of weird tales. Then it is a survey of modern folklore, showing the continuation of traditional themes. An overview of this material reveals its conformity as a whole to the tradition of daimonic manifestations. Finally, most valuable of all, is Harpur's power of communicating a worldview, not just his own personal view or some clever notion backed by empirical evidence, but one recognizable as an authentic rediscovery, or restatement, of the perception that inspires the Perennial Philosophy, whose symbols include the Grail.

There is pessimism in Harpur's writing, and it serves its purpose in preserving his contacts with human reality. The menagerie of foul creatures and monstrous images that occupies the modern imagination is clearly apparent to him. He is quite honest, and if he saw no hope for the future he would certainly say so. It is impressive and a relief, therefore, to find the good news at the end. Nature will prevail and the alchemical process will work its way through. The daimonic tradition, as Harpur refers to it, has passed into our own times through an unbroken "golden chain" of mystics and poets, and even if it were entirely lost it would spring up again spontaneously from human nature. At certain moments in history, in times of crisis and need, the tradition is once more revealed. The very fact that it is now being written about and discussed—which was hardly the case twenty years ago—is an indication of its rebirth. The transformation of minds, once duly started, is a rapid, almost a sudden process.

—JOHN MICHELL

The Complete Gospels. Edited by Robert J. Miller. San Francisco: HarperSanFrancisco, 1995. Paper, 464 pp., $18.00.

THIS VERY USEFUL BOOK offers something unique and refreshing for the library of the well-informed student of early Christianity. *The Complete Gospels* is just that: a collection of all the gospels, canonical and apocryphal, in one handy volume. What sets this work apart from similar efforts is the fact that all of the books are given in a new translation called Scholars Version. One hesitates to call the translations definitive, if for no greater reason than their sometimes jarring unfamiliarity. The Scholars Version is a work in progress, and before it is officially "set" (if it ever is) surely all of these translations will be revised. That said, they are among the best English translations available today, their main feature being faithfulness to the sense of the original with no attention paid to the often stifling and distorting interpretations of later church tradition. Their *style* may be improved in many cases, but their accuracy is extremely good. Thus the gospels of Mark, Luke, Matthew, and John come across with a liveliness practically unknown to readers unversed in New Testament Greek. Even so, it is the inclusion of the other gospels which gives the book its real value: the Gospel of Thomas, the Gospel of Peter, Dialogue of the Savior, the Secret Gospel of Mark, the Egerton Gospel, the Gospel of Mary, and many others. These gospels, with their concise and informative introductions and notes, place into the student's hands the raw materials for a new understanding of the literary realities of the early church. The editors are to be commended for including as well two "theoretical" gospels: Q and Signs. Q is the scholar's abbreviation for an early document which served as the source for many of the teachings of Jesus as given in the New Testament. The Gospel of Signs is a theoretical "miracle book" which, as scholar Robert Fortna has argued, lies at the basis of the Gospel according to John. This is the first English translation available of Fortna's reconstruction of this work. In addition, many fragmentary and newly-discovered pieces of gospel tradition are present which are not found in older collections of apocrypha. If *The Complete Gospels* is any indication, we may eagerly await the publication of the rest of the Scholars Version New Testament.

—SHAWN EYER

The Five Gospels. Edited by Robert W. Funk. New York: Macmillan, 1993. Cloth, $30.00.

THIS IS THE FIRST MAJOR REPORT of the Jesus Seminar, a group of scholars who have worked for over a decade to analyze and assess the historical reliability of the surviving Christian gospels. During this time, the scholars have deliberated mainly over the sayings of Jesus recorded in the gospels. This task, though performed individually by every critical reader of the Bible for well over a century, has generated controversy in conservative religious circles, probably because the scholars represented comprise a formidable proportion of recognized experts in the field of Christian origins. The Jesus Seminar has been depicted by some as a star-chamber group attempting to mandate matters of faith, but even the most casual examination of *The Five Gospels* shows that it is an accessible and reasonable work which makes few demands on the reader. The five earliest gospels—Matthew, Mark, Luke, Thomas, and John—are given in the new Scholars Version translation, with all the sayings of Jesus color-coded according to the statistical analysis of the democratic ballots cast by the fellows of the Seminar. Red means Jesus said it. Pink means he said something like it. Gray and black respectively mean that Jesus probably or definitely did not say it. Gray and black sayings are explained as the work of the gospel writers, or the offspring of oral tradition in the primitive church. Each section of every gospel is followed by an informative commentary which also discusses very openly the reasons for the Seminar's assessment. Another feature of the book are the very good sidebar essays which encapsulate some of the latest and most exciting scholarly understandings about the meanings of certain key Greek and Hebrew terms such as "the kingdom of God" and "Messiah," as well as historical discussions of Gnosticism and its possible relationship to the gospels. Probably no one, not even on the Jesus Seminar, agrees with every single assessment found in *The Five Gospels*, but it is an excellent guide to contemporary scholarship regarding the historical Jesus, and a valuable resource to anyone who wants to explore the latest learned opinions on this complicated and compelling topic.

—SHAWN EYER

Boehme: An Intellectual Biography of the Seventeenth-Century Philosopher and Mystic by Andrew Weeks. Albany: State University of New York Press, 1991. Paper, $19.95.

German Mysticism from Hildegard of Bingen to Ludwig Wittgenstein: A Literary and Intellectual History by Andrew Weeks. Albany: State University of New York Press, 1993. Paper, $19.95.

GERMANY has produced an astonishing array of theosophers, philosophers, and literary artists over the centuries, but there are relatively few books in English about these traditions and their interrelationships. Hence it is good to see these two works by Andrew Weeks, who has given us both a survey of German mysticism in general and a close reading of the great German theosopher Jacob Boehme.

In *Boehme*, Weeks aims to consider the visionary cobbler Jacob Boehme (1575–1624) "by interpreting his work with reference to the environment in which and for which it arose." Although at times his focus on the "specific time, place, culture, and character" of Boehme's writings threatens to submerge the enduring broader meanings of Boehme's works, much illuminating cultural context and reasonable interpretation is offered here. In reminding us that Boehme's writings emerged in a particular social milieu, Weeks's goal is to disentangle Boehme from the legends and "occultism" that have developed around him; and while Boehme's broader significance to us today would have made an interesting element in this book, the author's aim is to show us Boehme as he was, without legendary accretion or reductionist dismissal. In this, Weeks is quite successful.

Weeks's other book, *German Mysticism*, is a broad survey that, as the subtitle promises, stretches from medieval through modern times. This is a daunting task, particularly in under three hundred pages, and although the author necessarily had to sketch vast areas of intellectual terrain in an extremely economical way, he touches not only on well known figures like Hildegard of Bingen and Meister Eckhart, but also on less widely recognized writers like Daniel Czepko and Johann Georg Hammann. At times this brevity approaches injustice, as when Weeks devotes only a couple of paragraphs to, for example, a figure as profoundly important as Franz von Baader, and none at all to Leopold Ziegler.

There is such a dearth of good books on these authors and subjects that this reviewer longs to see more, to see them considered in detail, enabling us to make the subtle distinctions that are essential for fuller and more complete understanding of this neglected field. Weeks's two books represent a long overdue introduction to an area of study whose implications and whose importance, particularly as regards European–Asian cultural dialogue, have not yet been adequately recognized.

—ARTHUR VERSLUIS

Books in Brief

DAVID FIDELER

Access to Western Esotericism by Antoine Faivre. Albany: SUNY Press, 1994. Paper, 369 pp., $19.95. This historical and analytical overview of the Western esoteric traditions features an attempt to introduce a rigorous methodology for the academic study of these traditions.

Alcinous: *The Handbook of Platonism.* Translated with an introduction and commentary by John Dillon. New York: Oxford University Press, 1993. Cloth, 226 pp., $48.00. This is a translation of *The Platonic Doctrines* of "Albinus" with a massive commentary five times the length of the text. John Dillon discusses the background of the authorship debate (was it Albinus or Alcinous?), and explains why he has now come over to the Alcinous camp since the publication of his 1977 book *The Middle Platonists.*

Art and Symbols of the Occult: Images of Power and Wisdom by James Wasserman. Rochester: Inner Traditions, 1993. Paper, 128 pp., $19.95. Contains many fine color plates relating to the Western esoteric traditions. Without a doubt, the highlight of this book are the reproductions of the twenty-two manuscript illuminations from the alchemical text *Splendor Solis*, one of the great treasures of the British Museum; the complete set of paintings is published here in color, for the first time anywhere.

Astronomies and Cultures. Edited by Clive L. N. Ruggles and Nicholas J. Saunders. Niwot: University Press of Colorado, 1993. Cloth, 344 pp., $39.95. A stimulating volume of learned papers from the third Oxford International Symposium on Archaeoastronomy. Three favorites: "Astronomies and Rituals at the Dawn of the Middle Ages"; "Medicine Wheel Astronomy"; and an article on "Astronomical Knowledge, Calendrics, and Sacred Geography in Ancient Mesoamerica."

At Home in the Universe by John Archibald Wheeler. Woodbury: American Institute of Physics Press, 1993. Cloth, 371 pp., $24.95. Essays on science, cosmology, and physics by John Wheeler, the colleague and confidant of Einstein and Bohr, pioneer of nuclear fission theory, and staunch champion of black holes. There is much of interest here, but his cheerful, optimistic address on dealing with the risk of nuclear power makes this reviewer quite nervous! (It was delivered before the Chernobyl disaster.)

At the Center of the World: Polar Symbolism Discovered in Celtic, Norse, and Other Ritualized Landscapes by John Michell. New York: Thames & Hudson, 1994. Cloth, 184 pp., $24.95. John Michell continues his research into sacred geography, the symbolism of the center, and its significance in ancient cultures.

A Beginner's Guide to Constructing the Universe by Michael S. Schneider. New York: HarperCollins, 1994. Cloth, 352 pp., $30.00. This amazingly accessible work is an introduction to sacred geometry, specificially the archetypal patterns present in the first ten numbers, and how these harmonious patterns underlie the forms of nature. The book contains hundreds of illustrations which analyze the geometrical forms of nature and show how these geometries have been used by artists, both ancient and modern. Simply and clearly, step by step, the author shows the reader how to evoke these geometries with a compass, marker, and straightedge. This lucid, well written, and engaging book is a "must have" for everyone interested in geometry, harmony, and the philosophy of whole systems. Highly recommended for all readers from the complete novice to the advanced student.

The Biophilia Hypothesis. Edited by Stephen R. Kellert and Edward O. Wilson. Washington: Island Press, 1993. Cloth, 484 pp., $27.50. In his landmark book *Biophilia*, Edward Wilson suggested that our tendency to focus on life and lifelike processes might be a biologically based, genetic need, integral to our development as individuals and as a species. This hypothesis, if substantiated, provides a powerful argument for the conservation of biological diversity, and implies serious consequences for our well-being as society becomes further estranged from the natural world. The very fact that people need a theory like this shows just how far we *have* become estranged from the natural world!

Book of the Heart: The Poetics, Letters, and Life of John Keats by Andrés Rodríguez. Hudson: Lindisfarne Press, 1993. Paper, 240 pp., $16.95.

Chaos, Gaia, Eros: The History of the World According to Chaos Theory by Ralph Abraham. San Francisco: HarperSanFrancisco, 1994. Paper, 256 pp., $16.00. This book deliteralizes history so we can see it not only as a sequence of events, but as a flow of ideas and cultural myths, and their social and ecological consequences.

Claiming a Liberal Education: Resources for Realizing the College Experience. Edited by Stephen C. Rowe. Needham Heights: Ginn Press, 1994. Paper, 219 pp., $33.00. Readers interested in the topic of liberal education will profit from this useful anthology of essays about the philosophy of education and what a liberal education means today. One of the highlights of this college textbook is the introduction by the editor, "Access to a Vision: Unlocking the Paradox of a Liberal Education." As he writes: "Without knowing it, most students at most institutions have an option: they can simply go to school, get a degree, and miss a liberal education, or they can spend the same time and money and become liberally educated. But they cannot exercise this option unless they know a choice exists. And they cannot exercise that option wisely unless they see the significance of what is at stake: the possibility of their own personal transformation. For the aim of a liberal education is nothing less than that: a transformation that enables us to achieve our full human potential, gives us access to what is great and sustaining in the Western tradition, and moves us to participate directly and positively in the drama of unfolding world civilization."

Cosmic Enigmas by Joseph Silk. Woodbury: American Institute of Physics Press, 1994. Cloth, 213 pp., $29.95. Wide-ranging, accessible essays on the mysteries of contemporary cosmology by a leading astronomer. From the big bang to galaxy formation to the large scale structure of the universe, it's all here, in another fine volume in the Masters of Modern Physics series.

Courting Disaster: Astrology at the English Court and University in the Later Middle Ages by Hilary M. Carey. New York: St. Martin's Press, 1992. Cloth, 282 pp., $49.95. This book, based on previously unexplored manuscript material, explains the role played by astrology in late medieval England. Having discovered horoscopes relating to English monarchs from Edward II to Edward V, Hilary Carey shows how astrology fought hard in this period to retain some kind of academic respectability, while in the end becoming overwhelmed by the dangerous politics of the late medieval court.

The Dilemma of Narcissus by Louis Lavelle. Translated from the French by William Gairdner. Burdett: Larson Publications, 1993. "Lavelle demonstrated a positive spiritual and metaphysical side to Narcissus' self-love, one which compensates the negative ego-centered and mundane physical side. He shows that our dilemma may well be that these two sides belong to each other as if they are total complex, a marriage of opposites. The Narcissus myth thereby teaches that discovery of mundane significance comes only, yet really, by means of image, reflection, and appearance. This is a very provocative notion, especially now, when imagination is demeaned and often demeaning."—David Miller, Syracuse University

Early Greek Myth: A Guide to Literary and Artistic Sources by Timothy Gantz. Baltimore: The Johns Hopkins University Press, 1993. Cloth,

909 pp., $60.00. This massive scholarly handbook takes the Greek myths apart and summarizes the written and visual evidence in which the specific details of the story appear. A masterpiece of learning and erudition, this work will be valuable to professional scholars, but holds little interest for the general reader, because there is nothing in it to awaken us to the spirit or significance of myth. As Thomas Moore once said, "Mythology is something that you study, but myth is something you live."

The Elements of Gnosticism by Stuart Holroyd. Rockport: Element, 1994. Paper, 121 pp., $9.95. A short introduction to Gnosticism and its significance in Western culture.

The Encyclopaedia of Middle Eastern Mythology and Religion by Jan Knappert. Rockport: Element, 1993. Cloth, 309 pp., $29.95.

Everyday Spirits by David Appelbaum. Albany: SUNY Press, 1993. Paper, 195 pp., $14.95. These meditations on household objects are a welcome and refreshing attempt to humanize philosophy and bring us back to the tangible reality of everyday things. Appelbaum is both a professional philosopher and a poet, and presents us with thematically arranged, associational reflections which reflect an innate mode of human consciousness that has been ignored by professional philosophers in general (who usually want to know "what's the *argument?*"). Consequently, there is considerable therapeutic value to be discovered in this beautiful, sometimes wry, poetic narrative.

The Eye of Heaven: Ptolemy, Copernicus, Kepler by Owen Gingerich. Woodbury: American Institute of Physics Press, 1993. Cloth, 442 pp., $24.95. Did Ptolemy fake his data or merely, as many other scientists have done, mold them into consistent form without intent to deceive? Was Copernicus's heliocentrism an inevitable response to crisis-ridden Ptolemaic cosmology, or was it an original, unexpected leap of the imagination? Are scientific discoveries merely the unveling of physical reality, or are they more akin to artists' creativity? These are some of the provocative questions explored in the twenty-five essays assembled here.

Fortean Studies 1. Edited by Steve Moore. *Fortean Times* (PO Box 754, Manhasset, NY 11030). Paper, 350 pp, $44.00 postpaid. Ever since the London-based *Fortean Times: The Journal of Strange Phenomena* "went commercial," there has been no decent venue for scholarly studies of strange phenomena. Now the vacuum has been filled by this scholarly anthology, which is supposed to be published once a year.

The Future of the Body: Explorations Into the Further Evolution of Human Nature by Michael Murphy. Los Angeles: Jeremy Tarcher, 1992.

Paper, 785 pp., $17.95. An encyclopedic overview of extraordinary human functioning drawn from medical science, sports records, parapsychological experiments, anthropological and comparative religious studies. Fortunately for the reader, this magnum opus is very well organized.

Gnosis: An Esoteric Tradition of Mystical Visions and Unions by Dan Merkur. Albany: SUNY Press, 1993. Paper, 387 pp., $19.95. The author presents a systematic history of the spiritual technique of "active imagination" in Western culture and argues that the paired use of visionary and unitive experiences, dependent for the most part on active imagination, constituted the *gnosis* at the core of the gnostic trajectory in Western esotericism. There is much of interest and merit in this volume; stylistically, however, the author's attempt to achieve an encyclopedic overview results in a text that often feels more like a collection of notes than the well-integrated historical thesis the book puports to be.

The Gnostics. Rhinebeck: The Numinosities Catalog (PO Box 417, Rhinebeck, NY 12572), no date. Four part video history: 1) Knowledge of the Heart, 2) The Goodmen's Heresy, 3) The Divinity of Man, 4) A Crack in the Universe, $99.00 for the complete set. This BBC documentary explores ancient Gnosticism and the discovery of the Nag Hammadi Library; the Cathars; the Hermetic tradition in the Renaissance; and the significance of Gnosis in the contemporary world and its influence on the thought of C. G. Jung. Includes interview footage with well-known scholars (Gilles Quispel, Elaine Pagels, James Robinson, Hans Jonas, etc.) and the remarkable peasant who discovered the Nag Hammadi cache (who tells us about how he once killed a man in revenge and ate his heart!). The videos are well-written and informative, and are marred only by interspersed dramatic reenactments which, for the most part, are quite annoying. If you can find some way to ignore these intrusions (e.g., a blond-haired Jesus twirling around and delivering lines from the Gospel of Thomas in Shakespearian English), the series is quite worthwhile.

The Golden Fleece and Alchemy by Antoine Faivre. Albany: SUNY Press, 1993. Paper, 140 pp., $12.95. A study of argonautic motifs in the Hermetic tradition.

Hermetica. Translated by Brian P. Copenhaver. Cambridge: Cambridge University Press, 1992. Cloth, 320 pp., $74.95. A new, one-volume translation of *Corpus Hermeticum* with extensive notes. The introduction draws upon recent scholarship which recognizes the genuine *Egyptian* background of the Hermetic writings; the author also provides a good overview of the influence of these texts, and their ideas, in the history of the Western world.

How Much is Enough?: The Consumer Society and the Future of the Earth by Alan Durning. New York: Norton, 1992. Paper, 200 pp., $8.95. "While the consumer society has been stunningly effective in harming the environment, it has failed to provide us with a sense of fulfillment. Consumerism has hoodwinked us into gorging on material things because we suffer from social, psychological, and spiritual hungers. Yet the opposite extreme—poverty—may be even worse for the human spirit and devastates the environment too, as hungry peasants put forests to the torch and steep slopes to the plow. If the Earth suffers when people have either too little or too much, the questions arise: How much is enough? What level of consumption can the planet support? When do more things cease to add appreciably to human life?"—From the cover blurb.

Iamblichus: *On the Pythagorean Life.* Translated with notes and introduction by Gillian Clark. Philadelphia: University of Pennsylvania Press, 1989. Paper, 122 pp., $14.95. This is a fresh, up-to-date translation of Iamblichus's *Life of Pythagoras* from the Greek with good notes. The version in *The Pythagorean Sourcebook* (Phanes, 1987), while fine for most purposes, is a revision of the old Thomas Taylor translation.

The Illustrated Encyclopaedia of Arthurian Legends by Ronan Coghlan. Rockport: Element, 1993. Cloth, 256 pp., $29.95. This stunningly beautiful volume, illustrated in full color throughout, is a helpful guide to the figures, places, and subjects of Arthurian legend, written for the general reader. Scholars will find *The Arthurian Encyclopedia* edited by Norric Lacy (Garland, 1986) to be a better source for in-depth information, but this illustrated encyclopedia, reminiscent of an illuminated manuscript, is a book that will be enjoyed by all.

Integrity in Depth by John Beebe. College Station: Texas A&M University Press, 1992. Cloth, 165 pp. $19.50. A psychological and philosophical exploration of the concept of integrity by a Jungian analyst.

The Jewish Alchemists: A History and Source Book by Raphael Patai. Princeton: Princeton University Press, 1994. Cloth, 617 pp., $35.00. A truly monumental history and sourcebook; discusses individual alchemists, the relationship between Kabblah and alchemy, and much more.

Kepler's Physical Astronomy by Bruce Stephenson. Princeton: Princeton University Press, 1994. Johannes Kepler revolutionized the most ancient of the sciences by being the first to understand astronomy as a part of physics. By closely analyzing the texts of Kepler's great astronomical works, in particular the *Astronomia nova* of 1609, Bruce Stephenson demonstrates the importance of Kepler's physical principles—principles now known to be incorrect—in the creation of his first two laws of planetary motion. This book explores and explains the development of Kepler's planetary theory and the physical hypotheses central to that theory. (See also below, *The Music of the Heavens: Kepler's Harmonic Astronomy*.)

The Letters of Marsilio Ficino: Volume 4. Translated from the Latin by members of the Language Department of the School of Economic Science, London. London: Shepheard-Walwyn, 1988. Cloth, 184 pp., $27.00. The Letters of Ficino are distributed in the United States by Paul & Company Publishers Consortium, c/o PCS Data Processing, 360 West 31 Street, New York, NY 10001. Vol. 1: $27.00; vol. 2: $25.00; vol. 3: $25.00; vol. 4: $27.00. The publisher tells us that volume 5 has just been released (224 pp. with five color plates): $39.95.

Lost Christianity: A Journey of Rediscovery to the Centre of Christian Experience by Jacob Needleman. Rockport: Element, 1993 (reprint of 1980 edition). Paper, 228 pp., $15.95.

Marcilio Ficino: Three Books on Life. Translated and annotated by Carol V. Kaske and John R. Clark. Binghamton: Medieval and Renaissance Texts and Studies, 1989. Cloth, 507 pp., $32.00. We love Charles Boer's lively translation of, and introduction to, Ficino's *Book of Life* (Spring Publications). But this handsome edition contains the facing Latin text, extensive notes, indexes, and a fat bibliography. "No one should doubt that we ourselves and all things which are around us can, by way of certain preparations, lay claim to celestial things. For these lower things were made by the heavens, are ruled continually by them, and were prepared from up there for celestial things in the first place" (Book 3, "On Obtaining Life from the Heavens," chapter 2).

The Masters Revealed: Madame Blavatsky and the Myth of the Great White Lodge by K. Paul Johnson. Albany: SUNY Press, 1994. Paper, 288 pp., $16.95. Argues that Madame Blavatsky's occult "Masters," rather than being discarnate entities or her own invention, were actual individuals, including leaders of secret societies in Europe and America, religio-political reformers in Egypt and India, and even British government agents.

Muhyiddin Ibn 'Arabi: A Commemorative Volume. Edited by S. Hirtenstein and M. Tiernan for the Muhyiddin Ibn 'Arabi Society. Rockport: Element, 1993. Cloth, 380 pp., $65.00. An anthology of scholarly papers celebrating the 750th anniversary of the great Sufi philosopher and mystic.

The Music of the Heavens: Kepler's Harmonic Astronomy by Bruce

Stephenson. Princeton: Princeton University Press, 1994. Cloth, 260 pp., $39.50. Challenging critics who characterize Kepler's theories of harmonic astronomy as "mystical," Bruce Stephenson offers the first thorough technical analysis of the music the astronomer thought the heavens made, and the logic that led him to find musical patterns in his data. In so doing, Stephenson illuminates crucial aspects of Kepler's intellectual development, particularly his ways of classifying and drawing inferences. The book also discusses earlier theories of *harmonia mundi*.

Mystical Monotheism: A Study in Ancient Platonic Theology by John Peter Kenney. Hanover: Brown University Press/University Press of New England, 1991. Cloth, 216 pp., $40.00.

Mysticism Examined: Philosophical Inquiries into Mysticism by Richard H. Jones. Albany: SUNY Press, 1993. Paper, 304 pp., $19.95.

Neoplatonism and Gnosticism. Edited by Richard T. Wallis and Jay Bregman. Albany: SUNY Press, 1992. Paper, 531 pp., $21.95. A collection of scholarly papers exploring the relationships between Neoplatonism and Gnosticism: the opposition between the two systems was certainly not as sharp as Plotinus claimed. Where, why, and how the lines were drawn is discussed in the light of new historical evidence.

Nicolas Flamel: His Exposition of the Hieroglyphicall Figures (1624). Edited by Laurinda Dixon. New York: Garland, 1994. Cloth, 125 pp., $29.00. A new edition of this alchemical text in Garland's English Renaissance Hermeticism series.

Nothing is Too Wonderful to Be True by Philip Morrison. Woodbury: American Institute of Physics Press, 1994. Cloth, 446 pp., $29.95. These friendly, readable essays by one of the great science writers and physicists of our time not only offer illuminating perspectives on science in the modern world, but also prove that some academics know how to *write*.

The Oneirocriticon of Achmet: A Medieval Greek and Arabic Treatise on the Interpretation of Dreams. Translated by Steven M. Obehelman. Lubbock: Texas Tech University Press, 1991. Cloth, 314 pp., $39.00. In addition to the carefully-annotated translation, this volume contains a wealth of background information which helps to place this work in context, including an excellent chapter on dreams in Greek thought before Achmet.

Orpheus with his Lute: Poetry and the Renewal of Life by Elisabeth Henry. Carbondale and Edwardsville: Southern Illinois University Press, 1992. This wide-ranging, lyrical, and keenly insightful study shows that there is still an an amazing amount of gold to be mined by unfolding the implications of the Orpheus myth. Drawing upon hundreds of sources, this volume sympathetically explores the archetype of the divinely inspired poet-musician, to answer the question "what is a poet?"—a question which is raised again at the end of each chapter. "The truths apprehended by the poet concern the creation of the world and all living beings, and the mathematical and musical relationships on which the creation rests. Poetic forms, like spatial ones, can express underlying harmonies not perceptible to ordinary consciousness, and so quicken awareness of the divine life which animates the universe."

The Oxford History of Classical Art. Edited by John Boardman. New York: Oxford University Press, 1993. Cloth, 406 pp., $45.00. This sumptuous, oversize volume explores every aspect of classical art in every period, and is illustrated throughout with superb plates in color and black and white. A fine, first-class production.

Paranormal Experience and Survival of Death by Carl B. Becker. Albany: SUNY Press, 1993. Cloth, 257 pp., $19.95. This lucid, well-balanced study also discusses the taboo on scientific discussion of such research within the social sciences, and proposes a new paradigm for a more holistic view of the field. "The question of personal survival of physical death is actually the question of the nature of personhood, and the relations of consciousness to reality and the body with which it normally seems affiliated."

The Passion of the Western Mind: Understanding the Ideas That Have Shaped Our World View by Richard Tarnas. New York: Ballantine, 1993. Paper, 544 pp., $14.00. Since the way that we think about the world determines the type of world we create, understanding the philosophical and intellectual history of Western civilization possesses a vital cultural relevance. This book is a remarkable achievement, because it provides a comprehensive, exciting, intellectual history of the Western world in one volume, and describes profound philosophical concepts simply without simplifying them. In a deeply perceptive and hopeful epilogue, Tarnas draws on recent psychotherapeutic discoveries to discuss the archetypal process which underlies the genesis of more inclusive cosmologies and world views; he argues convincingly that the fragmentation and confusion of the modern world is not a mistake worthy of regret, but an intrinsically necessary phase foreshadowing the emergence of a new conception of our place in the cosmos. This book has received widespread critical acclaim, and for good reason. Highly recommended.

Peri Tôn Mathêmatôn: Essays on Ancient Mathematics and its Later Development. Edited by Ian Mueller. Edmonton: Academic Printing &

Publishing, 1991. Paper, 251 pp., $23.95. Essays on Greek mathematics, including a paper by Andrew Barker on "Three Approaches to Canonic Division" (the monochord) and a paper by Ian Mueller on mathematics and education in Plato.

Person, Soul, and Identity: A Neoplatonic Account of the Principle of Personality by Robert Bolton. London: Minerva Press (2 Old Brompton Road, London SW7 3DQ), 1994. Cloth, 279 pp., £14.99. An investigation of the problem of personal identity from a contemporary Neoplatonic perspective, the conclusions of which are in opposition to a wide range of theories of the self which would serve only to desubstantialize it.

Plato: *Republic.* Translated with an introduction and notes by Robin Waterfield. New York: Oxford University Press, 1994. Paper, 475 pages, $5.95. This is perhaps the most readable, contemporary English translation of the *Republic.* The only bad thing is that it's reproduced in small type on newsprint. If you want to read this excellent translation, our advice is to order the hardcover.

The Parthenon Frieze by Ian Jenkins. Austin: University of Texas Press / London: British Museum, 1994. Cloth, 120 pp., $29.95. Most of what survives of the Parthenon frieze is now in the British Museum or Athens. This book reconstructs the frieze in its entirety according to the most up-to-date research, with a scene-by-scene commentary. The superb quality of the sculpture is shown in a series of close-up photographs.

The Primavera of Sandro Botticelli: A Neoplatonic Interpretation by Joanne Snow-Smith. New York: Peter Lang, 1993. Cloth, 297 pp., $39.95. This study of the Hermetic and Neoplatonic allegorical underpinnings of the Primavera takes an interdisciplinary approach; it contains fine plates, many in color, and a useful bibliography.

Proclus: *A Commentary on the First Book of Euclid's Elements.* Translated with an introduction and notes by Glenn R. Morrow. Princeton: Princeton University Press, 1992. Paper, 355 pp., $19.95.

Proclus' Commentary on Plato's Parmenides. Translated by Glenn R. Morrow and John Dillon. Princeton: Princeton University Press, 1992. Paper, 616 pp., $24.95.

Proportion and Style in Ancient Egyptian Art by Gay Robins. Austin: University of Texas Press, 1994. Paper, 296 pp., $19.95. A comprehensive, highly-illustrated study of the canonical grid system used in Egyptian art. The author seeks to show that, despite the use of canonical grids, innovation and stylistic variation played a significant role in Egyptian art. This book makes a significant contribution to our understanding of the grid system, but there is no discussion of dynamic symmetry or the use of geometrical ratios, which were used in conjunction with it.

Ptolemy's Universe: The Natural Philosophical and Ethical Foundations of Ptolemy's Astronomy by Liba Chaia Taub. LaSalle: Open Court, 1993. Paper, 188 pp., $14.95. While much has been written about Ptolemy's mathematical work, few attempts have been made to understand his philosophical and cosmological ideas. This learned but very accessible study examines Ptolemy's ideas within the broader context of Greek philosophy, mathematics, culture, and scientific thought. The final chapter is on "The Divinity of the Celestial Bodies and the Ethical Motivation for the Study of the Heavens," and concludes with the observation that "In Ptolemy's universe, mathematics is merged with moral philosophy, allowing the mathematician to function as philosopher, all the while striving to imitate the divine." In other words, he was something of a Platonist.

Quest for the Red Sulphur: The Life of Ibn 'Arabi by Claude Addas. Translated from the French by Peter Kingsley. Cambridge: Islamic Text Society, 1993. Distributed in the U.S. by Atrium Publishers Group. Paper, 347 pp., $19.95.

The Rebirth of Nature: The Greening of Science and God by Rupert Sheldrake. Rochester: Inner Traditions, 1994. Paper, 260 pp., $12.95. There is much of interest in this book to students of the Western cosmological traditions. Drawing on recent scientific theory, Sheldrake presents powerful arguments for more organic cosmological models and is particularly effective in showing just how anthropocentric the inanimate, mechanistic worldview of the Enlightenment is. Highly recommended.

Rediscovering the West: An Inquiry into Nothingness and Relatedness by Stephen C. Rowe. Albany: SUNY Press, 1994. Paper, 222 pp., $19.95. Philosopher Stephen Rowe argues that the Western intellectual tradition, by entering into dialogue with Zen, can expand its conceptual horizons. Moreover, such a dialogue can help us rediscover what is truly great in our own tradition, and not available elsewhere. Accessible and extremely engaging, this book is an attempt to rescue the Western philosophical tradition from intellectual system-building and restore philosophical inquiry as "the practice of relatedness." Highly recommended.

The Reenchantment of Art by Suzi Gablik. New York: Thames & Hudson, 1991. Cloth, 191 pp., $22.50. The author describes how the future of art is dependent on our culture's spiritual and ethical renewal. As Gablik describes it, "The psychic and social structures in which we live have become too profoundly anti-ecological, unhealthy, and destructive" to indulge the modernist sense of alienation and social antipathy. Her way out of this cul-de-sac points to a new cultural paradigm whose imperatives include a renewed sense of community, an enlarged ecological perspective, and greater access to the mythic and archetypal underpinnings of spiritual life.

The Rose Cross and the Age of Reason: Eighteenth-Century Rosicrucianism in Central Europe and its Relationship to the Enlightenment by Christopher McIntosh. New York: E. J. Brill, 1992. This book deals with the relationship between the philosophy of the Enlightenment and the complex of ideas known as Rosicrucianism, which historians have often depicted as a Counter-Enlightenment force. Dr. McIntosh argues rather that it was part of a "third force," which allied itself sometimes with the Enlightenment, sometimes with the Counter-Enlightenment. Drawing on many unpublished materials, this book is the first comprehensive study of the German Rosicrucian revival and in particular of the order known as the Golden and Rosy Cross. Dr. McIntosh shows how the order exerted a significant influence on the cultural, political, and religious life of its age.

Sacred Architecture by A. T. Mann. Rockport: Element, 1993. Paper, 192 pp., $19.95. This introduction to sacred architecture, aimed at a popular audience, is illustrated throughout with beautiful color plates. If approached as a contribution to our knowledge of sacred architecture, this book will disappoint the reader; but if approached for the illustrations, this is a delightful and worthwhile volume, which successfully reflects the underlying harmony on which these structures are based.

Sacred Drift: Essays on the Margins of Islam by Peter Lamborn Wilson. San Francisco: City Lights, 1993. Paper, 167 pp., $12.95. Engaging essays on the fringes and margins of Islam at its intersection points with the Western world. Inspiring, weird, deep, and oftentimes hilarious—you won't find this material in the official history books.

Sacred Geography of the Ancient Greeks: Astrological Symbolism in Art, Architecture, and Landscape by Jean Richer. Translated by Christine Rhone. Albany: SUNY Press, 1994. Paper, 319 pp., $19.95.

Seal of the Saints: Prophethood and Sainthood in the Doctrine of Ibn 'Arabi. Cambridge: Islamic Text Society, 1994. Distributed in the U.S. by Atrium Publishers Group. Paper, 192 pp., $17.95.

Socrates' Ancestor: An Essay on Architectural Beginnings. Cambridge: MIT Press, 1993. Paper, 193 pp., $14.95. This beautifully designed book is an investigation of the relationship between ancient Greek philosophy, cosmology, and the beginnings of architecture. The author's approach takes us into a world in which philosophy, architecture, literature, and myth were not university departments or separate fields, but unified. "*Kosmos* was, as we have seen, also political, with the making of the *polis* and its emblem, the temple, the very embodiment of the building and navigation of a boat, the weaving of a cloth, or the tracing of the figure of a dance."

The Soul of Beauty: A Psychological Investigation of Appearance by Ronald Schenk. Cranbury: Bucknell University Press, 1992. Cloth, 176 pp., $34.50. This learned, wide-ranging book is an important contribution to both a philosophy and psychology of beauty, which can help overcome the split in modern consciousness between perception and action, appearance and meaning, matter and spirit, subject and object.

Sphinx 6: A Journal for Archetypal Psychology and the Arts. Edited by Noel Cobb and Eva Lowe. London: London Convivium for Archetypal Studies, 1994. The latest volume of *Sphinx* contains papers from the Ficino Conference held at the villa Careggi in 1993. It also includes a translation of Ficino's "The Book of the Sun" (*De Sole*) and his essay "The Star of the Magi," translated by Thomas Moore. Essential for all Ficino admirers and students of Renaissance Platonism; see advertisment in this issue for ordering information.

The Star Guide: Learn How to Read the Night Sky Star by Star by Robin Kerrod. New York: Prentice Hall, 1993. Cloth, 160 pp., $25.00. A beginner's guide to how to get around the night sky (and what you'll find once you get there). Includes facts and figures about the planets and other celestial phenomena with charts and fine illustrations on every page. The text should be accessible to bright children and young adults, but is not overly simplified by any means. If you're looking for a solid introduction to observational astronomy for the entire family, this would be an excellent choice. Includes a planisphere.

The Stones of Time: Calendars, Sundials, and Stone Chambers of Ancient Ireland by Martin Brennan. Rochester: Inner Traditions, 1994. Paper, 216 pp., $19.95. An important and beautifully illustrated study of the megalithic chambers in Ireland and their astronomical significance.

A Taxonomy of Fundamental Polyhedra and Tesselations by Charles E. Peck. Spiral bound, 51 pp., $8.00 postpaid from the author (PO Box 47186, Wichita, KS 67201). Presents a new taxonomy of the five Platonic solids, the Archimedean solids, and the Archimedean duals, arranged by the symmetries of the polyhedra and their tesselations. A fascinating and copiously illustrated visual grammar of polyhedra and their interrelationships.

The Theosophical Enlightenment by Joscelyn Godwin. Albany: SUNY Press, 1994. Paper, 448 pp., $19.95. This is an intellectual history of occult and esoteric currents in the English-speaking world from the early Romantic period to the early twentieth century. It contains a wealth of previously unpublished material, delightful observations, and photographs of the entertaining characters discussed. The book's ambiguous title points to the author's thesis that Theosophy owed as much to the skeptical Enlightenment of the eighteenth century as it did to the concept of spiritual enlightenment with which it is more readily associated.

The Therapy of Desire: Theory and Practice in Hellenistic Ethics by Martha C. Nussbaum. Princeton: Princeton University Press, 1994. Cloth, 558 pp., $29.95. An engaging and in-depth study of emotion in Hellenistic ethics that touches upon the role of philosophy in public and private life.

Three Books of Occult Philosophy by Henry Cornelius Agrippa of Nettesheim. Translated by James Freake. Edited and annotated by Donald Tyson. St. Paul: Llewellyn, 1993. Paper, 938 pp., $29.95. This welcome new edition of the classic Renaissance textbook of celestial correspondences and white Christian-Neoplatonic magic is an edited, corrected, and highly-annotated version of of the English translation of 1651. The editor has done an admirable job of presenting the text, although at times has introduced some minor inaccuracies in his notes (e.g., the Orphic poems are described as "forgeries of Christian grammarians and Alexandrian philosophers"); taken as a whole, however, this is a solid effort. The publisher, unfortunately, has misleadingly put a *black* cover on the book (as if to suggest sinister connotations) and inserted a considerable amount of tasteless advertising hype in the back. Regardless, it is good to have this important sourcework available in an inexpensive edition.

Trialogues at the Edge of the West: Chaos, Creativity, and the Resacralization of the World by Ralph Abraham, Terence McKenna, and Rupert Sheldrake. Santa Fe: Bear & Company, 1992. Paper, 175 pp., $12.95. Behind the playfulness of these edgy trialogues, there is some very serious and exciting cosmological thinking going on. Highly recommended.

Turkoman Figural Bronze Coins and Their Iconography (Volume 1: The Artuqids) by William F. Spengler and Wayne G. Sayles. Lodi: Clio's Cabinet (PO Box 123, Lodi, WI 53555), 1992. Cloth, 193 pp., price unknown. This highly-illustrated book may be of interest to some readers of this journal on account of the planetary and zodiacal symbolism which appears on many of the coins. Discussion of the individual coins includes numismatic commentary and art historical analysis.

A View of the Universe by David Malin. Cambridge, MA: Sky Publishing /

Cambridge: Cambridge University Press, 1993. Cloth, 266 pp., $39.95. This book, by one of the world's leading astrophotographers (Anglo-Australian Observatory), presents the finest collection of color photographs of nebulae, star clusters, galaxies, and galaxy clusters ever assembled in one volume. The author explains what we are looking at and describes the photographic techniques employed in recording the plates. Many of the photographs have a three-dimensional quality, especially the nebulae. Hopefully, it won't be too long until a similar, lavish anthology is published of images from the Hubble Space Telescope. Until then, this is the finest around.

The Vision of the Fool and Other Writings by Cecil Collins. Edited with an introduction by Brian Keeble. Golgonooza Press (3 Cambridge Drive, Ipswich, IP2 9EP, UK), 1994. Cloth, 191 pages, price unknown. Essays and plates by one of the great visionary artists of this century.

Visit to a Small Universe by Virginia Trimble. Woodbury: American Institute of Physics Press, 1992. Cloth, 336 pp., $24.95. In this varied collection of essays, astronomer Virginia Trimble demonstrates how we really understand much of what our universe is like on a large scale, and that the unanswered questions are at least as exciting as those we think we have answered. (Masters of Modern Physics series.)

The Voice of the Earth: An Exploration of Ecopsychology by Theodore Roszak. New York: Simon & Schuster, 1993. Paper, 367 pp., $13.00. This wide-ranging, seminal work by historian Theodore Roszak explores the intrinsic (yet overlooked) relationships between the fields of psychology, cosmology, and ecology. Highly recommended for its breadth, depth of genuine insight, cultural relevance, and compelling argument.

Who's Who in Classical Mythology by Michael Grant and John Hazel. New York: Oxford University Press, 1993. Paper, 367 pp., $14.95. This handsome and reliable A–Z guide to classical mythology contains over 1,200 entries, and would make a fine addition to any library. However, if the reader wants to dig deeper, he or she is out of luck, because the entries lack citations to the primary sources. Thus, for anyone but the casual reader, I would recommend Edward Tripp's *Meridian Handbook of Classical Mythology*: it is extensive, well written, cites the ancient sources with precision, includes a pronouncing index, and lists for $12.95.

About the Contributors

Ralph Abraham holds a Ph.D. in mathematics from the University of Michigan and has taught at the University of California at Berkeley, Columbia University, Princeton University, and the University of California at Santa Cruz, where he has been a leader in the new theories of nonlinear dynamics, chaos, and bifurcation. His books include the pictorial introduction to dynamics, *Dynamics, the Geometry of Behavior*, and the recently published *Chaos, Gaia, Eros: The History of the World According to Chaos Theory* (HarperSanFrancisco, 1994).

John Carey taught for some years in the Department of Celtic Languages and Literatures at Harvard University, and has more recently held research fellowships at the Warburg Institute (London) and the Institute of Irish Studies (Belfast). At present he is based at the Dublin Institute for Advanced Studies. His articles have appeared in many publications including *Temenos*, *Avaloka*, and *Gnosis*. His essay on "The Waters of Vision and the Gods of Skill" appeared in *Alexandria* 1.

Shawn Eyer is a scholar of Hellenistic religions, translator of Greek and Latin texts, and part-time archaeologist who lives in Defiance, Ohio. His translations and articles have appeared in *Alexandria* 2, the *Pig Iron Anthology*, and other publications. He has delivered papers at the Nashville Panathenaia Festivals (convened around the full-scale replica of the Parthenon in that city's Centennial Park) and at conferences of the Ohio Academy of Religion.

Marsilio Ficino (1433–1499) produced the first Latin translations of Plato, the Neoplatonists, and *Corpus Hermeticum*. An influential philosopher in his own right, Ficino's work blended reason with the faculty of imaginal insight, to deeply inspire the culture of Renaissance Florence.

David Fideler is a philosopher, historian of the Western spiritual and cosmological traditions, and editor of this journal. He is the author of *Jesus Christ, Sun of God: Ancient Cosmology and Early Christian Symbolism* (1993), and is currently writing a book on the history of the World Soul and the contemporary reawakening to the living universe. Over the last decade, under the Phanes Press imprint, he has published thirty-nine books which relate to the spiritual, philosophical, and cosmological traditions of the Western world.

Ignacio Götz is Professor of Philosophy and Comparative Religion at New College of Hofstra University. He studied Indian music and philosophy at various colleges in India where he earned two baccalaureate degrees, and he received his M.A. at Columbia University (1965) and his Ph.D. at New York University (1968). He is the author of numerous scholarly articles on philosophy, education, and religion. His books include *The Psychedelic Teacher* (1972), *Creativity* (1978), *Zen and the Art of Teaching* (1988), and *Conceptions of Happiness* (1995).

Michael Hornum, educated at the University of Pennsylvania (Oriental Studies, B.A. 1985) and Bryn Mawr College (Classical and Near Eastern Archaeology, M.A. 1987; Ph.D. 1991), is an archaeologist with a special interest in ancient religion and philosophy. He is the author of *Nemesis, the Roman State, and the Games* (E. J. Brill, 1993), the introduction to the Phanes Press edition of *Porphyry's Launching-Points to the Realm of Mind* (1988), and previous contributions to *Alexandria*. His main interests include vegetarianism, Hinduism, philosophical paganism, and the relevance and vitality of Neoplatonic thought, particularly that of Plotinus, for the modern world.

Lee Irwin teaches comparative religions in the Philosophy and Religious Studies Department at the College of Charleston in Charleston, South Carolina. He has published two books, *The Dream-Seekers: Native American Visionary Traditions of the Great Plains* (University of Oklahoma, 1994), on the Plains vision questing, and *Visionary Worlds: The Making and Unmaking of Reality* (State University of New York, 1995), on esoteric spirituality. He manages an esoteric discussion list on the Internet (*Hermetica*, contact Hermes_owner@cofc.edu), plays guitar, flute, and piano, and lives happily with his artist wife and two cats on an island off the coast of South Carolina. His article on "The Orphic Mystery: Harmony and Mediation" appeared in *Alexandria* 1.

Jane Leade (1623–1704) was a visionary mystic and the center of a Christian theosophic circle that called itself the "Philadelphian Society." Her visions were recorded in numerous books published around the turn of the eighteenth century, including *The Revelation of Revelations* (1683), *The Laws of Paradise* (1695), and *A Fountain of Gardens* (1696–1700). The two excerpts from *A Fountain of Gardens* reproduced in this issue were kindly provided by Arthur Versluis.

Terence McKenna studied ecology, resource conservation, and shamanism at the University of California at Berkeley. After graduation he traveled extensively in the Asian and New World tropics investigating shamanism and the ethno-medicine of the Amazon Basin. He is the founder and director of Botanical Dimensions, a nonprofit research botanical garden in Hawaii devoted to the collection and propagation of plants of ethnopharmacological interest. His books include *Food of the Gods* and a collection of essays, *The Archaic Revival.*

Bruce MacLennan is an Associate Professor in the Computer Science Department at the University of Tennessee, Knoxville, where his research and teaching are centered on nonverbal knowledge and cognition and on their representation in the brain and in computers modeled on the brain. His approach to epistemological problems combines insights from the philosophies of the Presocratics and the phenomenologists with "holographic" models of neurodynamics, and he is also a devoted student of ancient Mediterranean philosophy, art, mythology, literature, and religion. He is the author of three books and several dozen articles, and is currently writing a book on the role of the continuous and the discrete in the history of epistemology.

John Michell is the author of over fifteen books, many of which deal with the worldviews of ancient civilizations and the contemporary quest for a more inclusive cosmology. His most recent volume is entitled *At the Center of the World: Polar Symbolism Discovered in Celtic, Norse, and Other*

Ritualized Landscapes (Thames & Hudson, 1994).

Melissa Nelson studied biology, global ecology, and ecophilosophy at the University of California at Santa Barbara and the University of California at Santa Cruz. She is the editor of *The Ecopsychology Newsletter* and executive director of The Cultural Conservancy.

Oliver Perrin is an independent researcher who lives in Atlanta, Georgia. He left school and home at age 16 to pursue life. The seven years spent since then in such capacities as co-publisher of *Thanateros*, bouncer, bookbinder, taiko drummer, and motorcyclist, on both the East and the West coasts, have helped to broaden his horizons. He is currently researching the Art of Memory and its relationship to Western culture. Email: Semyaza@alamut.is.net

Peter Ramus (1515–1572) was a French humanist who lived during a time when the revolt against scholasticism was in full swing, and received a degree based on his thesis "Everything that Aristotle taught is false." His subsequent lectures drew upon him the hostility of conservative theologians and philosophers, who charged him with undermining the foundations of philosophy and religion, a matter that was brought before the parliament of Paris, and finally before Francis I. He was found guilty of having "acted rashly, arrogantly, and impudently." He withdrew from Paris, but returned after the decree against him was cancelled. Later, after his adoption of Protestantism, he had to flee again, during which time his house was pillaged and library burned. He finally fell victim to his opponents in the massacre of St. Bartholomew (1572). Ramus published fifty works during his lifetime; nine appeared after his death.

F. Christopher Reynolds (289 Wyleswood Dr., Berea, Ohio 44017; email: an167@cleveland.freenet.edu) is a teacher and songwriter. He has published articles on nurturing adolescent creativity and on using computer-aided telecommunications in the classroom. He has released the cassette recordings "A Suburban Nigredo" and "Ex Uno Plura," from which the two lyrics in this issue are taken. He is studying patterns of initiation in adolescence and is working to develop a program to bring soul to public education.

Christine Rhone is a writer, translator, and artist interested in ancient cultures and landscape symbolism. She is the author, with John Michell, of *Twelve-Tribe Nations and the Science of Enchanting the Landscape* (Phanes Press, 1991) and the translator of Jean Richer's *Sacred Geography of the Ancient Greeks: Astrological Symbolism in Art, Architecture, and Landscape* (State University of New York Press, 1994).

Anthony Rooley is a lutenist who specializes in discovering forgotten masterpieces of the Renaissance, the director of the Consort of Musicke, and joint director of the new CD label Musica Oscura. According to our reckoning, he has appeared on well over eighty recordings of Renaissance music. Recently he co-directed a video, *Banquet of the Senses*, featuring the Consort of Musicke performing erotic madrigals by Claudio Monteverdi in the setting for which they were written, the Palazzo Te in Mantua. He is the author of *Performance: Revealing the Orpheus Within* (1990), which was reviewed in *Alexandria 2*.

Peter Russell is the author of numerous collections of poetry and criticism. He has lectured around the world and, until the overthrow of the Shah of Iran, was teaching in association with the Imperial Iranian Academy of Philosophy in Tehran. One-time editor of the poetry review *Nine*, and a friend of, and authority on, Ezra Pound, Russell now resides in an old Italian mill, and subsists exclusively from the sale of his books and pamphlets (and the occasional odd lecture). To receive information on his publications, including the newsletter *Marginalia*, write to him at La Turbina, I-52026 Pian di Scò, Arezzo, Italy.

Michael S. Schneider is an educator and workshop presenter who takes delight in pointing out the harmony which embraces mathematics, science, nature, art, and self. He holds degrees in mathematics, is the author of the recently published book *A Beginner's Guide to Constructing the Universe* (HarperCollins, 1994), and designed the geometry harmonizing the statues at the entrance to the Cathedral of St. John the Divine in New York City.

Rupert Sheldrake holds a Ph.D. in biochemistry from Cambridge. As a research fellow of the Royal Society, he carried out research on the development of plants and cell aging at Cambridge, and was principal plant physiologist at the International Crops Research Institute for the Semi-Arid Tropics in Hyderabad, India. He is the author of *A New Science of Life*, *The Presence of the Past*, *The Rebirth of Nature*, and *Seven Experiments that Could Change the World*.

Dianne Skafte received a Ph.D. from the University of Colorado and currently chairs the clinical psychology program at Pacifica Graduate Institute in Santa Barbara, California. Dr. Skafte's research focuses on the depth-psychological dimensions of historical topics, particularly those touching upon spiritual traditions and women's experience.

Arthur Versluis is the author of numerous books including *American Transcendentalism and Asian Religions* (Oxford University Press, 1993) and *Theosophia: Hidden Dimensions of Christianity* (Lindisfarne, 1994). A native of Grand Rapids, Michigan, he holds a doctorate in literature from the University of Michigan. He recently completed an anthology of Sophianic works, most of which have never been published in English before.

Karen-Claire Voss is Adjunct Professor of Religious Studies at San Jose State University where she taught for five years. She is the author and co-author of articles dealing with Western esotericism, feminine gnosis, mysticism, alchemy, and transdisciplinarity, and is a member of the editorial boards of the journals *Theosophical History* and ARIES. Current work-in-progress includes a doctoral thesis on the life and work of eighteenth-century French *illuminée* and theosopher, Bathilde d'Orleans, Duchess of Bourbon (1750–1822). She currently lives in Istanbul, Turkey.

Robin Waterfield, translator of Anatolius's work *On the Decad*, has translated many works of Plato. His versions of the *Philebus*, *Theaetetus*, and other dialogues have been published by Penguin Books. More recent translations include the *Republic*, *Symposium*, and *Gorgias* (Oxford University Press) and *Statesman* (Cambridge University Press). His translation of *The Theology of Arithmetic*, attributed to Iamblichus, was published by Phanes Press in 1988.

Dana Wilde has taught literature and writing at the university level, is completing a doctorate at Binghamton University in New York, and lives in Troy, Maine. His writings have appeared in academic as well as interesting magazines, and in two books of fiction and poetry. His article on "Galaxies and Photons" appeared in *Alexandria* 1.

Peter Lamborn Wilson teaches at the Naropa Institute, edits for *Semiotext(e)* and Autonomedia, and does radio for WBAI-FM in New York. Recent publications include *Angels: Messengers of the Gods* (Thames & Hudson) and *Sacred Drift: Essays on the Margin of Islam* (City Lights). *The Drunken Universe: An Anthology of Persian Sufi Poetry*, translated by Peter Lamborn Wilson and Nasrollah Pourjavady, was published by Phanes Press in 1987.

List of Subscribers

THE FOLLOWING INDIVIDUALS have made *Alexandria* 3 a reality by joining THE ALEXANDRIA SOCIETY, the sole purpose of which is to support our publications program. We thank these individuals for their generosity and support, which has made this forum possible.

Semi-Divinity ($500+)
"Hebe," Cup-Bearer
  of the Gods

Patron ($250)
Lorna D. Mohr
Dennis Walton
Roger Harmon Weeks

Benefactor ($100)
Frederick C. Adams
Maria Babwahsingh
Tamara Daphne Boneta
J. H. Bruening
F. P. Cruikshank
Kathleen G. Damiani
A. Jay Damon
Lance deHaven-Smith
Edward C. Deveney
Federico González
Mickey Bright Griffin
Dr. John J. & Constance
  J. Harper
James Hindes
Jacob Hopkins
Jim Kaelin
Reah Janise & Hadan Kauffman
Arnold E. Kern, D.C.
Theo Kouros

William R. Laudahn
Forrest McIlwain
Doss McDavid
Ruth McMahon
Jeffrey G. Mead
Patricia J. Middleton, M.D.
Ann Ovodow
Betty Jo Papagna
Dr. Joseph M. Perry
John G. Pladel
Prof. Peter Russell
Alexander Szabo
C. Eric Walburgh
Tom Whiteside

Sustainer ($75)
Anonymous (1)
David Ciarlo
Armand Courtois, Sr.
Frances M. Evans
John Fogarty
David A. & Marie J. Garcia
Meredith Hardin
R. Nemo Hill
Alan Klimek
Sharon R. Michaels
James B. Robinson
Val Savenko
Robert Swanson

Julian Watson

Supporter ($50)
Anonymous (1)
Shawn Abbott
Marc Adamchek
John Alwill
L. J. Annarino
Robert C. Armstrong
William R. Bacher
Darwyn J. Batway
Chester L. Behnke
Joanne Stroud Bilby
Mr. F. G. Bitter
Estella Bourque
Carolyn B. Brafford
Robert V. Broughton
Dean Brown
Randy F. Buchanan
Hall C. Burbage
Arnaldo A. M. Cacha
John Carey
Roland Carter
Kimbal R. Clark
Leroy Clark
Celeste Conboy
Robert T. Cooke
Joseph Costion
Robert Craft
Robert E. Craig
Tracy Cranick
Mary Cupp
Greg Danyluk
Nancy Denton
Michael Díaz
Harry Doumas
Bill Downey
Arthur Durant
Peter Dussik
David A. England
Antoine Faivre

Robert Firth
Viva Fisk
Norman Frank
Virginia Gaines
Robert Galbreath
Brenda Galindo
Karen Gardner, Ph.D.
Thomas J. Germine
Annie Gladden
Dan R. Glass
Lydia Sessions Gottardi
Ignacio L. Götz
Geoffrey Gough
Sara & John Michael Greer
Schuyler E. Grey, CLU, Ph.D.
Julann Griffin
Mrs. Yvonne Hack
Dr. Hans T. Hakl
Marge Haller
Robert S. Hand
Ethel B. Hankey
Ken Harbour
Patty Ann Hardy
Carol Harrison
Mary Hart
Dr. Thomas Head
Elena Heckathorne
Michael C. Hergoth
George Hersh
Joanne Hinkle
Joseph & Stephanie Hoggert
Alvin Holm
Michael Honea
Richard & Ruth Hornaday
Lance Hurst
Evangelyn D. Johnson
Constance Papson Johnston
Quentin Jones
Dr. Roger W. Jung
Christopher Kaiser
Robert Kaladish, M.D.

Sylvia Kalb
Raymond Peter Kane
Marianna Kaul-Connolly
Alma Kearney
Scot Kelly
Tan Choon Kiat
Mark Kindt
Patrick Kinmonth
R. Russell Kinter
Maurice Krasnow, Ph.D.
Nelson E. Lamborn
Dr. Melvin Land
Sidney Lanier
Huguette Lapierre Lanoue
Lawrence J. Lardieri
T. Jerome Layfield
Claudette Le Blanc
John S. Lemmon
Gerald F. Leska
Flora R. Levin
Roger Lipsey
Bruce R. MacKenzie
Bruce MacLennan
Peter Madren
James J. Malpas
Perry D. Manack
Carla Mathews
David E. Mathieson
Rosa McGehee
Owen McKinney
Rev. Malcolm McLeod
Donna Lee Mendrygal
Ralph Metheny
David Millard
Richard Morris
Alexander Moshos
Bob Murk
Paul Nagy
Thomas Nary
D. D. Nelson
Frank G. Neves

Katherine Neville
Charles Newlin
Dan Noreen
Philip Nyman
G. Antoinette O'Heeron
Scott Olsen
Kevin Oster
Arthur Ostergard
S. C. Perry Parojinog
Walter Parrish
Charles E. Pasley
Harold W. Passonno, F.R.C.
Dr. Laura Peterson
Hohl Philipp
Barry Popik
Randall N. Pratt
Karen K. Prince
Michael Randall
Philip J. Romei
Joseph F. Rorke, M.D.
John R. Ross
Betty Roszak
Gregg W. Saunders
JoAnne Schmitz
Charles Schwamb
Arthur Setteducati
Carolyn Sims
James Skinner
Gerard Smith
Ruth Smith
William Smith
Jeffrey J. Snyder
Rev. X. Ruddy E. Soloria
Audrey M. Stone
Jon T. Strehlow
James Strickler
Gerd Stumpf
William F. Sturner
Ray Styles
Terrence M. Sullivan
Linda Sussman

Göran Svarvell
Loyd S. Swenson
Billy E. Taylor
Erol Torun
Lill Van Eps
Jean-Pierre Vila
Ubaldo Vitali
John T. Walker
Jeffrey Weidman
Larry R. Welker
Eugene H. Whitehead
Terry Williams
Larry C. Williamson
Ruth G. Wiskind

Member ($35)
Anonymous (3)
David L. Ackerman
Robert Adams
Robert B. Albertson
A. Alexandrakis
Kathleen S. Allen
Carl R. Anderson
Norman Anderson
Linda Anson
Joan Appel
J. Michael Applegate
Linda Ardito
H. Scott Armstrong
Andrea Ashtine
Ann Ashworth
Pieter Asselbergs
Philip R. Atkinson
Steven G. Ayre, M.D.
Delton I. Baerwolf
Wm. Joel Bailey
Sherry Ackerman Ballou
Alexander Bardosh
Sarah Batchelor
Patricia Baum
Taylor Baxter

Janet Bayliss
Charles Beck
Thomas Beckett
John & Darlene Berges
Gail Bering-Porter
Tracy M. Berkland
Rudolf A. Binnewies
Marco Bischof
H. Avoise Blackway
John M. Boersma
Dr. Robert Bolton
Josep M. Gracia Bonamusa
Tracy Boyd
Rex Boyer
Mr. & Mrs. William Braden
Jay Bregman
Elfriede Bretthauer
Thomas Merton Brightman
Francis P. Broussard
Dennis Brown
Richard Brown
Richard Brzustowicz, Jr.
Susan Buchanan
Willam S. Buehler
Neil Bull
Dusty Bunker
Dennis J. Burke
Bob Burnside
Rose Mary Byrne
Yves Cambefort
Robert Capps
Antonia Cardona
Jim Carpenter
James Cartwright
M. Casey
Michael D. Castelli
Ruth Chandler
Maria Ellen Chiaia
Walter R. Christie, M.D.
Robert Clark
Vernell Cocanour

T. Coffman
Christopher Michael Collins
Andrea L. Conners
Howard Cooper
Catherine Cope
Priscilla Costello
Joseph Coyle
Kirk Crady
Mark Crann
David Crawford
William Crouch
Douglas S. Crow
Francis Paul Czawlytko
Carl O. Daggett
Johanna De Graaf
Anne de Vore
Ronald Decker
Keith DeVito
John Di Gravio
Marcella Dodd
Frank E. Dougher
Tony Edwards
Kacki Ehrhardt
Arni Einarsson
Jacques H. Etienne
Evangeline Farrell
Don Fausett
Robert Ferguson
Stephen Flowers
F. G. A. Fluitsma
Sonja A. Fogg
Rory Fonseca
Brett Forray
Lawrence Fothe
Alastair Fowler
Farida Fox
Mark Framstad
Martin Franklin
Marco Frascari
Nancy Freyer
Jeffrey I. Friedman, D.C.

Elisabeth Furbush
Diane Gaboriault
Michele Gagnon
Dolph Gaines
Byron D. Gallup
Bernard Gauthier
Prof. Dr. Helmut Gebelein
Heljä Geib
Demetra George
Steve Georgiou
Suzanne Getz
Prof. Paolo Gianfagna
Pam Giese
Derek Gilman
Sarah Gilmer
David F. Godwin
Dr. Nicholas Goodrick-Clarke
Julie Grabel
Dr. Sydney R. Grant
Liesel Gras
Sam Gray
Joseph Groell
R. C. Guarino
Zev & Heidi Guber
Marilyn Gustin, Ph.D.
Christian Haenseil
Leo Hansberry
Chip Harmison
Peter D. Harrison
Richard Harrison
Steve Hart
Janet Hartley
John R. Haule
Mary Ann Hawk
S. C. Hedger
Fritz Heinegg, M.D.
David Henderson
Cristóbal M. Hernández
Ingrid Hess
Jane Hill
W. Ladson Hinton

Frederick M. Hoagland
John Hodgson
Ray Hogenson
Paul Evans Holbrook
Karl F. Hollenbach
J. W. F. Holliday
Arlene Hopkins
Charles Horton
Alice O. Howell-Andersen
Elizabeth Huddleston
Stephen G. Hughes
Nancy S. Hurd
David Patrick Hurley
Paul Huson
Daniel Huston
Gisela G. Ibrahim
Marta Illueca, M.D.
Albert Jacobbe
Nancy Jaeger
Len Jenkin
Evert Johnson
Charles Joiner
Roger S. Jones
Robert C. Jorgensen
Marie Louise Kagan
Karen Keith
Kathryn Kelley
Carson Kelly
Nanette Kemp
Margaret Kerns
Andrea Kielpinski
Michael Kimbell
Richard M. Kline
Laura Louise Klohn
Dr. Roger B. Knapp
Brace I. Knapp, M.D.
Bob Kogel
William P. Kuentzel, M.D.
Sandy La Forge
Clem Labine
Martha Lahana

Jean Hinson Lall
Enrique R. Larde
Charles Larry
John A. Leaman
Douglas Leedy
Frank Leib
Chris Lemoine
E. Kaufman Levy
Dr. Robert Lima
Richard Lipton
James Maclellan
Scott E. Mann
Thomas Mansheim
Jon Marshall
Robert Mathiesen
Kevin A. McCarthy
Art McCornack
Lois R. McCalmont
Carolyn A. McColley
Riley McConnell, Jr.
Dr. Adele McCormick
Howard W. McCoy
Bonita J. McEnaney
Karen McGrane
E. J. McInnis
Ms. G. McKemey
Ed McKeown
Dr. James L. McNamara
Conti Meehan
Alison Melville
E. Elias Merhige
Patrick Miner
David Mitchell
Steve Mitchell
Frank Modica
Dr. John L. Moffat
James & Janet Moffett
Thomas Moore
Cynndara Morgan
Gary Moring
Dr. Amy E. Morrow

Judith E. Moss
Jim Moyers
Curt Musgrave
Paul Myers
Richard Myers
Jorge Najera
Deanna J. Neider
Richard Nelson
Stephen Neuville
Raymond G. Newak
John Nicholas
Vanya Nick
Nancy Nietupski
Sandra D. Niiler
Richard P. Nolan
Jan Noyen
Katherine O'Brien
James O'Meara
Haven O'More
George Osterman
Catherine Owens
Rev. Anna Louise R. Pagano
Richard Palcanis
William G. Peacher, M.D.
John Peck
Sharon Pellerin
Sabra Petersmann
James Peterson
Carroll Phillips
Rik Pickrell
Allen Pluth
Frances W. Porter
Michael Praetorius
Nicholas Psillas
R. H. Pulliam
Rose Marie Raccioppi
Valerie Rawlings
Ruth Raymer
Rebecca Reath
F. M. Redd
Howard Rhodes

Christine Rhone
David Richards
Mary Lynn Richardson
Lloyd F. Ritchey
Elisa Robinson
Paul Robinson
Dorothea Rockburne
J. L. Rogers
Paula Roosa
Mary Lou Skinner Ross
Elisabeth Zinck Rothenberger
Andrew E. Rothovius
George Rowe
Audrey Sabot
Mark Sanders
Hugh Savage
J. Scott Sawyer
William Schaa
R. Murray Schafer
Barry M. Scheben
Michelle Majerus Schmidt
Leslie Schnierer
Peter F. Seerie
Shirley Self
Robin Van Löben Sels
Elizabeth Sewell
Dr. M. Sharma
Stephen J. Shartran
Rev. Milton R. Shaw, Ph.D.
Jay Sherry
Mark Siegeltuch
Robert Simon
Eugene Smith
John L. Smith
Dr. Michael G. Sollenberger
Alvin Souzis
J. Sowers, M.D.
Louis Spiegel
David B. Spurgeon
Willard Stackhouse
Barton Stanley

Jesse Stanowski
Kevin Stein
Robert Stein
James E. Stevenson
Ted Stimpfle
David Stobbs
Carol Stoddard
Valerie Stromberg
Joseph H. Sulkowski
Catherine Swanteson
Sondra Ford Swift
Toby Symington
Frank Tarala
Norman Taube
D. W. Taylor
Howard Teich
Rev. A. H. Thelander
Rosalind Wholden Thomas
Lee A. Thomassen
Gretchen Thometz
Monte Thompson
Shawn Tillman
Phillip Tod
Henry P. Trantham
William J. Turgeon
Harold A. Tyman, Jr.
Louise B. Ulh

Christiane A. Usher
Ned Van Der Oudermeulen
Lerie Alyn Van Ells
George Viney
Jaromir Vonka
Rod Wallbank
Jim Walsh
Len Ward
Daniel N. Washburn
Bonnie Weber
Joseph Weitner
Luiz Weksler
B. Robert Welton
Andrew White
Joseph F. White
Richard Stanley Wilkinson
Thomas Willard
Charla Williams
Ric Williams
Christina F. Winter
Beatrice S. Wittel
Clifford P. Wolfsehr
Jeff Woodart
Lorraine Yee
Stuart Yerian
Steven Young

SPHINX 6

A Journal for Archetypal Psychology
and the
Arts

Editor: Noel Cobb with Eva Loewe

SPHINX 6 is dedicated to the life and work of that Doctor of Soul, Marsilio Ficino, Renaissance philosopher, musician and astrologer. Most of the writing here is taken from the London Convivium's Florence Conference on Ficino, a celebration over five days in 1993. Accompanying papers from the conference at the Villa Medici, are also first English translations of Ficino's "The Star of the Magi"and"The Book of the Sun". The renaissance being brought about now in psychology by the provocations, reversals, inversions, subversions, incursions, excursions, revisionings and general outrageousness of archetypal psychology has much to do with this"loveless, humpbacked, melancholy teacher who lived in Florence, still one of the most neglected important figures in the movement of Western ideas." (J. Hillman) As usual, there is also a large section devoted to contemporary poetry and translations.

Published by

The London Convivium for Archetypal Studies
P.O. Box 417, London NW3 7RJ
Registered Charity No. 298266

Illustrated, 272 pages, ISSN 0953--6582, £13.95 or $28.00 postpaid.

THE
ETERNAL
HERMES
*From Greek God
to Alchemical Magus*

ANTOINE FAIVRE

TRANSLATED BY JOSCELYN GODWIN

Now Available

Cloth, 216 pages, limited to 250 copies, $35.00.
Paper, 216 pages, $18.95.

Enclose $3.50 postage if ordering direct.

Phanes Press • PO Box 6114 • Grand Rapids, Michigan 49516

THE ETERNAL HERMES

HERMES—the fascinating, mercurial messenger of the gods, eloquent revealer of hidden wisdom, and guardian of occult knowledge—has played a central role in the development of esotericism in the West. Drawing upon many rare books and manuscripts, this highly illustrated work explores the question of where Hermes Trismegistus came from, how he came to be a patron of the esoteric traditions, and how the figure of Hermes has remained lively and inspiring to our own day.

Great erudition blended with a highly refined metaphysical sensibility brings the great Hermes to life and allows this powerful psychospiritual archetype to speak once again (and perhaps even play a few much-needed tricks on us).

> —Jacob Needleman, author of *The Heart of Philosophy* and *Money and the Meaning of Life*

Faivre's remarkable achievement in this single volume is to combine the historical richness of the Hermetic tradition with its relevance to understanding the circumambulations of the psyche today as it pursues its spiritual quest.

> —June Singer, author of *Boundaries of the Soul: The Practice of Jung's Psychology*

This book is an impressive and compelling contribution to the puzzling question of both the source and perdurance of Hermes in his variety of shape-shifting guises. From Alexandria to Amsterdam, Athens to America, this thrice-great Hermes keeps showing up, perhaps even more than in antiquity!

> —David L. Miller, Syracuse University, author of *The New Polytheism*

Antoine Faivre, the most prominent scholar of esotericism to have appeared since Mircea Eliade, is Director of Studies at the Ecole Pratique des Hautes Etudes (Section des Sciences Religieuses, Sorbonne), University Professor of Germanic Studies at the University of Haute-Normandie, and director of the series Cahiers de l'Hermétisme (Albin Michel).

Contemporary Neoplatonism Conference

Vanderbilt University
May 18–21, 1995
Nashville, Tennessee

How are Neoplatonic themes significant in our present century? What is alive and dead in Neoplatonism? Place on the program will be provided for strong critics of Neoplatonism (as long as it is evident that they understand what they are criticizing), as well as for exposition of the ideas of contemporary philosophers, writers, and artists, who hold essentially Neoplatonic views.

It is hoped by the organizers that this will be the largest Neoplatonic conference held in history.

For information on registration and housing, write:

Professor John Lach
Contemporary Neoplatonism Conference
Department of Philosophy
Vanderbilt University
Nashville, Tennessee 37235

Sponsored by
The International Society for Neoplatonic Studies and
The Center for Neoplatonic Studies at Vanderbilt University